Charlotte's Story

Charlotte's Story

One girl's life in Germany from 1943–1951

CHARLOTTE WITTMUTZ LOWE

Edited by Michael W. Lowe

iUniverse, Inc.
New York Lincoln Shanghai

Charlotte's Story
One girl's life in Germany from 1943–1951

iUniverse books may be ordered through booksellers or by contacting:

iUniverse
2021 Pine Lake Road, Suite 100
Lincoln, NE 68512
www.iuniverse.com
1-800-Authors (1-800-288-4677)

The views expressed in this work are solely those of the author and do not necessarily reflect the views of the publisher, and the publisher hereby disclaims any responsibility for them.

ISBN-13: 978-0-595-43793-1 (pbk)
ISBN-13: 978-0-595-88123-9 (ebk)
ISBN-10: 0-595-43793-1 (pbk)
ISBN-10: 0-595-88123-8 (ebk)

Printed in the United States of America

Contents

Introduction. vii

PART ONE 1

PART TWO. 219

Michael's Epilogue 335

Introduction

My mother, Charlotte, had to be coaxed to write this memoir. Over the years she had told our family many of the stories which you will soon read in this memoir, but it was difficult for us to remember all of them. I imagine it is the same in many families. Certain stories continue to be told and others fade. Individual family members remember only their favorite stories or remember the same story in different ways. Over time a few persist and become family legends, but so much is lost.

I did not want that to happen in our family. I know that my sister, Diane, shared my sentiments. Each of us in our own way encouraged "Mom" to write down her stories so that we could better remember them.

Finally, tentatively, she began to write. At first she confided only to our father, Stanley, and only sought his assistance. She laboriously wrote down her recollections by hand in spiral notebooks and worried constantly whether or not her written voice was adequate.

After many months of carefully choosing her words, several restarts, and three hundred hand-written pages, she reached what she believed was the end of her memoirs. They started with a letter from my grandfather, Willi Wittmutz, in January of 1944 and ended in December of 1945. Those pages covered an amazing twenty-four months of her young life. When I finished reading them for the first time I was impressed by what she had seen and experienced. At an age when I was going to school, playing with my friends and sleeping in a warm, dry bed, my mother was huddling in air raid shelters, shivering in the cold, and dodging Russian military patrols.

But she was not yet finished.

After a pause my mother realized that she had more to tell. The effort of recalling the past had prompted many other memories to surface. She also wished to close on a more positive note than the bleak ending to 1945. So she set about writing an additional three hundred hand-written pages, one section covering the time before January of 1944 and one section covering the time after December of 1945.

What you hold in your hands is the sum of the two efforts my mother made to record the memories of a significant part of her life. It is difficult to truly appreciate what she went through, but I am very grateful that we now have a chance to preserve her memoirs and create the opportunity for future generations to learn from them.

Thank you, Mom, on behalf of all of us.

Michael Lowe
February, 2007

When I started to write my memoirs, recalling my experiences from November 1943 until December 1945, I had no idea that I would complete over six hundred hand-written pages. I did not realize that I had so much to write about.

I marvel at all the things I do remember. Some are so clearly pictured in my mind; it is as if they happened yesterday. I only wish I could have expressed myself better. Anyway, I tried my best.

Charlotte Wittmutz Lowe
April 3, 2006

PART ONE

Berlin Nord, 1943

One cold and wintry day in November of 1943 I stopped at the library on my way from school, where I found three books to read. As I walked home through my neighborhood I was looking forward to reading my books after supper. I never anticipated that in only a few hours my neighborhood would not be there anymore and all the familiar places would be gone, totally destroyed. Neither did I think that I had spent my last day in school on this Monday, November 22, 1943. I would not return to school until the fall of 1945. Maybe it was better not to know what was to happen in only a few hours and maybe not.

At the beginning of the war, the soldiers belonging to a special military unit came along and started constructing our air raid shelter. It was located in the front cellar of our apartment house, in a large room under the entrance hallway. The tenants from the side and back of the building had to downsize their cellar space in order to give the tenants that lost their cellars to the shelter some storage space.

My friends and I found it quite interesting to watch the construction. The soldiers brought big tree trunks into the cellar and reinforced the ceiling and the walls with them. The soldiers kept telling us that we should feel quite safe in that shelter.[1]

We were then required to attend regular air raid drills with the *Luftschutzwart* (air raid warden) on how to handle emergencies during an air raid and how to use a gas mask and so on. During the drills the only one who took it seriously was the warden, while the rest of the people responded rather nonchalantly. But I believe that is to be expected from people, always doubtful about something that has

---

1   A couple more rooms were added later on, but they were not as strongly reinforced as the first one.

not yet happened, thinking that it cannot be all that bad. We were all so guilty of that.

Up until September of 1943 my family had been living quite peacefully, going about our daily tasks just as we had done before the war. The biggest of our worries and concerns was about my dad's welfare. He was serving in the German military and fighting in Russia. We looked forward every day to receiving a letter from him, letting us know that he was alright.

Our neighborhood had not been affected very much by the air raids. A house here and there had been bombed or burned down, but not enough to make us worry about it. The gym at my school was one of the first buildings in our area to get bombed. It was located across the street from the school. It was rebuilt and used for storage.

We had become very lax in our attitude towards the warnings of impending air raids. At the beginning of the war we had very obediently followed the rules and gone to the shelter when an air raid was announced. It happened mostly during the night while we were asleep and it would last for hours. It gave us the impression that they were only sending one airplane to bomb us at a time, but of course this theory was not logical. It just appeared very strong to us. Later on, we could easily tell that more than one airplane was involved in the bombing.

Eventually we did not bother going to the shelter anymore and we slept through the alarm many times. I remember my mother telling me to go back to sleep after we had been awakened by the wailing sound of the siren. Then she would wake me up when she could hear the hum of an airplane. Not really a good decision. By the time she heard an airplane it might have been too late to save ourselves. As I said earlier, we had become very lax. Too much so!

All of the children, including me, would get excited when we heard the antiaircraft guns blasting away on top of the *Flakturm* (antiaircraft gun tower). It meant that we would find shrapnel pieces the next morning. A new game for us. Where we used to trade lacquer-pictures or marbles with our friends, now we were trading with shrapnel pieces. I found some interesting pieces. Deadly too, if one fell on your head.

I used to look forward to going to the shelter. There were tables and chairs set up in the back and we would play games or work on some crafts. It seemed like fun for awhile.

Not so much for the adults who had to go to work. At that time, an air raid was not accepted as an excuse for not coming to work on time. Many times my mother, along with other employed people, would leave the shelter to go to work before the "all clear" was sounded. If it had been quiet for a while and nothing was happening, the air raid warden would give his approval for them to leave. My mother used to mention how many people would be on the street, all hurrying to the train station to catch their train, filling up the cars to capacity.

The government also did not want the workers to fall asleep while at work. Therefore the shelters contained bunk beds for sleeping. Although some people did use the bunk beds in the shelter, most lost precious hours of sleep.

When my dad was drafted into the military, he tried to talk my mother into quitting her job, but she kept saying, "Just a little while longer." She worked so she could get whatever was needed for our home to make it nice. It had been rough for them for many years, ever since the time of the Depression. They were just beginning to get back on their feet when the war came along. When my dad came home on leave in the spring of 1942, he tried again to talk my mother into quitting her job, only by then it was not so easy anymore. They needed people to work to keep supplying the war effort. My mother requested a release several times, but was always turned down.

When my dad returned to his company in Russia, he was able to persuade his commanding officer and the doctor at the field hospital into writing a couple letters. One letter was to the Deutsche Waffen munitions factory, where my mother worked. The other letter was to the principal at my school. They must have been very impressive letters because they worked. My mother was released from her job. It was so incredible that my mother had trouble believing it.

My dad must have used me as the reason to get my mother released from work, arguing that she needed to be at home with me. I was very surprised when all of a sudden I was the center of a lot of attention from my principal and teachers and I was called into the principal's office. She was a very nice lady and she had always treated me nicely. But now she was acting very concerned about me and my welfare. She told me repeatedly to be sure to come to her office if I had a problem. At first it had me quite puzzled. Something like the following was said: "A poor child, on my own all the time, with my mother away for most of the day and my father, a frontline soldier, fighting for the Fatherland." The way everyone was fussing over me, I suspected that I had been diagnosed with some kind of an emotional problem. Actually, I had been on my own all of my young life, coming home to an empty house, and it had not given me any problems. But whatever, I did not mind being used as a reason. I was very happy to have my mother at home. A great change.

Someone else was extremely happy and that was my dad. The letter he wrote must have been received by someone at the munitions factory who was very understanding in order for them to grant my dad's request.

Tante Grete, Inge and the Heinz Family

The air raid that took place in our neighborhood in September of 1943 was indeed a much needed wake up call. We were extremely lucky that it happened early in the evening and not while we were asleep in our beds. On that day in September, my mother and I were at our friend's apartment on the ground floor of our house. Her niece Edeltraut was also present. We were helping Inge Heinz prepare pears for canning. We had become good friends with Inge, ever since she and her husband Peter moved into our building at the end of 1940 or perhaps the beginning of 1941. They were in their early twenties and they had just gotten married.

I have a picture postcard taken on *Pfingsten* (Pentecost) in 1941. The photo shows my mother and I cruising on a steamboat on Berlin's largest lake, the Muggelsee. We were going to an island to spend the day. We were with our landlady, her daughter, and the daughter's two young children. Inge and Peter Heinz and their niece Edeltraut, who was a year younger than me, were also with us. Even though we were at war at the time, there was no sign of it. Berlin was still quite peaceful. My dad was stationed in Norway and getting ready for the big invasion of Russia, and here we were cruising on Lake Muggelsee! But just a short time after our excursion, Peter Heinz was drafted into the German military. So my mother and Inge shared the same fate.[2]

Sometime during the summer of 1941, my mother came home to find three people sitting on their suitcases in our entrance hallway—Tante Grete Heinz, her sister Hanna Heinz, and their mother. They had stopped off in Berlin to visit Inge. Peter was Grete and Hanna's brother. But Inge was not at home. They had been traveling by train from Silesia, going back home to Alt-Ruppin. My mother invited them into our home to wait for Inge's return, and that is how we first

---

2   I never heard if he survived the war alive or if he returned back home. The last time that we talked to Grete Heinz, Peter's sister, she had not heard from him.

met Grete and the rest of the family from Alt-Ruppin. We were to become good friends.

During our conversations on that visit, they learned that I was still recovering from a bout with yellow jaundice and that the doctor had ordered *Luftveranderung* (a change of air) to help in my recovery. The illness had left me very weak and with little appetite. Grete and the others also heard about all the trouble my mother had in trying to arrange a trip to the country for me. In response, Tante Grete invited us to come to Alt-Ruppin to see if the country air there would help me.[3]

We did soon visit Alt-Ruppin. We filled out a form at the local police station and we were issued a *Reisepass* (travel pass) which allowed us to travel to Alt-Ruppin. When we arrived in Alt-Ruppin we had to go to the local police station and report our arrival and fill out an *Anmeldung* (registration). The same procedure had to be done in reverse when we returned home. If we were staying longer than three days we had to report to our local police station to get an *Abmeldung* (notice of departure) or permission to leave our local area. This was how everyone's location was monitored and how the police could locate someone in an emergency. The fact that telephones were not owned by private persons was one reason for this. Another was that "Big Brother" was always watching over us.

Alt-Ruppin was a nice little town, close enough to Berlin for people to come and spend the weekends. Neu-Ruppin was a much larger city than Alt-Ruppin. It had an airport where a *Segelflugzeug-Schule* (glider plane flying school) was located. Ruppiner See was between Alt- and Neu-Ruppin. This lake was about five kilometers long and quite wide. Everyone seemed to own a *Kahn* (small boat).

Almost every house in Alt-Ruppin was located on the lake or on the two streams that fed the lake. Most of the houses were one or two stories high. The church steeple was the highest point around. Pine woods surrounded the town. Good mushrooms could be found under the pine trees after it rained. There were also plenty of blueberry patches. During the blueberry picking season, a group of women would get together and have a farmer with his horse and wagon take them deep into the forest. They would leave early in the morning and return in the evening. They paid the farmer with blueberries, with everyone contributing a certain amount.

---

3   I do not know if *Luftveranderung* was really the answer to help me regain my energy and appetite, but that was always the remedy prescribed by doctors. I have since learned that being near water, like the ocean or a lake, gives me an insatiable appetite.

My mother and I went along a couple of times. I did alright picking berries from the bushes, but when I started eating them, that was the end. My belly got filled, but not my basket. Luckily my mother was a good berry picker or we would not have been able to give our share to the farmer.

Tante Grete's mother showed me how to find *Pfefferlinge* (mushrooms) after a rain. They tasted good when fried and then added to a gravy. They would also dry them to use later during the winter. Many women would take baskets of blueberries and the mushrooms to the markets in Berlin and sell them for a little extra income.

Some people from the town were *Klein Bauern* (small farmers). Others worked in the ammunition factory with Tante Grete and some people were employed at the *Panzerkaserne* (tank barracks). A training center, it consisted of several two-story buildings, well hidden in the woods. I would jump out of bed early in the morning when I heard the German soldiers from the *Kaserne* come marching down our street. They would be on their way to the training area on the other end of town and they would be singing loudly, "*Auf der Heide bluht ein kleines Blumelein und das heisst, Erika!*" ("On the heath blooms a little flower and it is called Erika!") or perhaps, "*Fruh morgens, wenn der Hahne kraht.*" ("Early morning when the cock crows.") I would open the outside shutters and wave to them along with other people from the houses along the street. They always sang such cheerful songs.

Tante Grete's home was small, but we managed. Inge Heinz' niece, Edeltraut, and I were friends. We always ended up sleeping on the floor. We thought it was fun. The street that Tante Grete lived on—Wilhelmstrasse—was the main road entering and leaving the town. Small *Rotdorn baume* (pink hawthorne trees) grew on both sides of the road. When they were in bloom they looked so pretty and had a nice fragrance. I could reach out of our bedroom window to cut some branches off and bring them into the home. They looked nice in a vase.

Everyone had a small garden behind their house. I enjoyed weeding and watering the flower and the vegetable beds. Many afternoons on weekends we would have our *Kaffee und Kuchen* (coffee and cake) break in the gazebo by the water. A small *Strom* (stream) flowed by our house. It was not very deep. The neighbor boys and I would wade around by the edge and look for frogs and crabs. The boys would use them for bait when they rowed out into the lake to fish.

During one visit to Alt-Ruppin, Tante Grete's husband Hans was home on leave. He invited Edeltraut and me to come along on a fishing trip. Rowing the boat out onto the lake was fun, but then sitting very still and waiting for the fish to bite was very boring to us. Onkel Hans decided to take us to the nearby island to explore it. We did not find anything of interest there either, only lots of very hungry mosquitoes. Needless to say, it was not a good idea to take us along on a fishing trip.

I recall that Alt-Ruppin had two grocery stores, one bakery, one butcher shop, one pharmacy, one beauty shop, one barbershop and three hotel-restaurants. Hotel Hubertus turned one of its large halls into a movie theater. It did not matter what was playing, it always sold out. The soldiers from the *Kaserne* saw to that. The other hotel-restaurant *"Zum Weissen Rossle"* ("To the White Horse") was about four houses away from Tante Grete's place.[4]

In Tante Grete's backyard was a small, one-story building. It had a tall chimney. I do not remember what it once was used for. It was totally empty and had been for years. A stork family took up residence on top of the chimney. They were fun to watch, especially when the *kleiner Storche* (baby storks) arrived.

1943—September

Back to the evening in September. We were having a good time, sorting through baskets of pears and telling funny stories. Inge was always a lot of fun to be with. We heard the wailing siren, announcing an air raid, but we ignored it, like all the other times. It was still daylight outside and unusual for an air raid to be so early in the evening. The windows were wide open but we were not paying attention or listening for any noises, like the hum of an airplane.

All of a sudden it happened—the blasting of the antiaircraft guns on top of the *Flakturm*, a terrifying sound, followed by a huge, earth-shaking explosion. Everything around us shook, including us, an indescribable feeling. I feared that the end had come for us.

Edeltraut and my first reaction was to save ourselves. We crawled under the bed. But my mother and Inge pulled us out and all together we ran down the stairs and took shelter in the cellar of our building. We joined the other people who had been caught in their homes like us when the attack started. It was a frightening experience. We felt many smaller explosions. We huddled together in

---

4   After the war, the Russians turned it into the *"Kommandantur"* (Commander's Office).

the dark and prayed. I know I made a promise never to take an air raid warning so lightly again.

During this attack, my mother ran back up to our apartment on the first floor to grab the bag that held our important papers and most valuable possessions. She was concerned about not having them with us.

I do not know how long the raid lasted but it seemed a long time before it calmed down outside and the "all clear" was sounded. When we came out of the cellar, we could see how the sky was glowing in a deep orange color in the direction of my grandparents' house, which worried us immensely. We started to go there, but the air raid warden caught us in the doorway. He was very upset with us for failing to come to the shelter during the air raid. My mother assured him that it would never happen again and we both meant it.

The warden advised us that if we were going out to take along a damp cloth for protection from the smoke and dust in the air. He was right. We were soon glad to have the cloth along. The wind started to blow hard and it blew lots of dust, ashes and cinders around us.

When we came to the end of our street we heard loud screaming coming from the bridge underpass. Some people had stepped in a pool of phosphor, a liquid material that would burst into flames upon contact. It was horrible hearing their screams. I saw someone totally engulfed by flames and people trying to help him. Others had become hysterical, running away and kicking their shoes off out of fear of this dangerous material.

We had heard about phosphor and what it was capable of doing, but we had not come into contact with it until that night. Some time later I noticed a boy, about my age, walking around in our neighborhood. I wondered about him because his face was badly distorted. I was told that he was the boy who was so severely burned under the bridge underpass, and that the rest of his body was likewise disfigured. It was a miracle that he survived, but at what cost?

My mother and I backed away from the underpass. We chose to walk the upper route to my grandparents' house. We walked by the Schwartzkopf Plant, a large factory complex. It appeared to be undamaged, along with my former school. We stopped and looked to the other end of the street from my school and we saw huge fires and lots of smoke. Three of my former classmates lived in that burning area. I was praying that they were alright.

We were also getting quite anxious to reach Hochstrasse. Arriving there, we breathed a big sigh of relief when we saw that the houses were intact. My grandparents had just reached their apartment when we arrived. They were very glad to see us. It had taken my grandfather all this time, since the "all clear" was sounded, to get back up the four flights of stairs. He was totally exhausted.

They had gone downstairs to the shelter in the middle of the bombing and experienced it all while on the stairs. It had been a frightful time. Their street was close to ours and to where the bombing had taken place. Knowing how it had affected us, it must have been twice as traumatic for them. My grandmother swore that she would never get caught like that again. She would go to the shelter as soon as the siren goes off. My grandfather just gave a nod. His poor health would certainly make it difficult for him to go down to the shelter every time a siren wailed.

We decided to spend the night with them and they seemed glad about it. My grandmother, who normally was very easy going, was visibly shaken up. It was the first time that we experienced such a devastating attack in our neighborhood and it had frightened everybody. It reminded us to be more alert, that we were at war and not to take things so lightly.

The following morning, when we were going back home, we had to take the upper road, the lower one being blocked off. We stopped beside my former school. From there we could see the damage from the previous night and it looked bad. When the area was later reopened, my mother and I went to have a look. I cannot describe our feelings as we looked at the devastation. It covered such a large area. Where my classmates used to live, nothing more was left, other than a big heap of rubble. We were told that two *Luftmienen* (air mines) or blockbuster bombs had fallen onto their houses. Then the incendiary bombs had started the fires that were still smoldering. Everyone in the houses had been killed. It would be some time before they could dig for them because of the intense heat. I felt sad about my classmates and their families. I had gone home with them many times after school, working on homework together or just playing. I felt quite emotional, looking at the heap of rubble and knowing that they were buried underneath. It was so cruel.

The blockbuster bombs became our biggest fear. Wherever they fell, they brought total destruction and death to everyone. There was no chance to survive a direct hit from a blockbuster and no air raid shelter could give protection from such a powerful bomb.

And now my story returns to November 22 and 23 of 1943. The two nights that brought disaster to us. Two unforgettable nights. I remember them just as clearly now, sixty-two years later, as if the events of those two nights had taken place yesterday. It changed everything for us. We would struggle for years to overcome the loss and the damage to our lives.

Monday, November 22, 1943

After supper I got ready for bed, anxious to start reading one of the books that I had taken out earlier at the library. My mother was sitting near the stove, reading the newspaper.

It was 7:30 when our quiet evening was interrupted by the wailing sound of the siren announcing the impending air raid. I was not happy to be forced to leave my nice, warm bed and the good book, but I grudgingly got up.

Normally we would wear our best clothing, but I was grumpy and chose not to. Instead, I wore my old, brown pleated skirt and a yellow sweater. My mother had just bought a new winter coat, hat, scarf, and gloves for me, but I left them in the closet and wore my old coat instead, a decision which I later regretted very much.

We picked up our bags and suitcases by the front door. They were always kept packed and ready at the door to take along to the shelter. Our suitcases contained various articles of clothing, shoes, towels, and a small blanket. Our bags were also packed with our most valuable possessions—documents, money, bank books and jewelry—plus pictures, my dad's last letters and some not so important items of sentimental value.

We noticed how quiet it was when we were walking across the courtyard to the shelter. Just a little hope was stirring within us that our unwelcomed visitors had changed their minds and were not coming to drop bombs on us after all.

Since the attack in September people were going to the shelter again. The wake up call was working. Indeed, it was not unusual to have two air raids in one night and one raid during the day. Some days we spent more time running to the bunker than doing anything else. On this evening we met other neighbors along our way. At the bunker the civil defense men were at their post and ushered us into the shelter.

It may help to understand that there were three sections of a house. The front was called the *Vorderhaus*, the side wing was called the *Seitenflugel*, and the back of the building was called the *Hinterhaus*. It may also help to know that our house was No. 111 and our shelter was at the front of the house. House No. 110

operated a coal business out of their front basement and with it being the month of November they were well stocked for winter. House No. 110 had their shelter at the back of the building.

House No. 112 had their shelter at the side of the building. House No. 112 had a nice *Speiselokal* (a small restaurant and pub) in the front of the house. The front basement was used for their storage. A trapdoor in front of the restaurant was used for deliveries. When unexpected visitors dropped by it was quite convenient to have a pub and refreshments so close. I would take a metal can from the kitchen and get it filled with draft beer or delicious *Apfelsaft von Fass* (apple cider from a barrel).

All the way at the rear of house No. 112 was a small *Molkerei* (dairy) and a large barn for their horses, cows, pigs, and chickens, plus a noisy rooster. He served as our alarm clock. The dairy had a small shop where they sold fresh milk in the mornings and evenings. Just as we did with the pub, we had to bring our own containers.

The tenants living in our house were mostly elderly people. It was the landlord's choice not to have young families living in his house. He was a very strange man. I grew up being afraid of him. He was very much against my parents moving into my great-grandmother's apartment. They pleaded with him but he was very stubborn with his decision until his wife intervened. Then he finally changed his mind and allowed my parents to move into the apartment with me. They had to promise to keep me quiet and never allow me to be a disturbance to the other tenants.

Upon entering the house, one could not miss looking at a large arch over the door leading to the courtyard. On it was written in large fancy letters, "*Es wunscht mir Jeder, was er will. Ich wunsche ihm nochmal soviel!*" ("Everyone wishes me what they will. I wish them again as much!") He was a wicked old man. His name was Sunder (Sinner).

I used to know all the last names of the tenants living in our house. Their names were listed on a board in the hallway along with the location of their apartments. I am guessing that there were thirty-five apartments altogether in house No. 111, along with a bakery, a smoke shop, and a grocery store. Plus more or less sixty-five people living in the house.

I was home alone a lot. I had to find things to amuse me, but I had to be careful not to be seen by the landlord. He did not tolerate any kind of playing in his house or in the yard. If the landlord was not around, I would play in the hallway. It was a beautiful entry. Dark wood, tile and mirrors covered the walls on the sides. A large, curved staircase led up to the first floor. Halfway up was a beautiful stained glass window. I would practice walking down the stairs, like a princess would, of course. Or I would take the names of the tenants and make some silly phrases with them. *"Frau Laabs, setzte eine Maske auf, stieg in eine Droschke und fuhr zur Kur!"* ("Mrs. Laabs, put a mask on, stepped into a hack and rode to take a cure!")

Our neighbor, Tante Maske, my mother and I sat together in the room that was added after the original construction of the bunker. About eight or ten people sat in the room with us. It was not as well reinforced as the one under the entrance hallway, but it offered a little more space. We had brought our own chairs to sit on. They were a little more comfortable than the benches the bunker construction provided.

As always, everyone sat quietly and always in the same spot. If someone spoke, it was done in a very low voice. I believe that was because everyone was doing the same as I was—listening. It was hard to believe that the same women at other times could stand for hours outside the front door and talk. I used to dread going out and coming back through the door and having to greet them nicely with a curtsy every time I ran past them. It was ridiculous! But mercy me, if I ever tried getting by without a proper greeting, my mother would have heard about it right away.

The air raid warden and the civil defense men had remained by the door at the top of the stairs. We all heard a loud banging on the heavy steel door. It was secured from the inside with swinging steel latches, but it was possible to peek out through a small opening. The noise was made by our neighbor Inge Laabs, who was about sixteen years old. She came bouncing down the cellar stairs into the bunker, all out of breath. She had just gotten off work at the telephone company and she was halfway home when the siren went off. The civil defense patrol tried to get her off the street and into another shelter but she convinced them that she only lived a block away and they let her run home. She complained to her mother about being hungry and was told that her supper was being kept warm in the oven.

Frau Laabs had become a very withdrawn woman since shortly after the September attack when she received word that her son, a German Air Force pilot, and his plane had been reported as missing. Everyone felt sorry for her. She had worshipped her son, with her husband and their two daughters always taking second place. She was a very loyal party member, wearing her party badge at all times, even pinning it to her silk blouses. We always knew when Horst, her son, was home because his uniform could be seen hanging in their window.

She had become hysterical after the September air raid when she returned to her apartment and found that her son's photograph had fallen off the wall. She cried and took it as a sign that something bad had happened to him. Everyone tried to calm her down, blaming the picture's fall on all the shaking from the bombs, but she would not listen. Sadly, her intuition came true. I was very sorry to hear about Horst. I always liked him. I used to pretend that he was the older brother I did not have. He was a nice fellow, always taking time to talk to me when we met. He also looked quite handsome in his uniform.

Inge looked at me and asked if I wanted to come along to get her supper. It was still very quiet outside. The two of us ran quickly upstairs. Instead of going with her into her apartment, I decided to go into ours. I did not need a key. The apartments were kept unlocked during air raids so that the civil defense men could go into apartments to check for *Brandbomben* (incendiary bombs). My grandparents, living on the fourth floor, once had a bomb come through their kitchen window and fall into the sink, which was a good place for it. Unfortunately that did not happen very often with most *Brandbomben*.

I went into our apartment and I walked from one room into the other, looking all around, as if it was for the last time. I certainly behaved strangely. I was very proud of our nice home, and I would get just as excited as my parents when they were able to buy something new for our home. In anticipation of my dad's homecoming for Christmas, my mother had put up curtains on the windows, against the fire rules, because she wanted it to look homelike. She had also been saving our sugar, flour, and butter rations, so she could bake cake and cookies for my dad.

The biggest surprise that awaited my dad was our remodeled bathroom. Gone were the old, ancient fixtures and the exposed pipes. Instead we had a nice new bathroom. We were very fortunate to know some people who had a plumbing business. Otherwise it would have been impossible to have the work done. We were very excited about our new bathroom and we knew my dad would be pleased too.

When I walked into the bedroom, I picked up one of my dolls, a small baby doll. I had many nicer ones, but I chose that one. I opened the closet and took out my mother's silver fox stole, which my dad had sent to her from Norway. It was normally packed away in a trunk along with my dad's and other seldom used clothing and stored in our private cellar. But she had worn it over the weekend when we had gone to see a play at the theater. I draped the stole around me, took my baby doll and walked back into the kitchen. I remembered that we bought the cocoa ration earlier that day. Such a ration was only for children. It was a small bag containing only a few ounces that had to last for a month. I always liked my sweets and this cocoa was a small substitute for the candy we could not buy. I grabbed a teaspoon and the small bag of cocoa and headed for the door.

This all gives the impression that we were gone a long time, but it really was only a few minutes. A few minutes too long. Just before I reached the front door, I heard the hum of an airplane. I quickly turned off the light. Inge came out of her place at the same time as I did. She had heard the hum too and without turning the hall lights on we ran down the stairs. But not fast enough, for when we reached the hallway door, the antiaircraft guns started to blast, creating a deafening noise. Everything shook, including the door and the wall I was leaning against.

We were both afraid to run across the yard for fear of getting hit by falling *Granatsplitter* (shrapnel pieces). Luckily, at that moment our superintendent, his wife and his son came out of their ground floor apartment. He urged us to run along with them across the courtyard. I looked up once and I saw the searchlights criss-crossing the sky, searching for airplanes.

The air raid warden met us halfway, scolding all of us. He had come to get us. By then I was feeling very sorry that I had placed myself in such circumstances. We were lucky to be safely back in the shelter as the situation was about to change rapidly.

On this night our neighborhood was definitely the target of the air raid. I could hear the whistling sounds of the falling bombs before they hit and exploded. I was told not to worry about the ones that we could hear, as the ones we could hear would not hit us. Instead, we were told, we would not hear the one that would hit us. I did not like hearing that whistling sound. It was such a threatening sound. But I wanted to believe the theory. It helped to calm me a little.

The lights were flickering on and off with every explosion. We felt the vibrations and everything shook. The airplanes were clearly unloading their bombs over us. I could see the fear on everyone's face. We were all afraid. I was praying, ever so pleadingly, *"Lieber Gott, habe Mitleid mit uns!"* ("Dear God, have mercy on us!")

Our small group decided to move into the main shelter for a little more protection. It was, after all, the sturdiest section of the shelter. The civil defense men left their post at the door and followed us.

We moved just in time. The next powerful explosion was very close by. It made the ground heave up and down. My mother was standing in front of me, leaning against one of the big tree trunks that had been used to reinforce the shelter, and I saw it swaying from side to side. And then the lights went out, for good. It was *Todesstille* (deathly quiet). No one said a word, except for the civil defense men telling us to remain calm, giving us encouragement.

My mother and I just held onto one another. We knew that we had been hit because of the crashing sounds above and around us. The house was breaking apart. All I could pray for was for us not to be buried alive under all the falling debris.

The bunker area was filling up with dust from all the fallen debris and we were having trouble breathing. My mother took out towels from our suitcase and we groped our way to the barrel of water. The water in the barrel was supposed to be changed periodically, but that had not been done for a long time. At this time of need, we did not care. We were ever so glad to have this foul-smelling water for wetting our towels. Pressing the towels to our mouths helped our breathing a lot.

There were many more near hits but none as powerful as the one that hit our house. There never was any panic among us; everyone was trying to help one another. But we all knew that we had to get out soon or it would end disastrously for us.

The civil defense men brought us bad news back from their search for a way out. Our exit was blocked from fallen debris. The whole wall lined with the tree trunks, where we had been sitting, had caved in, along with a part of the ceiling. We had been very fortunate to move from that room when we did, or we would be buried now, under all the debris.

They decided to break through the *Durchbruch* (emergency exit) leading to house No. 110. When the shelter had been constructed, bricks of a portion of the connecting wall had been carefully removed and then lightly mortared together again. That made it easy to break through in case of emergency. The escape exit was clearly marked with white paint. A pickaxe was hanging on the wall next to the exit. We could go from our cellar to the one in No.110 and they in turn had the same set up as we did. It was possible to go from one building to the next and beyond until safety was reached. It was an escape route.

The civil defense men started to break through the bricked up exit. Just when one man got ready to step through our opening a breaking noise was hear from the adjoining cellar wall from house No. 110. He waited until the other wall broke open, and my mother and I recognized the man that came stepping through from the other side. It was the father of one of my friends, Inge. He was glad to have met up with us. He told us that bombs had fallen onto our houses in the back and the side wing of No. 110. He was certain that everyone from No. 110 was dead except for him, his wife and daughter. They had been sitting by themselves in the walkway outside the shelter. They had stumbled in the dark through the long side wing cellar, over all the fallen debris and piles of coal to the front house cellar exit and found it blocked. Then they had made their way to this exit. They were exhausted.

We were all shocked and saddened hearing about the people's fate from No. 110 and about the houses in the back. It was what we had feared ever since we felt the huge explosion.

I remember seeing Inge's father stepping back to their side while the civil defense men held up their flashlight, which was the only lighting we had. The next thing we heard was a terrible scream and a big crash, followed by a huge cloud of dust that blew into our area. When he had reached for his wife and daughter to help them, the whole ceiling above them gave way and came crashing down on top of them, burying them under all the debris.

The poor man went out of control trying to get to them, but it was impossible. The civil defense men had to pull him away from the opening. It was so tragic that they had come so far through the cellars only to end up like that. We were all crying with him. It was heartbreaking.

Our thoughts soon turned to concern about our own situation. We were having more trouble breathing because of the new dust. We were desperate to find a way out before we suffocated. Luckily, the second barrel of water was found intact and usable. It was a big help. I could dip my towel into the water and suck on it a little to quench my thirst.

In order to get to the emergency exit to house No. 112, we had to go through the room where we had been sitting earlier. The men did their best to clear a pathway for us and we managed to climb over all the debris without falling. We were actually getting around quite well in the dark. Everyone was helping one another. Considering that most of the people were elderly, including the civil defense men, that had been important.

I do not remember anymore how many people were actually present. I know that some were absent, including our friend, Inge Heinz.

Just before we reached the exit to house No. 112, we again heard the sounds of someone breaking through. This time it was the proprietor of the restaurant. He had come looking for us because he had not seen anybody from our house outside. He told us that everyone was alright from house No. 112 and that they were using his private cellar entrance to get out. Their main exit was blocked. He urged us to get out immediately because the fire had reached the second floor (not counting the ground floor).

Some people followed him back to his exit. However, the civil defense men had managed to clear our own staircase and after a lot of pushing were able to get the door open. It had been blocked by fallen debris, but now there was enough space for one person to get through. Surprisingly the narrow door opening allowed enough light in to help us walk up the stairs, without the missing railing, helping Tante Maske along.

I was the first one out. What I saw was a big shock. There were fires burning everywhere and there was nothing left where the back of our house once stood. All around us was total destruction. Tante Maske came out next and looked in disbelief at the burning pile of rubble. My mother stepped out last and when she saw what used to be our home, she totally came apart. I had never seen my mother like that. She cried and wanted to go back into the rubble and look for her iron. My poor mother did not make any sense. An iron was the last thing we needed. I had all I could do to keep her from going back.

I am convinced that she went into shock when she saw the aftermath of the bombing and what it had done to her home. I had never seen my mother react so out of control and become so emotional, as she did then. I never saw her react like that again. It was difficult to comprehend. All those past years of working and saving to have a nice home and now it was gone, burned to ashes. She could not understand why this had happened.

It took a lot of begging to get her to move on. I was getting very worried about the floors above us. I was afraid that they might come crashing down on us, like we had seen happen just a while before. And what two blockbuster bombs did not destroy, the incendiary bombs were finishing up.

We finally made our way through the hallway and the once so beautiful entry, all filled with broken tile and glass, and out to the other side of the street. We could see that the top two floors of the front of the house were gone and that the fire had reached the landlord's apartment on the first floor. Big flames were erupting from the window openings.

We had made it out just in time. We had a lot to be thankful for, having escaped our blocked shelter. We were alive and not buried under all the debris of our house, unlike the people from No. 110 and the two houses behind us. But to be honest, when we were standing amidst all the destruction and watching the fires burning everything to ashes, we felt nothing but despair.

We were standing next to our landlords, Herr and Frau Sunder. They were both crying while watching the flames shooting out of their apartment, devouring all of their possessions. All around us, people were staring in disbelief at the merciless, devouring flames.

When we had escaped up the stairs, I had looked for our chairs, but they were gone. In all the confusion that took place, I had lost my bag of cocoa and the spoon, but I still had my baby doll and "Foxie," my mother's stole. Frau Sunder was clutching a featherbed, almost as strange as my mother would have looked holding an iron. I have often wondered about this. How did she get hold of a featherbed? She certainly did not get it from their apartment after we left the shelter. She must have had it in their own private cellar. I felt sorry for them, despite of all the times that he had been so mean to me. They both appeared to be two old, forlorn people.[5]

I looked around. I could see that most of the houses on our street had been destroyed and were engulfed in flames. The two houses where most of my friends lived appeared to have survived. The house between them was burning out of control, as were those on the opposite sides. People were running with pails of water from the street pump at the corner and brigading them up to the rooftop, trying to protect the roof from flying embers.[6]

The wind had started to blow hard, blowing dust and cinders around. The air was so full of smoke that it burned our eyes. The civil defense patrol came along and asked us to go to our assigned shelter. They were concerned about people getting hurt from collapsing houses.

When we got to the corner of our street, we saw several fire trucks lined up on the street, alongside the AEG factory. They were just sitting there with the firemen standing by and watching the neighborhood burning down. Unbelievable! My mother walked up to them and asked why were they not helping the people

---

5   At least they were not totally homeless, like the rest of us. They still owned a nice cottage and garden in Finkenkrug, a suburb of Berlin, where they could go and live.

6   I remember that every apartment had to have a pail of sand outside of the door, probably meant for putting out incendiary bombs.

extinguish the fires and save their homes? Their answer was that they could not. They had strict orders to protect only the factories. What a cruel order. Many homes could have been saved with their help. There was plenty of water available in a *Loschbecken* (a huge, deep cement basin filled with water to use for extinguishing fires). It was located right next to the Catholic church in the little roadside park, by my *Gartenplatz* (garden square).

I have often thought about the locations of the basins. They were always located close to the factories. We had really been fooled into believing that the basins had been installed to protect our homes. But the Hitler regime did not operate that way. They did not care to save people's homes. Their priorities were the factories. In all our troubled times, I never recall seeing a fire truck come to help put out the fires. I would have surely noticed, as I stood in front of burning houses many times.[7]

When my mother and I were by the *Gartenplatz*, I happened to look up. I saw the church steeple on fire and it worried me. I was afraid that it might come crashing down on top of us. I wanted to walk faster to get by this dangerous spot

---

7   I remember when they built the basin near our house; it was very deep with sloping sides, wide on the top, narrow on the bottom. We would go there after the workmen left. We had to sneak by the guard's shed, but we were not too worried about him. He was an old man and we could easily outrun him. But we could not outrun his dog, so we had to be watchful for it. We had fun running up and down on the sloping sides until the cement was poured.

When the basin was finished they installed a fence around it, but it did not keep the boys out. In the summer, they would go swimming in it and in the winter after it froze over, they ice-skated on it. Of course, it was forbidden to use the basin for these activities and rightly so, for it was dangerous.

My girlfriend Ursula and I stood watch a few times, while they were having fun, except for one evening when we acted by impulse to tease them. The boys were swimming without bathing suits and we decided to take their pants and hide them. It did not go over too good. We were scolded by a couple of nuns who were looking out of their windows across the street from the basin. So we took the boys' pants back to them, but not before we had their promise that they would not beat us up. The boys kept their promise, but excluded us from all their games for quite a while. It became a very boring time. They certainly knew how to punish us. The worst of it was not being able to go for embroidery lessons anymore at the home of retired nuns. Some time before we had been asked by the nuns to join four other girls to learn embroidery and work on a long altar cover. Each of us were given a section and started out with a basic cross-stitch. We had really enjoyed going there, but now we did not have the courage to face them.

but we could not because of Tante Maske. She had trouble walking. I kept my eyes on the church steeple as we moved slowly past.

The wind was blowing very hard now, making it more difficult to walk. Lots of dust and pieces of cinder were flying through the air. A couple of small pieces found their way into my eyes, which was very painful.

When we finally reached the shelter for the homeless, we found the house totally engulfed in flames. Now what were we to do? Looking around at all the destruction, with fires burning everywhere, it was difficult to comprehend. The same scene was repeated in all directions—blazing fires and people running while carrying pails of water. It seemed like a bad dream, one that would not go away. Very little of what I saw resembled the old neighborhood that I had walked through earlier that afternoon.

Someone stopped and took pity on us lost souls and told us to go down into their basement shelter for something warm to drink. We accepted their kind offer. It meant a lot to us that they would stop to care for us when they were so busy trying to save their own house from burning. In their shelter I tried rinsing my eyes out with water but it did not help much. My eyes still felt very sore and irritated. We did get something to drink. We had not realized how thirsty we really were until then, or that we were cold. It must have been chilly. It was the end of November.

I also do not have any recollection of time. I do not know how long the air raid lasted, how long were we stuck in the air raid shelter, or at what time we arrived at the shelter for the homeless. We both had watches but I do not believe that we ever looked at them. Time had become meaningless to us.

We were told of another shelter, near Stettiner Bahnhof, the train station. We were quite doubtful about its surviving so near the railroad. Nevertheless, I was hopeful that it did survive and that I would find a nurse there to help me with my eyes.

We set off on our way after thanking the people for their kindness and for taking the time to care for us. They all looked so tired, but they had managed to keep the fire under control. We wished them the best of luck.

Much to our surprise, we found the shelter undamaged, though surrounded by burning houses. Incredible! I was so relieved to see a nurse on duty. She took me right away to her station and cleaned out my eyes. What a good feeling to be able to open my eyes without the pain. The staff offered us hot drinks and sandwiches, and treated us very nicely. We then rejoined some of our neighbors and found ourselves an empty spot to settle down for the rest of the night.[8]

---

8   The NSV or *Nationale Sozialistische Volkswohlfahrt* (National Socialistic People's Welfare) was a truly well-organized group of women volunteers. They tried their best to help the homeless people. Within a short time after an air raid attack, they would arrive at the devastated areas and set up their field kitchens and first aid stations. They were very efficient and helpful.

Our first assigned shelter, the one we had found in flames, had also been the meeting place of the *HJ* (Hitler Youth) and other Nazi party offices. I had joined the Hitler Youth when I was ten years old. It was a lot of fun for a ten or eleven-year-old girl—going to weekly meetings, learning and singing songs, playing games. I enjoyed going on field trips, especially visiting hospitals. I remember our group visiting the Hermann Goering Kaserne, a place where members of the *Luftwaffe* (German Air Force) were recuperating from injuries caused by the war. They seemed to enjoy our visits. Most of the ones we met were not from Berlin and did not have families coming to see them. My girl friend and I went back a few times by ourselves and took them books and magazines that we collected from our neighbors.

I never owned a uniform, although I wanted one badly. It required textile coupons and according to my mother I always needed something else more urgently. The uniform was very simple, but it looked smart. A dark blue skirt, a white blouse, and a dark blue cardigan with red and green trim around the collar and bottom. The cardigan looked very similar to the style that was worn in Bavaria. Adolf himself must have selected it.

A *Fahrtentuch* (scarf) completed the uniform. It was held together with a leather knot, which had to be earned by doing different tasks within the community and receiving points. My first attempt at earning points was babysitting for a neighbor across the street from us. She had six children and one on the way, all under the age of six. It had already earned her *das Mutterkreuz* (the Mother Cross), the highest order of motherhood, presented to her by Adolf himself. He approved of her many children with favoritism to her family. Her husband was stationed in Paris, France, and he often sent big boxes of goods home to her. He also came home on leave often, a subject that was very upsetting to my mother, especially when she saw him strutting around the neighborhood in his boastful manner. Before he joined the military, he never held a job for very long. They were poor and dependent on welfare. Now she owned several fur coats and could invite neighbors to parties, serving French champagne.

I would not have normally done anything for the woman but I liked little children and they very seldom were seen outside. I thought my girl friend and I could take them to the park, but we spent most of the time cleaning them up and putting them on pots while their mother watched us. She was a messy housekeeper, and very lazy.

My mother did not know about this job until she saw my little booklet in which my babysitting was recorded and vouched for by this woman. She became very angry,

The full realization of what happened on that night of November 22, 1943, did not become immediately evident, but when it did, the cruel reality of it all was very painful. And yet we were thankful to have survived the frightening and life-threatening ordeal, despite our losses. Yes, we were thankful. My mother and I could easily have been buried under all the debris and died with the rest of the people. But we were alive.

Tuesday, November 23, 1943

We spent a rather restless night at the shelter. In the morning the NSV women served us a hot breakfast. Then we left Tante Maske behind and went back to our neighborhood. We just had to see what it looked like in daylight.

What a heartbreaking sight! The houses looked like skeletons from the front, while in the back there were just huge piles of rubble where main parts of the houses once stood. I could look right through from our street to the elevated railroad tracks. Houses used to block the view.

The fires were still burning, and because of all the coal in the cellars they would continue burning and smoldering for about three weeks. Someone told us that the owners of the dairy from No. 112 had lost all their animals. They tried saving the horses and the cows but the animals kept running back into the burning barn. Their effort had failed, sadly.

---

not so much with me, but with the woman. She did not waste any time. She marched over and told her how she felt about the whole deal.

My second attempt at filling up my booklet with points was at a small candy-making shop, wrapping pieces of marzipan. We were allowed to eat all we wanted, but could not take any home with us. We certainly ate our share of marzipan. It was delicious. But the job only lasted through the summer vacation. My mother would not allow it during school time. Needless to say, I never earned enough points to get my leather knot.

I do not regret belonging to the Hitler Youth Group when I did. They were good times, but it changed after November of 1943 to sad, unsettled times. The fire at the shelter not only destroyed our meeting place but also the files and records of the Hitler Youth Group. They never contacted me and I never tried joining another group. In the end I was glad that it turned out this way for me.

Looking in the daylight at what was left on our street was quite an emotional experience—and then to think how quickly the devastation had occurred. All for what purpose?[9]

We returned to the shelter. Tante Maske was anxiously waiting for us, hoping that we would tell her that our homes were still intact and that the previous night had been a bad dream. But sadly, we had to tell her the truth that it was all gone and nothing was left, only a burning pile of rubble. She looked utterly dejected.

Much to our surprise, her daughter came looking for her at the shelter. My mother was glad to see her and happy to hear her offer to take her mother home with her. She was finally showing some feelings for her mother. Ever since her marriage she had isolated herself from her, indicating that her mother did not fit into her new lifestyle. She would only drop in for short visits on her birthday or around Christmas. That was also the only time when she would bring the grandchildren along. Tante Maske never complained, but it bothered my mother to think of how she was neglected. I remember a couple of times when my mother took care of her when she was confined to bed with phlebitis in both of her legs. After repeated calls to her daughter, she finally came by to see her. She only stayed for a few minutes. She really had been an uncaring daughter and very ungrateful.

Tante Maske had lost her husband in the First World War and had raised her daughter by herself, working very hard to support them. She had looked after me while my parents went to work. She had shown a lot of patience with me, as I had not always been easy to handle. Her door was always left open for me to come

---

9   I remember what our street was like before the attack. Our street was a good-sized block that extended from the railroad bridge to the small roadside park or *Gartenplatz*. I recall ten or twelve houses on each side of the street. Almost every house contained one or two small businesses. Our house had a bakery, a smoke shop and a grocery store. All together there were five pubs, four grocery stores, two bakeries, two smoke shops, two produce markets, one butcher shop, one candy shop, two soap and miscellaneous stores, two dairy businesses, one coal business, one barbershop, and one small factory, the Kuehne plant. They made sauerkraut, mustard and pickles. The Kuehne plant (which is still in operation today in Berlin) had a small shop in the front of a house with the plant located in the back. The sauerkraut and the pickles were sold out of the barrel and put into containers, which we provided. My mother always planned ahead when she sent me to get sauerkraut. Instead of the one pound she really wanted, she would ask for a half of a pound more. She knew that her daughter would be sampling it all the way home.

and go, as I needed to. My mother told me that one of my first spoken words was "Masche" for Maske.

As a very young girl I would stand in my bed and pound on the wall calling for her. Her kitchen was on the other side of the wall and her sewing machine sat there. She supported herself by sewing men's shirts for a small company, keeping very busy. Many Saturday evenings, when my parents went out to be with friends in the neighborhood, I would lie in my bed and talk to her, listening to the hum of her sewing machine, until I fell asleep. It was comforting to know that she was close by.

I did not know at the time when we said our goodbyes that I would not see her again. We hated to part from one another. She was our friend and we had become very close over the years. My mother visited her a couple of times after our parting and found her in a very unhappy state. She did not like living in her daughter's home.

We received a note from her daughter sometime in early 1944, informing us that her mother had passed away. My mother and I both felt that she just never got over the loss of her home and had lost her will to live. We felt sad, losing our dear old friend.

After lunch, we returned to our street again just to stand around with our neighbors and look at the pile of burning rubble that used to be our homes. I cannot explain our behavior. Perhaps we were trying to get used to the reality of our loss. Late in the afternoon, Frau Linke, the mother of my friend, Kurt, came to the shelter with her neighbor and invited us and the Doring family, our superintendent, to come home with them. They lived across the street from us, at house No. 81, one of the two houses that survived and would eventually make it to the end of the war. The other house was No. 83, where many of my friends lived. I often wished that we had been living in those houses.

We accepted their thoughtful offer and went home with them. Frau Linke had sent Kurt and his brother Werner to stay with their grandparents, away from our torn up neighborhood. She gave us their room to stay in. They lived in the front of the house on the fourth floor with the attic above them. They had worked hard all night, carrying pails of water up onto the roof, protecting it from flying sparks and embers. The adjoining houses had burned out of control. It was a miracle that they were able to save their house.

The windows were all blown out in their apartment, along with other damage, but it was habitable. They had covered the window openings with cardboard and blankets. It made it very dark inside, but perhaps it was better that way. It kept us from looking across the street to where we used to live. I helped carry pails of water upstairs from the street pump for our personal use, the water pipes being broken and shut off, along with the gas and electrical lines.[10]

We had brought along sandwiches, distributed at the shelter, for our evening meal and we shared them with Herr and Frau Linke. I became aware of how nervous I was getting as the clock moved closer to the time when it had all started the previous night. I was thinking and reliving the horror of it all and I was praying that the airplanes would not return that night. We were all exhausted and we needed a good night's rest. But it was not to be.

Right on time at 7:30 the sirens went off, announcing another *Fliegeralarm* (air raid). We picked up our things and wasted no time heading out of the door. There we bumped into the Doring family as they came out of the next apartment. We ran down the stairs as fast as the darkness allowed us and into their air raid shelter, which was located in the front of the house. But I froze when we reached the entrance. I could not make myself go down into the cellar. Neither could my mother or the Doring family, despite our friends' encouraging words. The memories of the previous night were too vivid on our minds. We were afraid.

We ran out into the street and decided to go to the bunker in Humboldthain, but we only made it to the corner of our street, at the *Gartenplatz*, when the searchlights appeared over us. We knew what that meant. We joined a group of people running to take shelter in the tunnel that ran under the railroad tracks. It was a poor choice for a shelter. We would have been safer in the cellar with our friends or inside the bunker. Earlier that day, my friend Ursula's mother had asked us to spend the night with them at the bunker. We declined because we just did not want to inconvenience anyone, knowing that someone would have to give up their bunk bed to make room for us. After this night's awful experiences, we wished that we had accepted their offer.

The tunnel was a pedestrian walkway underneath the railroad tracks. It was a very convenient shortcut that avoided a roundabout walk of several blocks to reach the other side. The entrance to the tunnel used to be as wide as the tunnel itself, but as part of the air raid precautions a wall had been built in front of the entrance. This allowed less space to enter. When we reached the entrance,

---

10 We were very lucky to have the street pumps. They helped us out many times. I remember stopping for a cool drink or a quick wash up before going home after playing in the sandbox at the *Gartenplatz*.

along with many other people, the anti-aircraft guns on top of the bunker started blasting, which created a panic situation. People started to push and shove to get to the inside of the tunnel. The civil defense men did their best to keep things orderly. They asked our building superintendent to stay with them up front. They needed his help.

The tunnel was already quite full of people. In addition, we noticed, many pieces of furniture had been stored on one side. People from nearby houses had brought them there, hoping to save something before the fires burned up everything. We found ourselves a spot on the left side of the wall. When we heard the anti-aircraft guns it only confirmed our feelings that we were again the targets of the enemy airplanes.

The lights began to flicker on and off. We felt explosions all around us. The ground shook and the walls trembled. It was another night of terror. The facial expressions of the people standing near us showed fear, and we were afraid too.

The noise from the guns and the explosions was so much louder in the tunnel than it had been in the cellar the previous night. Every so often I felt a draft of air blowing through. I could not help wondering if it was *der Tod* (death) coming for us. As I stood there in the tunnel with my mother, a strange feeling came over me. It was as if "someone" was telling me to move away from that spot and go over to the other side. I asked my mother if we could. She agreed, without asking my reason, and we moved a little further down the tunnel. And just in time!

The next big bomb hit on the tracks above us, very close. The wall where we had been standing only a couple of minutes before came crashing down, revealing a big dark hole. Then the lights went out.

I held onto my mother. Hearing the people screaming for help we realized how close we had come to being where they were now. We had been saved from injuries, perhaps even death, by moving away from that spot, thanks to God our Savior. But we were not out of danger yet. We still needed a lot of help to get through this disastrous night.

The next sounds we heard were the sound of water and someone yelling that a main water pipe had been hit. In an instant chaos broke out among the people. Frightened people were pushing and shoving frantically towards the middle of the tunnel. There a set of steps led up to a walkover platform and other steps led back down toward the other entrance to the tunnel. My mother and I held tightly on to one another, while moving with the pushing and shoving crowd. We could still hear people crying for help and the sound of water gushing behind us. We knew that falling would be disastrous. We were familiar with the lay out of the tunnel, having walked through it countless times, but we had never done it in total darkness with such a frantic crowd of people.

We made it safely up the steps, across the platform area and down the steps on the other side without falling. I came close to losing my suitcase when it somehow became entangled with someone's bag. My mother told me to let go of it, but I pulled until it was free.

We were relieved to have reached the other side of the stairs, but then we learned that the exit was blocked by fire. We were trapped. Fire in front of us and water behind us.

There was a lot of smoke blowing into the tunnel. It bothered our eyes and our breathing. Everyone found a spot to sit on the ground, which helped a little bit.

We were sitting on the left side by the wall, and every once in a while I took a lick on the tiled wall. It felt cool. We were all very thirsty. We would have liked to have some of the water to drink that was filling up the tunnel behind us.

I never heard how deep it actually became before it was turned off. I overheard people complaining about the pieces of furniture. They had become an additional obstacle as the water pushed the pieces along.

The screaming and the crying finally stopped. I hoped that the people had been helped out through the entrance of the tunnel where we had entered. The anti-aircraft guns were also now silent, but we still felt and heard explosions going off around us. We found out later that the explosions we heard came from *Zeitbomben* (time-delay bombs).

Suddenly we heard someone calling Frau Doring and her son's names. She recognized her husband's voice and she answered him, directing him to where we were. It was good to see him. We had been concerned. He told us that the *Entwarnung* (all clear) had been given quite a while ago. He had managed to find his way across the railroad tracks to the door on the platform. Many bombs had fallen onto the tracks and it had been very hazardous walking.

I knew about the door on the platform. Many times while running through the tunnel with my friends we would open the door and take a peek. I had been thinking about this exit and wondering if it could be used as an escape route for us. But according to Herr Doring, it was too risky. He urged us and everyone else around to come along to the tunnel exit and leave this death trap behind. He was worried about the *Zeitbomben* that had fallen onto the tracks above us, further endangering our situation.

So we made our way to the exit, but when we stepped outside, I backed up. I saw huge flames leaping across the narrow street. From the facades of the apartment houses big chunks of burning debris were falling and flying through the air. I panicked when I saw this blazing inferno. I was terrified of running through it.

My mother took out a blanket from our suitcase and, throwing it over my head, took hold of my hand and pulled me along. Without my mother's help, I never would have had the courage to run through the blaze.

When we reached the end of the street, I collapsed into a heap on the ground, all shaken up. It had been frightening. I do not recall another time when I experienced such a panic attack. Chaussee Strasse, where we had moved to, was also ablaze, but being a much wider street it did not appear as frightening. A few people from the tunnel had followed us. Together we walked down the middle of the street with our heads held low. We were trying to keep the blowing pieces of cinder from getting in our eyes. I knew how painful that would be.

The wind was blowing furiously and mercilessly, adding to the difficulties for the people involved in rescue efforts and for those who were trying to save their houses from burning to the ground. We walked by so much devastation, just as we had the night before. The attackers had not left much untouched in our neighborhood. What had survived the previous night had been finished off on this second night.

The church steeple of the Catholic church by the *Gartenplatz*, the one that I had feared would fall upon us while walking by the night before, did fall down. But the rest of the church was saved from burning down by the nuns' water brigade. They carried pails of water tirelessly from the nearby concrete reservoir to the rooftop of the church. It was a shame that they did not have an easier and quicker way to move the plentiful water supply. The nuns did lose their convent, which consisted of several buildings on both sides of the *Gartenplatz*, including the home for the retired nuns, where I had enjoyed my few embroidery lessons.

Someone running by with a pail full of water told us where to find a street pump to get a drink of water, for we were still very thirsty. While standing in line at the pump, we were told that we could seek shelter in the subway station, which was located close by. This time I did not have a problem going down into the underground, probably because there was not an active air raid alert.

In the subway station we discovered that the lights were on, which surprised us. There were two trains sitting in the station with quite a few people either sitting or lying down inside on the benches. We found ourselves an empty spot and settled down for the rest of the night. I do not recall if anyone actually fell asleep, but at least we rested.[11]

Wednesday, November 24, 1943

It was one month before *Weihnachten* (Christmas Eve). We looked forward to this Christmas, hoping that our wish would be granted to have my dad home with us. In his recent letters he had written that he was still on the list for *Heimat-Urlaub* (home leave) and that he hoped he could be with us for the holidays. But it had been the same message and hope the previous years, and then at the last minute his leave would be canceled. Once he had to step aside for someone who had more than one child waiting at home. That was so unfair! The last time that we were together for Christmas was 1939—a long, long time ago. We had spent many sad and lonely holidays without him. And now we were homeless, resting in a subway train. It seemed so unjust.

---

11 After I began writing about my experiences, I came across a book entitled "*The Fall of Berlin,*" by Anthony Read and David Fisher (Pimlico 2002), written from the Royal Air Force's point of view. The authors write that the raid of November 22 had been the first real success of the Royal Air Force. That night 764 planes had taken off for Berlin. The following night, November 23, 383 aircraft were sent to Berlin. They did not need marker flares this time for dropping their bombs. Many streets were lit up by the glare of fires still burning from the night before. The British estimated that 3,000 buildings had been destroyed or damaged, with 175,000 people made homeless and an estimated 2,000 people had been killed. In January of 1944 a casualty list was issued. It held that the three raids in late November of 1943 killed 4,370 people.

Many Berliners felt the raid on November 23 had been even more awful than the bigger one the night before. Dr. Goebbels, our propaganda minister, inclined to agree in his diary, stating that the damage caused was extensive, with the inner city and the working class neighborhood getting the worst of it. That was my neighborhood! The Berlin Zoo was also hit on that night. Of the 2000 animals that were in the zoo, 750 were killed.

I have always known that the raids that took place on November 22 and November 23 were bad and very destructive to our neighborhood, but actually reading about it in that book confirmed my belief. And seeing the casualty list made me aware again at how fortunate my mother and I were to survive the horrible events of those two nights. I don't know why we had to endure so many hardships but throughout our difficult times, my mother and I never felt abandoned, God was always by our side.

When it became daylight, we moved on to our shelter. We were very doubtful we would still find it intact after last night's bombardment. The shelter was located on the same street as the entrance to the pedestrian tunnel, perhaps a block away. We had to take several detours. The area around Stettiner Bahnhof was a complex of burning and smoking rubble. In many places it was impossible to get through. But to our surprise we found the shelter still usable. Everything else around it was gone.

We lived in a very industrial neighborhood. Two large factory plants—Schwartzkopf and AEG (Allgemeine Elektrische Gesellschaft)—were located at either end of our street, and a second large AEG complex was one street away. Behind us, the railroad tracks led to a very important railroad yard and a railway link to the east—Stettin, the Baltic Sea, Lithuania, and Russia. In fact, my dad left on a train from Stettiner Bahnhof, after being home on leave, to travel back to Russia.

The railroad tracks did get hit, but were soon repaired and back in operation. The factories that were surrounded by our neighborhood survived any serious damage and continued working, while the houses lay in ruins. Complete devastation existed in our neighborhood. It was so bad that it was brought to the attention of Reichsmarshal Hermann Goering and Propaganda Minister Dr. Josef Goebbels. They were directed to visit our area and offer encouraging words to the bombed out people.

Hermann Goering was the first one to come. He rode around in his chauffeur-driven limousine, looking ridiculous in his white uniform and waving his marshal's baton. He stepped out of the car, at the *Gartenplatz*, where a group of people was standing. He tried to offer a few caring words to cheer everyone up. They remembered his boastful words from a speech at the beginning of the war. He had stated very adamantly that he should be called "Meier" should enemy airplanes ever fly over Berlin and drop their bombs onto its people. I am quite certain that he regretted ever making that statement when the people at the *Gartenplatz* started loudly shouting "Meier! Meier!" He quickly got back into his car and left hurriedly.

Needless to say his visit was not received well among the people and neither was the one by Goebbels. He also came and toured the area, promising the people an extra treat to make them feel better. What a joke! A few extra cigarettes and a bottle of schnapps for the men, some real coffee beans for the women and a sweet treat for the children. It was a sad attempt at consoling the people in our situation.[12]

I am sorry to say that my mother and I missed these visits, but perhaps it was for the best. Knowing my mother's state of mind, she would certainly have joined the angry crowd of people and possibly gotten into trouble. That was something I always worried about, as she was too outspoken. For a while, the visits of Goering and Goebbels were the talk in the neighborhood, especially how the people had responded so angrily. Even the fanatical party members kept quiet and out of sight.

At the shelter a lot more people had come since we left. It was getting very crowded. As we stood in line waiting for something to drink, we saw my grandmother come through the door. I believe that it was at this moment that we were brought back to reality. In the whole time since the bombing, we had never given any thought to going to my grandparents' house, only a ten or fifteen minute walk away. Instead we had roamed around like lost souls, adding more misery to our misfortune and bringing so much worry to my grandparents. It was not like us to be so thoughtless. Later on in life, we often talked about our strange behavior during that time. We could not find an explanation for it, no matter how we tried. It remained a mystery to us.

When my grandmother saw us, she broke down crying. She was so relieved and happy to finally have found us. We were feeling the same, very relieved. It was a wonderful feeling to walk into a home that we were familiar with and find my grandfather waiting for us. It had been an awful time for them, dealing with the uncertainty of our fate. It almost felt, despite everything that had happened to us during the last two nights, that it was not so bad anymore. We were still homeless, but we were no longer lost.

My grandmother had tried several times to get some information about us, without having any luck. When she heard that our street had been bombed the night of November 22, she immediately came looking for us after the "all clear" was sounded. She made it as close as the bridge, where the civil defense patrol would not let her walk any further. She tried a different way, but ran into the same situation. She never told my grandfather how devastated our street was or that

---

12 The *Sonderausgaben* (special treat) that we received after surviving the bombing reminds me of what my dad wrote in his letters. They too were treated the same way. After a successful battle with the enemy the survivors were rewarded with schnapps, cigarettes, coffee beans and candy. What a sad charade!

someone had told her that the people from those destroyed houses were all buried under the burning debris. It was upsetting enough for him when she returned home without us. But she refused to believe the rumors and again came back looking for us. This time someone told her to go and check out the shelter where we finally found one another.

After a thorough clean up, which felt so good, and a tasty breakfast, I fell asleep while sitting on the sofa. When my mother woke me up, I was lying down all covered up. I could not believe that I had slept all day. The fatigue had gotten hold of me.

After supper my mother told me that she had decided to accept our friend's invitation and spend the night with them in their room at the bunker. They had applied for a room at the bunker a long time ago and had only recently been given one. In the meantime, Ursula, her two brothers Guenter and Manfred, along with their mother, had been evacuated to *Ostpreussen* (East Prussia). They were seeking a safer place away from Berlin, something that *Ostpreussen* was still able to offer—a peaceful way of living. But they had found their accommodation very unpleasant with the farmer's family. They were not welcomed into the community. It was expected of them to work for their room and board, which was a very poor arrangement. But mostly it was the unfriendly treatment of the farmers that brought Ursula and her family back to Berlin. I heard many people speak unfavorably of their host families. As of 1943 the war had not come to their parts of Germany, so consequently they were still enjoying a peaceful life with little concern about their fellow citizens. A rude awakening awaited them when the war reached their homeland during the winter of 1944–1945.

We arrived at the bunker where we found Ursula waiting for us in the lobby. She took us upstairs to their room. It was a very small room, with two sets of bunk beds and just enough room to walk between. On every floor was a recreation area, with tables and chairs and a play area for small children. It was quite nice.

Guenter, Ursula, and I were playing a board game when I started to feel nervous again. I knew without looking at a clock that it must be close to 7:30. My anxiety was very apparent to the others, but I did not know what to do about it. And it was not long before the announcement came over the loudspeakers that an air raid alarm had been sounded. We were asked to leave the area and go into our rooms to create space for the people who were coming in from the outside, seeking shelter during the air raid.

This bunker was the communication and control center. It had *Horchgerate* (listening equipment) and searchlights. The other bunker, located on the opposite side of the park, had four towers. On each one of them was an anti-aircraft gun. There were at least four bunkers with this configuration located in Berlin.

We all decided to go to bed. I had not done that for quite some time. I had learned to seek shelter during an air raid. But then I was in a shelter, and it was a different feeling. My mother and I shared an upper bunk bed. Ursula and her mother shared one and the boys each had one to themselves. Manfred was about three or four years old, a very spoiled little boy, who insisted on sleeping by himself.

I lay awake for a long time, listening to a low humming noise, the only noise I could hear. I was very uncomfortable and apprehensive. The stillness bothered me most of all, along with not knowing what was happening on the outside. The tiny quarters were giving me a closed-in feeling. I was not aware that I had a little claustrophobia in me, which would explain my anxiety.

Thursday, November 25, 1943

We spent one more night with our friends at the bunker. In the morning we told them that we wished to try the other bunker. Using it would mean that we would remain at home with my grandparents until an impending air raid was announced over the radio. It was very thoughtful of our friends to share their room with us, but it really was very uncomfortable for everyone, especially with the room and the bunk beds being so small. But the main reason was my anxiety and claustrophobia. As soon as they told us that an air raid was imminent and we had to go into the room, I became very fearful. I really had a problem. I tried not to show it, but it was noticeable and I did not want to bother others with it.[13]

We had talked to our new neighbor, Frau Bottger, and she told us that she sought shelter with her two daughters at the *Flakbunker*. We decided to give it a try. We spent a lot of time at various city offices filling out forms and talking to officials, a typical bureaucratic nightmare. My mother had become very quiet. I had to do most of the talking and answer their questions. No matter where we were, our path would always lead us back to our street, as we had to reassure

---

13 I would like to mention that I never lost my fear of seeking shelter in a cellar during an air raid alarm. It also took years before I could listen to the sound of a siren without getting panicky.

ourselves again and again of the reality of our situation. We would stop at the bakery, located at the end of the street, near the bridge. The bakery had also been heavily damaged and had floors missing above it, but somehow they managed to be back in business, baking only basic goods. It had become a meeting place for former neighbors.

On one of those trips to our street, I scribbled our name and whereabouts on a piece of wall from our building that had been left standing. It was right next to where the entrance to the bakery used to be. It read *"3 X taglich frische Schrippen"* ("3 X everyday fresh-baked rolls").

A little remnant of what once existed.

It used to be so nice and convenient to have a bakery located within the house. Our apartment was always pleasantly warm during the cold months of winter, with the wonderful aroma of baking drifting throughout. The bakery was located in the side building. Many times I would stop in and have a look at what the three bakers, a father and his two sons, were making on long tables by the window. I liked watching them. And I liked getting my bag of *Kuchenkrumel* (cake crumbs).

When my mother was at work, she made an arrangement with the owner of the bakery, Frau Olechek, to give me whatever I wanted and write it in her book. My mother would pay for what I ate at the end of the week. It worked well, until some older girls, living in the next house, found out about it. In order to let me join in their games, they asked me to get them treats from the bakery. It worked for only a little while, because Frau Olechek became suspicious of my new taste for the fancy pieces of cake instead of the usual *Schnecken* (danish). She watched me leave the bakery and give the treats to the waiting girls. Well, my mother had a good talk with me. I could still get whatever I wanted, but not for others.

Other than special occasions, my mother very seldom baked. We would buy whatever we wanted to eat. The oven in our kitchen stove was unreliable for baking. It was difficult to get the proper temperature. It was either too hot or not hot enough. Sometimes, she would mix up a cake and take it to the bakery to have it baked for a small fee. Many people would do this, especially around Easter or Christmas.[14]

And then only a small piece of wall remained to remind me of what was once there.

---

14   In later years, when I was working and earning money, I bought my mother a stove top three piece *Backwunder* (baking wonder), that could be placed on a gas flame. A very unique oven, it baked wonderfully. No more burned cakes.

Friday, November 26, 1943

Friday evening the radio interrupted its program with the announcement that we would hear almost every night in the days to come—*"Achtung-Achtung, eine wichtige Luftlademeldung! Feindliche Flieger befinden sich im Anflug auf Berlin uber Hannover-Braunschweig!"* ("Attention, Attention, here is an important announcement about the air position! Enemy aircraft are approaching Hannover-Braunschweig destination Berlin!") We knew that three announced locations in particular—Konigswusterhausen, Hannover-Braunschweig or Magdeburg—always meant that they were flying to Berlin.

We quickly got ready and left for the bunker. We met Frau Bottger and her two girls on the stairs. She kept the baby carriage in the hallway downstairs, always ready for the bunker trips. Her oldest daughter Elfriede was about sixteen years old and the other one, Marlies, was a baby. Elfriede had just returned home from one of her recurring trips to a health resort, where she had received treatments for her illness, tuberculosis. She appeared so fragile.

I am guessing at how long it took to walk to the bunker, but I believe it was about fifteen to twenty minutes at a fast walking pace. Eventually we figured out a few shortcuts, trying hard to save a couple of minutes. At that time in 1943, we did not meet many people along the way, but before long it became a nightly migration of frightened people seeking a safer place, just like us.

When we left the house the *Vor-alarm* (forewarning) was announcing the impending air raid. Three short wailing sounds were repeated three times.[15] It usually was given when enemy aircraft had entered the airspace over the suburbs of Berlin. But it was not reliable or trustworthy. Several times during the daytime raids, I had a chance to see airplanes flying over us while the siren was still wailing. We learned not to rely on the system entirely.

By the time we reached the bunker, the "full alarm" was sounding. A long wailing alarm, it was a sinister sound. Full alarm meant that airplanes had entered the airspace over Berlin.

The big door to the bunker entrance was open and we were ushered in by smiling soldiers. The welcome melted my fear away immediately. While the rest of the bunker with its two side entrances was occupied by civilians like the bunker where we stayed with our friends, this section of the bunker was occupied by

---

15   The *Entwarnung* (all-clear) was a steady sounding siren without the wailing.

the military. It was only open to the public when an alarm was sounded for an impending air raid.

We walked into a large open area. Elevators were located on the right side and a wide staircase was on the left side. The baby carriages were stored in a designated area. Two horses were brought in and kept by the staircase. I suspect that they belonged to the Bunker-Kommandant, who probably rode them around the Humboldthain Park.

We were allowed to sit on the steps, in the hallways and in the lounges. Two people could sit on either side of the steps, leaving the middle open for access. Every available spot was used to accommodate the people. We found ourselves a place to sit, way up to the top of the staircase, as high as we were allowed to be and near the banister, where we could watch all the activities down below. I felt truly at ease in this bunker. Seeing the soldiers nearby made me feel safe.

My mother was not feeling well. She complained about chest pains. Perhaps the fast walk to the bunker had bothered her and caused her pain. It seemed unlikely, since she was used to walking, but I talked her into going to the infirmary to have it checked out. They did not find anything wrong with her, except for being anemic and exhausted. My mother had been through a lot in the past days and it had probably caught up with her. Their advice was to get a good rest. Good advice, but how were we to arrange that?

When we were informed that the "all clear" had been sounded and that we could leave the bunker and return to our homes, I begged the nurse to let us stay for the rest of the night. For us to stay I had to have permission from an authorized person in charge.

I was sent from one person to another. It was making me a little angry. The last one I spoke to was a major. He listened to my story, probably finding it to be a little amusing as I was quite charged up by the time I got to him. I know that I said more than I should have, especially telling him how lucky he was to be in this safe place, having a nice bed to sleep, while my poor father had to sleep on the cold ground in Russia. I must have touched a soft spot in his heart. He was very nice to me, despite my angry behavior. He made arrangements for us to stay that night and the following nights, for about one week.

Earlier I had told Frau Bottger to let my grandparents know that I was trying to stay at the bunker for the night and not to worry about us. My mother seemed a lot better in the morning. Everyone was very nice to us. They even brought us breakfast. I had the feeling from the way we were treated that they were aware of our homeless situation.

Saturday and Sunday, November 27 and 28, 1943

Saturday and Sunday we spent the daytime hours with my grandparents. We were still receiving our three meals per day from the field kitchens. It always was very tasty and plentiful, enough for the four of us. After supper we would go to the bunker. They had given us a pass. We would use the civilian entrance to get to our room.

Monday, November 29, 1943

We had no idea as we were leaving the bunker this Monday morning that it was going to be a very happy and joyful day. In fact, we were talking about what happened a week ago, remembering how everything had still been intact and then all that had taken place since. It was unbelievable.

We left my grandparents' house to do some errands, including a stop at the post office. It was a different location than before, as ours had been destroyed. We had not received any mail since Monday, November 22, and we were concerned that we had not heard from my dad. He tried to write a few lines every day to let us know that he was alright. At the post office we came away empty-handed and worried.

As we had many times before, we ended up on our street at the bakery. I remember it being full of people just standing around and talking. I was standing by the back wall and I was not really listening to the conversation until I heard the baker woman saying something about two soldiers. She had watched them come around the corner into our street. When they saw the devastation they threw off their knapsacks and dropped the parcels they had been carrying onto the street. They both ran towards the smoldering piles of rubble where their homes used to be and then they just stood there with a look of disbelief on their faces. The baker woman and her husband had stepped outside and taken their stuff to them. She recognized one of the soldiers. It was Alfons, the barber from house No. 110, and he had come home on leave from Africa. She did not remember the other one's name, only that he had come from Russia.

My mother asked her if the name had been Wittmutz and she thought it sounded like that. That is all it took! I do not think I ever ran that fast in my entire life. I flew out of the door to my grandparents' house and up the four flights of stairs. What a joyful moment when I opened the door into the kitchen and I saw my dad sitting there. He had turned to face the door when he heard it being opened, and he jumped up to meet me. It felt so good having his arms around me. I will always remember how happy I was to see him, but also how I came apart at that moment. For the first time since it all had happened to us I started to cry. I was sobbing while trying to tell my dad about us and being homeless and so poor!

I was not known for being a crybaby or getting easily upset over something, but I surely was overcome with emotion at this time. It took quite a while before my dad was able to calm me down. I remember him saying over and over that everything is replaceable and that the most important thing is that we were alive and that we were together. All the other things do not matter. So very true. Alfons, the barber, was not so fortunate. His family was buried under the piles of smoldering rubble from house No. 110.

My dad and Alfons had met at the railroad station Humboldthain. They had walked to our street together, feeling so happy and excited about coming home to their families. Alfons' wife and their children, including a baby who he had not seen yet, had been evacuated to the country to keep them safe. But they had decided to come back in order to be there when Alfons came home on leave. It was a fatal decision and created a very sad outcome to their planned happy reunion. My dad told us how horror-stricken they felt when they turned the corner into our street and saw the still-smoldering piles of rubble where their homes used to be. He also told us how relieved and thankful he was when he spotted my scribbled message of our whereabouts on the piece of wall. "*Wir leben. Wittmutz-Hochstrasse 36.*" ("We are alive. Wittmutz-Hochstrasse 36.")

Alfons kept asking the people that had been gathered around them about his family's whereabouts. But no one had the courage to tell him about the people from house No. 110. When he finally found out about the fate of his family and the rest of the people from the house No. 110, he totally came apart. Everyone felt so compassionate for the poor man's loss. He and his wife were well known in the neighborhood. They had worked together, until he was drafted into the military. His barbershop was in the front and her ladies salon was in the back. I used to get my hair cut there. He could not understand why the special salvage group was not at work, digging for the people; but it was not possible to do any digging, because of the intense heat from the coal fire. It would take two more weeks before they were able to start their digging. When they did, Alfons was there alongside the salvage group. So too was the father of my friend Inge. Together they were digging for their buried loved ones, a very sad task.[16]

---

16 My dad stopped by one day to talk to Alfons to console him in his grief. He was shocked at his haggard, unshaven looking appearance. He came away feeling heartbroken and very discouraged by not being able to help. Not long afterwards, he was told that Alfons had been arrested and put into confinement at the military prison at Lehrter Strasse. My dad went to see him and found out the reasons for his arrest. Alfons had been walking on the street, near Stettiner Bahnhof, when he absentmindedly walked by a young lieutenant without saluting him. He stopped Alfons and chewed him out for failing to salute him and for his unacceptable appearance, which he described as a disgrace to the German Military. He called over two guards standing near the station and ordered them to take him away to headquarters, about one block away.

Alfons had not told anyone about his personal affairs, he appeared very discouraged. My dad felt it was his duty to let someone know about Alfons' sad circumstances. He asked to see someone in charge, which resulted in the charges against Alfons being dropped. He was released with a warning not to walk around looking so disorderly while wearing a German uniform. They had also arranged for additional leave time.

My dad had waited for him and he walked back with him to our old neighborhood. Alfons thanked him for getting him released but he truly did not care about himself anymore. He simply wanted to continue digging. He wanted to find his family and give them a proper burial. He made it known to my dad that he had no plans of returning to the front and that he would use his revolver to end his life, because he no longer had any reasons to live. My dad tried to talk to him but found it difficult to find the right kind of words to say to this discouraged and grieving man. He kept wondering how he would have handled the loss of his loved ones.

Some time later, after my dad had gone back to Russia, we heard that Alfons had found his wife. By a strange coincidence, her right hand was not as severely burned as the rest of her body and he was able to identify her by her wedding band. When a couple became engaged in Germany, they would wear their rings on the left hand, usually a gold band. During the wedding ceremony, the rings were moved from the left to the right hand, where they were worn for life as a symbol of being married. When one spouse died, the surviving spouse would wear the partner's ring. Two wedding rings worn on the right hand indicated that the person had been widowed.

Alfons' wife was the only one of all the people from house No. 110 who could be identified. Everyone else's body was almost cremated except for a few bones and skulls.

Sadly, Alfons did end his life, just the way he had indicated he would.

It was a wonderful surprise to come home and find my dad sitting in the kitchen. He had written a letter telling us that he was coming but we never received it. We were all so happy to have him home with us. Even my grandfather, who usually was quiet and withdrawn, sat in his chair with a big smile on his face, talking non-stop. He had never talked much about my dad to me. He listened intensely when I would read my dad's letters to him but he responded very little. The way he was behaving on this day surely showed how much he had missed having my dad around.

My grandmother had gone shopping to the butcher shop and to the bakery. In her excitement she had told everyone about her son's homecoming. When she unpacked her purchases at home, she found an extra large piece of meat and a package of luncheon meat plus a larger sized loaf of bread. She was so surprised. Indeed it was so unexpected that it made her speechless. It was a nice gesture and very thoughtful of our circumstances. We all appreciated the gifts. Later on that day, in the afternoon, the baker sent a cake with his best wishes, a very special treat. We were all quite touched.

At the railroad station my dad had received a big box from the Red Cross nurses. It was given to every frontline soldier coming home on leave. It was packed full of all kinds of goodies—chocolate, cigarettes, a bottle of schnapps, butter, salami, ham, and so on. It, too, was very much appreciated.

My grandmother brought out her *Kaffeemuhle* (coffee-grinder) and prepared a pot full of good coffee to serve with the cake. We had ourselves a nice afternoon with *Kaffee und Kuchen* (coffee and cake), just like old times.

We had another pleasant surprise when my Tante Anna and Onkel Alfred stopped by on their way to check their apartment. They were happy to see my dad and also saddened to hear about the loss of our home. They offered us their apartment, which was directly underneath my grandparents' place. Tante Anna was a sister of my grandfather. She and Onkel Alfred did not have any children, only a large white poodle. Besides their apartment, they also owned a cottage with a good-sized garden, in Schonholz by Tegel. They used to spend only the summer months out there, but since Onkel Alfred retired from his superintendent's job, they had been staying there for longer periods. Especially now that the bombing raids were becoming more frequent, they felt a little safer living in the suburbs. They also had an underground bunker close by where they could take shelter.[17]

17 Onkel Alfred had served in Kaiser Wilhelm's army during World War One. He was somewhere in France when gas was used on the soldiers. His lungs had been affected by this exposure and were in bad shape. He had to go for treatments periodically at

a special sanatorium. My grandfather had one more sister, Marie, and one brother, Otto. Marie was the mother of my favorite, Uncle Gerhard. Otto was not married. He was a sailor in the *Handelsflotte* (Merchant Marine), sailing out of Hamburg, where he lived in a sailor's home, after his retirement.

My grandfather's sister Marie Masnek had two children, a son Gerhard and a daughter Wally. Wally was married to Kurt Kleist. He was a locomotive engineer and had been given the very privileged task of driving one of Adolf Hitler's special trains. Wally and Kurt had a son Klaus, who was about my age. They lived around the corner from us, on Liesenstrasse. We saw them quite often, but whenever they stopped by for a visit, I would hurriedly hide my favorite toys, especially my dolls. Klaus was a nice boy, but a little too rough with my toys, and I did not like that.

They moved away from Berlin to some place in Germany, which would several years later become a part of East Germany. They would come to family gatherings until the war came along and then I never saw them again. We lost all contact. After the war, when traveling was still possible between eastern and western parts of Germany, Klaus came to visit my grandmother and Uncle Gerhard. He told them that his father Kurt had returned home after a short imprisonment by the Russians. I do not remember hearing anything about Kurt's job assignment or how involved he might have become in the Nazi party. For some reason I believe that he was just a locomotive engineer. It probably was a good job to have, much safer than serving in the military and putting his life at risk.

Marie Masnek was widowed after her husband, the father of Gerhard and Wally, died in an accident. She was married again to a man named Berger. He was the typical kind of man that the Nazi party looked for as a loyal member. I never saw that man wearing normal clothes. He always walked around in his brown S.A. uniform. I do not believe that he was an evil person. He just got caught up in all the events and promises the party presented.

Before the war, my grandparents always had big parties and family gatherings at their home. They always had a full house. I remember seeing my grandfather sitting between the two brother-in-laws, Berger and Alfred Herzog, puffing away on big cigars and having serious discussions. I did not know what it all was about except that I wondered why Berger and Uncle Alfred would become so excited and red-faced. Meanwhile my grandfather never said anything, but always had this amused look on his face, like he was enjoying the discussion.

Years later, I learned about that curious three-part conversation and how everyone was amused about their controversial political theories and their heated arguments. My grandfather's position was that of a referee between Berger and Alfred. It was a family comedy! I do not recall ever hearing anything about Berger once the war started, but I am sure that Berger was very disappointed at the end of the war and burned his uniform last of all.

My parents happily accepted their kind offer. The chances of finding an apartment around this neighborhood were very questionable. Plus we wanted to be near my grandparents and in familiar surroundings. So the offer was a wish come true, and we were very grateful to Tante Anna and Onkel Alfred.[18] November 29 turned out to be a very special day!

My parents went downstairs to sleep, but I stayed with my grandparents. I was not ready yet for a change. We did not go back to our room at the bunker. We stayed at home. I did return the pass to the major on our next visit to the bunker, during an air raid. He actually seemed quite sincere when he asked me about our well being. He was happy to hear that my dad came home on leave. He wanted to meet him, but I told him that he had stayed with my grandfather to help him get to the shelter. The major really seemed to be a caring man.[19]

The four of us enjoyed every minute of my dad's presence. We were a family again, like old times. In the evening we would sit together and play cards or our favorite board game, *Mensch argere Dich nicht* (Man, don't be annoyed). My dad liked playing games and we had a lot of fun.[20]

I was still bothered with the anxiety problem, every evening around 7:30. I tried hard not to show it, but my dad became aware of it. He tried to help me by talking and telling funny stories to me, but it did not help. It was a struggle for me to overcome the nervousness and uneasiness. This problem lasted for quite a while with me. Eventually I was not so nervous anymore, but I still caught myself watching the clock. I also noticed that others were doing the same. Once the clock moved past 9:00, I started to feel a little more relaxed.

The fear of going down into an underground shelter during an air raid never left me either. It remained with me to the end of the war. The thought of getting buried alive underneath a bombed house was too frightening for me to consider.

Our evenings were interrupted many times by our unwelcomed visitors. My mother and I would join our neighbors for our journey to the bunker. My dad declined to go there with us. He did not think that he could handle being locked inside the bunker. He felt the same way about the air raid shelter in our house. He went downstairs with my grandparents, but then stayed by the door with the civil defense men. He had to see and hear what was going on outside. He

---

18 Eventually, they transferred their rental contract over to us and we became the rightful tenants.

19 "Herr Major" was the proper manner in which to address him.

20 I was told that he was a very good skat player.

would sometimes go along with the civil defense men, searching the rooftops for incendiary bombs.

It was a rude awakening for him to witness the air raids at home and see all the devastation that they were causing. Information about the air raids and the destruction had been kept from the soldiers. The bombing of innocent people also bothered him a lot. It just was not his idea of war. My mother told me that they talked about many of these things when they were by themselves and also about how worried he was about us. She promised him then that she would find a safer place for us to live, perhaps with Tante Grete.

I went back to my school to check on what was happening. I was told that the school was closed officially because of the constant air raids. It had become a matter of safety for the students. We were asked to stop by once a week and sign in. I guess it was to see who was still alive or not. The request was withdrawn once the daytime raids started. No one wanted to be caught away from home.

I do not remember when the nightly air raids became more frequent and a lot more violent or when the daytime raids started. I do remember how our daily lifestyle was affected by the constant raids, especially when the daytime raids started. We hardly ever went anywhere far. We remained close to home. It seemed that we were on the run, day and night. We had indeed become *Bunkerratten* (bunker rats)—a name that was given to us by some of our neighbors, who stood outside of our house. When we would run by, they would call out loudly, "Watch out for the *Bunkerratten*, they are on the run!" Yes, they would laugh about us and make funny remarks. We ignored them, but it was not very nice of them. As it turned out, in March of 1945 the very same people ceased laughing at anyone when a blockbuster bomb hit our house and they all died. A very sad and tragic ending.

On December 14, 1943 we celebrated my twelfth birthday. Having my dad home with us made it very a special one. The last time that he had been home for my birthday was in 1939, my eighth one. I cannot emphasize enough how happy it made me to have him there to celebrate my special day with me. Looking back, I am also glad that I did not know then that it was to be the last one that we would celebrate together.

No matter how sad and discouraging the times were and how hopeless everything appeared, he was always able to cheer us up and give us encouraging words. Since my dad came home, my grandfather was up and about. He did not stay in bed all the time; and he was in such a good mood that we enjoyed his company.

The days went by quickly. We did not talk about it, but we all dreaded the day when my dad had to leave. My mother told me later on that he suffered from severe pains in his head at times, the result of a head injury he received during a battle. She had tried to talk him into applying for a medical discharge from the front line. My dad thought that it was very tempting, but he did not feel comfortable with the idea. He felt that he would be disloyal to his fellow comrades. Many of them were in worse shape than he was and his conscience would not allow it.

I recall a letter my mother received, some time before, from his commanding officer, Captain Schulze, asking her not to send any kind of pain medication to my dad, on the doctor's orders. My dad was taking too many pills to ease the pain in his head and they were concerned about his alertness and ability to carry out his duties. It certainly would have given him a reason for a discharge request, but that was not his way; and he suffered greatly for it.

My dad was wounded twice, the first time in the fall of 1941 and the second time in the early spring of 1943. A hand grenade thrown by a Russian soldier landed near a big rock near where he had taken cover. When it exploded, it showered him with pieces of rock. One small piece, the size of a pea, penetrated his head. His left eye was also torn. The rock pieces could easily be removed from his body, except for the one in his head. He was advised against an operation, being told that it was too risky, with possible unforeseen problems afterwards. The doctor told him that the pain in his head occurred when the small piece was moving around in his head.

A very good eye surgeon who happened to be there the day that my dad was brought to the *Feldlazarett* (field hospital) took care of his eye. He had done an excellent job. It seemed a little bit smaller than his right eye, but he did not have any problems with it.

The second injury also happened during a fierce battle with the Russian army over a hill, which was an important strategic location overlooking the surrounding territory. If I remember correctly, an explosion lifted him up in the air and he came back down hard onto the ground. He felt as if something had hit him in the back, but when he touched himself all over he thought he was alright. He kept right on fighting until he felt the warmth and stickiness in his trousers. He crawled to the back of the line so he could stand up and pull his trousers down for someone to take a look. He was told he needed medical attention, along with a few stitches. The *Sanitater* (medics) were very busy caring for his severely wounded comrades, who were much worse off than he was.

So he decided to walk himself to the field hospital. Only he misjudged his condition. Evidently he had lost a lot more blood than he thought and he collapsed on the way. He had also strayed away a little from the path. Luckily for him, two soldiers came along with a *Panjewagen* (a horse pulled cart) and found him. They took him to the hospital. A couple of days later two soldiers from his company stopped by with a list of names, conducting a routine check to see who was present and who was missing. They discovered my dad lying in bed on his stomach. They were glad to see him and to find that he was not missing, as had been reported.

Thank God that the letter about his being missing had not been mailed yet. It would have been immensely painful to receive. We lived from day to day with that dreadful thought on our mind. He tried to write every day a few lines to let us know that he was alright, but even then we did not get his letters every day. Sometimes we waited four and five days and then we would receive several letters all at once.

Normally, when a soldier was wounded, he would get a special furlough to go home. Only in my dad's case, it did not turn out that way. They were very short of men and could not spare anyone at the time. So instead of a *Heimat-Urlaub* (homeward journey), he was granted a few days of rest behind the front line. A small compensation.

Weihnachten—Christmas, 1943

We decorated a small Christmas tree. It was to be seven years before we had one again. My dad had purchased gifts from people selling goods in the station in Latvia, when his train stopped there on the way back to Germany. They were beautiful handcrafted gifts and he had one for everyone. Mine was a pair of boots, made from soft reindeer leather. They were fur lined and they were pretty. My mother and grandmother both received nice, warm house shoes. My grandfather got a leather bag filled with tobacco. We did not have any other gifts to exchange between us, but seeing how much my dad was enjoying himself giving us his, was a gift in itself.

We enjoyed a very blessed, peaceful Christmas. We were thankful that we were together, and even our unwelcome flying visitors gave us a peaceful holiday.

Then the dreaded day arrived when we had to take my dad to Stettiner Bahnhof for his departure back to that awful cold country. We arrived at the railroad station and found two trains sitting on both sides of the platform, already filled full of soldiers. We ran up and down the platform looking for an empty spot on the train. My mother was loudly proclaiming her feelings about the situation to my dad. *"Bleibe hier. Lass die Anderen kampfen in diesem Krieg!"* ("Stay here. Let all the others fight this war!") She was serious and meant every word of it. How I wish that my dad had listened to her and stayed behind. When we got back home we found a telegram that had been delivered during our absence. It was from Captain Schulze, granting him ten extra days of leave because of the loss of our home.

A couple of soldiers standing by a window called to my dad, saying that they would make room for him, only he had to climb up and in through the window. So we helped him up and through the window, handing him his *Rucksack* or *Tornister* (backpack). The two soldiers let him stand by the window, as they did not have anybody at the station to see them off. I believe that the trains rolled in from some other place already full; otherwise there would have been a lot more people on the platform seeing the soldiers off.

When the train started moving, very slowly, the band started playing the farewell song. *"Muss I denn, Muss I denn, zum Stadtelein hinaus, und du mein Schatz bleibst hier"* ("Must I then, Must I then, leave my home, and you my darling are staying here.") We felt bad enough without the band reminding us of our situation. We really did not need that song to add to our sadness.

We ran alongside the train, trying hard to smile, with tears running down our faces. I saw my dad's sad smile, and it turned out to be for the last time.

We stood at the very end of the platform, waving until the train rode out of our sight. We knew that it was rolling slowly past our old neighborhood and across the big bridge that we walked underneath almost daily. It was rolling towards the east, to Stettin and then back to Russia. I know that he had one last look at our neighborhood, where our home used to be, because the window that he was standing at faced that direction.

It has been very difficult to write about this episode. The memory of that day at the station still brings tears to my eyes, even after all the years that have gone by. The memory of the sad look on my dad's face as the train was moving away from us has always been with me.

My Father the Soldier

It upsets me every time I hear someone describing all German soldiers as Nazi soldiers. My dad was a German soldier fighting for his homeland and not for the Nazi leaders. I also believe that many German soldiers did not wish to be called Nazi soldiers. That name belonged to Hitler's special group of soldiers, the SS.

We were living a good and happy life before the war came along. I was envied by my friends for having such a nice and friendly father. He never passed by us on the street without saying something to us. He was quite the opposite from the other fathers, who always looked so grumpy. I avoided running into them as best I could.

My dad was employed as a crane operator at the Borsig-Werke in Tegel. When the war started, in September of 1939, he received his *stellungsbefehl* (draft notice), but with the help of the Borsig-Werke, it was postponed until the spring of 1940. Then he was drafted into the infantry, probably because of his good physical condition. For years he had been riding his bicycle to work, and it was a fair distance from our home to Tegel.

He took his basic training in Potsdam, a beautiful old garrison town in the suburbs of Berlin. He lived in a big old *Kaserne* (barracks), which was cool and pleasant during the summer and probably not so hospitable during the winter.

I loved visiting him there on weekends. It was such an interesting place. There was so much to see and do. I enjoyed every minute of it. We would attend outdoor concerts or we would take walks around the beautiful gardens of "*Sanssouci*" or "*Sorgenfrei*" (Without Worry), the Palace of Frederic the Great. I found it very exciting being amongst all the men dressed in their uniforms. I guess, even as an eight-year-old girl, I had this admiration for men in uniforms.[21] But most of all I looked forward to our visit to a cafe or *Konditorei* (pastry shop) in the afternoon, for *Kaffee und Kuchen* (coffee and cake). Then for supper I would have a delicious *Kommisbrot und Leberwurst* sandwich made by my dad in his room at the *Kaserne*. At home I would not touch a liverwurst sandwich. It did not taste as good as the one my dad made for me in his room.

I remember one Sunday when we came to visit him and found him in the courtyard. He was marching back and forth in a small group of men to the commands of a *Feldwebel* (sergeant) and saluting over and over again. He told us

---

21   My dad did not share my enthusiasm. He thought it was very tiring to have to constantly lift up his arm to salute.

later that most of the recruits were country boys and used to working at their own pace, never hurrying for anything. They were nice fellows, but because of their slowness they got into a lot of trouble, for which the whole group was punished. On this particular Sunday, they were being reprimanded for not giving a salute properly. For this the whole group had to march and salute until the sergeant was satisfied with their performance. It must have been a little embarrassing to have to practice this in front of the visitors who had gathered around the courtyard to watch. But the biggest disappointment was not being issued a pass to leave the grounds and therefore missing out on a visit to the cafe.

The good times at the *Kaserne* did not last for very long. All too soon we had to say our goodbyes. The night before my dad's departure to "an undisclosed destination", he surprised us at home with a visit. He took quite a chance, but it went well with the help of his comrades who covered for him. Most of the fellows in his group were not from Berlin and therefore did not have the same opportunity to go home, as my dad did. He waited until dark to climb out of his first floor window, which looked out onto the street, and then walked to the next railroad station, Bahnhof Babelsberg, to avoid the controls. It was worth the risk and it was wonderful to have him home with us for just a little while longer. He had to go back long before daybreak to climb back up into his room without being seen.

As it turned out, we would not see him for almost two years. He was shipped off to Norway where he spent the next few months in a training camp on the outskirts of Oslo. My dad liked Norway. He made friends with some of the Norwegian men who worked at the camp. The German soldiers had been cautioned about venturing away from camp by themselves. They were advised to go only in groups, supposedly because the Norwegian people were hostile towards the Germans occupying their country. But my dad never encountered any problems with them. He got along with them just fine.

One of the Norwegian men arranged for him to meet a jeweler in Oslo where he was able to buy several new pieces of jewelry. He was so excited about being able to get these pretty pieces for us, but his monthly allowances were not enough to pay for these purchases. My mother had to send him some money in her letters. It could not be too much at one time or whoever censored the letters would become suspicious. Trading outside the base was not allowed. The shopping had to be done in secrecy behind the back of the German authorities, as they did not approve of such purchases.

After he bought the jewelry he sent the pieces along with a comrade who was going home on leave to Berlin. It was the safest way to get them to us. The pieces of jewelry that he selected for us were beautiful watches, rings, a necklace and a broach. My watch had a gold band and a dark face. My ring was gold and had a good-sized ruby setting. It was my first watch and ring. I wore it on special occasions and it made me feel so grown up. The necklace had a heart-shaped locket. My mother's watch had a black velvet band and a light face. Her ring was gold with an onyx stone and a diamond in the center. The broach was for my grandmother with a very pretty design made of several different stones.

The same Norwegian also got him some beautiful material for a suit. It was cut in three pieces—a jacket and two pairs of trousers. That made it easier for someone to bring it to us. My poor dad was dreaming of the day when he could trade his uniform for a nice suit. Sadly, that time never came.

My mother's stole "Foxie" came from Norway and so did my much-in-demand *Fussball* (soccer ball). He also sent many packages home with cans of different kinds of sardines, which was quite a treat. We used some for trading.

He was always thinking of us, trying his best to help whenever possible. When my dad was drafted into the military, he made arrangements for my mother to receive most of his pay, while he only kept a small amount for himself. I do not recall that we ever had any financial problems. We always seemed to have money for doing things. My dad's paycheck must have been sufficient to take care of us.

My dad spent his first *Weihnachten* away from home in Norway. He had to give up his turn to let fathers with more than two children go home. It made me feel very angry and resentful. We had not been together since the summer of 1940 and I wanted to see my dad just as much as three or more children did. It was very unfair.

It was a very lonely time for all of us. To cheer us up a little, his friends dressed up like Santa and one by one came by our house. They brought us some small gifts, mostly for me. One of them serenaded us just outside our door with his violin. It was nice of them to think of us on Christmas Eve.

My dad was the only one in his group of friends that had been drafted into the German military. And I was the only one among my friends whose father was serving in the military. Very strange, I think. A very popular song during the war years was, *"Weit ist der Weg zurick ins Heimatland, so weit-so weit!"* ("Far is the road back to our homeland, so far-so far!"). Sung to the tune of "Tipperary", its words were so true.

In Norway my dad received further instructions in warfare and he also learned to cross country ski. Unknown to him at the time, all of this preliminary training was in preparation for "Operation Barbarossa," the German assault on Russia. That was when he saw his first real action of the war.

The next time that we saw my dad was when he came home on leave in 1942. That was the first time we learned of the injury to his head. He probably would not have mentioned it, but my mother found him pacing the floor during the night. He could not sleep because of the pain in his head. It was then that he told her of the injury I have already described. It had occurred while he was fighting on the Kandalaska front near Murmansk in the fall of 1941. We also learned for the first time about his trip to the hospital in Helsinki, Finland, to have his tonsils taken out when he became ill with tonsillitis. He had kept it all to himself, never wanting us to worry.

My dad told us during this visit where and how he spent the Christmas of 1941. He had felt so sad and depressed on Christmas Eve that he poured himself a couple shots of cognac. Not something he should have done soon after the surgery as it brought on some unpleasant results. The doctor who was called in by the nurses scolded him. They thought that he had had a relapse or was suffering complications from the surgery, due to his feverish appearance. But that was just my dad. He never made out well drinking alcohol.

One evening in March of 1942, after our supper, my mother and I went across the street to a friend's home. She was an elderly lady who claimed to be able to see the future, a *Wahrsagerin* (fortuneteller). After visiting with her for a while, my mother asked her to look into her cards to see if my dad might soon be coming home on leave. We were asked to sit at a small table and to put our hands on it and to keep our eyes closed, while she mumbled unintelligible words. We were waiting for "knocks" to answer her questions.

I never believed in any of this. I thought that it was amusing; especially when I opened my eyes and saw how weird we looked sitting there. I was then scolded for interrupting her concentration and asked to leave the table.

When she laid out her cards, she became quite excited over what she saw. She proceeded to do it again after which she told my mother that, "Yes, your husband Willi is on his way. He might be arriving any minute!" Of course she knew that was exactly what we wanted to hear. But she was so adamant about her prediction that we did not want to show her our doubts and hurt her feelings. I had trouble believing that the ordinary cards she was using could tell her that my dad was coming home on leave. We left her shortly thereafter. On our way back home we talked about her prediction and agreed how nice it would be if it turned out to come true.

When we walked up the stairs we could not believe our eyes. There, in front of our door, sat my dad's *Rucksack*. My mother's friend's prediction had come true! We became ecstatic. We could not open Tante Maske's door fast enough. Running down the long hallway to her kitchen we found him with a big smile on his face. Oh it was so good to see him! We were overcome by our emotions, crying and laughing all at the same time. We had waited for this a long time, almost two years.

My dad explained that he did not tell us beforehand because he was worried that his leave might get canceled at the last minute and we would have to cope with another disappointment. He looked great. He had a nice suntan, which seemed strange considering that he came to us from Russia. Everyone who later saw him thought he had come from Africa instead of Russia. He told us that the winter had been very long and icy cold, with hip deep snow that never melted. When the sun finally came out (they were close to the Arctic Circle), it felt good just lying in the sun. It thawed them out quickly, and it gave him his tan.

That night I stayed up way past my bedtime. I was too excited to go to sleep. When I finally did, both my mother and I overslept. She decided not to go to work and she told me I could stay home from school, but I decided to try to make it before the bell rang at 8 o'clock. I ran all the way, but I was late by five minutes. I was then still so charged up from the excitement of having my dad home that I forgot to follow the school rules. Running inside of the school building was not allowed, but I ran to my room. Upon knocking on a door we were expected to wait before entering the room until we heard "*Herein!*" ("Come in!"). Then we had to stand at attention and give a proper "*Heil Hitler!*" salute. I failed all of those rules as well. I knocked on the door, but I did not wait for the "*Herein!*" Instead, I bounced into the classroom with a very sloppy "*Heil Hitler!*" salute.

Frau Fritz was a loyal follower of Adolf Hitler. She considered me to be the "unruly Charlotte". We were all intimidated by her, especially me. But I had never been disobedient to Frau Fritz, despite her awful ways towards me. Inside the room I walked up to her, ignoring the displeased expression on her face. She sat at her desk and listened to my explanation for being late. When I was finished she gave me such a mean, cold stare. Then she told me that my reason for being late was not acceptable as an excuse and that I had disobeyed school rules. For that I had to be punished!

She ordered me to get the *Stock* (cane) from the closet, which would result in me holding out my hands and getting several slaps over them with the cane. I stood there in disbelief at what she said to me, more so at this time than at any other time. For once I really had expected her to show some understanding. She surely must have been a very deranged woman.

When she repeated her order, "*Na, wird es bald—hole den Stock!!*" ("Well, will it be soon—get the cane!"). I stomped my foot on the floor and I said loudly, "No, I will not get the stick!" With that said, I ran out of the room, leaving my bag behind.

I ran down the teacher's staircase, which was located adjacent to my classroom. It was forbidden for us to use it. When I ran by the office window and out of the door, I heard someone shouting behind me, but I kept right on running towards home and my dad. I knew that my dad would take care of this awful situation between Frau Fritz and me. And he did. We went back to the school after my mother first unpacked some of his clothing for him to wear. His civilian clothes were stored in a trunk in our basement for safekeeping. My poor dad could not wear his uniform. The pants were so badly worn that they showed his underwear, which was very embarrassing. When he had gone through the *Entlausung Station* (delousing station) the chemicals that they were using had totally destroyed his uniform. They did not have any spare new uniforms to give him. So he had to find himself another one to wear from a pile of discarded ones. For a new replacement he would have to go to the headquarters building in Berlin, where he would be outfitted correctly once again.

When we arrived at the school we stopped by the office and my dad asked to see the principal. We did not have to wait long before we were greeted by the *Herr Direktor* and asked to step into his office. My dad explained the reason for his visit and I was asked to tell about what happened earlier in the classroom between Frau Fritz and me. Frau Fritz was then asked to come to the office and I was asked to leave and wait outside. When she came out of the principal's office she told me to go to my classroom and get my *Schultasche* (schoolbag) and the rest of my things from my desk.

I felt a little strange walking into the room and gathering my things together while my classmates watched me, but I hurried in order to get away from there. When I left I found my dad and the principal standing in the hallway and saying their goodbyes. The principal was wishing my dad and our family a pleasant and relaxing time while he was home on leave. My dad told me as we were leaving that he had asked the principal to give me time off from school so we could spend as much time together as possible while he was home. Not only was I happy to have my dad home, but with those words I was relieved to know that I would not have to return to Frau Fritz's class. With Easter fast approaching and my having been accepted to private school, I could now look forward to entering fifth grade at the private school after my Easter vacation.

While my dad was home we heard several interesting stories, particularly when a fellow comrade stopped by and visited with us for a couple of days on his way home to Silesia. My dad did not talk much about his experiences. When he did, they were always told in an amusing kind of way, never giving an indication of how serious the situation actually had been.

I remember one story quite well, and just thinking about it makes me shiver. It was so unjust and barbaric it could have had serious consequences. At the time this incident took place, the company had been placed temporarily under a Finnish commander. I do not remember the reason for this arrangement. It was well known amongst the German soldiers that the *Finlander* held so much anger and hatred for the Russians that they showed no mercy for them and never took any prisoners. My dad had taken a ski-patrol out to survey an area when they were surprised by two Russian soldiers. They were a couple of young boys who came out of their well-hidden hiding place, held up their arms and surrendered. They had been so well hidden that they could have easily killed several in his patrol. My dad took the Russian soldiers back to his unit and gave his report, whereupon he was harshly criticized for having them brought back as prisoners. He was told he should have eliminated them on the spot. He was ordered to take them out back and shoot them dead.

My dad refused to obey the order. He was not going to shoot unarmed men, especially not after they had surrendered to him. The Finnish officer went into a rage and ordered my dad's arrest for disobeying orders. It came to a trial and it looked quite bad for him until his commanding officer, Captain Schulze, helped him out of this very critical situation. The captain delivered a report written by a doctor describing my dad's head injury. Although my dad had a good conduct report, the doctor's letter was the main reason my father was let off. They made it look like he was not responsible at times for his actions, due to his head injury. For his punishment he served a couple of weeks behind the front line, doing odd jobs, like scrubbing the white camouflage coveralls clean, using cold water. He was glad when the two weeks were over.

The comrade who was visiting with us had been along on that fateful ski-patrol and he had also given his testimony at the trial. He and the rest of his comrades agreed with my dad's decision concerning the Russian soldiers. They strongly condemned such an inhuman order. My dad and his friend both agreed that the Finns were good soldiers but they did not like serving under Finnish leadership.

We were quite shocked at hearing this story. We were also thankful that things had turned out in my dad's favor. I remember asking about the fate of the two Russians and my dad and his comrade just shook their heads. A very cruel and unjust way to deal with other soldiers.

The following two stories are a little more on the lighter side. The comrade who was visiting with us was a young and handsome fellow. He had taken up several correspondences with girls living in Berlin. He laid out a whole stack of pictures on the table and asked me to help him choose one to call upon for a date. I felt honored and I had fun helping him pick one. I do not know the outcome of the dates, but I remember that at least three girls came by asking about him after he left. I hope he had a good time while it lasted.

My dad's friend also told us about an old *Grammophon* (record player) that they had at the front line. They also only had three records. According to his comrade, my dad enjoyed aggravating "Ivan" and knew how to quickly get the Russians' attention. He would crawl to the end of the German line and set up the *Grammophon*. First he would play the record of classical music, followed by the second record—a dashing march. Everything would be deathly silent on the Russians' side until the third and last record started playing. Then he had to hurry back fast because they started firing immediately. They did not care to hear *Deutschland uber Alles*, the German National Hymn and they would react extremely angrily to the song that followed it, "*Die Fahne hoch!*" (Raise High the Flag!), by Horst Wessel, the anthem of the SA.[22] I think they were all starving for a little fun in their otherwise cheerless lives and trustless world.

---

22 Raise high the flag! The ranks are closed and tight, Storm Troopers march, with firm and steady step. Souls of the comrades, shot by Reds and Counterforces, are in our ranks, and march along in step.

Open the road for these, the brown battalions. Let's clear the way, for the Storm Troopers. In hope, to the swastika, rise the eyes of millions. Dawn breaks for freedom, and bread for all man.

This is the final bugle call to arms. Already we are set, prepared to fight. Soon Hitler's flags will wave, o'er every single street. Enslavement ends, when soon we set things right.

After my dad returned to Russia from that leave in 1942, his company was moved to the area around Lake Ladoga near Leningrad. In the spring of 1943 he was wounded there for the second time. That was also where he came from when he came home on leave in November of 1943. He spoke of heavy fighting and big battles that took place around the Lake Ladoga area and huge losses of men. He also mentioned that he was the last one left alive from the group that left Norway for the attack on Russia. They had all either been killed or taken prisoner. Not a comforting comment for us, and a very uncomfortable situation for him.

The biggest problem for my dad and his comrades was the shipment of supplies. There were shortages of everything. With very little ammunition to fight off the Russians, hearing the Russian soldiers' eerie battle cry of "Urrah-Urrah" was frightful. They would end up using their shovels to defend themselves.

My dad was awarded a couple of Close Combat Badges, more for being a survivor of the gruesome hand-to-hand fighting than in actual recognition of a successful defense. My mother and I buried those badges along with the other medals in the forest at Grabow in 1945. He left them at home in 1943. He suspected that the Russians were well aware of their meaning and he did not want to be caught wearing them.

I asked him once about his feelings on shooting someone. He told me that he had thought a lot about whether he could do it or not while he was in training. It had worried him. But when the time actually came and he was facing the enemy's gun, there was no hesitation to making that decision. It was an "either him or me" decision.

I understood what he was telling me, but I had trouble seeing my dad doing it. He never liked to see the sight of blood. It bothered him. Whenever I needed someone to take care of my bloody wounds, cuts and scrapes, it was my mother who would look after me. A war can surely change people.

I wanted to write a little bit about my dad to give some insight into his character. He was a wonderful, loving man with a good sense of humor.

December 1943

When we arrived back home from our trip to Stettiner Bahnhof, my grandmother handed us the telegram from Captain Schulze, granting him ten extra days of leave. We hurried back to the station to ask the Red Cross for their help. They promised that they would try and get in touch with the Red Cross in Stettin and have my dad sent back to Berlin. Not an impossible task to fulfill, but it did not happen. It was very upsetting. We spent the rest of the day waiting and hoping that he would walk back into our home. It would have been nice to have him for ten days longer. My dad was never told about the extra days of leave he had missed. He only learned about it from my mother in a letter, and then he too expressed great disappointment.

New Furniture

After my dad left I moved downstairs to stay with my mother. I would have rather stayed upstairs with my grandparents, but it was a little crowded for all three of us. I had been searching around our neighborhood for a furniture store that still had something to sell. I found a small shop on Brunnenstrasse near Bernauer Street where I used to change trolley cars on my way to school. The proprietor, an elderly man, seemed quite amused about my apparent excitement at having found a two-piece kitchen cupboard in his shop which looked almost like the one we had before. There also was a nice table and four chairs, two twin beds and a small sofa.

I begged the shop owner to hold the furniture for me while I ran home to get my mother. She agreed to buy the furniture, more to please me than her. She did not mind using my aunt's furniture but she knew that I did. We would be reimbursed by the government as long as we could show proof of our purchases. The only bad part to my good find was that the shop owner had no way to make a delivery. But I was able to talk the owner of a small produce shop on our street into lending us his two-wheel pushcart.

We made several trips with our pushcart. It was a long way to push the cart along Brunnenstrasse, then through Humboldthain Park, and finally on to Hochstrasse. Then we had to carry the furniture upstairs. Again we were in luck. When we arrived with the sofa we met our superintendent in the hallway, who offered his help.

We moved my aunt and uncle's furniture into the back room and set up our new furniture. It did not replace what we had lost, but it was our own. The furniture was actually of good quality, except for the beds. They were typical wartime production pieces—made from light wood and just stained a brown color.

Dad's First Letter—January 12, 1944

We finally received my dad's first letter after his departure, written January 12, 1944. We have been waiting anxiously to hear from him. We had been writing every day to him because we know that he worried about us. I wished that he had not experienced our constant air raids and seen the awful devastation to our neighborhood. It all added to his worries about us.

January 12th, 1944

Liebe Friedel and Lottchen!

I am letting you know that I arrived back at the front on the 7th of January. I am sorry for not writing sooner but it was not possible. I will tell you more about it in my next letter. I hope, that you are both alright. It is my biggest worry now, that something could happen to you, it is such a dangerous place to be for you.

I received a care package from the division, all kinds of good things. I was quite surprised and very glad about it. I will pack a box right away and share some things with you. I hope, it doesn't get lost, let me know when you receive it. It seems quite risky anymore to be sent something. I found it extremely difficult to leave you both, knowing your helpless situation at times. We must (remain) not become discouraged and remain brave, to live means not to give up and to keep on fighting. A very hopeless situation at times.

Dear Friedel, please write every day, so I don't have to live in constant fear about you. I have been ordered to another post, temporarily. My Field-post-number for now is 3000. Enclosed are two Air-mail stamps.

Many Greetings and Kisses to both of you from your Pappa.

His mention of a new posting was a reference to his being temporarily ordered to an assignment guarding Russian prisoners at a prisoner of war camp. He was never told the reason for this transfer to the rear of the line, but I suspect that it had something to do with the loss of his extra days of leave. My dad came to like his new post and wanted to stay permanently. He had the consent of the officer in charge, but he did not get a release from his unit. They wanted him back at the front. No chance of a break for a weary soldier.

January 13th, 1944

Liebe Friedel and Lottchen!

I have mailed two packages to you yesterday, with all kinds of good things. I hope you will get them. It must be a bad situation with the postal service.

I am curious when I will receive the first mail from you?

Dear Friedel and Lottchen, my worries about you increases more and more each day. Maybe it would be better if you would go someplace safer. I am so concerned about your situation. Otherwise, I will not rest here and I will blame myself, should something happen to you both.

It is very cold here, freezing cold and lots of snow on the ground, very uncomfortable. I cannot send any coffee beans to you, for awhile, because they brew the coffee for us at this post. Tomorrow, I will pack your birthday box.

Please, don't forget to write every day, let me know what's happening at home. Many Greetings to Father, Mother, Aunt Anna, Uncle Alfred. I write everything under Postant N20, just so you know. I was not able to exchange anything during my return trip, we traveled only at night.

Many Greetings and Kisses to both of you from your Pappa.

The new year, 1944, brought us many changes. We were experiencing shortages of everything, except air raids. They had become more frequent. It was not unusual to have two raids in one night. They were also a lot more violent.

We spent a lot of our time on the run to the bunker in our effort to stay alive. We also made many trips to the bunker for false alarms, but we never complained. We became sky watchers, doing our own predictions of whether a raid was likely or not. A certain kind of cloud formation would give us hope that we would have a restful night. We especially welcomed fog. It was the best guarantee for a quiet night, and such a night was a treat.

Weihnachtsbaume—Christmas Tree Flares

I remember one bunker trip very well. It stands out in my mind from all the other ones for its spectacular display of firepower and how it gave us such a run for our lives.

On that particular evening we had received the announcement late that enemy aircraft were approaching the vicinity of Oranienburg, a suburb of Berlin. By the time we were leaving the house, the siren was wailing full alarm, which meant we really had to hurry. When we reached my former school, we debated whether we should go into their air raid shelter or take a chance and go on. It was very quiet yet, so we decided to keep on running to the bunker.

We were about halfway through the park, when all of a sudden the big searchlights on top of the bunker lit up. It really surprised us and we knew what that meant. The lights were criss-crossing the dark sky, searching for the enemy planes. It would have been fun to watch if it did not signal the danger we were in. I turned my head to look over my right shoulder and I saw an airplane in the beam of the searchlight. The firing of guns on top of the bunker began instantly.

The bunker was located almost in front of us. It looked as if the guns were firing over our heads, and the noise hurt our ears. We could see the big red fireballs with every blast plus the illumination from the flares. Those were followed by more flashes from bomb explosions. The whole sight was spectacular.

It was our first time seeing the *Weihnachtsbaume* (Christmas tree) flares. They hung like a large cluster of lights, shining brightly in the sky, an awesome sight to see. If only we could have watched it all from a safer place than our dangerous location.

The road through the park seemed endless and my mother was giving up, crying out that she could not go on anymore. She wanted to toss her suitcase aside. I could not let her do that. So I grabbed it. Then I was running with two suitcases and my shoulder bag, which was heavy too.

When we finally reached the bunker entrance, we banged on the door, using our last bit of strength, until they opened the small passage door. The soldiers quickly pulled us in, whereupon we collapsed. Our chests were hurting badly. We had much trouble breathing. The soldiers brought us chairs to sit on and water to drink. We were exhausted, except for the baby, Marlies, who slept through it all.[23]

A Sad Day

On one of my visits to my old neighborhood I noticed that the cleanup was in progress. I was able to get to the area where the courtyard of our house used to be. The salvage crew was still digging and so was my friend Inge's father. They were using some of the large bowls from the bakery to gather what little they had found, only bones and few skulls.

I was looking at a smaller skull and it made me think of Inge, because she had teeth that stood out a little and they seemed to show on the skull. When I looked up Inge's father was standing next to me and he nodded. Neither one of us spoke, but I knew that he had the same feeling about the skull. I looked at the bakery bowls and remembered what they had been used for only a short while ago. Now they were being used as containers for what used to be people.

I felt sorry for everyone whose life had ended so abruptly in those cellars, but I sympathized with Inge's father and Alfons, the barber. They were the survivors

---

23 At different times we were late in getting to the bunker but we had never before been caught in such a dangerous situation. And we were very lucky. Had it been March 18, 1945, we would not have made the run to the bunker alive. On that day, during a daytime raid, the enemy's target was the bunker and its surrounding area. If the bombs that fell on top of the bunker and in front of the entrances had penetrated the bunker, they would have killed many of the 30,000 people that were packed inside. After that raid the park looked like a battlefield, but the bunker itself survived. It was indestructible. It also survived a heavy rocket barrage from the Russian forces. After the war it was eventually blown up and destroyed, a decision with which I did not agree.

I had always felt safe in the bunker and it did save our lives many times. Years before my parents and I had watched the construction of the bunker. None of us ever imagined that this building would someday become our protector, including that day in March of 1945.

and they had to deal with the loss of their loved ones. It was a lesson for all of us—that everything can be taken away, in a flash of a moment, and be forever gone.

I did not stay for very long at this depressing site. It was so sad.

January 14th, 1944

Liebe Friedel and Lottchen!

I have just finished packing another small box for you, with a bottle of liquor and 12 cigarettes. It is my birthday present for you. I don't want you celebrating without a toast. Cheers!! To a healthy Wiedersehen! This is the third package that I have mailed. I am anxious to hear if you will get them and when.

How are you both doing? Are you still going to the bunker? At times, when I think about our misfortune of losing our home and everything in it, I find it very difficult to believe. But we must not give up and lose faith, we are not alone in this situation.

Please don't forget to write every day.

Many Greetings and Kisses to both of you from your Pappa.
Many Greetings to Father and Mother and Grete

We received some of the seven small packages that he had mailed to us, but not all of them. The mail service had become very unreliable. It would have been better if he had kept the treats for himself, but he wanted to share them with us.

January 16th, 1944 "In the Field—Russia"

Dear Friedel and Lottchen!

I write just a few lines again, because I know that you are also waiting for mail from me. I am still without any kind of news from you. I probably will have to be patient for the next fourteen days.

I feel so sad, my thoughts are always with you. I live in constant fear that something could happen to you.

I hope that you will get all my packages I have mailed to you. There are three of them, the fourth one I just finished packing. I just need to get a twenty penny stamp.

I will close for now and I hope that we will see each other again, soon, and in good health.

Auf wiedersehen!

Many greetings and kisses to you both from your Pappa

My mother stopped going back to our old neighborhood. She did not even talk about it anymore. She went to visit Tante Maske instead. Now and then I would go back to my old neighborhood to see my friends. They all wished that I had sold my *fussball* (soccer ball) to one of them. It would have survived with them and we could have played ball.[24]

---

24 Items like balls, bicycles and musical instruments could only be bought during the war with special permits. When my dad sent the soccer ball to me from Norway, it made me very popular in our neighborhood. The boys showed how nice they could be if they wanted to play with my ball.

We liked playing *Volkerball*. There were two teams with two goalkeepers. I do not remember the rules anymore, only that the player had to catch the ball and not drop it. Well, that is where the end of my soccer ball began. I caught the ball in my stomach area and it was not always thrown gently. I became ill with *Gelbsucht* (yellow jaundice). When my mother asked the doctor what brought this on the good doctor replied, "Perhaps pressure in the stomach area could be the cause." "Aha," my mother said, "the ballgames". She marched home to deflate my soccer ball and throw it up on our *Hangeboden*, a little storage area in our hallway. And this was the end of our *Volkerball* games. They were missed by everyone.

The "Gelbsucht" made me very sick to my stomach and I was yellow all over. I looked awful. Cooking odors bothered me and I did not have any appetite. I did not even want to look at food. My mother had a hard time trying to find something I could eat. She finally fixed some noodles and poured some tomato sauce that she made over it. That was the first meal that tasted good to me. The yellow color lasted a long time before it went away.

January 19ᵗʰ, 1944

My dearest Daughter!

How are you both? I am still without any kind of news from you. Which is simply terrible for me, not knowing how you are doing. I am so worried.

I have mailed four packages to you, so far, I hope that you will get them all.

Please try to leave Berlin, find a safer place to live. It would be better for you and also for me. I wouldn't have to live in constant fear about you.

Please send a few twenty penny stamps so I can mail some more packages to you.

I will sign off for today, hoping, that this letter will reach you both in good health.

Many greetings and kisses to you both from your loving Pappa.

Many greetings to Oma and Opa.

Shortages were beginning to be felt more and more. I do not, however, remember being hungry. We were getting the essential food we needed and after every heavy air raid in our neighborhood we would get some extra rations, along with sweets for the children, coffee beans and cigarettes for the adults.

We ate lots of fish. It was available without ration cards. There was a big indoor *Markthalle* (marketplace) close by. They sold different kinds of nice fresh fish. We liked flounder best of all.

Somehow, I always managed to get sick during *Schulferien* (summer school vacation). *Ziegenpeter* (mumps), *Masern* (measles), *Windpocken* (chickenpox), and *Gelbsucht*. I had them all and I did not miss any school. It was not any fun spending my school holiday in bed. I am sure it made me feel twice as bad.

I would get a prescription from our doctor for cod liver oil. He would smile while writing it. He knew what it was used for. We would fry the fish and potato pancakes with the oil. It smelled awful, but it tasted alright.

Of all the changes that came along with the new year the power outages were the worst to deal with, especially during the winter months when it turned dark so early. The electric power and the gas were turned off more often and for longer periods. We never knew when the power or the gas would be turned on or off. It could be anytime during the day or night. Without power we could not read or listen to the radio. Many evenings were spent sitting in the dark, with only the glow from the kitchen stove around us. Flashlight batteries were not available in stores anymore, only emergency personnel could get them. All we had for light were some small candles. They were shaped like metal lids, about one inch high. They were filled with wax and held a piece of wick. They did not give off very much light.

A bigger problem than the lack of entertainment was that we could not listen to the radio and receive the early air raid warnings. Then one day my grandfather remembered having an old battery operated radio stored away in the basement. We were so excited when we found this priceless treasure. I took the battery to the radio shop for re-charging and it worked. We were in touch again. We knew once again before the sirens told us about airplanes flying towards Berlin, coming to visit us. They surely liked our city, coming back again and again, bringing us tons of fireworks. They did not even feel offended by the greetings from the antiaircraft guns.

Evenings would find my grandfather sitting in his comfortable wicker chair near the warm kitchen stove, his earphones on, listening to the radio. When a report came through, he would raise up his hand and report the message to us. Eventually as the *Luftangriffe* (air raids) increased and came at any time in the night, the adults set up a watch schedule. My grandfather would listen until midnight. Then my mother would take over for the rest of the night.

> *Actung—Actung! Hier ist eine Luftlager meldung!!*
> *(Attention—Attention! Here is an air position announcement!)*

As soon as an announcement came through, my mother would wake me up first and then our neighbor Frau Bottger. She would then knock on the ceiling with a broom handle to let my grandparents know. Next she would run down three flights of stairs, across the courtyard, and back up three flights of stairs to wake up another neighbor. She and her baby girl joined the rest of us *Bunkerratten* on our run to the bunker.

My mother or Frau Bottger also knocked on Frau Girndt's door to let her sisters and husbands know about approaching airplanes. They would get ready and leave for the *Erdbunker* (underground bunker) where Frau Girndt and her daughters were. The *Erdbunker* was a little closer to walk to from our house than the *Flakbunker*. It used to be a huge gas tank, but had been converted into an underground bunker with several floors.

After this wake up call, my mother returned to our apartment to get our baggage and me. She could not depend on me being ready to go. Many times she would find me back in bed. I would put on a coat and off we would run. By this time we did not fully undress anymore when we went to bed. We only took off our dress, skirt, sweater or blouse. We kept the rest on. There was not enough time to change bedclothes for street clothes and then get to the bunker.

Looking back and reflecting on those evenings living in the dark, I still marvel at our ability to get around as well as we did without injuring ourselves. When we were leaving the apartment, hurriedly, for our trip to the bunker, we knew exactly how many steps to take from one landing to the next, using the railing to guide us down the three flights of stairs. We would run along one hallway, cross a courtyard and then maneuver through a second hallway before getting to the front door of the house. We never had any time to waste from the time an announcement was made of an impending air raid to when we actually got going. I must say we did well on our trips in total darkness. I do not recall that anybody ever missed a step or ran into a wall.

At the beginning of the war, a lot of accidents happened outside during the *Verdunkelung* (black out). My mother had a bad accident one dark morning around 5:30 while on her way to work. She rode the S-Bahn from Humboldthain to Tegel. Thinking the train had stopped, she stepped off the still moving train onto the platform of the station. She fell down, hit her head against a pole, and injured both her knees and her shoulder. She went on to the plant where she stopped at the first aid station. How she ever managed to walk there was a puzzle to us. They had her lie down and bandaged her knees and after a while she was sent home to see her doctor. He was furious with their careless treatment. She should have been taken to a hospital for proper care. She had a mild concussion and a wrenched shoulder, but her knees were the worst. She took a long time healing. It was very lucky that she did not get killed.

"Don't let the enemy see anything." Well, I do not think the *Verdunkelung* worked. They found everything they wanted to find, even in the dark.

January 21st, 1944

Dear Friedel and Lottchen!

Unfortunately, I am still without some news from you, which bothers me very much. Nevertheless, I am hoping for the best. I have just finished packing a small box for you. It is meant to be your birthday present. Some sweets and 12 cigarettes.

I hope you will get it on time. I would have liked to send a small bottle of liquor along but I couldn't get any stamps.

How are you both doing? What are the news at home? Please, write every day to me!

Greetings and kisses to you both from your loving Pappa.

Many greetings to Oma and Opa
Aunt Anna and Uncle Alfred
Grete

My dad's letters were arriving at our house regularly but as of the 21st of January he had not received any mail from us. He must have been so worried.

January 22nd, 1944

I received some stamps today and packed two small boxes for you. One bottle of liquor, a very good one, and one bottle of vermouth wine. Now I am very anxious to see if you receive them alright.

At any rate, a little celebration and a toast on your birthday will be good for you and for Mother and Father.

There is so much sadness around us. The most important wish is that we will see each other again, in good health. And all the rest, like our lost home, we will procure again.

At present we are having violent snowstorms.

I will sign off for today.
Many greetings and kisses to you both from your Pappa.

My mother's birthday would be February 11. I believe that 1940 was probably the last time they were together on her or his birthday (March 9th).

January 25th, 1944

Dear Friedel and Lottchen!

I am still without some news from you. I live in constant fear about you. Perhaps the mail service is to blame. Well, I am hoping for the best.

It is snowing here, every day and night. We haven't had this much snow in quite a while.

I have not heard from Karl Heinz yet either. Also the package from Mrs. Hoffmann has not come yet. Probably very little hope of getting it anymore.

I will try and be patient and hope to hear from you very soon.

Many greetings and kisses to you both from your Pappa.

Karl Heinz, his comrade, was one whose life he had saved, along with Hoffman. They had both been shot and wounded and were lying in the line of fire on the battleground. My dad crawled out to them and pulled them back to safer ground.

He was honored with a medal for this, which did not excite him very much. He was happy that he was able to do this for them, his comrades. Their families were very thankful and stayed in touch with him and with us.

January 29th, 1944

Dear Friedel and Lottchen!

I received your first dear letter today written on January 23rd!

I am so glad to read that you are both alright. I have been so worried! In your letter you mentioned the 10 days additional furlough for me, that the telegram arrived when you returned home from taking me to the railroad station. I don't know anything about it, no one here has told me. Very unfortunate!

Sorry to hear about Alfons, that he shot himself, it gave me quite a shock. He kept his promise and I can understand his feelings, his situation.

It is all so heartbreaking!

Therefore I would like for you to leave Berlin, somewhere safe.

Maybe stay with Grete?

Now it looks bad for Gerhard too. I hope he pulls through. I wish him all the best.

Dear Friedel, I have mailed 7 packages to you. I hope that you will get them.

Did you receive the 35 Marks that I mailed from the border?

In three weeks I am going back to my Company. Already I shudder thinking about the awful coldness in the Bunker.

One meter away, near the stove, glowing red hot, stood the pail with coffee and it froze solid. You can imagine all the rest.

Last week, Ivan launched a big attack. He was beaten back under heavy losses. Perhaps you heard about it on the radio? By the way, has Lottchen received an answer yet on her request for a radio? You know what I mean.

Many Greetings and Kisses to both of you from your loving Papa.

Many Greetings to Father, Mother, Family Herzog, Grete

While my dad was home on leave I mentioned to him how much I missed having a radio. He jokingly suggested that I should write a letter to our Propaganda-Minister, Dr. Goebbels, and ask him for one. At first I laughed at this funny suggestion, thinking, "When did we ever get something from a Nazi organization?" But then I thought, "Why not?" Who knew what might happen? It was at least worth a try.

We had heard about Dr. Goebbels' *Spenden* (donations) for needy people. Well I certainly was one now. I just never thought that we would have a chance as non-party members. So I wrote him a letter. I do not remember anymore what I said, but I am certain that I was quite explicit about our situation and about the location of our bombed out home, remembering that he had visited our neighborhood. Within a few days I received an answer from his office to come and pick up a *Volksemplfanger* (public radio) at the designated address. What a surprise! I had trouble believing that I had received a response, but I did not waste any time going to pick it up.

I was still feeling a little doubtful when I arrived at the office, but they really presented me with a radio. Of course it came with a little speech about the generous *Spenden* from Dr. Goebbels. I listened politely to their propaganda talk. I did not mind so long as I had a radio to listen to again. I know that Dr. Goebbels did not personally read my letter, but someone in his office who had the authority to allow me the *Spenden* certainly did.

I was very happy with my radio and so was my dad when he heard about it. He also was very surprised. He really never expected it to happen.

February 1st, 1944

Dear Friedel and Lottchen!

I want to let you know that I have only received one letter from you, so far.

I am quite certain that my mail is lying at the Company. I am going back there soon, then I will be able to pick it up myself. I put another package together for you, today. It is number eight.

Perhaps you should inquire at our former post office about the packages that I mailed before coming on leave.

Maybe one of them made it yet!

I will sign off for today with my hope to be with you again soon and maybe then forever.

Greetings and kisses to you both from your loving Pappa.

February 3rd, 1944

Dear Friedel and Lottchen!

I have received your dear letter of January 25th with many thanks. It is the 2nd letter from you. I am glad to hear that you have received the first two packages. It would have been regrettable, should they have gotten lost. I hope that all the other packages arrive yet too, especially the one for your birthday. It is a very good liquor and I want you, Mother and Father to enjoy a glass together and think of me.

I sent a crocodile to Lottchen. She doesn't have to be afraid, it is very tame. Ivan made it for me. A Russian prisoner of war.

I would feel so much better if you and Lottchen would leave Berlin. I live in constant fear about you. And Lottchen might be able to go back to school, otherwise she is falling behind too much.

I will sign off for today.

Greetings and kisses to you both
Your Pappa

Many greetings to Mother and Father.

After reading my dad's letters about his concern for us and our safety, my mother decided it would be best for us to leave Berlin and let my dad have a little less to worry about us. My grandmother's cousin lived in Kottbus, not far from Dresden. We asked her to help us find a place to stay.

I do not know the reason for not going to Alt-Ruppin to our good friend Grete's home. Maybe Alt-Ruppin was not such a safe place. It was on the direct air attack route to Berlin. Airplanes flew over the little town all the time, although they had not been bombed yet. They probably would have flattened the place had they known about the underground ammunition factory where Tante Grete worked. We did not know about it until after the war, when she told us about it. They were sworn to secrecy. It was a little farming village that portrayed such a peaceful image, while harboring a very deadly secret.

My mother wrote to my dad and told him about our decision. I really did not want to go. I felt quite safe in the bunker, but I also wanted my dad to feel less worried about us.

February 7th, 1944

Dear Friedel and Lottchen!

Today I received a letter from you of January 10th. I see from your letter that I was to have ten more days of furlough. Regrettable that the telegram arrived after we left for the Railroad Station. It really was bad luck.

In a few days I am returning to my Company. Who knows where they will put me again. I really would like to stay here in this camp for Russian prisoners. I have already spoken to the Chief and he told me, that he would take me back any time. It is up to the Company to let me go.

During the time while I was on leave and since I returned many of my old comrades have left. Either wounded or killed. New people are coming in all the time and they are such young boys. If only the war would soon come to an end, that is everyone's wish.

It is all so difficult for me anymore; I am so tired and feel so exhausted.

I have written to Mother and Father and I sent him a bottle of Schnapps and some cigarettes. Please send me some cord to wrap packages with. Otherwise I don't need anything. I have food to eat, cigarettes and Schnapps.

Whatever is wrong with the Postal Service? I have only received three letters from you, so far.

Many greetings and kisses to both of you from your Pappa.

Many greetings to Father, Mother, Aunt Anna, Uncle Alfred, Grete.

February 10th, 1944

My dearest Daughter!

I received your dear letter of January 24th, with many thanks. It is letter #2, #1 I have not received yet. I see from your letter that you are both well.

Above all, I rejoice with you that you will get a radio soon. "Volksempfanger"!

Tomorrow is Mutti's Birthday, too bad, I cannot be there with you. But in my thoughts I will be and I will have a toast on her birthday. Cheers! For a healthy wiedersehen!!

I am enclosing a few marks for you in this letter!

Many greetings and kisses to you both from your Pappa.

Many greetings to Oma and Opa.

February 11ᵗʰ, 1944

Dear Friedel and Lottchen!

Today is your birthday and I would like to be there with you to celebrate but unfortunately, I cannot. Perhaps, when you celebrate the next one, with the four zeroes? I have packed up two more packages for you. In one of them is a bottle of Rum, some pipe tobacco and 10 razor blades. It is for Father, please give it to him. I hope that it all will get there alright, especially the bottles. Please let me know when it does.

Tonight I will in my thoughts and with a full glass have a toast with you for a happy, healthy reunion, to be together again.

You have not written yet, whether you received the 35 Marks or that you have not. It is the money I sent back from the border, had to send the money back. I wrote to Lottchen yesterday and enclosed some money for her, in the letter.

Many Greetings and Kisses to you both from your loving Pappa.

Many Greetings to Father and Mother.

I received the money and was happy about it. I could not buy myself anything with it, but I took it to the bank and deposited it into my account, where all the gifts of money went that were given to me. I am quite sure that I would have spent some of the money had there been something in the stores to buy. By the end of the war my account showed 500.00 marks. Eventually the banks were paying back ten percent of the total bank account balance. I received about 50 marks, not even enough to buy a loaf of bread on the black market.

February 13th, 1944

Dear Friedel and Lottchen!

Your dear letter of January 26th and one from Lottchen written on the same day finally arrived here. Many thanks! Also for the stamps!

I was so happy to read that you are both alright. I also heard from Gerhard yesterday. He told me that they had to take his leg off and that he was in a lot of pain. I feel sorry for him, but at least the war is over for him.

I still think it would be better for both of you to leave Berlin. We don't have anything to lose anymore but our lives. You both could use a little change, a nice rest, from all those air raids. You don't have to worry about money; they will forward it to wherever you go.

I don't have my old position anymore. Soon, we will be relieved up front.

The funny story that Lottchen sent along in her letter, was amusing. She is right, we must not lose our sense of humor.

I will sign off for today. Enclosed are some air mail stamps.

Many greetings and kisses to you both from your Pappa.

February 15ᵗʰ, 1944

Dear Friedel and Lottchen!

I received your two letters of January 29ᵗʰ and a letter from Lottchen of January 3ʳᵈ with many thanks. They finally got here! I also received the package from Mrs. Hoffmann. It took over three months to get here. I really didn't expect it anymore. Everything was in good condition.

I see from your letter that you have decided to leave Berlin with Lottchen. It is a good decision, much better to leave than to stay in Berlin. I am relieved too and I hope that you will find a good place to live. With the money that you get every month, you can live anywhere. You don't have to worry about that.

Mrs. Hildebrand wrote a letter to me. She told me that Karl-Heinz made Unter-Offizier. I am glad for him. He never would have made it in our Company.

Please let me know your new address as soon as you can.

Es grusst und kusst euch, Euer Pappa.

We got ready for our trip to Kottbus. When I said "good bye" to my grandfather he looked at me and replied "*Auf Wiedersehen*, see you in about one week." I guess he knew me better than I thought he did.

We took the train to Kottbus and we found my Oma's cousins without any problems. We stayed a couple of nights with her, sleeping in a huge, high bed. Even I, the tallest girl in my school class, needed a stool to get into it; and then I disappeared into the big feather beds, two feet thick at least.

We went to the housing authority for evacuees and they found us a couple of possible places to live. We took the trolley car to the suburbs of Kottbus to a farming community. I was not thrilled about living in the country. I liked going to Alt-Ruppin for the weekend, but any longer it became boring. I knew I would miss my life in the city and my friends.

We chose one of the places, a small house owned by an old lady. She rented us a furnished room with kitchen privileges. It was nice but very old fashioned—gas lights and no indoor plumbing. We had a washstand, complete with bowl and a pitcher for water, which had to be carried in from a pump in the yard. I probably could have gotten used to this way of washing up, but I struggled with the "outhouse situation" and I was afraid of the gaslight. On our first night I laid in bed, keeping my eyes on the hanging gas lamp. It made a hissing sound. I was not familiar with such lighting fixtures and it frightened me and I was afraid of falling asleep while it was turned on.

My mother went in to the village to the meeting place to see what she could find out about any news or what might be happening elsewhere. She learned little. We felt very isolated.

On another evening we walked to the meeting place when the sirens went off. It was the location for the only air raid shelter in the whole area. Very few people were in the shelter. Most of them stood outside, talking. They were not very friendly towards us outsiders coming from the city. Nothing happened during the air raid. After this experience we did not bother going to the shelter anymore. Neither did our landlady.

We had heard stories from returning people that were evacuated to the country about how unwelcome they felt. The government made the arrangements with the farmers to take in evacuees from cities, mostly mothers with their children, but it did not always turn out satisfactorily.

My mother always said, "One never knows what lies ahead. Things can change so quickly, and it can happen to anyone, whatever the situation is." They laughed at us *Bunkerratten* (bunker rats) for running to the bunker and made fun of evacuees leaving the cities for safer places to live. It turned out before long that many of these people were forced to leave their homes, their farms, their land and livestock, thrown out by Poles, Czechs and Russians. Then they became the *Fluchtlinge* (refugees), traveling from one spot to another, trying to find a place to stay.

I was very unhappy. I did not like living in this unfriendly place and I missed my grandparents and seeing our *Bunkerratten* friends. I pleaded with my mother to take us back to Berlin. My grandfather was right with his prediction, for I was home within a week. He smiled when I walked into the kitchen. Maybe he was glad to see me back. I know that I was.

February 24th, 1944

Dear Friedel and Lottchen!

Today I received several letters from you and the package with the cake. Many thanks! I am sorry I cannot write more often anymore. It is almost impossible to find the time. And the bunker is so small it is difficult to move around. The cake was delicious and good eating. I packed a box for you too with a few cigarettes and some tobacco.

I had believed that you and Lottchen were long gone from Berlin.

Well you must know what is best for you both. I don't feel well at all, it is so exhausting for me anymore. I am very tired, but I will have to clench my teeth and bear it.

Hearty greetings and kisses sends to you your Pappa.

Many greetings to Father, Mother

March 14th, 1944

Dear Friedel and Lottchen!

First of all, my best thanks for all the letters! I also received the package with the cookies with many thanks.

It arrived on my birthday, a very special treat. The time allowed for writing has become extremely scarce, so please be patient.

I see from your letter, that you didn't find a good place to live, away from Berlin. Please go and stay with Grete, it is too dangerous living in Berlin.

I have not heard from Mother. I hope that nothing bad happened to them, and that they are alright.

Here by us it is very cold, colder yet in our bunker.

What did Lottchen say about the crocodile?

Please write often, it is about the only joy that I have left here.

Es grusst und kusst Euch, Euer Pappa.

Viele Grusse Vater, Mutter, Tante Anna, Onkel Alfred, Grete

I did receive the box with the tame crocodile. It was carved from a piece of wood, very simple, but a neat idea. And now, fifty-six years later, it can be found resting comfortably in Florida, near real live crocodiles. It is enjoying a well earned rest, having spent many months hiding in suitcases during air raids, fleeing across Germany, being inspected by Russian soldiers, having its head torn off, returning to Berlin via Alt-Ruppin, living for years on dry land and far away from other crocodiles, and then flying across an ocean from Germany to America. The small wooden tame crocodile, carved in Russia for my dad by a prisoner of war will always be a very special keepsake for me.

March 18th, 1944

Dear Frau Wittmutz!

I have the duty to make this very grievous announcement to you, that your husband, Corporal Willi Wittmutz, Feldpostnummer (FPN15297c) has been missing after a scouting mission since the night of the 15th–16th of March.

The scouting mission under the leadership of a sergeant had been ordered to reconnoiter the Russian positions. Shortly before reaching the enemy position, they suddenly came under heavy fire, whereby five of the seven men were wounded.

The sergeant, badly wounded himself, was the last man to fall back from the enemy position. Because he saw no one else on the battlefield, he felt assured that everyone else had pulled back. Everyone made it back to their position before they realized Cpl. Wittmutz was missing. We quickly organized a search party under my command and we returned to the battleground and searched the entire area, unsuccessfully. We found nothing in the whole area, except a track in the deep snow that looked as someone had been dragged towards the enemy position.

This indicates he may have been captured. Other clarifying results could only partly confirm my suspicions.

It is very sad for the whole Company, that we lost a first class comrade over whose whereabouts we are uncertain.

He was to all of us, whether officer, sergeant or man, because of his cheerful willingness, wonderful comradeship and his experience in many areas, very special, close to our hearts.

Dear Frau Wittmutz, we are unable to measure the heavy suffering that has come upon you again, in such a short time after the "bombing damage". I beg you to accept our sincere sympathy from the whole Company. The hard sacrifice can only be for us front line soldiers an obligation to duty. May the exemplary performance of duty from your husband be a little comfort in this difficult, grave hour.

Should you have any kind of wishes, I gladly stand at your disposal at any time.

In deep sympathy,
Your Werner Schulze, Captain and Co-Chief

I find it very difficult writing this down, this very sad part of my life, even after all the years that have gone by. It is a wound that has never healed. Our reaction, when we received the letter telling us about my dad's fate, was to feel heartbroken. We could not understand why this was happening to us. It seemed so unfair and so cruel so soon after the loss of our home. We were filled with despair and felt so discouraged.

When we told my grandparents we became very concerned about "Opa", my grandfather. He lost what little color he had. He turned deathly white, shook uncontrollably, and his breathing became more strenuous than ever before. We feared a heart attack coming on. He looked like a very old man at age sixty-four.

We were all visibly shaken. We did not know how to cope—not getting letters from him anymore—not knowing about his wellbeing—not knowing his whereabouts. I prayed to God harder than I ever did before, to keep him well and strong so that he might survive the dreadful prison camps, that his captors would be kind, and that he would come home to us.

My dad was not a young fellow anymore at age thirty-six. He felt worn out after spending two and one half years in Russia as a front line soldier. He had already endured the awful cold winter months without proper warm clothing. For that he and the other soldiers who survived had only received another medal.

This was the third time that he had been wounded, only this time he had been taken prisoner by the enemy. He had always strongly objected to this possibility. He never wanted to become a prisoner of the Russians and be marched off to Siberia to work in their mines until death had mercy. He told my mother repeatedly that he would always try and save the last bullet for himself before being captured. My mother would try to talk him out of this but he was very determined. No prison camp for him. But this wish was not granted to him. He had to go through this painful humiliation and endure the awful treatment at a time when he already felt tired and exhausted. How much strength was left in him to survive such an ordeal?

I remember that the last letter was written March 15, the fatal night. I do not know what happened to the letter. It is no longer with the rest of the letters. I saw my mother reading the letters from time to time. I remember that he wrote, apologizing for writing a very short letter. He had just come off duty and was going back out on ski patrol, taking a comrade's place who was too sick to go. I wished that he had not taken his comrade's place! He probably was already tired and not as alert anymore to notice the enemy hiding under the cover of snow, surprising them. I heard him tell about the Russians in their white camouflage *tarnanzug* (overalls). They would lie motionless under the cover of snow, totally hidden, and cause surprise attacks.

The Red Cross notified us after the war, in either 1948 or 1949, that a comrade from my dad's company had returned to Berlin, having been released from a Russian prisoner of war camp. We got so excited we could not get to his place fast enough, hoping to find out something about my dad's whereabouts. He told us that he saw my dad in 1945 in a prison camp near Finland. They had assembled outside but he was not allowed to walk over to him or try to talk to him. He appeared alright. Comforting words!

He also told us that a couple of days after my dad's disappearance he was speaking to them, his fellow comrades, via a loudspeaker and giving a propaganda speech, the same kind as they had heard before. They could tell that he was being forced to say these words as he spoke very slowly, a long pause after every word. "Come on over Comrades! It is great here. Good and plenty to eat, lots of vodka to drink, and beautiful women!!" My poor dad. What a humiliating ordeal for him to endure. I wished that my dad still believed we were in a safe place away from Berlin, when this happened to him. He worried so much about us. It might have made it a bit easier for him.

He must have been unconscious when the Russians dragged him away; otherwise he would have made his presence and his situation known to his comrades. I guess we will never know what happened to him on that awful night, at least not until we meet again in heaven.[25]

Property of Corporal Willi Wittmutz

1 Cardigan	*1 soap dish*
4 hand towels	*1 tooth tartar cleaner*
3 pair socks	*2 pocket calendars*
1 handkerchief	*Letters*
1 pair ladies stockings	*Writing paper*
1 bag shoe polish kit	*Envelopes*
1 box shoe polish	*1 bag coffee beans*
2 razor blades	*1 package tobacco*

---

25 Many years later, fourteen to be exact, my grandmother, his mom, died on March 14, 1958. A very strange coincidence.

2 shaving brushes	*1 pipe*
1 pocket mirror	*1 lighter*
1 comb	*Cigarette paper*
1 hand brush	*1 sewing kit*
3 cans skin cream	*1 breast pouch*
4 tubes tooth paste	*1 pen*
1 toothbrush	*1 pencil lead*
2 bars soap	*1 pencil*
1 can opener	*1 knife—Finnish*
1 deck cards	*1 pair shoe laces*
1 tin Hapland	*2 pair shoe soles*

We received my dad's *Eigensachen* (personal property), which added one more sad day to the rest of them in our lives. His comrades should have kept the items for their own use. Earlier we had received the letters and photos that had been in his possession. I received back the birthday card that I had sent to him just before his capture.

When I saw the tubes of toothpaste and tartar remover I was reminded of his advice to me to take good care of my teeth. He was so insistent, and it worked. Whenever I felt apprehensive in later years about visiting the dentist I remembered his words—and went to visit the *Zahnartz* (dentist).[26]

---

26 He started taking me to the *Zahnartz* for checkups at a very early age. Sometimes, he would send me ahead across the street to the office to wait for him. And wait I did. I would take my place in the waiting room and when my turn came and my dad had not come yet, I let the next person go ahead of me. The dentist knew that I would not come in without my dad by my side. I was not afraid of anything. I just needed to wait for my dad.

I do not believe my mother ever took me to the dentist, probably because my dad worked the night shift and was home at times during the daytime hours. I liked having my dad home during the day even though he was sleeping and I had to be quiet. It felt good knowing that he was there. My mother worked the daytime shift. When both worked the same shift I was home alone all day long. Tante Maske, our next door neighbor, looked after me or at least was there if I needed something. It was difficult, but we trudged on, living from day to day, making the best of it!

Life Moves On

Onkel Gerhard was in a rehabilitation clinic in Werder, not far from Potsdam. We rode the S-Bahn there to visit him on a nice warm sunny spring Sunday. Werder was known for its fruit orchards, very popular for outings during the *Baumblute fest* (tree-blossom festival). Sundays were still quite safe to go about our normal activities without worrying over interruptions from air raids. My mother and I walked along under the fruit trees, full of blossoms. It almost seemed that the good old times had returned. But when we looked around us and saw all the soldiers missing arms or legs we were reminded of our present situation and what this awful war was doing to us.

Onkel Gerhard seemed very glad to see us. We took him for a walk in his wheelchair through the orchards, then took a rest and sat for awhile on a bench, having a nice talk with him. He felt very sad about my dad's fate. They had always been very close to each other, more like brothers than cousins. Both grew up as only children in their families. When we went back to the clinic, Onkel Gerhard showed us the beautiful handbags he was making. Something they had taught him to do as he recovered. They were made from twine. I was hoping that he would make one for me, a shoulder bag.

He was having a lot of trouble with his artificial leg. He could not get used to it, but he seemed cheerful and joked about it. In the years to come he never overcame this problem and would just use his crutches to walk with. He eventually had two or three additional operations on that leg. The first surgery on his leg was a little above the knee. Eventually there was not much left of that leg.[27]

Now and then I would go back to my old neighborhood to see my old friends. The sidewalks had been cleaned up, the debris taken away. It felt strange looking at what was left of the houses that once stood there.

I missed going to school. I did a lot of reading, trying to keep up a little bit. I signed up for Confirmation classes with Pastor Werder from the *Himmelfahrtkirche* (Church of the Ascension). Pastor Werder had also confirmed my dad. Unfortunately, the church, located at Humboldthain near the bunker, was bombed and burned out. The parsonage was across the street and it had survived, so classes were held

---

27 He found a job sitting in a booth in the S-Bahn station Waidmannslust, punching tickets. After the war, he opened a kiosk selling newspapers, and magazines. Later on he added cigarettes, candy, and ice cream bars. He was quite successful, adding three more kiosks at different locations near factories. The whole family became involved with this business.

there. For the first time I attended a class together with boys. It was quite different. I also went for English lessons across the street from us. A retired English teacher was giving private lessons. Her husband operated a "Smoke Shop" in the front of the house and their living quarters were in the back of the shop. I tried very hard to ignore the peculiar, strange smell that lingered throughout their place and the teacher's fat dog. Its name was "Mops". It always sat on a pillow across from me and right next to her. It would slobber and stare at me. It was such a homely looking dog. I finally decided that I really did not want to learn *English sprechen* (English conversation) bad enough to put up with all that!

We began to become much better acquainted with some of our new neighbors and I spent a lot of time with their children. Right next door to us lived a young couple. They had a little boy, Jurgen, about four years old. Frau Bottger had her two girls, Elfriede and Marlies, with Marlies being about ten to eleven months old that spring. Marlies could not walk yet, but she would stand in her crib and call for me, saying "Rotti, Rotti" very fast. My name was her first word. I felt honored. There were times when her mom would come and get me to put her to sleep or to calm her down when she was upset and crying. I would sprinkle my magic potion over her and to everyone's surprise she would calm down and fall asleep. Oh my!

On the second floor, below us, lived Frau Girndt. Her apartment was the one that my mother would also alert when we heard of an air raid on the radio. She had three girls who were three, five and seven years old. Frau Bottger and Frau Girndt's husbands were serving the military. Frau Girndt had taken into her home both of her sisters and their husbands. They had lost their homes too, like we did. Frau Girndt had a room in the underground bunker where she and the girls went every evening to spend the night. Her sisters and their husbands stayed in the apartment. They were a bit crowded in the daytime, but they managed.

I became quite the "Nanny", although without pay. The mothers trusted me with their children and the children liked being with me. On nice days, I would take them all to the small street-side park and let them play in the *Buddelkasten* (sandbox). Sometimes we would go to Humboldthain, where there was a larger play area and a *Planschbecken* (wading pool). My mother told me about my dad being scolded by a policeman when he found him wading in the kiddie pool in the early morning hours on his way home with his friends from a Fathers Day Celebration outing. Whenever I saw this pool, I could see my dad wading around in it. He liked having a good time.

Humboldthain was a nice big park with lots of trees and a beautiful rose garden. My dad helped get it planted as a member of a depression era government sponsored workgroup. It also was a good place for sledding in the winter. There were long and short *Rodelbahnen* (sled trails). The three long ones were called *Lebensbahn* (Life Threatening Run), *Knochenbahn* (Trail of Bones), and *Todesbahn* (Dead Man's Run). The runs were lots of fun, but very dangerous. They passed between trees, were very bumpy, and often quite icy. The names chosen for these runs were not exaggerated.

My dad remembered sledding on those runs when he was a young boy living across the street from the park. I was told to use the smaller runs. They were safer, but not much fun. When I was older, I went to the park and rode the longer runs. It really was not all that bad, except for some older boys acting very malicious. They would hang around on top of the slope and, just as one of us girls pushed off, they would slide behind and throw themselves on top of you. Of course then one would lose control of the steering and crash into a tree. That is how I ended up with a broken sled and nearly crushed my leg. Just before hitting the tree I was able to pull my leg up. Otherwise it would have been between the sled and the tree. Those boys were very irresponsible and mean. They spoiled our fun. I was told that before the war and the black out that the trails were lighted and the "older generation" would go sledding after dark. It must have been fun.

One day that spring the superintendent asked us if we would like to plant some flower seeds in the backyard. We thought it was a great idea. We worked very hard as we took our task very seriously. And it paid off. We all grew some nice flowers.

Then we had another bad experience from an air raid in our neighborhood. The street behind us was bombed and we suffered a little damage. We lost the glass in our windows. That meant we were considered *Leichtbeschadigt* (lightly damaged). Until then we had been lucky to have the glass panes survive. My mother nailed cardboard over the openings. She also helped my grandparents clean up all their shattered pieces of glass and to cover their windows. A couple days later, a *Glaser* (glazier) came by and installed some kind of material into the window frames which allowed light to come through a little better than cardboard.

For my grandfather, however, this seemed like more than light damage. Poor Opa, he could not see anything anymore unless the window was open. The window is where he sat and watched the activities below. He could see the workers from the small businesses behind us and the happenings in that part of our neighborhood. He hardly ever went downstairs anymore. Even during the air raids he would stay upstairs. He had become very feeble with shortness of breath. Going up and down the stairs or doing any kind of walking would exhaust him.

About this time our neighbors lost their little boy Jurgen to scarlet fever. It happened so fast. He complained about his throat hurting. He would just whisper. Then he asked for me. I went and sat by his bedside and read stories to him. He looked so feverish. Every time I tried to leave, he would get upset. The doctor finally came and they took him to the hospital, but he did not make it. We all felt so sad. I did not tell anyone, but I pretended that my little friends were really my brothers and sisters. He was such a good little boy. I missed him a lot.

Jurgen's father once told us about a very sad experience. He worked in Oranienburg as an engineer for a big factory. During the air raids they would seek shelter in *Luftschutzgraben* (air protection trenches). These were long covered trenches, reinforced with tree trunks. They would sit on long benches on either side. On this particular occasion he was sitting by himself at the entrance when a "blockbuster" bomb exploded close by. He felt himself being lifted up and dropped back down again, along with a big rush of air. He only heard one big sigh from the rest of the people in the shelter. When he called out no one answered to his calls. He found his flashlight and went looking for the people. They were sitting in the covered trench, apparently undisturbed, but dead, every one of them. Their lungs had apparently collapsed from the effects of the explosion.

We heard that this happened time and time again when blockbusters were dropped on or very close to this kind of shelter. I do not recall how many people could seek protection in one of those trenches but must have been a fairly large number. He was the sole survivor in his *Luftschutzgraben*. His story is quite similar to the one I told about the night when we were bombed out and everyone was killed in the house next to us, except the father of one of my friends, who was the only survivor.

That spring I also became quite upset about the allied bombers when they managed one night to hit our *Badenstall* (bathhouse). That meant that I could no longer go there for a *Brausebad* (shower). I liked taking showers much more than baths. The bathhouse was a big building that covered an entire city block and stood five stories high. It had one big indoor swimming pool in the center. Bathing cabins, tubs and showers were located along the sides. One side was reserved for girls and women, and the other side was for boys and men. The two sides were not allowed to mingle. After the bombing we tried to have a look but the area was all roped off. There was lots of water running along the street, but it did not bother our house. Our street, *Hochstrasse* (High Street) stood behind its name.

Tante Grete came early on Saturdays, riding the train from Alt-Ruppin to Berlin. She would bring us fresh fruit and vegetables from her garden, which we appreciated very much. We would return her favor by taking her *Lebensmittel Karte* (ration card) to our grocery store and get the items that she could not find due to a shortage of such items in the country stores. We were still better supplied with certain selections. Then she would return on the train to Alt-Ruppin in the late afternoon.

One day I saw a small group of Russian prisoners cleaning up the debris from the bombed out building behind us with only one guard watching over them. I noticed that they looked into the garbage can, the one marked for *Schwein* (pig).[28] When I saw them looking into the can I figured that they were hungry. I took some bread and asked the guard if I could put the bread for them on top of the can. He nodded and turned his back while I laid it on top of the lid. I felt like I was being watched as I did so. I went back upstairs and when I looked out of the window, I saw that it was gone. From that day on, I took something every day. I could tell that they were waiting for me to come. I never had a guard deny me or chase me away. We could not truly afford to share our food rations with them. They numbered eight or ten. I would ask the people in our building and the lady from the bakery and the lady in the grocery store to help. No one ever turned me down. I received mainly bread, boiled potatoes, and some fruit. Everyone tried to come up with something to eat for them.

One of the guards asked me one day if my family could use some firewood. He said that he would have the prisoners cut some up for me. We certainly needed some firewood. It had become quite scarce. A neighbor let me use her small wagon and I took it with me when I made my food delivery. The Russians would stack

---

28 At the beginning of the war people were asked to separate their garbage. The authorities provided a special can with a cute sign of a pig above it, listing all the things a pig could eat. *"Ich fresse"* ("I eat") potatoes, vegetables, fruit peelings and table scraps. Berlin was surrounded by *Bauernhofe* (farms) and that is where the garbage was taken. Long before this was done, I remember a man walking through our street with a horse pulling a wagon and calling out loudly, *"Brennholz fur kartoffel schalen!"* ("Firewood for potato peelings!") People would come and bring their baskets with potato peelings and receive a small bundle of firewood in exchange. The peelings were used for feeding pigs.

it full of wood and I would pick it up before they left. I shared the wood with everyone that gave me food to give to them.

I never liked seeing people begging. I wanted to help, which was not always possible. But on this occasion, it felt good being able to help. I also hoped that a kind person somewhere in Russia was helping my dad too.

October 1944 *"Schwerbeschadigt"*

It is hard to believe, but there really were areas in Berlin where the houses did not get bombed and people never lost their homes. Unfortunately we lived in an area that was a sought after target. In October of 1944 our school street was hit again by *Luftmienen*, blockbusters and *Brandbomben* (incendiary bombs), the bombs landing only about five houses away. The dental school across the street, near Bahnhof Humboldthain, was a total loss. I wondered where I was now to go for my dental checkups. The dental school had been very convenient for me to get a dental checkup. The students were so glad to have us come that they gave us the royal treatment.[29]

When we walked back to our neighborhood from the bunker and into our street it looked pretty bad. The whole corner of the block was gone. The houses were just piled up in a big heap of rubble, which was burning furiously. We were lucky on this night. Our house was still standing, thank goodness.

Inside the house things looked very different. To allow us to see things better the power was turned on for us as we returned. After walking upstairs to our apartment, we found our front door lying a half floor below. A strong wind greeted us though the open windows. Yes, they were blown out again. We never did find the blankets that we used to cover up our windows and comply with the *Verdunkelung* (black out). The kitchen floor was covered with broken bits and pieces from our dishes. Everything movable was sitting some place else. The big heavy wardrobe (my aunt's) was blocking the entrance to our bedroom.

The superintendent helped us with our door and with the wardrobe. My mother nailed some more cardboard over the window openings. I had to hold it in place. The wind was blowing very strong. Then we hurried upstairs to help my grandmother, as my grandfather was not capable of doing anything. He had not gone downstairs to the shelter with my grandmother. He had taken refuge in the

---

29 I must confess that I never went alone. I always found someone I could talk into going with me.

bathroom when the fireworks came closer and louder. It was a good decision that he left his post by the window. The top of the kitchen cupboard would have hit him and showered him with broken glass and dishes. Opa did not have much to say about the bombing, but he did admit that it was a frightful experience.

Their home was in worse condition than ours was. They had more things to move around and break. First of all we had to cover the windows to keep the cold and smoky air outside. That air was very bad for my grandfather's breathing problems. As long as the power stayed on and we had the light we attended to the worst of the clean up. The light allowed us to move around without stepping on the pieces of broken glass and dishes that seemed to be everywhere.

The lights were turned off by the time we went back downstairs to our own home. We just swept the broken pieces from the kitchen cupboard into a corner of the kitchen and called it enough for one night. We were both very tired. We hoped that the unwelcome visitors would let us sleep for the rest of the night.

I was already lying on my bed when my mother lay down. She and the bed together collapsed onto the floor. It really was not funny but she looked so surprised I had to laugh. Of course she did not find it amusing. She lost control and started to cry, which did not happen very often. She kept asking how much more we could endure. We did not know it then, thank goodness, that it was only the beginning. There was a lot more to come for us. Nevertheless, we were now *Schwerbeschadigt* (heavily damaged).

We felt better the following morning, especially after we took a look in the daylight at the damage to our street. The bed frame had no doubt been damaged during the air raid, as the bomb that hit five houses away had unleashed a very powerful force. Where it landed the houses were all gone, along with the people who had lived in them. Wherever a blockbuster hit, it left no survivors. We considered ourselves lucky to have survived another bad night. We still had a roof over our head and a bed to sleep in, even if it was down on the floor.

By this time there were more and more people going to the bunker. Baby carriages and strollers had to be left outside. They took up space that was needed for all the people. Those seeking shelter even rode in on the S-Bahn when the forewarning was given. During the daytime raids the surge of people looked like a *Volkerwanderung* (migration of people) coming from all directions and moving towards the *Bienenkorb* (beehive) a name the Allies gave the bunker. The name was written on leaflets they dropped from their airplanes. I saw one once that someone found. It was strictly forbidden to pick one up or to keep one. I do not remember anymore what it said, but I do remember something about *Bienenkorb* and that lots of people would die because of the bombing and that we should surrender. "Stand up against Hitler and his group!!" So easy for them to say.

The block warden and his volunteers had the same orders, keep the people in the shelters until everything was checked and clear. Often we were kept in the bunker until long after the *Entwarnungs* (all clear) siren had sounded. I believe that this delay was not just for finding the *Zeitbomben* (time delay bombs), but also for finding and disposing of the leaflets. Many people saw the papers floating down. There were lots of them, but they were quickly picked up.

My mother and I would always try and get a place to sit on the top floor of the bunker, right under the *Flakturme*. There I met and talked to some of the young boys who helped man the *Flakturme*. They were called *Flakhelfer* (flak helpers) and yes, they were very young, perhaps fifteen or sixteen years old. Most of them were from the country—*Bauernjunge* (farm boys)—looking healthy and strong. It was a very dangerous position, working on the towers and serving the guns. They acted so proud that they were able to serve their country.

On one of our visits to the bunker we were sitting on the stairs when we heard loud shouting and much commotion coming up from below. When we looked down we saw a group of strange soldiers, dressed in unfamiliar uniforms, being led by German soldiers to the elevator. The people along the hallways were yelling and acting very angry towards these men. Rumors were passed along that they were American airmen captured after they had parachuted from a disabled airplane. I cannot explain why I did not feel anger towards them, after all they had put us through, but instead I felt sorry for them.

People were becoming more and more short-tempered, with very little courtesy left for one another. During one daytime air raid the siren wailed at the same time that the sound of airplanes could be heard over us. A large group of us who were waiting outside the bunker were caught by surprise. Panic broke out. At once most of people started pushing and shoving to get to the doors and to the inside of the bunker. My mother and I tried to stay together, but we became separated. A woman started yelling at me, accusing me of stepping on her foot. I just ignored her. I had no idea whether I had or had not done it. It certainly seemed so unimportant at that particular time.

Then I heard more loud shouting and one voice that sounded a lot like my mother's. When I looked back, I saw my mother arguing with the woman over my supposed action. Incredibly, when my mother pointed her finger at her the women bit it. She almost bit the top off. It was unbelievable. The top of mother's finger just dangled there, bleeding. It looked awful.

We were let through quickly into the bunker and taken to the first aid station. The doctor took care of it. They bandaged it up and it healed alright, but it left quite a scar on her fore finger. It is a wonder that more of this sort of thing did not happen, people hurting one another because of stress or fear. I asked my mother afterwards how she got involved in this argument and she told me that it was because the woman called me some bad name. I told my mother again that she must learn to ignore such incidents. They were not worth fighting over and getting hurt, but she never did listen to me.

Since the time we had started going to the bunker only twice did we not make it. Both times I was very nervous and also afraid, feeling unsafe outside the bunker. One time, my mother was sick with *Hexenschuss* (lumbago) in her back. She could hardly move. It took us forever to get downstairs into our *Luftschutzkeller* (air raid cellar). The second time we were on our way to the bunker and just as we were entering the park the anti-aircraft guns on top of the bunker started firing. That meant the airplanes were nearby. After my former school closed a civil defense group took up temporary quarters in the building. We walked back across the street to and went down into their shelter. I had become apprehensive about pipes. I was not comfortable sitting in the cellar of my former school, looking at the big pipes running along the ceiling over our heads, wondering what was in them and what would pour out of them were they to burst.

Amazingly, the school building survived the *Bombenangriffe* (bombardment). As I mentioned earlier, the *Turnhalle* (gymnasium), which was located across the street from the school, was hit sometime in 1941. It burned and destroyed all the equipment. However, the roof was replaced and the building was then used for storage. The storage facility was not the type one would have expected. After losing our home in late 1943 we received an invitation from the office of Doctor Joseph Goebbels. His "*Spenden Program*", the same one that would give me a radio, invited us to visit this storage facility. Because we had lost everything we were told that we could pick and choose from the contents of the storage facility furnishings for our new home.

The storage facility was filled with all kinds of furniture, some of it very fancy and expensive. It was not the kind of furniture one would find in our neighborhood. Several pieces of bedroom furniture stand out in my memory.

White with gold accents, perhaps French provincial, they were beautiful pieces of furniture that would have looked ridiculous in our home.

My mother and I, along with many other people, wandered through this huge storage facility, my former *Turnhalle*, just overwhelmed by the amount and quality of all the furniture. We could not help asking ourselves, "Where did it come from and who were the donors?"

Our letter of invitation allowed us to select and take whatever we needed. We looked and looked, but we did not make a selection. We had a very strange feeling about the contents of the storage facility. Many years later, turning Doctor Goebbels' apparently generous but actually incredibly sinful *Spenden* down was a very wise decision. The strange feelings we had that day did not betray us. I would feel very sad had we had benefited from a program that had taken this furniture from the homes of Jewish people. The Lord works in mysterious ways. The feelings that we experienced as we walked through this storage told us that we did not want any part of this "give away". To this day, I thank the Lord for His guidance.

One additional time we received a letter of invitation to come to a warehouse to select whatever we needed and could use. Several floors of this warehouse were filled with all kinds of household goods, neatly arranged on long tables, everything from spoons to clothing. I remember seeing tables full of children's items, a very sorry collection from many households and families. Again, I am so thankful that I have been spared the horrible feelings I know I would have had if we had accepted any of these items. Doctor Joseph Goebbels "donations" indeed!

I have often wondered why we were given these letters of invitation in the first place. We were not party members. We never received such privileges except for the one time when I wrote the letter to Goebbels asking for the radio and I received one. Perhaps my name was on a list because of that request.

I never had any kind of association or contact with Jewish people except for one family who lived on our street. I do not know of anyone else. I was not aware that this elderly couple was different from the rest of us until one day when I saw the old gentleman with this strange yellow star on his coat saying "Jude". When I asked my Mother about it she just told me to ignore the emblem and to act and treat him the same way as before. I did not have a problem doing so. I liked the elderly couple. They were always friendly to us children. And I never heard my friends say anything improper to them or about them. I remember that one day I noticed that I had not seen the old man for some time. Only the old lady appeared on our street and she acted so sad and dejected, not at all the way I knew her. When I inquired about him, I was told that the Gestapo came one early morning and took the old man away for questioning. I was told that he was probably sent to an *Arbeitslager* (labor camp) for whatever reason known only to the Gestapo. I felt sorry for both of them. I then discovered that the old lady was a gentile and that their two sons were considered as *Halbjuden* (half Jews). That may be the reason they were allowed to serve in the German army.

My mother told me later how difficult it was for everyone, neighbors and shopkeepers alike, not to talk to the couple anymore. Very few followed the order, but the couple withdrew from any kind of socializing and kept to themselves. When they came into a neighborhood store where they had been customers for years and would have taken time to chat with everyone, they would enter quietly and stand in the back of the shop waiting patiently until everyone else was served. A very awkward situation for everyone involved. When our neighborhood was bombed in 1943 their house too was destroyed. We never saw or heard about her again. A very sad and tragic circumstance.

I experienced one other incident where a Jewish family was indirectly involved. I never saw or met them. I was just a witness to a kind deed done for a family in need. Our neighbor Inge Heinz, the good friend of ours who was related to Tante Grete in Alt-Ruppin, invited me to go along to visit relatives living at *Alexanderplatz*. When we arrived at their house and walked up to the third floor, we passed by an apartment on the second floor. As we did so, Inge laid down the large bag she had brought from home by the door of the apartment, rang the doorbell and walked on. She did not offer an explanation to me about her strange behavior, but I could not help being curious. Later on I asked Edeltraut, Inge's niece and my friend, if she knew what it was all about. She told me, after my promise not to say a word to anyone, that a Jewish family lived in the apartment with small children. It was forbidden to speak to them or to help them. But people were trying to help, the same way as Inge did, by leaving things on their door threshold. Another sad and tragic case, and ultimately so inhuman.

It is hard to explain how people would become so intimidated by the use of one simple word—*Arbeitslager*. Yet it was a word and a place that was feared by everyone. Just saying the wrong words against the *Reich* (German Empire) or its leaders at the wrong time when one could be overheard by the wrong person could result into a trip to the *Arbeitslager*. I used to worry about my mother, as she had a tendency to be very outspoken.

There was one of the notorious *Arbeitslager* in Sachsenhausen. When we rode the *Bummelzug* (the slow train) that stopped at every station on the way to Alt-Ruppin, we would stop there. I could see a gate not far away with a welcome sign that read, "Arbeit macht Freude!" ("Work brings enjoyment!") Yet another charade.

In a way I have been thankful that we did not have any close friends who were Jewish who would have asked us for help or a place to hide. I know that we would not have turned them away, but if found out by the wrong person the alternative could have been disastrous everyone involved. It makes me shudder when I think of it, now that I have learned the truth about the *Arbeitslager*.

After the war we lived at No. 37 Seestrasse. We used to sit on a bench outside the house where we met and talked to a woman living in No. 36, the house next to ours. She occupied an apartment that was identical to ours. One day, as we were sitting together, she started to tell us the following story, very similar to the story of the old man and the old lady on our street. It also reminds me a little of the "Diary of Anne Frank".

The woman and her husband were good friends with a Jewish family. One day the doorbell rang and there they stood, the mother and her teenage son, asking for a place to hide. Her husband had already been picked up for "questioning" and had not returned. Our neighbor said that she took them in and hid them in a small room meant for storage. We had one just like it in our apartment. It was a room without windows.

The woman's apartment was on the third floor in the *Hinterhaus* house to the back of the building. Her husband was serving in the German army. She was employed and went to work every day, which of course the neighbors around her and above and below her knew. So whenever she left the apartment for work or to run errands, the two left behind had to be extremely quiet—no moving around, no running water, no using the toilet, only total quiet. The neighbor woman shared her ration card with them and bought a little extra on the black market. She always had to be careful not to over do it so that people who thought that she was living by herself would not get suspicious.

During air raids the entrance door to the apartment had to be kept unlocked by the order of the air raid warden. I am not certain how this was accomplished in her case during the daytime air raids while she was at work. My guess is that she had to leave a key with the *Hauswart* (superintendent). And all the while the Jewish mother and he son were upstairs in the apartment.

Luckily, No. 35 and No. 36 Seestrasse did not get bombed, although the church next to No. 36 and the house next to No. 37 were hit. The fear and the anxiety had to have been a tremendous strain on them all. Not very many people survived such an ordeal. I do not remember when they went into hiding, but I know that they stayed with her until the war was over. They kept in touch until the mother and son emigrated to Israel. They never received any information about the husband. The neighbor woman also told us that after they left for Israel she never heard from them again. She felt quite disappointed after all what she had done for them, risking her own life to save theirs. But who knows what happened. Maybe in time they remembered their friend and contacted her. I admired the woman for her courage and kindness.

Hochstrasse in the Fall of 1944

We were starting to have shortages of heating supplies, especially wood. We would look around our neighborhood in the daytime. If we saw something that we could use and that we could carry away, we would go back after dark and get it. One time we spotted a work area a couple streets away from our house. They had put up a wooden barricade to keep pedestrians out. My mother and Frau Bottger decided to go there after dark and get one of the long "poles" that made up the barricade. They planned to go around 10:00 pm or later to make sure the guard in the trailer was asleep—along with his dog. Frau Bottger's niece and I were to come along to help. I did not like this plan. I was worried about the dog hearing us and letting the guard know. The whole affair was frightening to me, but my mother and Frau Bottger were determined and would not listen to my lamentations.

It was a clear moonlit night. We were able to see, but all the bombed out houses made the night feel eerie. It was quite spooky. We managed to pick up a long pole, but it was very heavy. I continued to fear that the guard would awaken and send his dog after us. I was a nervous wreck by the time we reached the house. Then when we carried the pole into our *Hausflur* (hallway) it was too long to fit. We could not close the door!

We did not want the neighbors to see our booty, but we had to cut the pole into pieces. I cannot believe they did not hear us sawing away on the long pole. We all took turns with the saw, and we finished without being found out. It took quite awhile. We carried all the pieces into our cellar. It made nice firewood that we shared with my grandparents, but we did not tell them where and how we got it. We also did not try going after the remaining poles, thank goodness.

I seem to remember the close of 1944 bringing an early winter, with lots of snow and very cold temperatures. Elfriede and her friends, the two sons of our superintendent, invited me to go with them a few times to Humboldthain, for sledding. I had a lot of fun with them. I knew the two boys from before I moved into this house. They used to be my grandparents' neighbors until my Uncle Alfred retired from his superintendent position and their father took over the job. I never knew the boy's mother. She died when they were very young. Their father remarried a few years later and they moved into a larger apartment in the front of the house. She was the woman with the baby that joined the rest of us *Bunkerratten* on our runs to the bunker.

My friends also asked me to come along to the S-Bahn station across the street from our house. It was where the local teenagers came together and just hung around and talked. I do not recall what they talked about. There really was very little to do. Most of them had jobs as apprentices, learning some kind of trade. I suppose they talked about their work. The boys never finished their apprentice jobs because they were eventually drafted into the military service. I do not know if they survived the war and came back home. We lost touch with one another after March of 1945.

December 14, 1944—My 13th Birthday

I could not celebrate my thirteenth birthday without thinking about my twelfth birthday and how happy I had been having my dad home to celebrate it with. I wondered where he was and whether he knew what day it was. I doubted it strongly. A calendar in a prison camp was hard to imagine.

I found it very difficult to talk about him to anyone. I kept all my thoughts to myself. I probably did that so well that I know that some people, including my mother, felt that I did not care. I just could not share my feelings with everyone. Not one day went by that I did not think of him, wishing him back home with us and praying that he was alright. I missed him very much.

My mother decided to have a birthday party for me. She invited Oma, Opa, Onkel Gerhard, my sister Lieschen and my cousins Trautchen and Guenter. She had saved up enough from our daily rations to treat everyone with cake and sandwiches. She hung curtains over the cardboard windows, rolled out the carpet and made a nice cozy fire in the *Ofen* (stove) in the living room.[30] My Mother made the cake a couple of days before to give it enough time to "age". It was "*Zwieback torte*". Layers of zwieback[31] and apricot flavored pudding in a spring form. The pudding softened the zwieback. It was delicious. We enjoyed it along with a cup of "*Muckefuck*" coffee, correctly called *Ersatz Kaffee* (coffee substitute). Berliners gave it the common name. It was made from roasted barley ground up just like coffee in a grinder.

Even the power came on for awhile that day. Plus the Allied bombers let me have a peaceful day and night without their interference, which was very much appreciated. I received a very nice present from Onkel Gerhard. It was something I had wished for—a shoulder bag that he made. It was very pretty. He had learned to dye the twine since we visited with him at the rehabilitation clinic and he was now putting color in his designs, making them very nice. For supper we enjoyed *Belegte Brote* (an open sandwich) and *Apfel Saft* (apple cider). We were still able to buy the juice in the *Kneipe* or *Local* (pub) around the corner from us. We brought our own *Kanna* (jug) and they filled it from a big *Fass* (barrel).

I do not recall my other birthdays as I do my twelfth and my thirteenth ones. Especially my twelfth birthday. It will always have a very special place in my memory.[32]

---

30 Normally we only heated the kitchen. We were also not normally allowed to have curtains on the windows or rugs covering the floor as a precaution to prevent fires started by incendiary bombs coming through the windows.

31 Zweiback was double baked bread with a slightly sweet flavor. The bread was baked, sliced and then baked again.

32 I really did not like having a birthday ten days before Christmas. I would have preferred having it in the summertime, perhaps in July like my grandmother's. She would receive beautiful bouquets of fresh flowers while I would get potted plants, like mums. Primrose sounds better in English than in German—"*Rimel*"—as does cyclamen—"*Alpenveilchen*". The potted plants were nice, but not as much as a bouquet of *Sommerblumen* (summer flowers).

And then there was always the big question—"What would I like for my birthday?" I had to decide whether I wanted one big present or one small present. If I chose "*ein grosses Geschenk*" (a big present), then I was told that I would only get "*ein kleines Geschenk*" (a little present) for Christmas—or the other way around. It never turned out this way, but my Oma like playing this game with me and I went along with it. She was lot of fun. I enjoyed being with her.

Christmas 1944

I do not have much to tell about *Weihnachten*. All of us felt very sad and we were glad when it was over. *"Der Weihnachtsmann blieb auch weg."* ("Father Christmas also stayed away.") But the Allied bombers gave us a peaceful holiday, for which we were thankful. We thought about going to a Christmas Eve church service, but the churches in our neighborhood were all destroyed and gone. Besides, we liked staying close to home.

Around the corner from our house was a small but very nice and *Gemutlich* (congenial) *Speise Local* (pub serving meals). Only by then there was no menu of choices. The chef would get whatever was available at the market and prepare it. He would set a blackboard in front of his place and write upon it, *"Hier kocht der Chef!"* ("The Chef cooks here!"), and then write what the meal for the day would be. *"Mittagstisch"* or *"Mittagessen"* (lunch table or lunch meal) *"Heute gibt's Eintopf."* ("Today we serve stew."). Mostly they were very simple meals like *Eintopf* (vegetable stew, one of my favorite meals) or *"quer durch den Garten"* (literally "across the garden", meaning all kinds of vegetables thrown into the pot). *"Der Chef ladet eine zum Mittagstisch or Mittagessen"* ("The Chef invites you in for dinner.") My mother and I would go there from time to time. If we chose the meatless *Eintopf* we did not have to use our *Fleishmarken* (meat ration stamps). It was a little change in our daily life. We would meet the same people coming there, and all for the same reason—a little social get together.

I have been asking myself over and over again, "What did we do for entertainment?" I honestly cannot think of very much that we did do. Very seldom would I go back to my old neighborhood to see my friends. Not because my mother stopped me from going, but because I knew that she worried if I went too far away from home.

I also worried about getting caught away from home and my mother during an air raid. The thought frightened me. Ever since that dreadful day when we received the letter telling us about my dad's fate I had been afraid of losing my mother and becoming an orphan. That thought bothered me very much. My mother and I decided that should I ever get caught away from home and an air raid siren was sounded that I should go directly to the bunker and meet her there. I was not to try to come home. Thank goodness it never happened.

1945

The new year meant that there were only four months to go until the end of the war, but of course we did not know. If we had known, it would have seemed a long time to wait. We were all getting very tired of the life we were living. We lived from day to day, without any plans, only prayers that the war would come to an end soon and that we could resume living a normal life.

Whenever people came together for a little chat, the topic was always our present situation. Everyone knew by then that we were losing the war. The big question was *who* would come to Berlin—the Allied forces or the Russian army. Many horror stories were circulating throughout the city. They had been brought back from refugees fleeing from the Russians, who by then had invaded and captured their hometowns in *Ostpreussen* (East Prussia). Everyone hoped that the Americans would be the ones to enter our city and not the Russians.

Remembering the time when I had taken food to the Russian prisoners, I found it hard to believe that the Russian soldiers could be so horrible and treat others so cruelly. But after my mother told me about the talk that she had with my dad before he returned to Russia after his leave, I started to think about things differently.

My dad believed Germany's chances of winning the war were very doubtful. He worried that the Russians might get to Germany before the Allies and he believed that would be catastrophic for the German people. The German soldiers would never get back home again and the future for Germany would be hopeless, with lots of suffering and pain. He made my mother promise that if this should happen and she should have a choice, that she should try her very best to flee to the Allied front, staying far away from the Russians. *"Falle nicht in deren hande!"* ("Do not fall into their hands!") He told her to avoid this at all costs.

These were very serious matters for me to consider. I wondered what would happen if Germany lost the war? I wondered what would happen to us, the German people? And what about our homeland? I was a thirteen-year-old girl who just wanted to do something fun.

In later years, I often wondered where my dad got this foresight of our future. What he had predicted to my mother all came true. For months, we had been trying hard to survive the bombing raids, looking forward to resuming a normal life again, being a family, having my dad back home with us. Not unreasonable wishes. And yet they would turn into unfulfilled dreams.

February 11, 1945

It was my mother's fortieth birthday, the "Four O's". The birthday my dad wanted to be home to celebrate with her! But he was not granted this wish. My dad had written a poem in my "posie album" when I was six or seven years old. Four of its lines read:

> *Vertrau auf Gott*
> *Verliere nie den mut*
> *Habe sonne im herzen*
> *Es wird alles wieder gut*

> Believe in God
> Never lose your spirit
> Keep the sun in your heart
> Everything will again be good.

My grandmother gave me a beautiful piece of blue fabric; enough to have a dress made for Easter. She just happened to find it in her treasure chest in the cellar. She had always been a very caring and thoughtful "Oma" with a never-ending supply of surprises for me. I was so overjoyed and excited that I took the fabric right away to our dressmaker and looked thru her catalogues for a pattern. I had a lot of fun.

Some time before, my dad's cousin Ilse had stopped by and presented me with a very nice blue spring coat, almost the same shade of blue as the dress fabric. Ilse was the adopted daughter of Onkel Paul and Tante Anna Laube, my grandmother's sister. They also had a son of their own, Erwin. Ilse was a pretty woman, about 30 years old, who always wore very stylish, expensive clothes. She had married into a well-to-do family. Her husband was a pharmacist and they owned their own *Apotheker* (pharmacy) in Oranienburg, a suburb of Berlin.

She had also brought some shoes along—"pumps"—just the kind I had been wishing for. It had become quite difficult to get *Bezugsschein* (ration coupons) for shoes. When we were able to, we had to buy practical ones.

My mother had been doing a good job as a *Schuster* (cobbler), repairing my shoes. I was told many times that I was very rough on shoes. They were forever in need of a heel or a *Spitze*, the front part of the sole. My mother had one of those cast-iron forms that shoes fit over. She would take the worn parts off, cut new pieces from a piece of leather and nail them on. It took weeks to get shoes repaired by a *Schuster*. My mother worked much faster.

Ilse was the child of an unwed mother who was a distant cousin of Onkel Paul. Ilse's mother lived across the street from them and they seemed to have a friendly relationship with one another. I remember seeing her at family gatherings. I never really knew the connection until I was older. They favored one another, like sisters. I overheard my Oma and Tante Anna talking about "Ilschen"—as she was called by everyone—and her trips to Switzerland or the *Ostseebad* (Baltic seashore). I do not know of anyone from our circles who went skiing in the Alps. The working-class people back then were happy to spend their weekends or holidays in nearby Tegel or perhaps at Wannsee on the beach or in the water. But I am glad that she could enjoy all this while she was young because as she became older she suffered badly from asthma attacks. I also appreciated very much that she gave me the nice coat and the pumps.

When our schools closed in the city I heard that the schools in Oranienburg were still operating. Some of my classmates were considering going there. My mother and I went along with them. We rode the S-Bahn from Humboldthain, all the way to the end station, Oranienburg. It was a long ride that took at least one and a half hours. The school offered the choice of morning or afternoon sessions, which meant that I would have to leave on a very early train to be there by 8:00 am or go to the afternoon session and get home late at night. It was not a practicable schedule. Tante Ilse invited me to stay with them during the week. They had a big house and room for me. I thought it over and decided not to do it. As much as I wanted to go to school, I did not want to be away from my mother during those dangerous times. I believe that I made a good decision.

Ilse's brother was my Onkel Erwin. I am sorry to say that I know very little of him and cannot report anything of interest. I remember him as a likable man of few words, characterized by his mother, Tante Anna, as a very weak person around women. He was married to Else, a very dominating, imperious woman. They had a son, Guenter, about three or four years younger than I was. They treated him like a little prince.

I will never forget one Christmas when we were all gathered at the Laubes' home. The gathering of the family was something we did every year, either at my grandparents' home or at the Laubes' home on the day after Christmas at two o'clock. *Der Weihnachtsmann* (Father Christmas) had brought a train set for

Guenter. His father along with my dad was setting it up on the kitchen floor. All four of us played with it for awhile and then the fathers left Guenter and me alone playing with the train. Before long Tante Else appeared in the kitchen and told me quite frankly that she did not want me playing with Guenter or his train. I felt so hurt. I tried hard to keep the tears back until I got to the bathroom. I could not understand why she treated me so mean. I never told anyone about this incident until many years later. When I did tell my mother and grandmother they were upset. My grandmother told me later, when we were alone, that perhaps Else carried a grudge against me because my dad broke their engagement when he met my mother. This could very well be the answer for her behavior towards me and my mother, who she also treated very coldly. Families! No wonder that my dad preferred being with friends more than relatives.

I am sorry to say that Tante Else did not live very long after our unpleasant encounter. I do not remember seeing her again until we went to her funeral service. She had died of breast cancer. I do not know why my grandmother took me along. I am sure that there must have been a reason. It was a traumatic experience for me. One I have never forgotten. On two occasions I was staying with my grandparents while my mother was in the hospital and my dad worked. Maybe this was the reason that I was taken along.

Onkel Erwin did not remain a widower for very long. A divorced woman with three boys of her own living in the same apartment building latched onto him. He married her just before receiving his draft orders into the Wehrmacht. His mother, Tante Anna, was not pleased at all about this new marriage and rightly so, knowing her son's weakness. She had been taking care of her grandson since his mother became too ill to look after him and now they came, her son and his new wife and took Guenter away with them, against her wishes. Such a trauma for the little boy that just lost his mother, taken away from his grandmother and brought into a strange home. His father soon departed for the military and he was left in her care. She was a wicked step-mother. She would not allow any visits between Guenter and his grandmother. Tante Anna tried unsuccessfully through social services to obtain visitation rights but was turned down as a "bad influence on the boy." Her son had sided with his new wife and he had given her all the needed signatures. It was a heartbreaking situation, but the worse was yet to come.

The *Bose Stiefmutter* (wicked step-mother) sent a note to Tante Anna that she had sent Guenter to a children's home somewhere in Germany, saying that it was a safer place. Once again Tante Anna tried to find out his location, but without having any luck. Eventually Tante Anna was without any information on his location and it was not until after the war that the Red Cross, which she had asked for help in finding him, located him in a *Waisenhause* (orphanage) and they were finally reunited. Guenter was about 12 years old by then. After all those years spent in different homes with strangers he was in bad shape. His physical health and his mental state were poor. His feet were in very bad condition. They were frostbitten, and improperly fitted shoes had done more damage. He had to have surgery on his toes. It took a lot of care and love from his grandparents to undo the awful damage that was done to him.

His father, Onkel Erwin, returned home from a prisoner of war camp, also not in good health or spirits. His wife did not welcome him back. Eventually their marriage ended in a divorce. Erwin's mother was angry with him and did not wish to forgive him for causing Guenter's troubled years and taking a normal childhood taken away from him. This seemingly happy and successful family ended up so terribly torn apart.

Onkel Erwin was very remorseful about it all. He would visit my grandmother and confide in her. He had found a job and was living in a small apartment. It was not like Tante Anna to be so angry and unforgiving, but she had reasons to be, after what happened to Guenter. My grandmother was finally able to reunite him with his family, but then he died of cancer.

My grandmother and Tante Anna were very close to one another. They would get together at least once a week at one or the other's house, or perhaps go some place together. Many times they took me along. One of my favorite outings was the trip to the cemetery in Tegel. It included a ride on the trolley car and a stop at the *Garden Local* (an outdoor café). I liked wandering around the cemetery. It was like a park. There were benches everywhere and lots of flowers to look at. I never thought of it being a sad place. My grandmother and Tante Anna would busily fuss around the burial site. They would plant flowers in the spring, summer and fall. When they were done, I was allowed to water the plants. In late fall everything was cleared and a blanket cover made from evergreen was laid on the grave. This was repeated every year as long as there were family members around to take care of it. On our way back home we would stop at the *Garden Lokal* for *Kaffee* and *Kuchen*. I liked being with them. They were lots of fun and are part of my memory of the good times we had before the war came and interrupted it all.

March 9, 1945

My dad's thirty-seventh birthday. A very, very sad day.

Sunday, March 18, 1945

I remember this as a beautiful sunny day with a feeling of spring in the air. I begged my mother to let me wear my new dress. Easter was still two weeks away, but it was such a nice day and perfect for wearing a new dress. The *Schneiderin* (dressmaker) had done a nice job. The dress had turned out beautiful. When my mother agreed, I went upstairs to show my grandparents my new dress. They liked it, too. Opa even gave a nod of approval. Then I went outside, hoping that some of the neighborhood boys would be around and see me in my new dress. I especially wanted to be seen by the ones who used to give me a bad time when I was younger and would walk by their houses on my way to visit Oma and Opa, but I did not meet anyone. Without a coat on I began to feel a bit chilled. Disappointed, I went back inside.

My mother was preparing our Sunday dinner—roast beef with gravy, potatoes and red cabbage. The radio program interrupted the preparations with the announcement of an air raid. "*Anflug von feindliches Flieger in Richtung Berlin.*" ("Approach of enemy airplanes, direction Berlin.") My mother asked me what we should do, eat our dinner in a hurry or wait until we returned from the bunker and enjoy eating it then. We decided to wait and eat it afterwards, which turned out to be a very bad decision. My mother wrapped the pot with the boiled potatoes in old newspapers and a towel and put it in our bed to keep warm. The rest of the meal could be reheated.

I kept my new dress on and wore the spring coat that Tante Ilse had given me. I took the pumps off and put my ugly walking shoes on. We were going out the door when, for some unknown reason, I reached for my winter coat hanging on a rack. I do not know why I did this. I certainly was warm enough with the spring coat I was wearing and it really was a burden carrying it along.

We took our time walking to the bunker. Many people joined us. It was no longer like it was when we first started going, back when it was just the seven of us from our neighborhood. We were still the only ones from our house, No. 36 Hochstrasse. Frau Girndt and her three little girls went to the *Erdbunker* on Chaussestrasse.

Vor-alarm had not yet been sounded. We were hoping that the Allied visitors had changed their destination and were not coming to Berlin. When we reached the bunker we found a spot near the entrance and sat down on our suitcases in the sun, enjoying the warmth. Just a little ways from us was an odd looking group. Standing in a circle, a group of old men were being sworn into the "*Volkssturm*"[33] by some members of the Wehrmacht. Many smart remarks were shouted out loud from the crowd watching this performance, not directed at the poor souls standing there, but to the recruiting officials. "This surely is a sign that the war is lost when we are sending old men to defend us! *Gott habe Mitleid!*" ("God have Mercy!") They were raising their arms for the oath when the antiaircraft guns above us let loose and the sirens started wailing. We jumped to our feet and made our way to the bunker door just before being pushed thru the entrance. I turned my head slightly to take one last look at the beautiful sunshine day we were leaving behind and there, to my left, I saw the airplanes sparkling in the sunlight, a beautiful and frightening sight. I wondered what had happened to the early warning system.

It was lucky that we had been so close to the entrance. We were able to quickly get inside before they closed the big door. The small door could only let one person in at a time. I believe that everyone was safely inside before the bombs began falling on us and around us. It was quite obvious to everyone that the *Bienenkorb* bunker was their target.

We reached our spot on the top floor directly under the antiaircraft batteries when the bombs hit above us. The lights went off only briefly and then came back on. We swayed a little as if we were on springs but that is all we felt. It was very quiet. Not a sound was heard from anyone. Except for the noise from the guns it was *Todesstille* (deathly quiet). We knew that we had been hit and that it had to be bad when we saw the soldiers running up to the tower. They were running to replace the wounded and the killed soldiers, many of whom were the young *Flakhelfer*. The mood around us was quite tense. We saw soldiers being carried down on stretchers from the tower. Everyone looked very serious. We found out later that some of the young *Flakhelfer* lost their lives when the bombs blew them off the tower.

---

33 The Volkssturm (literally translated as *People's Storm*) was a German national militia formed during the last months of the Reich. It was founded on Adolf Hitler's orders and drafted all men between the ages of 16 to 60 years of age as part of the German Home Guard.

We felt a few more swaying movements but we did not hear any bomb explosions. The bunker was holding up well. It was *Bombersicher* (impenetrable) and it saved our lives.[34]

We were kept in the bunker long after the *Entwarnung* (all clear) was given. Bombs had been dropped precisely at all three entrances to the bunker and had left big deep craters. A walkway had to be built across the craters and that took some time. It also was a lot slower exit path for people to move along and we were among the last to leave from the top floor.

What a sight greeted us. The beautiful sunshine was gone. In its place were dark clouds. There was dense smoke everywhere and a strong wind blowing, which made the smoke worse. We made our way across the big hole in the ground and looked for our neighbors' baby carriages. Several rows of carriages had been lined up by the entrance, but they were totally blown away. There was nothing left of them, other than a few feathers blowing here and there in the wind.

We tried walking across the footbridge over the railroad tracks at the upper end of our street but it too was gone. We could see that the houses on the other side were all on fire. We turned back into the park and found it devastated, with deep bomb craters and huge uprooted trees blocking our path. It took us a long time to climb over all the debris, helping our neighbors along. It was especially hard for them to carry their babies and their bags.

When we finally came out of the park we asked a man standing there to tell us what we would find around the corner. "Is anything left on our street?" He just shook his head. That was a bad sign. We could not get there fast enough and yet we were afraid of what we would find. We were so worried about my grandparents.

When we turned the corner by the *Bahnhof* we could see that we had been hit again. We stood across the street from our house, No. 36, which by now, at least

---

34   Years earlier, I remember going with my parents after dark to Brunnenstrasse and standing there, along with the other curious people, watching the construction of the massive concrete structure. They used big searchlights to work after dark. Everyone was wondering and guessing at what it would turn out to be and for what purpose it would be used. My mother told me later that there were all kinds of rumors going around. I remember my dad holding me up so that I could see the construction. This must have happened during his visit home in March of 1942, because that is roughly when the *Flakturm* was constructed.

two hours after the "all clear" was given, was totally engulfed in flames. So, too, were the houses on each side, No. 35 and No. 37.

We kept asking the people walking by if anyone knew where the people from the burning houses would be, but no one knew. At this moment we did not even think about being homeless again. Our main concern was to find Oma and Opa. Someone thought to go around to the back, the area where I used to take food to the Russian prisoners. When we walked through the hallway into the open courtyard we saw my grandmother standing near the big pile of rubble that used to be our home, but we did not see Opa or our neighbor's husband. Oma started to cry when she saw us. She confirmed our suspicion that Opa and the superintendent were still inside, underneath all the debris. While she was still in the cellar Opa had not responded to her calls. She had just gotten out herself with the help of some people and appeared very confused. She feared the worst for Opa unless the specially trained rescue group arrived soon and rescued the two from the cellar.

We held our breath when we saw someone being helped out, but it was one of the men that had come to help. He had tried again, but it was getting too smoky in the cellar and no one answered to his calls. Most of all, a light was needed to find someone in the debris filled dark cellar. We felt so helpless.

Everyone avoided answering our neighbor's friend's questions of her husband's whereabouts. No one was able to tell her the truth. At last the special group showed up with about four men from the Red Cross unit. After looking the situation over they asked the people to form a water brigade to slow the fire from coming into the area where the two men were trapped.

Opa told us later on that he had drifted in and out of unconsciousness. He had trouble breathing but he was able to free himself from the debris that had fallen on him. He slid down to the ground, hoping it would help his breathing. He thought that he must have drifted off again when the superintendent's screams brought him back and he realized that the fire was creeping up on them. At the same moment he saw a light coming towards him and a man coming to help him out of this death trap. He told us how the superintendent had helped him by talking to him, keeping him awake and waking him up.

All the while the superintendent's wife was standing near the opening helping pour buckets of water into the hole while Frau Bottger watched her little girl. We all heard the loud screams and she recognized her husband's voice. She started screaming and calling his name, trying to go down to him. It was heartbreaking!

The men had a hard time holding her back. They kept promising to keep on with their efforts to bring him and my Opa out. That was when my grandfather saw the man come towards him, with the light. He helped him to the opening, but Opa would not fit through it while wearing his heavy coat. So he had to take it off, which of course we did not know. We saw a bundle being lifted out but to our dismay it turned out to be only his coat. Then they lifted Opa out, this lifeless-looking body. We were convinced that he was dead, until he opened his eyes and saw us. He lifted his hand and waved to us. The Red Cross nurse came right over and attended to him. He was very weak and his breathing was very labored. We saw his lips move but we could not hear him.

We made him as comfortable as possible, covering him up with everything we had, including my winter coat. He seemed afflicted with *Schuttelfrost* (fever) and was shaking badly.

My mother spotted my grandparents' sofa on top of the pile of rubble. The size of a loveseat, it was just sitting there as if it still sat in their living room. The two of us managed to climb up and bring it down and set it off to the side, a little away from all the activities. We laid my grandfather on it. The oxygen mask was helping. His breathing was getting better.

Opa was very lucky to have survived in the small cellar. Everyone in the large cellar died.

We were thankful that he did not stay upstairs in the apartment like our neighbor, an elderly deaf woman, who was later found crushed under the debris, still sitting in her chair. Her husband was one of the survivors from the small cellar. On this fateful day he had come down into the shelter, but instead of going into the large cellar where he normally sat, he stopped at the doorway to the small room where Opa was sitting in his wicker chair. He pulled up a chair to sit with Opa for a little chat. *So Wie das Schicksal es bestimmete.* (So fate determined it.)

The houses were hit in the *Seitenhaus* (side house) and towards the *Hinterhaus* (back house). The big cellar was underneath the side and a small portion of the front of the house. The small cellar was located under the *Hinterhaus*, with a walkway passage joining the two cellars. They had heavily reinforced the big cellar and everyone was encouraged to take shelter there instead of in the small cellar, which had not been supported as well. We had tried to convince my grandparents to go into the big cellar, but they felt crowded there. They preferred the smaller cellar where they could bring in their own comfortable chairs. Oma and Opa both told us later that when the bombs hit they heard one loud outcry from the people in the big cellar and then not another sound was heard. Total silence.

I remember once when we had to take shelter in the *Luftschutzkeller* because of my mother's bad back. We sat in the small cellar for awhile, until the fireworks became too violent. I could hear everything so clearly, even the bombs' low whistles, plus feel the ground quivering. We moved into the larger cellar. It felt a little safer. Thank goodness for the bunker. I felt so much safer in there and more protected.

The men were still trying desperately to free the poor superintendent from all the debris. He was covered up to his waist. The heat from the fire was intense. A fire truck would have been a big help, but as I wrote earlier, I cannot say that I ever saw one coming to help put out the fires. If they had, many houses and lives could have been saved.

Now and then we could hear his screams. It was such an agony for him, his wife and everyone else. We heard afterwards how he begged the men to shoot him and put an end to his misery and pain. It would have been better if he had been in the large cellar with the other people. They did not suffer.

We saw Tante Anna come walking into the courtyard. We were so glad to see one another. It had taken her quite some time to find us. She had not known where we were and, while standing in front of our burning house, had been agonizing over whether we were alive or not. Her street, too, was bombed. One bomb fell directly in front of the house and tore up the gas and water lines. Their house had survived in a damaged but livable state. Now she wanted us to come back with her to their home

My mother asked the Red Cross nurse about some kind of transport to carry Opa to Tante Anna's house, but they did not have anything. All around us there was much confusion. With all that was going on, very little help was available from anyone. Everyone was busy trying to take care of his or her own needs.

My mother went looking and found a two-wheeled cart in the next courtyard, chained to a post. She borrowed an axe from a Civil Defense solder and with it she was able to break the chain, just in time for the owner of the cart to appear. He was very upset and angry words were passed between him and my very tired mother. When he finally allowed himself to listen to the reason for her action, he became very cooperative. He even helped us lift Opa onto the cart. We promised that we would return the cart to him.

It took us quite awhile to get to Tante Anna's house. Under normal circumstances it was only a thirty-minute walk, but on this day it took a lot longer. We had to take lots of detours around all the debris and big bomb holes in the streets. It was very hard pushing the cart through and around all of this. Not much was left intact in our neighborhood.

We dropped Oma and Opa off at Tante Anna and Onkel Paul's house and went back to get the sofa and the two rolled up oriental rugs my mother had retrieved from the pile of rubble. When we walked into the courtyard we saw right away that they were gone from where we had left them. We were hoping that someone had simply moved them to a safe place. That was what had happened, but not for our benefit. They were gone for good. We asked around, but no one had noticed them being carried away. One of us should have stayed behind to keep an eye on our things, but it really took all of us to push the cart through the torn up streets. We took the cart back to the owner and he was pleased.

The rescue work had come to a halt. The fire had taken over. They could not get to the poor man anymore. I saw that they had made the opening to the cellar much larger and that they had hoses hooked up to an outside faucet across the yard. The water could reach the opening, but it was not enough water to stop such a big fire. I did not see the superintendent's wife and baby anywhere in the area. Someone must have taken them away. Frau Bottger too had left with Marlies. Her relatives had come and taken them to their home. Elfride was spared this awful experience. She was away again getting her treatments at a health resort.

We walked back to Tante Anna's house without the sofa. We surely could have used it. The couch would have helped Oma and Opa's sleeping arrangement in Tante Anna's home. As it was, Opa would end up sleeping on their sofa and Oma would share a bed with Tante Anna.

I helped carry pails of water from the street pump around the corner to Tante Anna's apartment. Again, I would like to mention what a blessing those street pumps turned out to be for the people without water in their homes. Even during the winter months, when houses and homes were unheated and the water lines froze, the street pumps supplied us with precious water.

Tante Anna and Onkel Paul's home seemed very small. Perhaps it was just filled with a lot of furniture. It always seemed difficult to move around without bumping into something. Instead of sleeping on the floor, my Mother and I decided to go downstairs and sleep in *Luftschutzkeller*. Like all the others, it had several bunk beds set up for people that wanted or needed to lie down.

During the early years when air raids lasted for hours, people who had to be at work early in the morning would lie down and sleep. These beds were located in an area of the cellar where it was possible to sleep away from the rest of the people that crowded the shelter. When it was announced to be safe they would leave for their work places. This plan was supposed to allow workers to continue to be productive in spite of the raids. It may have worked at first, but not later on.

At first it felt a little spooky, all by ourselves in a dark cellar that was unfamiliar to us. Our small candle did not give off very much light. But in the end we did not have a problem adjusting to our new bedroom. We were exhausted and we fell asleep quickly.

Homeless again!

What began as such a beautiful Sunday ended up as a dark and dismal day filled with so much sadness. We were thankful to be alive, but also very discouraged and disheartened.

We spent the daytime hours upstairs with the rest of the family and the nighttime hours downstairs in the shelter, where many times we were joined by others during air raids. I did not mind sleeping in the cellar, but I became extremely nervous during air raids. I did not like the feeling of being underground.

I am certain that the bunker saved our lives many times, but that fateful Sunday, March 18, 1945, turned out to be our last trip to the bunker.

March 19, 1945

We started out on Monday morning for our trip to City Hall, Rathaus Wedding, to apply for our *Total Ausgebommt Ausweis* (bombed out certificate). We stood in line for hours along with many other people. This certificate was an important piece of paper. It was proof of our situation. We had to show it to receive our daily food rations, apply for lodging and other kinds of available reimbursements.

The Red Cross provided us with food for one week, three times daily. Several stations were set up around the area. In the morning they served hot porridge, oatmeal or farina, hot *Ersatz Kaffee* or *Pfefferminz Tee* (peppermint tea) and rolls. At noontime, it would be hot *Eintopf,* made with vegetables, potatoes, peas, and beans! I liked *Eintopf* soups. They were very tasty. For supper they would serve *Belegte Brote* (open faced sandwiches). The drinks were always the same. Only young children under eleven years of age could get milk. Children eleven and older would get one daily cup of *Magermilch* (skim milk).

It was my job to get our daily provisions. I took Tante Anna's metal *Kanna* (jugs) and checked out the different stations. They did not all serve the same food. I would take back whatever looked good to me for the rest of the family. The portions were very generous, enough for all of us, including Tante Anna and Onkel Paul.[35]

My mother and my grandmother spent hours waiting in lines with the rest of the homeless people at the City Hall *Wohnungsamt* (housing agency) trying to find us a place to live. They had looked at two places for which they had been given addresses, but when they got there they found them gone, bombed out the previous night. The last place they were sent to was likewise heavily damaged. The ground floor was still standing and part of the second floor. The apartment assigned to them had one room with three walls left standing and that was it, nothing else. There was no kitchen or bathroom, only a partially intact staircase leading to the second floor. My mother felt as if it was ready to collapse with every step they took. It was nothing but a *Ruine* (ruin).

Why did the agency keep sending us to houses on streets that did not exist anymore? Why not send us to another location in the city, one that was not so damaged, where we could have found livable lodging? It was the Block Warden's duty to inform the agency of available places that were still *bewohnbar* (habitable). The report on this one obviously had not been updated since it was bombed.

---

35 Only a few houses away was a big bread-baking factory—*Wittler's Brot Fabrik*. They were working around the clock. I was told that they were the first to use the new ovens that could bake bread continuously on an assembly line basis. They must have had their own electric generators because they would be operating when we had no power in the whole neighborhood. The bakery made bread for the German Army. *Kommis* was a nickname for army. The bread they baked for the army was called *Kommisbrot*. It was a dark, course grain bread, baked in loaves. It is what my father used to make sandwiches for me when he was in training.

The bakery was not hit by any bombs and it survived the war. The Russians found out that the bakery was operational after the fall of Berlin. They rounded up all the former workers and made them bake bread for the Russian soldiers. It was a big change within a very short time. The Russians were eating bread baked from German flour by German bakers and the neighborhood was again treated to the good aroma. *Die Sieger bekamen das Brot zum essen.* (The winner got to eat the bread.)

We should have considered going to Tempelhof and asking Tante Martha and Onkel Herman for lodging. They would not have refused us. I cannot explain why we did not do so. They did not lose their house. It was slightly damaged when a bomb fell in front of their house, but it still was livable. They lived very close to Tempelhof Air Field but even it was not bombed. The area was quite the safe haven, a much better place to live than our neighborhood.

When my grandmother and mother returned to the *Rathaus* (City Hall) to report their findings, they had the unfortunate luck to be taken care of by the housing agency manager himself. He had a reputation for being difficult to deal with and that was exactly what happened. He did not even give my mother a chance to tell about the condition of the house that the agency had sent them to or what they had found. He kept saying to them, "So you are refusing our offer? And for the third time?" My mother tried to tell him that the place was not habitable, that it was a ruin, but he ignored her. He took my grandmother's pass and drew a line across it and he wrote on it *"Keinen weiteren Anspruch auf Unterkunfts-angebote."* ("No further demands for housing-offerings.") He told them that this was the third time they had turned down the agency's offer of placement and that was it. My grandmother started to cry at this decision, but this cruel, heartless man did not change his mind. He did not care.

They did not tell my grandfather about this episode. He did not need to be upset. I strongly believe that had we been members of the Nazi Party we would have been treated with more respect. They would have found us a place to live, one with four standing and intact walls.

Thoughts about the "Party"

I am almost convinced that we made a mistake by not belonging to the *"Partie"*. It could have been beneficial for us many times. Whenever we went to a public office to request something, the first question asked was, "Are you a member of the Party?" With our negative response we could almost immediately sense that our request would not be granted or would be put on a waiting list. The year when I became ill with the *Gelbsucht* (yellow jaundice) my recovery was very slow. Our family doctor suggested that a visit to an *Erholungsheim* (spa) would help me to recover. He wrote out a medical recommendation, which we took to the responsible office. After they asked us *"In welcher Partei sind Sie Mitglied?"* ("In which party are you a member?") and we answered, we were told that nothing was available at the time. They said they would file our request—probably in their wastebasket—and put us on a waiting list. My mother offered to pay for it out of her own pocket if they would give us the necessary permission to travel to one of the spas. Even this request was turned down.

My mother was asked repeatedly by our superintendent's wife to join the *Frauenschaft* (a woman's group in the party) or just to come along to their meetings. But my mother did not want to. She did not have any interest in doing so. Perhaps it was a mistake we made. Belonging to the *Partie* would have given us benefits in many ways and made it a little easier for us.

Back in 1944 we had heard of homes being built for *Ausgebommte* (bombed out) people, families like us. They were called *Behelpsheime* or *Behelfshauser* (makeshift homes to help accommodate the homeless). They were located in the suburbs of Berlin. We rode the S-Bahn to a couple of places to have a look at them. They were small white one-story cottages that looked neat and tidy. We went to the Housing Agency and filled out an application. We had the money to make the required down payment. Then we would have had monthly payments, just like the rent that we were paying anyway. Right away we were informed that to be eligible there had to be more than just one child in the family. "*Sei Partei Mitglied und Kinderreich.*" ("Be a party member and have lots of children.") If you met that standard you had it made! My mother wrote my step-sisters' names on the form. They were still her children even though they did not live with us. We told them about it afterwards and they promised to go along with it should we be so lucky to qualify for one. But we did not have to worry. We never heard from them. It was just a wonderful dream for a change in our otherwise dreary life that ended as another disappointment.

I do not recall that my family was "Anti-Hitler". They often talked about the good things he had done for Germany and the common people when he took over the leadership of the country. They were very thankful to be employed at regular jobs, earning a steady income and enjoying a normal life.

Before the war, every tenant in an apartment house had a small storage space in the attic and one in the cellar. We had a very nice attic space with a window in it. I believe that many of the things stored there had belonged to my great-grandmother. One was a big wicker chest with big fancy hats, bags, fur capes, shoes, and lots of neat things for playing dress-up. I also found an armband—the kind that the S.A. Members wore. When I asked my mother about it, she told me that when Hitler took over the leadership in Germany, he promised employment for all the unemployed people. Both of my parents had lost their steady employment right after I was born. It had been very difficult for them. Belonging to the *Partie* helped when it came to finding a job. My dad had joined the *National Sozialistische Arbeiter Partei* (National Socialist Workers Party) so that he could get a permanent job as a *Schlosser* (metalworker). Up until then he had worked for the Parks Commission, including, as I mentioned before, placing the *Rosengarten* (rose garden) in Humboldthain Park. My dad was not enthusiastic about joining the *Partie*. He started attending the weekly meetings, but after the Bergmann Company hired him he eased himself out of this commitment as soon as he could. He was never bothered by the *Partie* for not coming to their meetings or for not participating in their activities, and the armband was the only item that I came across in our home which referred to the Nazi Party.[36]

My parents also appreciated that the streets were again safe to walk. The pre-Hitler times were very unsettled in Germany. The crime rate was very high as a result of all the hardships caused by years of depression. My mother often told me how unsafe it was walking on streets at night after dark.

On one such evening, going home from my grandparents' house, my mother was pushing me in a carriage while walking past Humboldthain Park with my dad. A couple of men came out of the park with the intent to mug my parents. My dad told my mother to run and he fought off the attackers using the brass knuckles that he carried in his pocket—a forbidden weapon. Incidents like this were practically unheard of after Hitler came to rule. He cleaned the streets of these bad individuals and it became safe again to walk anywhere, at any time. Years later we walked through the same park on our way to the bunker in total darkness. Many times we did so all by ourselves while carrying all of our valuables with us. This was obvious to everyone and yet we never had a problem.

---

36 Living in the *Hinterhaus* (building in back) was also to our advantage. We were never ordered to display or hang *Fahnen* (flags) from our windows on special celebrations. Tante Maske still had two large portraits of Kaiser Wilhelm II and Kaiserin Auguste Viktoria hanging in her living room. I used to find them fascinating to look at. They presented such a calm, serene authority. I would let my imagination take over and visualize their life in their *Schloss* (castle). My friends and I spent many Sunday afternoons visiting the *Berliner Schloss*. We had to wear these huge *Filzpantoffeln* (felt slippers) so we would not damage the *Parkett-Fussboden* (parquet floors). When no one was watching us, we would pretend that we were on skates, sliding along on the parquet floor. It was fun!

March 26, 1945

It was our second week of being homeless. Our second week of living from day to day. I remember the weather being warm and sunny, helping us cope with our situation. I also remember the dust and the awful smell that lingered over our area. The smell was like that of a huge landfill dump, a burning, smoldering smell that never went away and at times was so strong that it burned our eyes. It would blow around with only the slightest little breeze.

There were more and more air raids that lasted throughout the night. People did not bother anymore to leave the cellar shelters. We had lots of company in our sleeping area. Only Opa could not be persuaded to go down to the cellar shelter. He still was not doing well.

My mother had decided to accept Frau Girndt's invitation to stay with her and her three girls at the *Erdbunker*. We would at least give it a try. Frau Girndt arranged to send one of her girls with the bunker pass to the entrance where we would be waiting around the early evening hours. With the *Ausweis* (pass) in hand we could then enter the bunker.

We walked through a foyer and past a window where we showed our pass to someone sitting behind the window. No one showed any special interest in us. We took the elevator down, though I do not remember how many floors we descended. I know that I was afraid and felt very apprehensive about the *Erdbunker* and being "down under". I tried hard not to show it. The girls' presence helped a little. They were excited to have me with them. They took me to the play area where we found games to play. That helped the time pass quickly until it was bedtime.

The bunker was quite nice and cheerful on the inside, all painted white. The rooms were very small, meant just for sleeping. When an air raid alarm was sounded, other people could come into the bunker and occupy the *Aufenthaltsraume* (recreation room). The bunker residents had to stay in their rooms.

I was surprised how quiet it was. I never heard any of the very familiar sounds that I had become used to hearing during air raids. We would often find out about an alarm when people started coming down to join us in the bunker. Otherwise we would sleep through the air raids. It was quite a restful change for us.

We would leave the bunker in the morning and go back to Tante Anna's home and spend the daytime hours there. We left our suitcases with Frau Girndt. Since she was homeless, she got permission to stay at the bunker during the daytime. It was their home "down under". She had not found a place "above ground" yet.

I believe that it had become impossible to find a place in our neighborhood that was vacant and in livable condition. There just were not many houses left.

Surprisingly, I adjusted to spending the nights in the bunker. I began looking forward to going there in the evenings and, most of all, to the uninterrupted sleep without any fear. The Girndt girls helped a lot. They were always waiting for me and glad to see me.

Our new arrangement was going well until the Saturday evening before Easter Sunday. The moment we entered the bunker that evening my mother spotted trouble in the form of the Housing Agency manager she had argued with a few days before. He must have spotted her at the same time. We learned later that he also was the Bunker Warden, in charge of the bunker. How lucky could we get?

We were walking in along with many other people, but he singled us out and ordered us to step aside. Margit, the girl that had brought us the pass, sensed trouble and took off to get her mother. He grabbed the pass out of my mother's hands and accused us of trespassing, saying we had no right to be in the bunker. My mother tried to tell him that we were sharing a bed in our friends' room, but he would not listen. Frau Girndt had meanwhile come to our aid. She too tried to reason with him, but it fell on deaf ears.

It became an ugly scene. He yelled and screamed, accusing us of taking beds away from needy people, and ordered us to leave. He treated us like criminals. My mother started yelling back at him. She told him what a coward he was, hiding out in this shelter, dressed in his S.A. Uniform and his polished, black boots, while all the good men were fighting to keep our country free from the enemy. The crowd standing around us was on our side, and they encouraged her. He finally stopped yelling when he realized that the people all around us were standing by us. He grudgingly allowed us to stay, but only for one more night and that was it. After this statement he quickly disappeared, probably into his safe haven—a comfortable apartment in the bunker.

He left us cursing our luck. A kind neighbor and friend shares her room and bed with us and the lunatic wants to throw us out onto the street. Someone should have come along and thrown the nasty man out into the streets during an air raid. How I wished at times like this that my dad could have been around. He would have set the man straight in a hurry.

We were also very worried about our friend losing her place in the bunker because of us and this incident. She had become dependent upon the room in the bunker. It was her only home.

Easter Sunday, April 1, 1945

We said our goodbyes to our dear friends, Frau Girndt and her three girls. We had become quite close to them. They were crying. They did not want us to leave.

When we stepped outside of the bunker we were greeted by a beautiful, sunny Easter Sunday. There we stood, homeless, with no place to go. The pretty Easter dress I had planned to wear on this special holiday was packed away in the suitcase. I no longer felt like dressing up.

We looked around us at all the horrible devastation, watching the women walking by us carrying pails of water from the nearby street pump. We wondered what would happen next. My mother looked at me and asked if we should try and find a way to travel to Alt-Ruppin, to see if Tante Grete would take us into her home. I was willing to give it a try. What other choice did we have?

We walked to the Laubes' apartment and told everyone about our decision. I had the feeling from their reaction that Oma and Opa did not want us to go away, but they did not try to stop us from going. It was not easy for any of us, not knowing if we would ever see one another again. With lots of tears and hugs, they send us on our way.

We walked to Stettiner Bahnhof. There we were told that we should take the S-Bahn to Oranienburg and then wait for the *Bummelzug*, the slow moving train, to take us the rest of the way to Alt-Ruppin. Train schedules did not exist anymore. The train would run only if it was not needed someplace else more urgently. We walked over to the S-Bahnhof and waited for the train to come along, which did not seem to take very long. We found a seat in a car without windows. Almost all the cars had blown out windows. They had been replaced with plywood, with only a small peephole in the center. Many times that too was *kaputt* (gone). We thought it was better having the wind blowing around us than sitting in a dark, boarded-up car for the ride. It was long, at least one and a half hours.

I remember that we had to leave the train a couple of times and walk along the side of the tracks to get around a blown up bridge or torn up tracks. We would get on another train waiting on the other side, performing a sort of *Pendelverkehr* (shuttle service). We finally made it to Oranienburg and found a train sitting in the station; only it was missing an engine. We were told that whenever an engine showed up, we would be on our way.

I believe there were three stops between Oranienburg and Alt-Ruppin. On any other day we would have been concerned sitting in a railroad station in

Oranienburg. It was a small town on a direct route for the allied bombers attacking Berlin. It had lots of industry surrounding it and had frequently been a bombing target. Not normally a good place to be. Except that it was Easter Sunday, a day that was meant to be celebrated in a joyful and peaceful manner. I do not recall that we were bothered that day with a visit from the Allied bombers.

At last we saw an engine, the missing part of our train, come huffing and puffing into the station. Before long we were finally on our way. It was late afternoon when we arrived in Alt-Ruppin. It had taken a long time to make the trip. Getting off the train and looking around, we could not help expressing our feelings of astonishment at how unchanged everything appeared. The town looked just the way we remembered it from our last trip during the summer of 1943. The war had not yet come to Alt-Ruppin. We also realized that we had made a big mistake by not coming there earlier. It would have been much better and safer for us than staying in Berlin. We should have listened to my dad.

We left the railroad station and walked to Tante Grete's house. We found her in the backyard feeding the rabbits. She was surprised to see us, but also genuinely happy to see us. We had been out of touch for quite awhile and she had been worried about us. She took us upstairs to her place and made us feel welcome. Then she fixed us something to eat, as we had not eaten all day, except for a piece of bread and a drink of water.

Tante Grete told us about all the new tenants who had moved into the house since we were there last. There was the landlord's sister—Frau Katerborn—who also was from Berlin. Like us, she had lost her home and a bookstore on Bernauer Strasse, next to the church where I was baptized.[37] Then there were the two young sisters, one with a baby, refugees from *Ostpreussen* (East Prussia). One of the sisters was married to an instructor at the tank barracks. They came to Alt-Ruppin to live near him. Another young woman from Lithuania and her son were also in the house. She, too, was married to a German soldier stationed at the *Kaserne*.

The following day was still a holiday, *2 Feiertag Oster-Montag*. Tante Grete had another day off from work and she helped us to settle in quite nicely. We could almost forget our present situation. Everything seemed so peaceful. However, this feeling did not last for very long. When we heard the tremendous humming noise in the air and saw the aircraft flying over us, it brought us back to reality. The war was not over yet.

---

37   *Bernauer Strasse* is also the street where the *Mauer* (the Berlin Wall) was built in 1961.

The air raid siren in our village would announce approaching enemy airplanes, but no one paid attention to it or went to the shelter. We would watch the huge formations of airplanes flying by the right side of the church steeple on their way into Berlin and returning from their mission by the left side of the church steeple. I do not think that they used the steeple as a marker. It just appeared to us like that. We were simply on their route. It really was an awesome sight and sound.

At night we could see the sky glowing red in the direction of Berlin. We knew what that meant. We felt so sorry for Oma, Opa and all the rest of the people. We prayed that they were safe and that it all would end soon, this horrible war. I missed Oma and Opa. It felt strange not being with them. Would we ever see them again?

Frau Katerborn used the air raid shelter as an information center. Neighbors would join her in the evenings hoping to hear of what was happening. That was when she had her radio tuned to the BBC. She understood English quite well. Many times the *Sender* (transmitter or signal) did not come in clear enough to understand, but she would keep trying. She undertook quite a risk, listening to the *English Sender*, as it was a forbidden undertaking. She also had a large map of Germany that she would lay open on a table. She used markers to guess where the approaching armies were, mainly the Americans.

It was everyone's wish and hope that the Americans would come to this town and not the Russians. I did not completely understand why everyone wanted the Americans to come and take over the town or even the whole country, instead of the Russians. After all, the Americans had been terrorizing us for years with their bombing attacks. But all the propaganda talks and caricatures that were shown to us never told us to expect inhuman, barbarous treatment from them. It was a different story about the Russians. We were warned about their behavior and were told some horrible stories by the refugees. I had a very difficult time believing that people could be so cruel, but I found out later on how true those stories were.

The peaceful picture was also changing on our street. We saw more and more refugees traveling through the town. There were farmers with horses and wagons and lots of people walking, mostly women and children, and carrying their belongings or pulling them along on small wagons. Everyone looked so tired and forlorn. We talked to some of them whenever they stopped for a rest. Many had been on the road for weeks or even months, traveling from one place to another. They left their farms and homes behind in East-West Prussia, Pomerania, Mecklenburg, and Schlesien (Silesia).

One time my mother was talking to a family from Silesia and she found out that they had come from the same area where she grew up. They knew the Schallert family well. The Schallerts were the owners of the large mill where they had taken their harvested grain for processing. Kurt Schallert, the son, had been killed on the Western Front. Ann Schallert had married an officer of the German Waffen SS. My mother mentioned on several occasions that she regretted not staying in touch with the Schallert family.[38]

Things were changing alright! German soldiers had joined the long lines of refugees, driving in any kind of vehicle that would still move. Was it a retreating army? Or was it an army trying to regroup with other units for one last stand against the enemy? We had heard that this route was the only way left to get into or out of Berlin. The Russians were in control of all other major highways. That was a very scary feeling.

The passing scenes on the street grew worse with every day. The column of people and vehicles moved past at a very slow pace. We saw wounded soldiers with blood-soaked bandages, badly in need of medical attention, some lying on the hood of the vehicles. All of the soldiers looked so tired and discouraged. We wished that we could have helped them but all we had to offer was water and *Ersatz Kaffee*.

The airplane activities had also increased. We saw large formations of aircraft, wave after wave, flying over us. It also brought us another frightening experience. The boys from next door and I were standing in the backyard, watching the airplanes. When all of a sudden the aircraft were bearing down on us and flying so low that I could clearly see the gunner sitting in a bubble of glass behind his machine gun. So low that for a moment I thought he was going to crash.

For a second, none of us could move, we were so scared. When we finally came to our senses, we started running towards the houses. The boys were yelling to me to come along with them and take cover in their greenhouse, which was closer

---

38 The part of Schlesien (Silesia) where my mother grew up would become part of Poland after the war. Sadly it meant that Polish people would take over the estate which had been in my mother's family for several generations. I always felt that these decisions were very unjust to the German people. I know of some people that traveled back to their former homestead, years later, and regretted doing it. They found their farmhouses, barns and fields totally neglected. The fields were uncultivated. The meadows were without grazing cows or horses. Schlesien had been a beautiful part of Germany and I always had hoped to go back to where my mother grew up. The stories that she told about the area sounded so nice, but I am sure that it had lost its charm.

than the house, but also a very poor shelter. I reached the back of the house where the cellar was located at the same time as my mother and everyone else from within the house.

We lay down on the cellar floor. Everything would shake and vibrate when the airplanes flew over us. The noise was deafening. They were using their machine guns, a frightening ordeal. *Tiefflieger Angriff!* (strafing aircraft attack)

Frau Katerborn was standing at the top of the stairs trying to keep the shaking door from opening. I do not know why she bothered. It made no difference. People did some strange things under these circumstances. Things that made no sense.

I am quite sure that the whole episode lasted only a few minutes, but to us lying on the floor, terror-stricken, it seemed a long time before it was over. This was our first experience with *Tiefflieger*. People that traveled on trains would talk about the danger of getting attacked by *Tiefflieger*. The missing, boarded up windows surely gave proof to their stories. From this day on we had to deal with events like this every day, until the war was over.[39]

I have often wondered about this incident. With the road crowded with military vehicles, German soldiers and civilians, we later suspected that it attracted the attention of the aircraft and caused them to target the area. What were the gunner's thoughts and his feelings as he sat behind his guns in the bubble of glass? We could see him clearly and I am sure he could see us just as well. He did not fire his guns at us. He showed mercy on us poor kids. And yes, the greenhouse got strafed. Luckily the boys had also gone into their cellar.

From this day on, we paid attention to the air raid siren. We would go to the shelter at night. During the daytime hours, my mother and I would go and hide in the woods, far away from the road. We would seek shelter amidst the new growth of pine trees that stood about five or six feet tall, where we could observe what was happening. On one of those trips a strange and somewhat funny incident occurred as we were hiding among the trees watching the *Tiefflieger* flying above us. Along the open path came this elderly woman carrying bags and acting very confused. My mother kept yelling to her to get down under a tree but she was wearing a *Bademitze* (bathing cap) and could not hear. My mother had to go to her and point out the airplanes above us and have her get down under a tree. Poor old lady.

---

39 I must add that I liked watching the airplanes when they were flying way up high much more than when they flew low to the ground and were bearing down on us.

April 20, 1945

Adolf Hitler's 56th birthday brought us another day of heavy aircraft activities. We did not even bother leaving the woods. The Americans gave him a big party with lots of fireworks. We could only hope that the rest of the Berliners survived the big celebration.

Fleeing westward

My mother kept talking about leaving Alt-Ruppin, joining the German soldiers and the refugees in their search for the American lines. We had heard that everyone from the tank barracks had moved out. I did not like the idea of leaving our place with Tante Grete and marching off into uncertainty. When we finally were able to leave our hiding place in the woods to return to the house, my mother told me that she had made up her mind. We were going to leave Alt-Ruppin before it was too late.

We packed two small suitcases and a couple of bags. We said our goodbyes to Tante Grete and everyone else living in the house. Frau Katerborn thought that we were foolish to leave when at any time soon the Americans would enter the town. She still plotted the American army's drive across Germany on her map. She believed strongly that they would come despite everyone else's doubts.

We walked to the corner of the street where a German soldier stood in the middle of the road directing the flow of traffic. I really do not understand why he was doing this. The traffic moved very slowly and only in one direction. Perhaps he was there to keep order. My mother told him that we would like to ride along on one of the trucks. He said he would ask the drivers of the vehicles if they had any room for us. We did not have to wait long before one of them said that there was room for us in the back of the truck. My mother threw our suitcases onto the truck. As we ran behind the truck, two soldiers held out their hands to help us climb in, but I came apart. I started to cry that I did not want to leave. The soldiers threw our suitcases back off and waved to us as we stood on the side of the street. Perhaps I was tired after our long and anxious day in the woods or just afraid of leaving our newfound home with Tante Grete and running off to somewhere unknown. It was an unspoken feeling that we all carried. What will happen next? What will happen to us?

Tante Grete was glad to see us come back. We spent another night with her, sleeping in a warm, soft and clean bed, our last night sleeping with such comfort. It would be six or seven weeks before we would come back to this comfort.

The following morning, after Tante Grete left for work, we were back at the corner to make another attempt at our *Fluchtversuch* (escape). The soldier found us space on a medium-sized truck with a canvas top. The two soldiers in the back helped us aboard. And so began our journey. We drove slowly down the road, thru the woods by the deserted tank barracks, and through the town of Neu-Ruppin. That was when the soldiers spotted a *Tiefflieger* circling above our column.

My mother became very concerned. The soldiers tried to reassure her. They told her not to worry because if we were hit we would not feel anything. It would be over fast for us. My mother wanted to know the reason for their prediction. They lifted the covers off the boxes we were sitting on and also pointed to the back of the truck where lots more were stacked up, all filled up with *Munition* (ammunition)! It certainly was a fast way to leave this place, but we were not ready for that journey, not yet anyway.

My mother moved into action once she understood what was being carried in the truck. She threw our baggage off to the side of the road and prepared to jump with me. The soldiers tried to stop us but my mother would not listen. We landed unhurt in the *Chaussee graben* (roadway ditch). Luckily, the ditch was dry.

So there we were, sitting alongside the road somewhere outside of Neu-Ruppin. We had no *Landkarte* (map) and no idea where we were headed. We could have walked back to Alt-Ruppin. We were not that far away, maybe twelve to fifteen kilometers, but I did not dare mention it to my mother. "*Wir warn au der Flucht von den Russen.*" ("We were in an escape from the Russians.")

We joined some other walking *Fluchtlinge* (escapees) without knowing where the road would lead. We walked and walked, passing road signs with the names of villages that did not mean anything to us. We were unfamiliar with the area, having never traveled beyond Alt- or Neu-Ruppin.

It was late afternoon when we came to a large *Dorf* (farming community). People were standing around talking about the airplanes that had been flying over their village and the area off and on during the day and wondering why. They acted very concerned and worried. They thought that they had been Russian airplanes. Up until then, people living like them in the country had enjoyed a very peaceful life. Just as it had been in Alt-Ruppin, until recently. These people probably had not seen the large flights of airplanes flying over because they did not live on a designated bomber route in or out of Berlin.

They did, however, offer us a place to rest for the night in their barn. We gladly accepted their offer as we were getting very tired. We found a spot near the entrance, pushed the straw around a bit and laid down for a little rest. I tried not to think about the nice bed I had left behind.

The *Bauer's Frau* (farmer's wife) brought us some boiled potatoes to eat. We were not just tired but also hungry, and we were grateful. My mother went outside to see if she could find out anything about our situation. Right after she left, I heard an airplane. I started to go outside to have a look when my mother came running back to get our things and me. The airplanes were back, flying circles over the village, and she did not like us being in a barn full of straw when we did not know what their intentions were.

It had become dark by then. We were on the run again, along with other people. A man standing in the middle of the road told us to seek shelter in the basement of the church that stood by the edge of the village. Some people took his advice but my mother wanted to take refuge outside, in the open field, where we found a mound of hay.

We only could see two or three airplanes. They flew very low, back and forth over the village, making a lot of noise as if they wanted to frighten people. But then they dropped their bombs. What an explosion! It made the ground shake. When we looked up from our position on the ground, we saw that the church had been hit. It did not take long before they had quite a fire burning in the village. After this attack, the airplanes flew away. We wondered why they had done this. It was just a farming village.

We stayed a while longer by the hay mound to make sure that they were not coming back. Then we made our way across the field to where we guessed the road was. All of a sudden a harsh voice was yelling to us to identify ourselves. What now?

My mother yelled back that we were just a couple lost *Fluchtlinge* (refugees). When we reached the road, we found a group of men from the *Volkssturm* marching single file under the trees on both sides of the road. Only the trees were still bare. They were not a good cover.

The *Volkssturm—der Fuhrer's letzte Hoffnung!* (the Fuhrers' last hope!) A group of old and very young untrained men and boys quickly called upon to go and meet the enemy and save Germany. Poor souls.

In Germany many of the smaller country roads had fruit trees growing on both sides of the road. Many times when we were on this journey, I kept wishing that the trees were full of apples or pears. An apple or pear would have tasted so good and taken care of our thirst.

We walked along with the *Volkssturm* for quite awhile, but we could not keep up with their pace and slowly fell behind. We were very tired. Before long we found ourselves all alone on the road. It was incredible. We were two lost hobos.

We came to a split in the road. One branch went to the left and the other one to the right. We had no idea which route to choose. We just guessed and took the one to the right. Then, after walking a while longer, we decided to take a little rest along the side of the road.

We had only been sitting for a few minutes when we heard heavy footsteps approaching. We were feeling a little uneasy, wondering who would show up. It turned out to be two young German soldiers about seventeen years old. They told us that they had become separated from their unit and were trying to link up with them again. By then we all knew that Germany was losing the war and everyone was trying desperately to reach the American lines. All the soldiers made up the same story. Some excuse.

We continued our walk with them and they offered to help us by carrying our suitcases. That was a big help. After walking for a while we came to a village where we were very surprised to find people up and awake, standing around and talking. It must have been well after midnight. Farmers were known to go to bed early, so something was keeping them up and had them wondering and concerned. They told us where we could find a barn and join the rest of the wandering migrating people to spend the night.

I do not remember anything after finding a place to lie down. I was the last one to wake up in the morning. I must have been tired out. My mother brought breakfast to my bedside, one cup of delicious milk and a piece of dark bread. With a little imagination it tasted like cake to me. Having bread to eat was a blessing and a gift and we were thankful whenever we received some.

The two soldiers came back to get their *Tornister* (knapsacks). They were ready to move on. Before they left they showed us on their map where we were and where they thought the Russians and the Americans were located. The Russians appeared to be a lot closer than the Americans, which was not a comforting feeling. We also noticed on the map that we had not come very far from Alt-Ruppin. It looked to me as we had been walking in a big circle. We said *"Auf Wiedersehen"*

("Till we meet again") to the two young soldiers and we wished each other "*Bleib am leben!*" (Stay Alive!) It was a wish that was spoken daily during the last months of war in Berlin and elsewhere when people met on the street or parted ways.

Earlier, while I was still asleep, my mother had been talking to some women who had also been staying in the barn for the night. They were from Neu-Ruppin and they had been working at a large dairy. They had "borrowed" one of the dairy's trucks to take them away *auf die Flucht* (on the escape). My mother had asked if they had room for two more on their truck and they said yes. We quickly gathered up our belongings and joined them outside, where they were about ready to leave. It was an open truck with long benches on each side. I do not know any more how many we actually numbered, but we must have been at least twelve adults, with perhaps ten women and two men, plus four or five small children.

They had brought along lots of good things to eat and drink, including cans full of milk and buttermilk, plus different kinds of cheeses and butter. I felt as if I had wandered into the *Schlaraffenland* (land of milk and honey)! What a treat to spread butter and cheese on our bread and have milk to drink with it.

It was not a good day for traveling. The roads were filled with horses pulling wagons, people pulling wagon carts, people pushing bicycles, and all loaded up with some of their "Hab' und Gut (belongings). "*Eine grosse Volkerwanderung!*" (A great migration of a nation!) We put very little distance behind us. And then that which had become our biggest fear since we started traveling arrived on the scene—*Tiefflieger*—terrorizing the helpless people. Several times we pulled off the road quickly into the trees for cover.

I do not know why we left the main road and took a side road that led to a large building that looked like a monastery. The driver must have known about the place. We parked in front of the building and walked through a large gate to an inside courtyard. Spaced around the courtyard were four connected buildings, each two or three stories high. German soldiers were occupying the building on the right side. We were told that we could have the building on the left side for our use. One soldier, probably the cook, was making something in the *Gulaschkanone* (field kitchen) that smelled delicious. He told us that there would be enough for all of us!

Inside the building were many small and large bedrooms and a big bathroom off the hall. I presume that the building was used as a *Jugenhaus-schule* (youth hostel-school). It reminded me of the ones where I had spent a couple of summer holidays. We chose a room that had two beds in it and immediately headed for the washroom. It felt wonderful to wash up. My hair needed a good washing too, but that was out of the question. I had to make do with just a good brushing. We looked forward to eating the cook's good-smelling meal and then sleeping in a real bed.

We decided to take a walk to the nearby village along with a couple of women from our group. When we came closer to the first *Bauernhof* (farm) we could tell that something was happening. They were in a big hurry, loading up their wagons. They told us that the Russians were not far away and could arrive at any time. We could see that the other people from the village were doing the same.

We hurried back to our place and found the soldiers packing up too. I was surprised to see so many army vehicles in the courtyard that had not been there before. I found out that they had been hidden out of sight in the woods behind the building. We went inside quickly to get our things. We did not want to be left behind to fall into the hands of the Russians.

When we came back outside the first trucks were already moving out through the gate. We joined the women who were begging the major to take us along, but he kept shaking his head. He could not do it. It was against army rules. Civilians were not allowed to ride with soldiers in army vehicles. They might become involved in combat with the enemy.

It turned into an angry tearful scene. I do not remember anymore what the reason was for not going on with the milk truck. Maybe we were low or even out of fuel or they hoped to move faster by traveling with the soldiers on the congested roads.

We were a sad looking group standing in the courtyard. Almost all of the trucks had left, including the major's vehicle. However, the soldiers from the two remaining trucks left in the yard did not have the heart to leave us behind. They ignored the rules, jumped off their trucks and helped us get on quickly. We sat inside, close to the cab, and they sat between the back and us. This was to be our hiding place and our new lodging for several days and nights to come.

Traveling on the roads had become very dangerous. We spent more time hiding in the woods than driving. The *Tiefflieger* were a big hindrance. But I am glad to say that traveling with the soldiers helped us to deal with the fearful situations. They were always trying to keep our spirits up by talking or singing to us. One of the soldiers had a *Mundharmonika* (harmonica), and he could really play it nicely.

Late one afternoon we stopped outside of a town called Perleberg at a *Bauernhof.* The cook fired the *Gulaschkanone* up and announced that he was serving *Erbsensuppe* (pea soup) for supper. I remember this afternoon so well, as if it happened yesterday. *Erbsensuppe* was one of my favorite soups. We asked our soldiers if we could get off the truck and wash up a little *am Brunnen* (at the well) in the yard. Only our two trucks had pulled into their farmyard. The other ones had parked in other yards. They took a look around and decided that it was safe for us to get off. I remember taking my coat off and holding my hands and face under the running water and how refreshing it felt. But then I heard a voice behind me asking, *"Seid wann befinden sich diese Mittreisende unter uns?"* ("Since when have these travel guests been with us?")

I was afraid to turn around to hear the major say that we would now have to stay behind. We had been with them for three days and nights and only now had been discovered by the major. One of our soldiers stepped forward and told him that we had been with them since we left the youth hostel. He looked at us and then turned away, telling the soldier that we were his responsibility and that he did not know anything about us.

What a relief! We were so happy that we could stay with them and that we did not have to hide anymore. That had been difficult, especially with the small children. One time during our journey the major had climbed into our truck and sat with the driver. We had been so worried the whole time he sat there that he might discover us. He only had to turn around and look through the little window. Thank goodness this worry was behind us now.

Our good feeling did not last very long. We noticed that the soldiers were acting concerned and worried. The cook was closing up the *Gulaschkanone.* Before long we were asked to get back into the trucks and told that we were moving out. We drove to a small stand of trees where they parked, the trucks in a circle. We were told that they were on alert and we were to stay on the trucks. We were told that the guns we had been hearing were Russian and that they feared we were surrounded by them.

The soldiers became very busy as they prepared for a confrontation with the enemy. They cut branches off the pine trees and covered up the truck with them. They dug trenches and set up their machine guns.

Was this to be the end of our journey? Were we not going to reach the American lines? Was all the trouble we went through during the past few days to be in vain?

I started to pay more attention to the sounds of the guns and, yes, they appeared to be much closer. We were all very quiet, even the children. Everyone was wrapped up in his or her own thoughts. A lot goes through one's mind in a situation like that. I thought about the *Erbsensuppe* that I did not get to eat. I also wished that the boys from my old neighborhood could see me now. I never imagined when I was playing army with the boys that I would some day be in a real life situation like this. But here I was sitting in a truck under some trees wondering what will happen to us next.[40]

I wondered why this was all happening. All I ever wanted was to be with my mother and father, my Oma and Opa, and be a happy family. I wanted to have fun with my friends, do things with my dad on the weekends, go to school and learn, and dress up in nice clothes. All of this was taken away so abruptly by a war that my family and I never wanted.

I remembered being at the Baltic Sea in September of 1939 and then having to travel all day on the train to get home. We had been told that we were at war with Poland but I had no idea what the word *Krieg* (war) really meant. I was alright until my dad opened the door. Then I broke down crying, "*Wir haben Krieg!*" ("We are at war!") Since that day in September of 1939 I had learned what the word *Krieg* meant. More than I ever wanted to know.

We spent all night in the truck listening and waiting. Eventually it became quiet. We must have then fallen asleep, because I remember it being day light and everything appeared to be very calm. We were alright. The cook fired up the *Gulaschkanone* and made us some oatmeal and coffee. It tasted great. I do not know what happened to the *Erbsensuppe*. Maybe they ate it while I was sleeping.

For the next two or three days and nights we continued our desperate effort to reach the American lines. We must have spent six or seven days on the road, but we lost all sense of time. The *Tiefflieger* were still our biggest fear, attacking us all the time. Our group lost some vehicles, but none of the soldiers. Many people and many horses were killed. They lay alongside their overturned wagons, with all kinds of abandoned belongings lying about. It was horrible to see, all the while wondering if we would be next.

---

40 I was always chosen to be their "nurse". Once I became a casualty myself. I was standing outside of my *Lazarett* (hospital), when the enemy came up from behind and hit me hard across my back with a board, knocking me to the ground. This had never happened to me while playing with the boys from my street, but this time they were at war with boys from another street. A mean group of boys.

The soldiers draped *Rote Kreuz Fahnen* (Red Cross flags) over the top of the trucks, hoping that the *Tiefflieger* would respect the symbol and leave us alone, but they did not. The *Tiefflieger* would just circle and come back for another kill. I wished that we had some anti-aircraft guns to eliminate a few of them. They were so persistent, and yet it was such a cowardly act. They should not be proud of themselves.

The people on the road did honor the flags. They moved aside to let us through, thinking that we were carrying wounded soldiers. It was not a very courageous act, pretending that we were a *Sanitater-Kolonne* (ambulance column), but one taken out of desperation and a desire to stay alive and survive.

During one of the *Tiefflieger* attacks a couple pushing their bicycles along the side of the road was killed while their little boy, about four years old, survived. He was standing by them crying. The driver of our truck stopped alongside while another soldier jumped out and picked the boy up, bringing him into the cab. I have often thought about this incident and wondered what became of the little boy. I am sure that the solider acted on instinct, wanting to move the little boy out of harm's way and away from the roadside.[41]

Neimandsland (No man's land)

Somewhere near Grabow we came to the end of the road. Ahead of us was the road that belonged to no one, *Neimandsland* (no man's land), and beyond it were the American lines. The soldiers must have known the location of the Americans. After all the days and nights of trying to get there, we had finally made it.

We got off the truck along with everyone else, trying to find out what to do next. There were many people and soldiers running all around, with total confusion everywhere. My mother and I had no idea where we were or what to do. We asked several different people, but no one knew anything.

---

41 I did not see the little boy again after we finally reached the American lines and walked through the gate. Hopefully a farmer's family took him into their care. My mother and I both felt relieved that there were just the two of us and that we did not have small children to take care of like so many other women. When I later worked at the *Rathaus am Wedding* (City Hall at Wedding), I would pause many times look at all of the pictures of children that were posted all over the walls of the foyer. They were either put there by parents looking for their children or by social workers trying to find the children's families. Most of them were very young, too young to know their own names. It was very sad. Just one more effect and consequence of the war.

Unfortunately, we wandered a little too far away from our truck and we became separated from our group. When we found some of the women they were on another fully loaded truck. They could only take our suitcases and stack them on top with the rest of the baggage. The driver had the cab full of children of all ages. He told us to stand on the *Trittbett* (running board), saying that we did not have very far to go and that he would not drive too fast. We did not want to be left behind, so we stepped aboard. We were able to put our arms through the *Blinkers* (turn signal extensions) which gave us something to hang on to and then off he drove.

It was a ride in style. Until we made this journey I had only been for a ride in a taxi car perhaps two or three times with my grandparents. Never did I dream that I would be traveling on a truck for a week and be standing on a *Trittbett* for a ride through *Neimandsland*. I felt a little adventurous with the wind blowing around me, almost free like a bird. Except that I found myself nodding off, because I was very tired. My mother, standing on the other side of the truck must have noticed it because she kept yelling at me, trying to keep me awake. It was not a good time to fall asleep.

Luckily for me, we soon came to a stop. Ahead of us was a roadblock, and on the other side of it were the American forces. Someone must have gone to talk to them because we were told that on the following day at 10:00 am they would open the roadblock for us to enter.

We spent a very anxious night, sitting around a campfire, with everyone in a very somber mood. We were very tired, but I did not see anyone sleeping. We were all thinking about tomorrow and hoping that the Americans would let us enter their territory and give us protection from the Russians.

I could not help wondering about the Americans. I walked a few times during the long night to the *Schlagbaum* (road block) and took a peek to the other side, but I could not see anything. It was dark and very quiet. Where were they? Why were they not guarding this roadblock? How could they trust us that we would stay put and not walk around the roadblock and disappear into the night? The German soldiers were still armed and could start another battle. The war was not over yet. I had all kinds of unanswered questions. It was a very long night.

The soldiers had parked the trucks off the road to the side. One small truck was packed full of boxes containing French champagne. They kept offering bottles of it to everyone, but very few felt like drinking or celebrating. So they entertained the children by smashing the bottles against a tree and making exploding popping sounds.

Another truck was equipped with all kinds of instruments, including radios. I believe the group we had been traveling with belonged to a *Nachrichtentruppe* (signal corps). They were busy destroying the equipment. I did not understand why they were smashing the equipment to pieces. It did not make any sense to me. People did lots of strange things during this time of uncertainty.

My mother decided to part with my dad's medals and to bury them there in the woods in *Niemandsland*. He had left them home with us on his last visit and we had been carrying them with us ever since. She did not think that we should have them in case our bags were searched.

My dad did not care about the medals anyway. He wore only his *Verwundet-Abzeichen* (Purple Heart) and one other badge for surviving the Russian winter. He was recommended for a promotion and for the *Eiserne Kreuz* (Iron Cross) for bravery and good service to the *Vaterland* and the *Fuhrer*. He missed the *Orden-Verteilung* (medal distribution) because he was in a hospital recovering from his second injury. He did not lose any sleep over it. He was supposed to get the medal when he returned to his company. But then his return to the front was delayed because he was given some extra time to recover and rest behind the front lines. Somehow it was then forgotten. He had a lot more important things to look after than his medal and he did not remind them about it either. So we buried them in the woods in *Niemandsland*, along with his Finish knife.

When we were sitting around the campfire, one of the young soldiers we had been traveling with noticed that his watch had stopped. My mother offered him my dad's watch. He tried to refuse it, but she would not hear of it. She kept saying, "Who knows what will happen to us tomorrow and in the following days." She must have been in a poor state of mind, very tired, mentally and physically. Looking back, it really was a foolish thing to do, especially when we saw what happened to it the following morning.

My dad had purchased the watch while he was stationed in Norway. He left it at home when he came on leave in 1942. It was a very good gold watch. He felt that it was too good and too valuable to be wearing it in Russia. On his last visit home he told us again how happy he felt about being able to get these pretty jewelry pieces for us. He also believed that they might help us out of a needful situation some day. Sadly enough, that day did come, and much sooner than we anticipated.

April 26, 1945 (?)—The Americans

Daylight finally came and with it came more unrest. People were walking back and forth and having, without a doubt, the same thoughts. Promptly at 10:00 am we heard and saw the first activities taking place at the barricade since we had arrived. The Americans were on time. They drove up in their jeeps, lifted the *Schlagbaum* up and drove slowly down the road, American flags flying on both sides of the vehicles.

I remember feeling very strange standing alongside the road, looking at them with great curiosity. It was my first glimpse both of an American and of a jeep! It definitely was a significant moment in my life.

Everyone was very quiet, just standing and looking, wondering what to do next. It was a strange sort of parade. They drove to the end of the road, turned around and drove by us again to the *Schlagbaum*, which was then left open. No one gave us any orders or instructions. We just gathered up our things and started walking towards the opened barricade.

When we came closer, we could see that they were waiting for us. I could not believe my eyes when I looked at the American soldiers standing there. They were doing what I had thought impossible—smoking a cigarette and chewing gum at the same time! I found it quite fascinating to watch and I probably was staring because my Mother gave me a "move-on" push.

I remembered having seen a picture, a caricature, of American soldiers from the German Propaganda Office. It was very close to the way these guys looked. The American soldiers were pointing to us civilians to go left and to the German soldiers to go the right side. We waved good bye to our soldiers. It was a very sober parting. We were all very happy and thankful that we made it here, but we also felt sad and so very uncertain about our fate. It looked so hopeless.

We could see that the soldiers had to put their guns and knives onto the ground and their watches in a box. Quite a surprise to us, and we wished that we had not seen it! We were not searched. They motioned to us to keep on moving.

We walked along this road for awhile until we came to small lake where we saw two German soldiers sitting on the bank and eating something out of cans. They turned around when they heard us approaching. We were very surprised to see that they were Orientals. They got very excited about our presence, shouting words that we did not understand. It was obvious that they wanted us to move on and away from them.

One of them really got to jumping up and down so that he lost his footing and started to roll down the bank towards the water. He reminded me of *Rumpelstilzkin*! It was a funny moment. I found out that I could still laugh. I had not forgotten how. Of course it was not a good time for laughing. We quickly picked up our things and moved on. We did not hear a splash so maybe he did not roll into the water.

Such a strange looking pair. Why were they wearing German uniforms? And why were they by themselves and not with the rest of the soldiers? My mother and I talked about this incident often and we wondered about it. We would have liked to have known the reason for their presence and for wearing German uniforms.

We walked along with a young woman pushing a bicycle. It was loaded up with two small children and their belongings. The children were very good. They hardly fussed. They come from a town on the other side of the *Neimandsland*. They had not been on the road as long as we had been.

We walked past lots of debris abandoned along the roadside by the German soldiers. There were many vehicles shot up, bombed and burned out, probably the result of the *Tiefflieger*. The worst of all were the dead horses that lay along the roadside. The smell was awful.

We walked through at least three small farming villages. We never saw anyone living in the villages or any kind of activity. We really wanted to talk to someone; we had so many unanswered questions. We were also getting tired and we wanted to find a place to rest.

When we came to the next village we tried the first two houses and did not arouse anyone, but at the third farm we found the *Bauer* standing in the yard. We asked him about lodging in his barn. He was very obliging. Too much so, I thought. He told us that we could sleep in his barn if we did not mind sharing it with his uncle. That seemed a very strange comment. We did not have any objection. We had become used to sharing accommodations with other people. But as soon as we opened the barn door, we could see why he acted so strange about his offering. His uncle was resting in a casket in the barn! We closed the barn door and told the farmer that we did not want to disturb his uncle's rest, after all, and then we walked on to look for another place. The farmer could not have known what was coming, but eventually the Russians took over this territory and I am certain that he lost his ill-mannered humor in a hurry under their rule.

We found another barn in the next village. The farmer family had turned over their house to the American soldiers, but they had been allowed to stay on their farm and live in the servants' cottage. The barn was full of straw. I climbed up a little higher on the straw pile, urging the others to come up to where it was soft and warm. Then to my horror a big rat shot out of the straw right next to me! I do not know who ran faster, the rat or me. And to think that only awhile before I had been complaining about being tired and unable to walk any further. I came to a stop way out in the field. My mother kept calling for me to come back, but I stayed put. She finally came to get me and I told her that I was not spending the night in the barn.

A young farm worker came walking by and asked what our problem was. After we told him about our experience he offered to fix a place for us in the *Waschkuche* (laundry room). We gladly accepted his offer. He brought straw and a couple of horse blankets. Later he came by and brought us some potatoes and milk for supper. He told us that he was from Poland and had been working for this farmer for several years. He was free to leave but he opted to stay a while longer because they needed him. He certainly was a nice and caring young man. He also cautioned us to keep our door locked because it might get very loud and noisy later on in the evening if the Americans staying at the house had one of their wild nightly parties. Indeed, it became very noisy later on. We were all asleep when the yelling, screaming and shooting woke us up. We were glad that the young fellow had warned us about it. Otherwise we might have been frightened.

April 27, 1945 (?)—The Refugee Camp

The small farming village seemed to me a strange place to find the American soldiers. But we did not know how far away the rest of their units were. For all we knew, they could have been close by. In the morning, our young friend came by and brought us milk and bread for breakfast. He also gave us directions to the refugee camp. He told us about a shortcut through the woods, but he cautioned us to be careful and watchful of a new threat around this area, especially in the woods. The Americans had opened the prison gates at the prison in nearby Ludwigslust and given every prisoner their freedom. That was very nice of them, but it also presented a problem to the people living in this area. Not all of the prisoners were imprisoned for political reasons. Many of them were thieves and murderers. They were now roaming around freely, robbing people of their clothes and valuables. We had survived the bombing raids and *Tiefflieger* attacks. We were looking forward to a little less worry in our daily life and along came this new threat.

We went on our way after thanking our young friend for taking such good care of us. We walked through another farming village and found the *Waldweg* (forest cart path) we had been told about. It went off to our right, leading us through the woods. We kept our eyes open for movement or for people in striped prison uniforms, but we were lucky and we did not see any. We were almost to the end of the path when we heard someone coming up behind us. It was our young friend on a bicycle, bringing us a bag that we had left behind. Too bad there are not more people like him in this world. He was a good and caring person.

We finally reached the refugee camp. It was on the big estate of Gauleiter Hildebrand and his family. He had been an important Nazi official, responsible for this area and the people living here.[42] Rumors were that he and his family had escaped to South America. The estate had a big, beautiful house with a courtyard, guest cottages, stables for horses and large impressive barns. Around the estate were several small cottages, including a schoolhouse. The people who had lived in them had worked for the family at the estate.

We asked at the entrance gatehouse for lodging and we were told that they were full, but were also told to inquire at the schoolhouse. There we found some empty spaces in the attic of the schoolhouse for all of us. Then we went to find us some straw to make up our beds.

By this point in time sleeping in a real bed had become something of the past, a dream. Our lifestyle had become so unsettled, so extremely different from what we were accustomed to, that it is very difficult to understand or explain. The attic of the schoolhouse was like a second floor. On each end were two large rooms occupied by two large families of all ages. Their chamber pot, a pail, sat outside of their doors and it was quite frequently used during the night. Sometimes we would wake up and first think that it was raining and that we had better close the window above our heads. In time we became used to those noise and all the other strange sounds around us. They did not wake us up anymore.

We were not so fortunate to have the usage of a *Nachttopf* (chamber pot). We had to go outside and walk to the outhouse, one of my least favorite places. Yes, we were living a very different lifestyle.

The American soldiers at the estate had inherited a *Gulaschkanone* from the German army and had set it up in the courtyard of the estate. We were informed

---

42   A *Gauleiter* was a Nazi provincial party leader similar to a Governor.

that we could come in the evening and get a hot meal, mostly soups or stews. We had to bring our own container, which of course was an item that we forgot to bring along on our trip. My mother asked the people staying at the schoolhouse if they had something she could borrow. They were mostly farmers and they had brought along everything but the kitchen sink. Someone gave my mother an enamel pot. We managed with that until we fished a mason jar out of the river flowing by across the road from the schoolhouse. We could then both stand in line and receive two helpings of soup. However, it still was easier to eat out of the *Topf* (pot). One of us would eat first from the pot. Then the next one poured the soup from the mason jar into the pot and ate it up. Luckily we both had our own silverware. My dad had left a set containing a fold up spoon and fork at home with us on his last visit. We had packed it into our suitcase along with a knife. The soldiers we were traveling with had given a second set to us. We were very grateful to the American soldiers for serving us a hot meal every day.

The people staying at the schoolhouse also had brought along a *Gulaschkanone* that had been abandoned by the German army. They had it set up in the schoolhouse yard. They kept the fire going all the time and they always had hot water for coffee or tea, but they never offered any to us outsiders. Not to mention any of the food that they cooked. We were only allowed to smell their cooking and not to eat it. I do not know what part of Germany they came from, but they were a very unfriendly group of people.

The day after we settled in the camp my mother and I walked over to the river across from the schoolhouse. We decided to take off our stockings and wade around a little in the water. It was very cold but it felt good. When I unhooked my stockings from my garter belt in order to take them off, I forgot about my ring. I had hooked the ring onto the belt to keep it safe in case we were searched when we entered the American territory. We were not searched and I forgot all about my beautiful ring until after I had taken my stockings off. I knew then that it was gone. The river took it away. It was my very first ring, a gift from my dad. I cried for a long while and felt very sad at losing it.

At the estate the Americans were living in the big house and all the rest of the buildings were occupied by refugees. As best as I can remember, we were not under any kind of curfew or restrictions. Although we were still at war, it did not feel like it anymore.

The road outside of the schoolhouse had become a busy highway with lots of traffic and all kinds of vehicles coming to the estate and going back to the city.

Trucks big and small drove to and from Ludwigslust. Perhaps that was where the American's headquarters was located.

There was very little for us to do. We did not like to go away for very long and leave our belongings unattended. The door to the attic did not have a lock, so one of us would always stay close by. I spent quite a lot of time with our new travel companions—Frau Sowieso's children. They were such good little kids. I am sorry to say that I do not remember their names.

Sometimes my mother would watch the children when Frau Sowieso and I would go to the next village for milk or walk to Ludwigslust to hunt for some food. The Americans had reopened the stores in the city and we could buy items in the grocery store and the bakeries with coupons from our April ration card. We could not use some of the items that needed to be cooked, but we used them for trading with the farmer at the schoolhouse. Sugar traded especially well. Of course, this would only last until the end of April. We did not have ration cards for May. Frau Sowieso did because she had left her hometown long after we did and consequently had received hers.

One time, while in town, we overheard some people talking that the shoe store on the main street was going to be open and selling shoes the next day. We marched back to town very early the following day. It was just starting to get daylight. Nevertheless, we found long lines already there. We wondered how many pairs of shoes they had to sell. It looked quite hopeless to us, but we decided to give it a try anyway. We stood in line for quite awhile but we did not have a chance. The store sold out before we even got halfway to the door. People were buying the shoes whether they fit or not because they could always be used for trading. On our way back we stopped at a textile shop where we were at least able to buy some stockings and socks which we could use for ourselves.

The road from Ludwigslust went through a section of woods. On one of our trips back from Ludwigslust, Frau Sowieso came up with the idea that we should walk a little ways into the woods and look for wild strawberries. I was walking along with my head down looking for *wild Erdberren* (wild strawberries) and thinking how good they would taste. I loved eating fruits of any kind. I did not notice the soldier standing ahead of me until I saw his boots. My eyes traveled upwards a long way before they saw who was standing there—*ein schwarzer Riese* (a black giant)! The surprise encounter frightened me. I had never seen a Negro in person and it must have shown on my face because he started to laugh. That only made it worse, because I saw bright white teeth, twice as many as I had in my mouth!

I finally came out of my stupor and moved backwards a few steps. Then I ran, yelling for Frau Sowieso. She had wandered a little deeper into the woods, but she came running when she heard me. We noticed a big army truck standing a little further down the road. The "black giant" was getting into the driver's side. What a frightful experience! And we never did find any *wild Erdberren*.

May 8, 1945—The End of the War

We lived from day to day without any kind of news of what was happening to Germany.

Then one day in early May we heard the sound of a lot of loud yelling and jubilation coming from the estate. We could tell something extraordinary had happened—and then we found out that the war was over! Finally!!

We felt happy and relieved that at last the terrible *Krieg* was over, but we were also worried about our own uncertain situation. The mood among the rest of the refugees seemed to be the same. I am certain that they shared our feelings as well.

The celebrations at the estate went on for several days and nights; and rightly so, they had reasons for celebrating. They were the *Sieger* (Victor) and they could look forward to going home victorious. One evening we were invited to join them at their celebrations. They had long tables set up in the courtyard and on them were plates full of all kinds of sandwiches. I had my first Coca-Cola at that celebration. I never had anything that tasted so good. I drank so many I was sure that I was going to be sick to my stomach.

We stayed quite a while listening to their music and watching the bonfire they had built outside of the estate in a field. We left when it started to get rowdy and wild. They were shooting into the air and it was not fun anymore. They were not drinking Coca-Cola and it was beginning to show. Despite all the noise and commotion we fell quickly asleep. We were awakened by flashlights shining into our faces. Several soldiers were walking around our bedroom, looking for their *Frauleins*. They had been partying with them and then they disappeared into the night leaving the poor guys by themselves. They acted quite angry.

Rumors of the Russians

The last time that Frau Sowieso and I went to the village to get milk we could not find the farmer in the cow's barn, but we did hear the chickens making a lot of noise in their coop. I looked inside. One chicken got off her nest and to my joy I saw that she had laid an egg. I grabbed the egg. It felt warm. I ran out excitedly to show the egg to Frau Sowieso. She took one look at it and started to laugh. I had been fooled by the *Henne* (hen chicken). It was a *Lockei*, an egg to entice the chicken to lay real eggs. Oh well, I was just a girl from the *Gross-stadt* (big city) *und nicht von Lande!* (and not from the country!) *Kein Landei!!* (Not a country person!!) I kept the "egg" as a souvenir to remind me of the day in the country when a chicken got the best of me.

When we did find the farmer he told us about some rumors that were going around. It was not something we wanted to hear. Frau Sowieso became noticeably upset about it. The rumors were that the Americans were soon going to leave this area and move back across the Elbe River. The Russians would be taking over this whole territory. These were very upsetting rumors!

As we were leaving the village we noticed an American soldier sitting on a bench outside a farmhouse. Frau Sowiso came up with the idea that I should go and ask him about these rumors. I did not like her idea at all, but she kept prodding me, so I gave in and gave it a try. I walked up to him and with my limited school English I tried my best to ask the questions about the rumors. I had the feeling that he understood me, but I did not have a clue what his answers meant. I did not understand a word that he said. It sounded so foreign to me. He kept trying, but it was useless. I felt so dumb. He finally took a stick and drew a big circle in the dirt and marked where the American and the Russian positions were going to be. He also drew the number "25" for how far away the Russians were right then. That is all that Frau Sowieso needed to see. Assuming that they were twenty-five kilometers away, she started immediately planning her get-a-way from the Russians. I had a hard time keeping up with her on our walk back to camp.

Back at the schoolhouse she told my mother about the rumors and that she was leaving right away for the other side of the Elbe River. She wanted us to come along. We gave it some thought but we decided not to run off again. We really wanted to go back home to Berlin to look for Oma and Opa. She packed up and left in a very short time, again on the road, pushing her children along on the bicycle. We were sorry to see them leave. We had become used to one another. She and her children were the only ones we associated with, the rest of the people being so unfriendly.

I have forgotten how long we stayed at the refugee camp. We arrived at the end of the April and lived there throughout the month of May. Then I remember being informed to come to the estate to hear what decisions had been made about us. An American officer told us through an interpreter that the time had come for everyone to return to our homes. The war had been over for a while. Law and order had been restored in the American occupied territories. But not, as we would soon find out, in the Russian occupied territories.

The officer also mentioned that cases of typhus had been reported due to our poor sanitary conditions. He promised us an escort through the *Niemandsland* and daily rations of bread. After that we would be on our own—and at the mercy of the Russians! Not a comforting thought.

Most of the people staying at the camp would never be able to return to the homelands they had left behind weeks or even months ago. It had been given to Russia or Poland or Czechoslovakia. Perhaps it was lucky that the people did not know that they could not return. Or perhaps it would have been better if they had known. They might have tried to settle in the area and foregone traveling through and to Russian territory. They had a rough road ahead. In a way, my mother and I were not much better off. We did not have a home to return to either, and we were wondering if we could find Oma, Opa, and Tante Grete again.

With all these thoughts going through our minds, I had to pick this time to get sick. I had a temperature and a very sore throat. My mother found out that an American doctor was going to be at the estate and that he would see us, along with other German people. We walked over very early to find a long line of people already waiting. We waited a long time before the doctor arrived and then longer to see him. But we were so thankful that the doctor would see us and help us. He was very nice. He looked into my mouth and throat and told us that I had *Mandelentzundung* (tonsillitis). I had had it before. He gave me some tablets to take and something to gargle with. My mother felt like laughing when the doctor told her to use warm water for gargling. Warm water! We had not had hot or warm water for our use since we left Alt-Ruppin. But of course the good doctor was not aware of our primitive living conditions.

The only people that my mother could think of to ask for warm water were the *Gulaschkanone* tenders at our schoolyard. My mother went to ask the woman sitting by the *Gulaschkanone* for a cup full of warm water. She told her that I was sick and needed the water for gargling. She refused to give my mother the warm water. She could not spare any, saying she needed it for herself. *Unglaublich!* (Unbelievable!) My mother could not believe that this woman could be so selfish and deny her a cup of water. A man from the woman's group was standing nearby and must have heard their exchange of words. He walked over and took my mother's cup and filled it up with hot water. He told her that she could help herself to hot water whenever it was needed. Why do people act so greedy and selfish, instead of helping someone? It is a very sad thing.

Back on the Road

The day arrived for our departure. It was time for us to leave the refugee camp and find a new place to live. I was feeling better but I was very weak. I did not know how I was going to walk, much less be able to carry anything. My mother walked from one wagon to the next trying to find some space for me. There were over thirty wagons, but no one had any room to spare. She was getting frustrated when finally one of the farmers allowed me to sit on the back of a *swartze Kutsche* (black coach) with our baggage. There was no room left for her to sit. She had to walk behind it, along with several other people who were also walking.

And so our caravan started on its way, moving along slowly, leaving behind the place that had sheltered us for several weeks. During the entire time that we had been living at the refugee camp, we had not heard anything about what had happened to Germany since the war came to an end. Everyone wanted to return to his or her home, but it was the unknown and the uncertainty that made us feel uneasy as we traveled down the road.

We had not traveled very far when trouble started. The axle on the back left side of the coach had lost a pin needed to keep the big wheel from moving out and falling off. No one had anything to make repairs with. The farmer handed my mother a mallet and asked her to walk alongside the wheel and bang it back on, to keep it from falling off. It kept my mother busy, but it worked. We made it to our designated stop for the night at a former German airbase, now occupied by the Americans. We were lodged in a hangar for our last night in a civilized manner—unknowingly, thank goodness—before we moved on and into the Russian occupied territory.

We were served soup and bread, with milk for the children. The Americans had taken good care of us during all the weeks at the camp. Beginning now, while traveling on without their help, we would not have anything to eat, especially us, the non-farmers. The farmers had their wagons to stock up on food items when it was available.

My mother and I found ourselves a spot in the center of the hangar and then went outside to have a look around before settling down for the night. We left our things behind, entrusted to a woman and her son who had been walking with us and were lying next to us. We walked outside and around the buildings toward the airfield where we came upon a whole row of German *Jagdflugzeuge* (fighter airplanes). They were hidden under camouflage covers, netting with pine boughs underneath. They looked in great condition, ready to fly away. The fuel shortage had probably kept them grounded.

We returned to the hangar and bedded down for the night on the concrete floor. Thank goodness for my winter coat, the one I grabbed off the hook before we left our home on that fateful Sunday in March. I really could not understand why I did it. I did not need it then, and it was something additional to carry. But I am glad that I brought it along. The coat served me well. It became the blanket I did not have, covering me during cool nights or making the ground a little softer to lie on.

I must have fallen asleep right away. I do not recall hearing any disturbing noises until a flashlight shone into my face. I sat right up to see this solder looking down at me. It really startled me. My mother pushed me back down and told him to go away and leave us alone. I am sure he did not understand what she said, but her gestures were clear. He staggered on.

It was quite disturbing having these drunk, noisy soldiers staggering over us and causing the small children to cry and be afraid. They meant no harm. They were just a nuisance. As had happened before, they were looking for the *Frauleins* they had partied with earlier in the evening. I do not know where these girls came from. I had never seen any girls of that age in our group. I presume that they came from the nearby towns looking for a good time with the American soldiers, enjoyed the food and drinks they had to offer, and then disappeared into the night, leaving the poor guys searching for them.

Into the Russian Territory

In the morning we picked ourselves up from our hard sleeping places. By then I had forgotten what it felt like sleeping in a soft bed or what it was like to undress and put on a nightgown. That all seemed so very long ago.

Our caravan moved on down the road towards *Neimandsland*. The coach had been left behind. We found instead a farmer who had room for our baggage on the back of his wagon. I do not know if this was the same road that we traveled along in April. I did not recognize anything familiar. If it was, then all the debris had been cleared away and cleaned up. The farmer and his wife, whose wagon we were walking behind, were a young couple with four children. The oldest was a boy about my age and the youngest was a baby, only a few weeks old. They had been on the road fleeing from the Russians since January, when they left their home and set off *auf der Flucht* (on the run).

We arrived in *Neimandsland*. Looking ahead I could see a *Schlagbaum* (barrricade) stopping us from entering the Russian occupied territory. It appeared quiet and deserted. I do not know if the Russians had been informed about our caravan wanting to enter their territory.

We had not been there long when an American truck arrived, bringing us the last provisions to take along on our trip. We were very thankful for their kind effort. They had taken good care of us. Without their help we would not have survived. We had also felt very comfortable around them. I never felt that they had been my enemy. Their treatment of us made it difficult to leave their safe haven and return to what we had fled from in April. As I found out in a very short time, my feelings towards the Russians were totally different. They were the enemy and the invaders of my country.

We waited for quite a while before we heard a truck come driving up to the *Schlagbaum*. We saw a couple of Russian soldiers jump off the back and walk over to the barrier, while the truck turned around and parked. Everyone in our group was standing and watching. Nobody said a word. It was so quiet. I am sure that everyone felt the same without saying it out loud. We were worried and scared of what lay ahead of us.

Before our turn came to move through the roadblock my mother became very concerned and afraid to carry along the few pictures we had of my dad in uniform as a German soldier. She wanted to discard them. I just could not let her do this. They were the only pictures we had left of my dad. We argued a little, but she gave in when I started to cry. I convinced her that I could hide them in my shoulder bag, the one that Onkel Gerhard had made for me. The lining was becoming loose a little on one side and it allowed me to slide the pictures inside. I wrapped our jewelry pieces in a couple of handkerchiefs and put them into the pocket of the coat I was wearing. I hung my shoulder bag to the back of me and draped my winter coat over my shoulders to try to cover up the bulge.

Finally the *Schlagbaum* was lifted up and the soldiers motioned for the wagons to come driving through. When the fifth wagon had passed through, they shouted a loud "*Staj!*" ("Stop!") to the next wagon and let the *Schlagbaum* back down. Then we saw something unbelievable and incredible. The truck was driving ahead of the first wagon, leading them some place. The soldiers leaned their guns against a tree and went running after that wagon.

We could not see very far ahead because the road curved to the right. If we felt worried and scared before, I cannot describe our feelings after what we had just seen. Too bad we did not turn around and head back to where we had come from! But where could we stay? The camp had been closed. We were caught in a difficult situation.

The same procedure was repeated several more times until it was our turn. We were with the last wagons to go through the *Schlagbaum*. We did not go very far beyond the curve in the road until we saw the wagons from our group all lined up waiting for us. The Russians took us to an empty area where we had to stop. Everyone was ordered off the wagons.

A group of Russian soldiers were ready to descend upon us like vultures. They jumped onto the wagons in search for treasures. Some were running around us demanding *Schnaps, Uhren* (watches), cameras, etc.

I was standing with my back to the wagon with the small children in front of me. I tried not to look scared, but I was. I was praying that they would not search me and that we would not lose what little we had left. Whenever I was in a situation like this and I needed help and guidance, I called upon our Father in heaven, but I also called upon my dad for help. My father had been right to encourage us to flee from these horrible men. They did not resemble the ones I had taken food to. They were shouting words that sounded so angry. We were all intimidated, especially the children. One came running to our farmer demanding his watch. I can still see this ugly soldier grinning at us with his mouth full of metal teeth as he pushed up the sleeves on his shirt and showed us his arms full of watches.

Another soldier came by and spotted our suitcases on the back of the wagon. He quickly pulled them down and just rummaged through them. At one point he stopped and acted excited, as if he had found something. He pulled out my crocodile. Then he tore his head off in his hurry and threw it down angrily when he saw what it was. Strangely enough, the crocodile was carved from wood by one of his fellow comrades and now it was broken.

My mother had to repack our suitcases by herself. I did not want them to discover my bag, so I kept standing still by the wagon. She almost had everything packed up again when another soldier came by and spotted "Foxie" in the suitcase. He grabbed it and draped it around himself. Laughing loudly, he danced off with it. My mother did not get upset. She was glad that they did not take my dad's suit material. The silver fox *stola* was the one that my dad had sent from Norway to my mother. It was what I chose out of all the things from our closet to take to the air raid shelter in 1943. It had been with us ever since and now it was around this Russian's neck. I hoped it would bite him.

We were told to get back on the wagons and to move out. "*Dawaj! Dawaj!*" They acted very dissatisfied. They did not find enough during their search, especially the *Schnaps* that they were looking for. Everyone helped put everything back on the wagons so we could quickly get moving and get away from there.

As we moved down the road and through the city of Neustadt-Glewe, we experienced a strange situation. It appeared like a ghost city. We were looking around, trying to find someone to talk to and ask questions about the situation in Germany, but we did not see a soul. Once I saw a curtain move away from the window and someone peek out, but only for a second. I waved, but there was no response. What an eerie feeling walking through a town, passing all the houses and not seeing a living human being.

What a day it had been so far and it was not over yet. I wished that the American officer who had assured us that it was safe for us to return could have seen our entry into the Russian territory and the horrible ordeal we had to endure. The Russians had not even tried to restore law and order! And as I soon was to find out, it was to get worse, much worse.

We spent the rest of the day walking behind the wagon, moving along at a good pace. A few Russian trucks passed us in either direction. The soldiers were always looking at us curiously, probably wondering if we had anything that they could rob us of. We tried not to look at them, hoping that they would drive on by and not stop us for another search.

When we came to a village we stopped at the first farmhouse and asked for permission to spend the night there. The farmer's wife was very nice and seemed glad to have us stay with her. She went back into her kitchen to cook a big pot of potatoes for us to eat. That was all she had left to offer to us. The Russians had taken away all her livestock, emptied her storage room and her cellar. They did not find her potatoes because they were stored out in the field.

I was relieved that we had stopped for the day. I was getting very tried and my legs were very swollen. I could not have walked much further. When we walked into the barn we noticed that there was very little straw. It, too, had been hauled away by the Russians. My mother and a woman and her little boy whom we had been walking with decided to go upstairs and find a place for the night. They thought that it might be a little safer than on the ground floor. But when I tried to climb up on the ladder, I found out that I could not bend my legs. They had become so stiff. My mother had to push me up while I strained to pull myself up, rung by rung. When I reached the top, I was totally exhausted. My mother helped me to lie down and that is all I remember.

She told me the next day that she tried to wake me up so I could eat some potatoes but I did not respond. She also told me that she got very little sleep during the night because she was kept busy shoving away the mice that were bouncing around us. She was afraid that I would wake up and become aware of them and that I would then run off in a hurry. She knew that I would be horrified.

The reason for their presence was the bacon in our bag, which my mother had hung on a beam next to us. The smell of it surely brought them out of their hiding places. Earlier in the day, while our caravan had stopped for a rest, she had made a trade with the farmer we were accompanying. She had offered him one part of the suit material for a slab of bacon. She believed that to keep up our strength we needed a little more to eat than just plain bread. She was certain that my dad would have agreed to this trade.

I was feeling better in the morning. My legs were no longer so swollen and stiff. I had always been a good walker and never had this happen to me.

The farmer had heard about my problem and said that my mother and I could take turns sitting on the wagon from time to time to make it a little easier for us. I was sitting up front on the wagon when a horse and wagon rode by us with two Russian soldiers sitting on it. They were really looking us over but they rode on by, or at least so I thought. I was unaware that they had turned around until I heard my mother's voice pleading with them not to take our suitcases.

The farmer stopped the wagon and I jumped off to help my mother when out of nowhere this rider on a horse appeared, shouting harsh-sounding words and cracking his whip. The rider looked like a *Kosak* (Cossack). The soldier dropped the suitcases in a hurry and ran after the wagon, which his comrade already had, moving. The *Kosak* then turned to us and told us to move on, "*Dawaj! Dawaj!*" It was a close call, almost losing our few belongings, and nothing that they could have used. They probably would have tossed it all away as soon as they opened up the suitcases. It was encouraging to see a Russian enforce some law and order. It gave us a little hope, but only for a short time, as we soon found out.

We next approached another good-sized town called Parchim. It did not mean anything to us. We had no idea where we were. We only knew that the caravan was heading towards Neu-Ruppin.

Again we were confronted with the same feelings we had the previous time when we entered a town. It seemed like another ghost town. Where were all the people? What had happened to them? The houses looked fairly untouched from the war, but there was no sign of life to be seen.

We were almost through the town when a Russian truck drove past us and stopped in front of the first wagon, signaling for us to follow them. Another search! They took us to an open area and told us to wait there. It seemed like we waited for quite some time while the soldiers paced back and forth. They certainly knew how to inflict scare tactics.

Finally, another group of soldiers appeared and they began walking from wagon to wagon, looking over the horses. They brought along a few very worn out looking horses and started to exchange them with the farmers' good ones. Most of the wagons had two horses, but they ended up with only one. A few wagons were left horseless. Our farmer had two good horses and they took them both and gave him a gray, worn out horse, which was better than no horse at all. Everyone looked on despairingly, but there was no point in pleading with the Russians. They looked unapproachable. They moved off with the horses and we were told to stay. They were apparently not done with us yet. What next?

A truck drove up with and a couple of very official looking soldiers got out. They exchanged words with the soldiers who had stayed with us. Then one of them announced in broken German that all men of the ages fourteen to sixty years of age were to step forward and line up. They were needed for work someplace. A heart-breaking scene followed, with everyone in tears. They had been through so much, leaving their homes behind, moving from one place to another trying to survive, and now this painful parting. The soldiers marched off with the men, including our farmer. He was one of the younger ones in the group, except for the boys whom the Russians also took.

Then we were ordered to move. The people whose wagons did not have a horse any more had to leave their wagons behind and find a ride with someone. Our farmer's oldest boy had taken over the lead and I was sitting next to him. My mother was inside the wagon trying to calm the farmer's wife and the children. They were all so upset. It was another sad situation.

After we left the town behind us, we rode along a road with trees on both sides. We had not traveled very far when we saw our group of men walking along on the side of the road. There were guard soldiers walking ahead and on the side of the group. We felt even sadder, if that was possible. The boy next to me started to cry when we passed his father. We all knew that our chances of seeing them alive again were very slim. Very few people returned from the feared and dreaded labor camps.

We heard a movement behind us. When we turned around to look, my mother gave us the "be silent" sign. Later we found out that our farmer had taken the chance to jump onto the back of the wagon and slip under the canvas cover. The guards missed seeing him escape and no one from the group gave him away.

We came to a road leading off to the right and saw the group of our men turning there. The road might have led to a railroad station. Our farmer hid under all the bedding with the children sitting close by him. He told us later on that he had not planned his escape, but that something told him to do it when he saw us driving past. He took a big chance. He could have been shot, but he was lucky that the guards missed seeing his escape.

My mother and I walked behind the wagon. We did not ride much. We were worried about the poor horse. He looked so tired.

When we stopped for a little rest, I could not help but notice how very quiet and discouraged everyone was, including the children. And with reason, having watched their husbands, fathers and sons marched off to a labor camp. Who knew where it was? Should anyone survive the camp, how could they find one another again? I felt very sorry for them.

It was decided among the people of the group that we should try and travel the country roads and avoid the towns in order to hopefully escape the Russians and their searches. That evening we found ourselves another barn to sleep in. This time the Russians had left the straw behind while taking everything else away.

Some of the people slept in their wagons, especially the children. A few of the people, along with us walkers, slept in the barn. My mother and I bedded down way up high in the barn. Luckily this time we did not disturb a rat's nest!

My mother woke up hearing voices and the strange sound of someone poking a stick into the straw looking for something. She immediately assumed the worse—that the Russians were searching around the barn. I woke up nearly smothered under all the straw that she had quickly covered me up with. As they came closer she could hear, to her relief, that they were speaking German. She let them know where we were to avoid getting poked. Then she told them where they could bed down.

Not long after their arrival daylight arrived and we met the two *Nachtschwarmer* (night revelers). The two German soldiers were trying to evade the Russians and their prison camps. They traveled only at night and hid out during the daytime hours in barns or wherever else. They agreed with our decision that we were a little safer from the Russians by traveling on the country roads. Then they stated that their destination was Ludwigslust. When they found out that we had come from there they had many questions for us. I hope that they were able to make it home safely without getting caught.

After walking for a while, my mother and I decided to take a little rest on the wagon. I was sitting next to the farmer's oldest boy when we again rode through a village. We both commented at how deserted it looked, another ghost village like all the rest we had traveled through. Just then this Russian soldier came tottering out from between two houses, headed towards us. We could tell that he was very drunk and very unsteady. I am very sorry to say that I made the big mistake of laughing out loud, which of course drew attention to the wagon and to me.

He stumbled towards us and tried to grab the horse by the halter and to pull me off. My mother became aware of the situation and came out from behind us. She took hold of the horse's whip and lashed out over the Russian's arm. He let go of my arm, stumbled backwards and fell down. She pushed me off the bench and took over the reins from the boy. His father had come out of his hiding place to try to help, but my mother did not need any assistance. She did not use the whip; she just kept calling to the horse. The poor animal must have sensed that we were in danger. He was trying hard to run faster. They were some very anxious moments! I was praying hard that we would get away and that he did not have any comrades nearby to witness the incident. It could have been disastrous for all of us. Thank

God that we were not followed and that we were spared any punishment. I was so sorry that I caused this incident and jeopardized the rest of the group.

My Mother's Way with Animals

My mother handled the horse well, but then she always had a special way with animals.

She grew up on a big estate in *Schlesien* where she did not have any children her age to play with. Instead, the animals became her playmates, especially the horses, dogs and cats.

She told me that there were some doghouses placed around the yard and *Wachhunde* (guard dogs) that were chained to them. All of the servants and hired hands were afraid to go near them, but my mother could even crawl into their houses while they lay out in the rain. They never bothered her and they also were very protective of her.

She picked up all kinds of stray dogs, and usually big ones. The dogs that she brought home were not always homeless, but she kept them anyway. She was not very fond of the smaller ones, the *Schosshunde* (lap dogs). They barked too much and for no reason.

She always told me not to show fear, to stand my ground, and to look into a dog's eyes. I tried to be brave when a barking dog was chasing me, but one look at those fletching teeth would send me off running. I did not have her confidence that they would not bite me.

One of her stray dogs was a big white furry one. She had named him Eislar and he was very devoted to her. Whenever she walked to the village she would take him along and have him wait by a large tree on a hill. It did not matter how long she was gone. He would always be there waiting for her. When she did not take him along and it became dark and she had not come back home yet, her aunt or uncle would send the dog to meet her. She would be walking up hill and feel so relieved when she spotted the white dog waiting for her. She was not afraid of animals but she was afraid of this so-called "Haunted Hill," where long ago fierce battles were fought. Supposedly, on special nights, one could hear the poor souls crying!

My mother told me that the women in the village would tell some very spooky tales while sitting together, working with their spinning wheels. It kept them amused and frightened the young ones, like my mother. Maybe they believed the tales. They were all so superstitious, way back then.

She also spent lots of time in the barn with the horses, brushing them and braiding their tails. Many times she fell asleep lying between their legs in their stalls. Those who came looking for her were hesitant about calling out loud to her. They were afraid that it would startle the horse and that it might then step on her. But the horses never moved while she lay there.

She learned at a very early age to ride a horse without a saddle. Her aunt was not in favor of this unladylike fashion, but her uncle just smiled and looked the other way. She would walk the horse by the house when her aunt and uncle were sitting on the veranda, but as soon as she was out of their sight she would jump on and ride away. Her uncle was aware of her games but he never forbid her, only cautioning her to be careful and to keep out of Auntie's sight. My mother could never understand why anyone needed lessons to ride a horse. For her it was something so easy to do.

The only animals that I know of that she did not like were the *Ganse* (geese). They had gotten her in trouble many times. The dislike must have been mutual because they would try and bite her whenever they could. When she was about six or seven years old she was given the task of watching twenty-five to thirty geese. She was to keep them from going into the garden. On several occasions she fell asleep in the field. The geese had promptly marched off to the garden, of course. They could make a terrible mess in a short time.

She had an accident once when she was about ten years old. I do not remember any more the reason for this encounter with a mean *Bulle* (bull). She was in the field when this bull came after her. Somehow he picked her up and threw her down, injuring her wrist with his horns. It dislocated her wrist bones and punctured a vein, which bled a lot. The wrist was not properly attended to and the injury was still noticeable years later. But she was very lucky. It could have been worse.

World War I came along when she was about nine years old. It changed quite a few things at the estate. Most of the younger hired help were drafted into the military service, so everyone had to help do the chores. One of the things my mother was taught was how to milk the cows. In years to come that skill proved to be quite useful. The army also came and drafted their good horses into the military service. It broke her heart to see her friends taken away. In exchange they left behind some very tired and worn-out horses. I remember her speaking of one, a *Schimmel* (a gray horse), and that he had lost the use of one eye. He was so pathetic looking that she took a liking to him immediately. In time she nursed him back to being a strong horse again, able to help with the farm work.

One day her uncle brought home a couple of Takener horses, a smaller breed. They were mainly used in East Prussia and Russia. They had long tails for braiding, only by then she did not have time for such things. They were kept very busy on the farm. She liked the little horses. They worked hard and appeared to be quite tough.

I wish that I had taken notes about some of my mother's stories. They were very interesting, often amusing, and could also be very sad. I used to remember them much better and more clearly than I do now. It is something that I regret very much.

Our Return to Neu-Ruppin

We were coming closer to Neu-Ruppin, guessing from the upside-down Russian writing on the road signs. Finally, our little caravan stopped in a village outside of Neu-Ruppin. Here we parted from the group. They were taking a different route, hoping that it would take them back to their homes. But from what I learned later on, I know that they were not allowed to return.

My mother and I walked on by ourselves. When we were almost through the village we took a rest, sitting on a bench near a house. A woman came out of the house and asked us if we were hungry and if we would like something to eat. We were both so surprised at this kind woman's offer that it made us speechless. We could only nod. She went back into her house and before long returned with two plates full of food—mashed potatoes, sauerkraut and pureed peas with bits of bacon it in. It was delicious! I have never forgotten how good it tasted. It had been a long time since we had eaten a home-cooked meal. We had not realized until after we ate how hungry we were. We could not thank the *Bauer* woman enough for her kindness. Before very long we were to find out that it would be months, perhaps years, until we would eat something so good again as that meal. Hard to believe, but so very true.

The meal, the woman's kindness and the realization of what had become of us brought tears to our eyes. We were thankful that we had survived the war, but at what cost? We were homeless, with our family separated. We did not know if my dad, Oma or Opa were still alive. It seemed that we had very little to look forward to, and our feelings of despair became stronger and stronger.

When we reached Neu-Ruppin we felt for the first time since we had started on our flight that we were coming back to familiar surroundings. The town seemed to have survived alright. We noticed very few damaged houses. We saw a few German people out and about, but mostly there were Russian soldiers walking around. Perhaps their presence was so obvious because we were walking by a *Kaserne* (barracks) which they had occupied.

When we reached the railroad station we saw that it was all closed up and that it did not look operational. We walked on and reached the road to Alt-Ruppin. There we sat down for a rest and tried to decide what to do next. It was four kilometers along the road and through the woods to Alt-Ruppin. The *Panzerkaserne* (tank barracks) was located close to Alt-Ruppin and was surely occupied by Russian soldiers. We did not think that we should walk along the road and past the *Panzerkaserne* by ourselves. It was too risky. We decided to wait, hoping that someone else would come along and we could walk together.

We were in luck. Before too long three people came along, a man and two women. We asked them if we could join them and they gladly agreed, adding that it was always safer to walk in groups.

As we walked closer to the vicinity of the *Panzerkaserne* we noticed that all the trees had been sawed off, but in such a weird way, with three to four feet left standing. It was a very strange sight. It exposed the *Panzerkaserne* and gave us a full view of all the buildings. Many we had never seen before. They had been well hidden behind all the trees that were now half gone.

Then we saw this huge pile of bathroom sinks, toilets and bathtubs in the woods. The people we were walking with told us that the Russians had torn everything out of the bathrooms and that we would soon see their new outdoor toilets. And that we did. It was an unbelievable picture, absolutely horrid. There in front of us sat the Russian soldiers on a long pole, doing their business with no privacy whatsoever, which did not seem to bother them. "*Germansky nix cultura*" ("Germans not cultured" or "Germans have no culture") was the phrase we were told often by them.

As tired as we felt, we found ourselves walking faster just to get by the disgusting place. I did catch a glimpse of the entrance to the *Panzerkaserne*. It too had been changed. The nice stone portal with tanks on either side was gone.

Instead, huge posters of Stalin, Lenin and Marx stood in its place. It looked more like the entrance to a circus.

We had often walked this road through the woods on our way to and from the railroad station in Neu-Ruppin. If we rode the *Schnellzug* from Stettiner Bahnhof it did not stop in Alt-Ruppin. Only the *Bummelzug* did. It had always been a pleasant walk with benches along the way as places to take a rest. But it had all changed.

We came out of the woods at the edge of Alt-Ruppin and were greeted by huge posters of Stalin, Lenin and Marx. They must have mass-produced them. The Hotel Hubertus was severely damaged with lots of bullet holes in the building. Also damaged were the other houses on the corner. But as we walked around a bend in the road we could see that Tante Grete's house was still there and that it looked intact.

The door to the house was locked. The window shutters were all closed. The house looked deserted. We knocked and knocked on the door and the windows. We had almost given up, thinking that everyone had left, when we heard someone on the inside and saw someone peeking through the *Kuckloch* (peephole) in the door. It was Tante Grete. She had not heard our knocking because she had just then entered the hallway from the backyard.

What an emotional moment for us, seeing one another again, *und am leben* (and among the living)! After all the weeks without any contact there were lots of hugs and tears. Then there were many more tears as we were reunited with the rest of the people living at the house. We all told our stories and related our experiences since we had last seen one another, and we cried.

The Russians' Arrival in Alt-Ruppin

Tante Grete and the people living in the house had suffered badly when the Russians entered the town. The difficulties of our time spent on the road or in the refugee camp were mild in comparison to what the people in this town endured when the Russians entered.

The townspeople had been—and were still being—severely punished because of a group of boys fourteen to fifteen years old. Members of the *Hitler Jugend*, they had positioned themselves on roof tops (one of them on the corner house across from Tante Grete) and had shot at the Russian soldiers as they were coming around a corner into the main street.

I knew one of the boys who had been involved in the shooting from the rooftops. He was the son of the owners of the grocery store located in the house. He had become very involved with the Hitler Youth Organization. He wore his uniform all the time and acted very conceited. He had come over once to see me, after he heard that we came to live with Tante Grete. But he had changed so much that we had absolutely nothing in common. He lived in his own world, out of touch with reality. A very lost soul. I felt sorry for his parents. He was their only child.

It was a very dumb thing to do, irresponsibly and insanely putting everyone in town in danger. In response, the Russians had acted barbaric and uncivilized. I was thankful that we were spared the horrible experiences of the townspeople. I owe it to my mother's persistence in wanting to leave before the Russians arrived and not listening to my lamentations about leaving our nice lodging. It still makes me shudder thinking about the consequences had we stayed behind.

Living Under the Russians

The townspeople were fortunate that the Russians did not destroy their town in retaliation to the hostile reception they received. Neu-Ruppin fared a little better because there the people at least hung white bed sheets from their windows.

The Russians had recently opened up a *Kommandantur* (Commandant's office) only about four houses away from Tante Grete's place. It was in the former *Gasthaus Zum weissen Rossle*. Since then it had become a little safer living in the area, especially at night, although we still had to keep our doors locked and the window shutters closed to avoid having unwelcome visitors.

Tante Grete's parents and sister lived in a small house with the woods right behind them. They had had a lot of unpleasant problems with the soldiers spooking around after dark. When the *Kommandantur* moved down the street from Tante Grete, they came to stay with her at night. Tante Grete's father worked at the *Kaserne* as an electrician and her sister Hanna was a nurse at the hospital in Neu-Ruppin. When she worked the late shift she would stay at the hospital instead of riding her bike home through the woods, a very risky ride.

The Russian soldiers marched through town early in the morning and late in the afternoons. They would be singing just as our German soldiers used to. But now we would not open our windows to wave at them. Sometimes I would peek through the shutters and I could see them looking around, but we had to be very careful to make ourselves invisible to them.

Their presence had brought big changes to the nice little town. People were hardly ever seen walking or standing around outside talking to their neighbors. There had been a little park across the street from us. People sat there on benches in the evening and visited with one another. It was gone. The little park had been made into a cemetery for Russian soldiers.

We were required to report to the *Kommandantur* and register our whereabouts. The Russians put my mother into a work program in order for us to receive a ration card. I still came under the children's category until the age of fourteen and did not have to work. The ration cards were a big joke. They were useless because the stores were almost always closed. They had nothing to sell. The only time that they would be open was when the Russians felt like giving the storekeepers something to sell to us. We would watch for the shutters to go up at the butcher shop and quickly run over hoping that he might have something edible for sale. But it was always the same, some awful smelly bones that had already been gnawed clean or some other horribly questionable foodstuff. We tried to cook a broth once from the bones to use as soup stock, but the smell was so bad it made us feel sick to our stomachs.

I remember it being a hot summer. It was everyone's belief that food items were held back deliberately from distribution to us until they were spoiled. Cottage cheese would be runny and bitter tasting. Margarine would be rancid. I am quite certain that I acquired my ability to recognize spoiled foods by tasting or smelling it during this period.

The bakery used a large cowbell to let the people know when they had bread to sell. There would always be long lines and many times they did not have enough bread for everyone. In the meantime, the bakery was baking bread every day for the Russians, tormenting us with the smell.

We were being punished daily for greeting the Russian soldiers, our "Liberators", with bullets instead of a white flag. Two other examples of their revenge upon us was the placement of the confiscated German *Gulaschkanone* in front of the *Kommandantur*, right on the sidewalk, instead of in the back yard of the building. And then the *Kommandant* (commander) ordered that the beauty shop be reopened for the use of his women soldiers only. He wanted them to look nice. There were quite a few of them walking around. The *Kommandant* himself looked like a polished round ball, puffing away on big cigars and using lots of cologne. He always left a big cloud drifting behind him when he strolled by our place.

The *Kommandantur* also gave everyone a piece of paper to be stamped every day to show that the person was employed. "*Dokumente!*" the Russians would demand. They always asked for your documents. They wanted everyone working. The day after my mother registered at the *Kommandantur* she had to report for work early in the morning. Off she marched to Neu-Ruppin in a group of women. They were to work at the airfield to help put it back into operation. This was not a paying job. *Schwerarbeit* (heavy labor) was, as I have said, the only way to receive a ration card. Tante Grete was better off. The Russian Army needed ammunition and she had been called back to the factory.

The airfield had been heavily bombed during the last days of the war, probably by Russian aircraft. Using only shovels, my mother and the other women were supposed to fill the huge bomb craters. It was hard work, very hot and dusty on the airfield, and they were treated like prisoners. If a woman became thirsty and wanted to get a drink of water, she would have to ask for permission from the Russian guard overseeing them. The only source was an old dirty barrel. My mother told me that the water smelled and tasted foul, but it was better than nothing at all.

At noontime the women were given watery soup and a piece of black bread. If the guard was a mean and spiteful one, he would let the soup sit in the hot sun until it soured and then dish it out. Many women became very ill from the spoiled soup, but that would not excuse them from work.

After a long day of hard work under these conditions they were marched back to town. I remember my mother coming into the house, totally exhausted. She would wash up and fall into bed.

I became very concerned about my mother's going off to work. Her legs began to bother her as the varicose veins in her legs started to swell up. Walking and standing were causing her some pain. By the end of the first week her legs looked awful—swollen, red and shiny. Not even the rest over the weekend helped. Monday morning she could not wear her shoes. Luckily Tante Grete still had a pair of her husband's slippers that my mother could wear.

She hobbled Monday morning to the meeting place to let them know that she was unable to go with the group to the airfield. They told her to see the Russian doctor. He looked at her legs and diagnosed it as *Venenentzundung* (phlebitis). He signed a paper allowing her to stay home for one week. After that she was to come back to see him. When she went back to see the doctor, her legs looked a little better but she still could not wear any shoes. He wrote out an order for *Leichtarbeit* (light labor). They found a job for her to do, right across from the *Kommandantur* and always in their sight—the Russian cemetery. She had to go there every morning and dust off the wooden crosses, rake the walkways between the gravesites, water the plants and sweep the roadside around the cemetery. I could tell that it was still painful for her to walk or stand, but it was an easy job compared to the one on the airfield. She never complained.

Of course as soon as the job was changed from *Schwerarbeit* to *Leichtarbeit* her ration card was also changed. It really did not make much difference. We could not buy anything anyway. We were all at the Russians' mercy.

I wondered about my mother's feelings about this job. I have often questioned God why were we traveling such a troublesome road and carrying such a heavy burden with no end in sight. It was so discouraging. I felt so sorry for her, seeing her hobble around the cemetery. I would have gladly gone to do the job for her but their work order issued by the *Kommandant* was made out in her name and it was stamped everyday after she completed the job. I could have helped if the *Kommandantur* had not been across the street from the cemetery.

During the last days of the war and just before the Russians entered the town, Tante Grete along with other townspeople had broken into an underground storage near the *Kaserne*. She made several trips back and forth with her bike and brought home one sack each of flour, salt, potatoes and rutabagas. It does not sound like much, but it surely helped a lot.

We were very thankful having the potatoes and the flour. For breakfast we would have *Mehlsuppe*, made with water thickened by flour and a little sprinkle of salt for flavoring. For supper we would cook a huge pot of potatoes. When they were done, we would put the pot on the table and help ourselves. We would peel them, sprinkle on a little salt and eat until they were gone. The amount we ate, just the three of us, would probably have been enough potatoes for a week under normal times. They filled us up and still our hunger. The feeling just did not last very long. All too soon we would be hungry again.

Sometimes we had delicious milk to drink. We could also use it to cook the *Mehlsuppe*. The opportunity to get the milk occurred in the evening when the Russian soldiers would herd cows through our town to a field outside of town for an overnight stop. We could hear the cows coming from far away. They were long overdue for milking and their loud mooing was easily heard. They looked miserable trying to walk along with their full udders almost touching the pavement. My mother would get her pail and stool and follow behind the cows along with other women from the town. When they came to a halt the women would approach the guard and ask for his permission to milk the cows. Most of the time it would be allowed, although sometimes he would chase them away.

Permission from the guard was not just a good deed for our sake to let us have the milk. It was also for the poor suffering cows to help them to be rid of their milk. My mother told me that the cows held very still when she sat down to milk them. That was not ordinarily the case with a milk cow. Under normal circumstances the cows would act quite fidgety. But in this case, she felt that they knew that she was making them feel better and helping them.

Once when I had gone along with my mother, the guard gave permission for her to milk the cows. While she was sitting and milking the cow, another soldier came riding by on a horse. He yelled at her and gave her a push. She fell over, spilling the pail of milk!

I was standing at the edge of the field when this happened. I was absolutely horror stricken, seeing her lying underneath the cow. I could not get to her fast enough to help her up. I arrived just in time for the soldier to come riding back to chase us both off the field. My mother did not get hurt. She was very lucky that the cow did not move and step on her.

We made sour cream from the milk. That was a nice treat on our potatoes. My mother also made a kind of cheese called *Kochkase* from the milk.

A couple of times my mother saw the soldiers butchering a cow and she asked them if she could have the parts that they were throwing away, such as the heart, liver and whatever else. Sometimes they answered with a "*Da*", and other times with a harsh "*Nyet*". It depended on what kind of mood they were in. We learned to deal with both kinds of Russian characters, the one who could be approached and the one who could be inhuman.

One time an older soldier asked for some *Schnaps* to complete the trade. My mother returned home and asked Tante Grete to search her cellar for some. She did find a bottle of wine, fermented with pieces of something floating in it. One had to be desperate to drink that stuff. It looked dangerous!

My mother and Tante Grete washed out the bottle and then poured the wine through a sieve into it and corked it back up. They returned and found him sitting by a fire, roasting a huge piece of meat. His eyes lit up when he saw the bottle of "*Schnaps*". I was anxious to see his reaction when he took a drink. I was also wondering if he would throw it back at us. Surprise, surprise, he liked the drink. He kept repeating "*Gut Schnaps, Gut Schnaps*", even after taking another swallow. But before we could leave with our trade, we had to sit down and listen to his stories. We guessed that it was all about the Russian *cultura*. We understood that much.[43] "*Russky Cultura gut. Germansky nix gut.*" He kept taking one swallow after another, until there was not much left in the bottle. This caused us great concern. We wanted to get away before he asked for another bottle of *Schnaps*. He finally motioned for us to go and take our cow parts, but before we left he stood up and took his knife and cut a big piece of meat—real meat—from the cow that hung nearby on a tree branch. What a treat!! The bottle of *Schnaps* must have softened up that old soldier.

We had a wonderful meal with that piece of meat. We invited Tante Grete's parents and her sister to share this delicious meal with us. It had been a long time since we had such a good piece of "real meat".

On another occasion, when the five of us were returning from picking blueberries, an old Russian soldier stopped his wagon and offered us a ride, but only to my mother and to Tante Grete's mother and sister. Guessing by his wild gestures and pointing to the long pants, borrowed from Onkel Hans, that Tante Grete and I were wearing, we figured that he did not like women to be wearing pants. He acted so angry, waving his rifle around and shouting at us. We just kept on walking. He finally drove on by us and we breathed a sign of relief. We could hear him talking loudly for quite awhile. He was a very weird Russian solider.

There were benefits to living in the country. It gave us more opportunity to find things to eat. Tante Grete and her father owned a piece of land outside of town where they grew potatoes and vegetables. The garden provided us with a few more things to eat than we would have in the city, something that we found out later when we returned to Berlin. I also remember how everyone grew vegetables in the flower boxes on their balconies. Peas, beans and tomatoes grew quite well that way.

I remember one rainy Sunday afternoon when we were sitting around and wishing that we had *Kaffee und Kuchen* for our *Kaffee Stunde*. My mother and Tante Grete decided to make some *Apfel Plinze* (apple blintzes). The only problem

---

43 It was very difficult communicating with someone who spoke another language. Some of the soldiers had picked up a few German words and we too had learned a few Russian words. But hardly enough to help us for better understanding one another.

was that we did not have any apples. I offered to go and find us some. We only needed four or five apples. We did not have any fruit trees in our yard, but the woman next door did. She was so selfish she would not willingly share with her neighbors. But she let the Russians come into her garden and take all they wanted and even helped them filling their bags!

The branches of one apple tree overhung our yard. They had been loaded with apples, an early variety. A green, crisp good-tasting apple, they had all fallen off and quickly disappeared, having been picked up very fast! There were a few of them lying on the ground under the tree, but on her side. So I took the rake and brought them closer to the fence. It made it easier to lift them over the fence into our yard. I knew that if she looked out of her windows that she would see me, but I did not care. Sure enough, she spotted me. I heard her squeaky gate and there she stood, yelling, calling me a thief, and wanting me to give her back the apples.

I picked up the apples and I told her what I thought of her selfishness, that I had only yesterday asked her nicely if she would sell us some of the fruit in her garden, with her answer a very unfriendly "No!"

She continued yelling at me, calling me names and saying how rude and naughty I was. Oh well. I left her standing there and hurried back to my house, thinking all the time how good the *Apfel Plinze* would taste for our *Kaffee Stunde*.

I have never forgotten that episode. I probably should have felt remorseful and apologized. I would have had she been a different person. I know what I did was wrong and under normal times I would have never thought of doing so, but we were not living under normal conditions. I have also wondered whatever happened to the old selfish woman. Who gave her a place to live when the Russians moved into her house and she had to leave? Sadly, there were a lot of German people like her. I always felt that had we helped one another more, it would have been easier for everyone.

Some one mentioned that the apples on the trees growing outside of town on the country road were getting ripe. We decided to go and try to get some. We almost had our bags filled when a couple of Russian soldiers came riding by on horses. We had kept our eyes open for any surprise visitors but we never noticed them until they were upon us. In their harsh language they demanded that we hand them our bags and gestured for us to get out of there. *"Dawaj! Dawaj!"* We understood the meaning of that word.

We wondered where they had come from so fast. Had they just been out riding their horses or were they patrolling the area? All the time that we had lived at the refugee camp with the American soldiers around us, we had never felt that we were under the kind of watch or control as we now were. We had been free to come and go as we pleased and it had been so different living under the Americans' supervision. Well, no matter what, we did not get any apples and came back home just the way we left, empty-handed and without our bags.

About this time I also had to part from my pair of shoes, my pumps, the ones that Tante Ilse gave me before Easter of 1945. I had heard the cowbell ring, which meant that the bakery had some bread. I quickly slipped into my pumps and started out the front door when I bumped into two Russian women soldiers walking by. I made it across the street when I heard them yell "Stoi!" I had also learned the meaning of that word and to do what it meant—"Stop!" They came across the street and kept pointing at my shoes. I tried to act dumb, pretending not to understand them, but they pushed me against the building and grabbed my leg to pull my shoe off my foot. They kicked off their boots and were trying on my shoe. To my horror, my shoe fit one of them. She demanded that I hand over the other one and then off they marched, leaving me standing in my socks. I wanted to cry, but I forced myself not to. Then the one wearing my pumps turned around and threw her boots back to me, laughing. My first instinct was to throw them back after them, but I restrained myself from doing so. I picked up those ugly worn-out boots and walked back across the street into the house. Then I cried, feeling so sorry for myself. I wanted revenge so bad but I knew that it was useless to feel that way. They were the *Sieger* (victors) and we were the losers. Now I had only one pair of shoes left, my walkers, and they were getting quite worn. My mother too had only one pair of everyday shoes and one pair of new ones, black pumps, which she had been carrying in her suitcase for a long time. They were meant for me to wear on my Confirmation Day.[44]

The *Kommandant* took a daily *Spaziergang* (constitutional) down the main street. On one of these walks the *Kommandant* was asked by a couple of women sweeping the sidewalk when the Russians would let the German men return home from the prisoner of war camps? His reply was that they would not return for a long time. They had much work to do, he said, to rebuild what they had destroyed. Then he asked why they wanted their men. "Do you need a man? Are

---

44   *Konfirmation* was a very special day for every young evangelical girl or boy. I had once been looking forward to that special day in my life, but I had become indifferent since April of 1945.

you lonely? Then take a look around. There are many good looking men available to fulfill your needs." He was such a creep.

I never had *Kopflause* (head lice) before this time, but someone in our group came in contact with those nasty bugs and soon we are all infected with them. We would take turns combing each other's hair with a special comb, then empty the comb onto some paper and crunch the running lice before they escaped to someone else's head. A lot of fun. When the pharmacy re-opened we were able to get something which burned like fire on our already sore scalps. Feeling the lice running under our scarf covers was worse. It was a miracle that we still had hair on our heads after the combing and the fire oil treatment.

The lady from the beauty shop told us that her Russian women customers had hair filled with head lice. They did not act too bothered by the lice, but she did not enjoy working on their hair. It bothered her very much. And to top it off, they were so hard to please. At times when she was finished and they were not satisfied she had to do their hair again. It was a very unpleasant job.

The Russian Military Funeral

My mother, caretaker of the Russian military cemetery, told me that a burial was taking place within the next day or so. The Russians had been busy preparing a burial place. So when I heard music on the following afternoon, I went to the window to have a look through the shutters. I noticed that soldiers were lining the street on both sides. Then it was a long wait until the funeral procession finally came into view.

The procession moved very slowly. Two horses were pulling a wagon that held the casket. Many followers walked alongside the wagon and behind it, all dressed up in their uniforms, their chests full of medals. It was an open casket with the soldier lying in it dressed in full uniform and surrounded by beautiful flowers. He must have been a high-ranking officer.

It was a different experience for me to witness this funeral procession, very dramatic and solemn. It was very impressive. They made their way to the little cemetery where a platform had been set up for the speakers with chairs all lined up in front of the platform and flowers everywhere. It was a long service. We could hear the music and the speeches for a long time.

I had never seen an open casket funeral before and I must admit I felt uncomfortable with the whole affair. It was a very hot summer day and we all believed that it was not healthy to hold a funeral in this way. We had heard that they came all the way from Neu-Ruppin, where they had places to bury people. We could not figure out their reason for coming to Alt-Ruppin.[45]

My First and Last Turkey Hunt

I do not want to forget to tell about the day when I caught, single-handed, a wild turkey (at least so I thought) in the woods. It was my very first and last hunt ever!

We had gone to the woods to gather kindling—branches and small twigs—which made it easier to start a fire in the kitchen stove. I heard a noise and when I looked up I saw this big turkey walking by. A turkey in the woods! I started after it and it started to run, with me behind it. I would get real close and it would quickly turn and run into another direction. Everyone was laughing, telling me that I was foolish and wasting my energy and that I would never catch this bird. I was getting tired and ready to give up the *Jagd* (hunt) when it ran into a pile of brush. I ran quickly to the other end and grabbed it when it came out. It must have been tired too, because it did not put up a fight when I put it into my burlap sack.

Everyone was astounded that I had managed to catch the turkey. I had no idea what I was going to do with it, but I did decide to take it home with me. The others had all enjoyed a good laugh on my account, which was good. It showed that we had not forgotten how to laugh.

With the turkey in the bag on my back, I started on my walk back to town. I was a little worried about walking by the back entrance to the *Kaserne* without attracting attention from the guards. The turkey had been very quiet, but as soon as we came closer to the gate it started to make turkey sounds—"gobble, gobble."

I made it safely back to the house and locked the turkey in an empty rabbit cage. It settled right down. It probably was relieved to be out of the bag.

My turkey soon became a very friendly pet. I do not remember what I named it, but it would come running when I called it. Hermann, the boy from next door, helped me make a pen for it. He also brought over a big box. We fixed up

---

45 Many years later, in 1992, we returned to Alt-Ruppin for a visit. The cemetery was still in its place, not as well taken care of as when my mother was the caretaker, but still looking basically as it did so many years ago.

a comfortable house for it. Hermann and his family were *Klein Bauern* (small farmers). They had lost all their livestock, taken away by the Russians. Hermann and his dad were put to work at the *Kaserne* doing odd jobs. All too soon they would also lose their home to the Russians. Big changes for Hermann and his family.

One day I finally found out what kind of *Geschlecht* (gender) it belonged to when it laid an egg. What a nice surprise—and such huge eggs! The only problem was that finding the eggs turned out to be like an Easter egg hunt. I only locked her up in the pen at night. She was free to wander around in the daytime, and she never laid her eggs in the same place.

One scrambled turkey egg along with fried potatoes was a nice meal for the three of us. Sometimes we would trade an egg for something else we could use, but not very often. Mostly we kept the eggs for ourselves. I know now that it was not a wild turkey that I caught. It was probably a domestic one that had escaped from the Russians and their stew pot.

Returning to Berlin

Since our leaving Berlin four months before, we had not had any contact with Oma and Opa. Not one day went by that we did not think about them, but the postal service had not been restored and neither had the train service. We did not get any kind of information. We were kept totally in the dark. We had no idea if they had survived the war or if there even was a city left after all the bombing raids and the Russians' battle for Berlin.

We had heard that there was a man in town fixing up a truck, a remnant from the German *Wehrmacht*, with the intention of taking people to Berlin. I guess there were other people besides us interested in going to Berlin. We went to see him and expressed our interest in going along if there was room available for us. He told us that he still had room for us and that we were welcome to come along.

When I took a closer look at the truck, I was not so sure that it could make the trip, much less transport a group of people. Hopefully, looks were deceiving and the parts that counted, like the motor, were in good shape. We paid the man in advance and he assured us that we would hear from him when we could leave.

We were getting quite anxious. We wanted to get back to Berlin and look for Oma and Opa. We also wanted to see what was left of our city. By then it must have been three months since the end of the war.

We could have stayed in Alt-Ruppin but the Russians had created a very inconvenient situation for all of us. The Russian *Kommandant* had served the people on our side of the street with an order that the houses be vacated immediately to be used as living quarters for Russian officers. It did not make any sense to us. German officers had lived at the *Kaserne*. Why could the Russians not live there? The *Kaserne* was only a few years old and had a lot more modern conveniences to offer than these old houses did. But of course the modern conveniences were all lying out in the woods. Maybe they did not leave the bathroom fixtures in the officers' living quarters either.

Somehow Tante Grete managed to persuade the Russian officers that were moving into the house, three or four of them, to let us move into a storage shed out back. She also offered her services for cleaning up the rooms and for washing and ironing their clothes. They agreed and she became their housekeeper, which meant that she did not have to go to work anymore at the factory. The Russians also allowed Tante Grete to use the house kitchen during the daytime hours when they were not there.

The landlord couple and Frau Katerborn went to live in Neu-Ruppin with their son and family. The Russians had reinstated him in his old position as the police chief. The two sisters and the little boy and the woman and her son from Lithuania and the three of us moved into the shed. We cleaned it up and hung sheets for dividers to give us privacy in our sleeping areas. We found cots in the air raid shelter, along with a table and chairs.

I wondered why Tante Grete went through all the trouble of moving into the shed and living under such primitive conditions when she could have gone to live at her parents' house. They had returned to live there quite a while earlier when the area had become safer and calmer.

I cannot exactly tell how long we stayed after our move into the shed but it was not for very long. We were glad when we heard from the man with the truck that he was ready to drive us to Berlin. We needed to get away from there. It had become very unpleasant. We felt very uncomfortable in our present situation. I am sorry to report that Tante Grete and the two sisters had become involved with the officers in the house. There were parties every night. We would not hear them coming to the shed before daybreak. I am glad that the little boy slept so well and did not wake up during the night asking for his mother.

My mother asked Tante Grete once what she was going to tell her husband when he returned from somewhere in Russia. In a small town like Alt-Ruppin it would not take long for him to hear about it. She just shrugged it off, saying she would deal with it when the time came and if he came back home. She had not heard from him for a long time. She wondered if he was yet even alive. She also said that she was tired of living from day to day, rummaging for food, with no hope in sight for improvements. She wanted to have a good time and forget our miserable existence, even if it was just for a little while. This attitude of hers and the two sisters had a lot to do with the horrible experiences they endured when the Russians entered the town. Tante Grete admitted the harm that had been done to them. They were not the same women anymore that they had once been. My mother strongly disapproved of their conduct, and especially Tante Grete's choice, but she also believed that if their conscience allowed them to live with those morally wrong doings, then it was of no concern of hers.

Despite our feelings about the current happenings, we parted as friends. Tante Grete had been so good to us, sharing her home and her food. We were indebted to her forever. When the time came, Tante Grete packed up two knapsacks full of potatoes, a few carrots and several heads of cabbages. She also packed a loaf of bread and a few Russian cigarettes for Opa. We only packed a couple of small suitcases and left the rest of our things with her. Sadly, I also had to part from my turkey friend. Tante Grete promised to take good care of her until I returned.

Having been away from Berlin for such a long time and all that took place during that time we did not know what we would find. We did not even know if we would find a place to stay. It was quite a chance that we were taking. We were leaving Alt-Ruppin after dark in hopes that the Russians would not be "spooking around" at that hour. We did not have proper *Dokumente* authorizing us to leave town and to travel to Berlin.

We avoided walking by the *Kommandantur*, and that meant we walked a long way to get to the meeting place. The truck was very noisy, or maybe it just seemed so to me because I was worried that a Russian patrol would hear us and come after us to arrest us. I could easily visualize our ending up in Camp Sachsenhausen. We had heard rumors that the Russians had reopened it and were filling it up with people that were disobedient.

Everyone on the truck was very quiet. We drove along slowly on the bumpy country roads with the lights partially covered up, like they drove during the war. A truck loaded full of illegal emigrants! A little light from a quarter moon helped us to see a little bit but it also made the countryside look spooky. My imagination could see all sorts of movements. I was just so afraid of us being caught without proper papers by the Russians.

I do not remember how long it took to get to Oranienburg but it surely seemed like a long time, longer than three railroad stops. When we reached the outskirts of the town the driver stopped the truck and we all got off. He told us that he felt it was safer for us to get off at this spot than at the railroad station. The Russians always hung around the train stations, for what reasons I do not know.

We made our way around Oranienburg walking through streets that had been heavily bombed and were still littered with rubble, with large craters everywhere. The town had been a much sought out target by the Allied bombers because of several big factories in the area. I wished that I had Tante Ilse's address. I thought that perhaps their house had survived and we could stop for the rest of the night, then continue our walk by daylight. But I had only been to her house once and I did not remember anymore where it was located.

It was difficult walking along in the dark, trying not to stumble and fall on the broken pavement. We were making very little time. We were also becoming concerned that we were getting farther and farther away from the railroad tracks and getting ourselves lost. We were also lucky that we had not met up with any Russian patrols. I would have been more nervous if I had known then that there was a curfew in effect from sunset until sunrise.

We finally decided to head back to the tracks and try walking on them. My mother and I felt a little more comfortable with this decision. We knew that the tracks would take us eventually to Waidmannslust. We could stop there and look up Onkel Gerhard and Tante Elisabeth, Traute and Guenter.

It was difficult walking on the tracks. We had to avoid holes made by bombs, broken tracks, and all kinds of hazards along this route too. Somewhere near Waidmannslust we had to take a detour because a bridge was gone and by walking around it we missed our original destination. We ended up in Tegel, but it was not too far out of the way. It was beginning to get light and we saw a sign for Waidmannsluster Damm. We were finally on familiar grounds. Only a little while before we had both been complaining about getting tired, but when we realized where we were, we gained new strength and walked right down the middle of the street. We both must have carried about a hundred pounds together. Our suitcases were light compared to the potatoes. They were heavy on our backs.

Waidmannsluster Damm was a long street leading from Tegel to Waidmannslust. Most of the houses on both sides of the street were one or two family homes. We had walked this road many times from Onkel Gerhard and Tante Elisabeth's house either to Tegel to take the *Strassenbahn* (streetcar) back to our house or to Bahnhof Waidmannslust to ride the S-Bahn train.

We felt very encouraged seeing so little damage to the houses on the street. Even the trees were in good shape. A big change from what we had walked through during the preceding hours. So when we reached their house we were totally unprepared to find their house gone, along with the two houses on either side. I remember just standing there in disbelief, looking at the ruins of what used to be their house. Had we been walking by other bombed or burned out houses, I would not have been so shocked. We looked around for a message that they might have left behind that they had survived, but we did not see one.

While we stood there a woman a couple of houses away walked out of her front door. We asked her about our relatives. She told us that they were alright and living in an apartment not far way, only about one block from the S-Bahn station. We were glad to hear that they were alright and we walked on to find their new location. We did not have any problems finding it.

When my Aunt Elisabeth opened the door the normally very talkative woman just stood there speechless, looking at us as if she was seeing two ghosts. I heard my Uncle Gerhard calling from inside asking who was at the door. Well that finally broke the spell we had cast over Tante Elisabeth. We all became very emotional, especially when my Uncle came hobbling to the door. I was so happy to see him.

After calming down a little, our first question was about Oma and Opa. To our greatest joy we were told that they were living only two houses away. When I heard that news I wasted no time in getting there. I rang the doorbell and Oma opened the door. She just gasped and I thought for a moment she was going to faint. We both started to cry, tears running down our faces as we stood clinging to one another. And more so when we walked in to see Opa. He was so overcome by his emotions when he saw us he could not speak. It was a very emotional *Wiedersehen* (reunion). I was known for not being very affectionate, for not showing my feelings so easily towards my family. But it surely was not the case at this time as everyone could see. We were all so happy to have found one another again and so thankful that we had survived the war.

Oma made some *Ersatz Kaffee* for us. By then Onkel Gerhard, Tante Elisabeth, Traute and Guenter had joined us. They had brought along our bags which we had left sitting in their doorway when we hurried off to see Oma and Opa. We had so much to tell each other and talk about and so many unanswered questions. It became quite a discussion.

Onkel Gerhard and Tante Elisabeth had come into the city right after Easter Sunday. They were looking for us because they had heard about the devastating air raid in our area. They found the house gone and when they asked people to tell them more about it, they were told the dreadful news that everyone was dead. They felt so bad. Even though we all lived with that thought in mind every time the air raid siren announced another air raid, it still was quite a shock to them.

They decided to go to the Laubes' home to talk to them. When they turned onto their street they were surprised to find the house still standing amidst all the ruins. To their joy and relief they found Oma and Opa there and heard the story of their survival. They also learned that we had left for Alt-Ruppin and Tante Grete's.

They convinced Oma and Opa to come back with them to Waidmannslust where it would be safer for them, away from the bombing and later on from any street fighting. They also asked Tante Anna and Onkel Paul, but they declined. They did not want to leave their home, what little was left of it.

Onkel Gerhard and Tante Elisabeth lost their house right after we did in March of 1945. They had gone to a public air raid shelter during a nighttime air raid. When it was over, they returned to their home, only to find it totally engulfed with flames. Neighbors were carrying pails of water from a nearby pump, trying desperately to save the houses on both sides of the burning houses, which they did. They stayed with neighbors until they found the apartment where we found them. They were using beds from the air raid shelter and besides a table and few chairs, it was sparsely furnished. But at least they had a roof over their heads. I wonder what the Russians thought when they went through the place looking for treasures.

I am glad that Oma and Opa decided to go to the Laubes' house. It was a good decision. Oma and Opa stayed with them until they found a nearby furnished room with kitchen and bathroom privileges. It was a very nice apartment. The landlady was widowed and a lot older than my grandparents were. Her husband had been a lawyer and they obviously had been well off. I remember admiring the beautiful furniture, the crystal and the china which had all survived the war and the search by the Russians. Not that they would have taken it away. They would have just broken it in pieces for fun, especially after a few bottles of *Schnaps*. Oma told me that the landlady had the crystal and the china all packed in big wooden crates and stored in her basement. Oma had helped her unpack it and bring it back upstairs just a short while before we arrived.

We stayed with Oma and Opa. My mother and I slept on the sofa. It was barely big enough for one person, but we managed.

I am glad that we had brought the potatoes from Alt-Ruppin even though they had been so heavy to carry. People living in Berlin had once again been issued ration cards. Oma and Opa fell into the "non-working" group and so had received the lowest calorie count card. It was just enough to keep one from starving to death. The potatoes we had brought provided some much needed food for us. I was beginning to see the difference between living in the city and living in the country. At least we could grow potatoes and vegetables in the country. That was not easy to do in the city. I do not remember my Opa being a big eater, but as I watched him eat the potatoes we had brought I could see that he surely was hungry.

One piece of important news we heard after our arrival in Berlin was that the city had been divided into four sectors. We had hoped and prayed that our city would be taken over by the Americans, but to our dismay the Russians had captured it. Now the four powers had divided Berlin into sectors. Waidmannslust and our former neighborhood were all to be placed within the French sector. I had never seen a French soldier and I wondered what they looked like. I also wondered what it would mean to live in the French sector. This division was a totally different aspect for us to think about.

During the night of July 4, 1945 units of the 7th British panzer division, the famous Desert-Rats (*Wustenratten*) who had defeated Rommel's Afrika Korps at El Alamein, moved into Berlin. On the same date, the American forces took over their sector. The French moved into their sector on August 21, 1945 with a big parade am Wedding in der Mullerstrasse. The British military forces that had occupied our sector took down their flag and the French flag was put up. The French then moved into the former Hermann Goring Kaserne which they renamed "Quartier Napoleon."

Before long we found out what living in the French sector was to be like under the rule of the French occupation forces. They were not very decent to us. We were being punished in retaliation for what the German soldiers had done during their occupation of France. I had a problem with this accusation. I had never done anything bad to the French people.

The best place to live in was the American sector, followed by the British sector, then the French sector, and lastly the Russian sector. The people in the French sector were supplied on an alternating monthly basis with food rations—one month by the French, one month by the British, and then one month by the Americans. We could always tell when it was the American's turn to feed us. The food was usable and edible. The people in the Russian sector were better taken care of than we were in the French sector as far as the food rations and the electricity and the coal rations were concerned. The leadership in the Russian sector was always trying to buy support from the people for the Communist Party.

Tante Elisabeth and Traute walked to Schonholz to check on Tante Anna, Opa's sister, and Onkel Alfred. They found them to be alright. They were living at their cottage, having survived all the tumult and excitement of the past weeks and months.

Oma had been talking a lot about Tante Anna and Onkel Paul, wondering about them and whether or not they had survived the end of the war. The lack of communication was very difficult to deal with. We were getting a little anxious ourselves and wanted to have a look at our former neighborhood. Around Oma and Opa's new apartment the area was quite untouched and peaceful, but what did it look like in the city? So we offered to go into the city and check on them.

We started out early in the morning as soon as it became daylight and the curfew was over. With our *Reise Proviant* (travel provisions) in hand—a couple slices of bread, two boiled potatoes and a bottle of water—we were on our way. We had to be very careful not to get caught by the French gendarmerie because we did not have any proper documents, like a valid evidence of residence. Many displaced German refugees were traveling daily through Berlin on a search for a new home. If they were unable to prove that they had a place to stay then they had to move on after three days.

We tried to avoid the *Hauptstrassen* (main streets) as much as possible. When we came closer to Tegel and Borsigwalde, where many of the big factories were located, we started to see lots of devastation everywhere. Unlike the main roads the side roads had not yet been cleaned up. It was a little worrisome walking by the ruins. They looked as if they were ready at any moment to fall on top of us. There were huge craters everywhere, with broken twisted pipes sticking up into the air and mountains of rubble.

But the worst of it all was the smell that hung over the area and followed us along. It was the smell of the dead, both human and animal, that still lay buried under all the rubble. It was a sickening smell, mixed with the odor from the burned-out buildings and the broken sewer and gas pipes. It was very strong. I also remember it being a very hot summer, which did not help the situation at all. It felt good when a little breeze would blow, but then we had to put up with lots of dust in the air.

When we came to the entrance of Borsig, the factory where my dad had been employed before he was drafted into the German Army, we stopped for a minute. We looked across the street at the familiar *Pfortner-haus* (gatehouse). We remembered it so well. I knew without mentioning it that we were both thinking the same thoughts. How many times my dad had walked through the gate by the *Pfortner-haus* and how much he liked working for this company as a crane operator.

Memories of a Better Time

The factory did not look badly damaged, at least from the front. Except for all the glass being gone from the windows it seemed okay. It had survived the bombardment better than the surrounding residential area. It did seem strange to see the factory so quiet and deserted, without any kind of activity. Not at all the way I was used to seeing it.

Every year at Christmas Borsig would have a big *Weihnachtsfeier* (Christmas party) for their employees and families. It was held in the afternoon on Advent Sunday. I looked forward every year to this event. The large factory hall would be completely decorated and look very festive. In the center of the hall long tables would be set up for *Kaffee* and *Weihnachtsgeback* (Christmas cookies). The children were served hot chocolate.

After the boring speeches given by the company supervisors and the visiting dignitaries—like Albert Speer and Dr. Goebbels—the fun time would begin. The candles on the big tree in the center of the hall would be lit. The band would play *Weihnachtslieder* (Christmas carols) and everyone would sing along.

The hot chocolate and the cookies tasted good, but the highlight of the *Feier* was the appearance of the *Weihnachtsmann* (Father Christmas). He brought with him a huge bag and in it was a small present for every child. Each one of us would be called by name to come to him and pick up the gift after reciting the little *Gedicht* (poem) for him.[46] It was a lot of fun.

Every year until 1944, even when my dad was away serving in the German Army, we would receive an invitation to join them at the *Weihnachtsfeier*. We also received a *Weihnachtsfest-paket* (Christmas party package) full of goodies. It always was a nice assortment of fruit, nuts, candy, cookies, a whole salami or smoked ham, and butter and cheese. The Christmas packages had been a tradition with each of the companies my parents had worked for. They would each receive one and they would be packed with different items. My mother and dad always had fun comparing the contents of their boxes.

The last two boxes were not filled as generously as the earlier ones. Some items like candy, butter, cheese and salami were missing. They were replaced with canned fish, which was good too. We were glad to receive the *Weihnachtsfest-paket*.

There were other occasions throughout the year when employees would get together for some kind of company sponsored activity. I remember going on boat rides to the Muggelsee and having lunch or *Kaffee and Kuchen* at a nice outdoor restaurant. There were many wonderful memories and enjoyable good times that ended too soon. I may not have seen my parents very much during the week because of their work schedule, but on weekends when they were home, they certainly spent a lot of time with me.

We walked on, leaving Borsig behind us with all the good memories.

Reunited with Tante Anna and Onkel Paul

The areas we walked through looked much like what we had already passed through earlier that day. Some areas had a lot of damage and others had very little. When we came closer to Reinickendorf and Tegeler Forest, where the Tegel Airport was later built during the Berlin Blockade, we started to see traffic—cars, jeeps and trucks. Until then we had not seen any vehicles and very few people on the streets. It had looked so deserted everywhere.

---

46   Gedicht fur den Weihnachtsmann   Poem for Father Christmas
     Lieber guter Weihnachtsmann   Dear good Father Christmas
     Schau mich nicht so bose an   Please don't look at me so angry
     Stecke deine Rute weg   Put your switch away
     Ich (name) will immer recht artig sein!   I (name) will always be good!

From what we could see, the Hermann Goering Kaserne, now the Quartier Napoleon, looked in good condition. I had fond memories of visits to the Hermann Goering Kaserne as a ten and eleven-year-old girl. It was a nice place, well hidden among trees from the Tegeler Forest and the Rehberge, a big park. On this day it was a very busy place. We kept ourselves at a good distance and tried to act "normal", whatever that meant.

We entered the upper end of Mullerstrasse, where one section was called the Afrikanisches Viertel (African Quarter). The streets were named after colonies in Africa that had formerly been under German control—Congo Strasse, Kamenener Strasse, Zanzibar Strasse, and Transvaal Strasse. The whole area looked good. Here and there a house was missing, but on the whole there was very little destruction. The windows in the houses even had glass in them![47]

After crossing Seestrasse we entered the district called Wedding. Before Hitler's era it was called *der Rote Wedding* (the red Wedding) because of the residents' strong Communist sympathies. The brown shirts of the S.A. had a difficult time marching through those streets. They were bombarded with everything that could be thrown from the windows, including burning mattresses.[48] This all came to an end when Hitler came to power. *Der Rote Wedding* quickly ceased to exist.

The Rathaus am Wedding (City Hall) had also survived the war. But when we turned into the street running alongside Leopold Platz, we began to again see a different picture. Many more burnt and bombed-out houses came into view and lots more destruction. The closer we came to the Laubes' home, the worse it became. We became quite concerned about what we would find.

To our surprise, while walking amidst all the rubble and debris, we started smelling the wonderful aroma of baking bread. Sure enough, the Wittler Brot Fabrik (Wittler Bread Factory) had been spared from destruction and was in full operation. The smell was tormenting our poor empty stomachs. It was a very cruel sensation, especially so because we could not go into the store and buy some bread for us to eat.

To our delight we found the Laubes' house still standing amidst all the burned out and destroyed houses. It was a miracle that their house survived. It

---

47 We walked by two streets in this section of the city—Transvaal Strasse and Seestrasse where, unbeknownst to us at the time, we would soon end up living, first on Transvaal Strasse and then on Seestrasse.

48 German mattresses came in three parts, making it easier to toss one through a window.

was, however, very dark on the inside. The windows were still covered up with cardboard and the staircase seemed to be quite rickety.

Tante Anna and Onkel Paul were very happy to see us and to hear that Oma and Opa were alright. They had not yet heard from Tante Ilse and her family and they were very concerned about them. Tante Anna made some *Ersatz Kaffee* for us and we talked about everything that had happened to us since we left on Easter Sunday.

I do not remember how long it had taken us to get to their house. Except for the little pause at Borsig's gate, we had been steadily walking along. I do recall that we decided we would not be able to make it back in time before the curfew went into effect. We therefore decided to spend the night with Tante Anna and Onkel Paul and start out early the next morning for our return trip.

We left them after awhile to walk to our old neighborhood to have a look around. The closer we came the more we realized that there was not much left. Even the little roadside park where I used to take the children to play in the sandbox and Opa would sit on the bench with the other old men did not exist anymore. It had been turned into a big hole, the creation of which must have swallowed up the trees and everything else.

Out of all the places that I had seen so far, I believe that this area, our old neighborhood, was hit the hardest during the bombing raids. It was a blue-collar working class neighborhood surrounded by factories and important railroad lines. The factories, strangely enough, had survived. I never could figure that out. It remains a mystery to me to this day.

Walking around the area we met our former neighbor and good friend Frau Girndt and her three girls. What a nice surprise! We had been thinking of them often but would not have known where to look for them. It was cause once again for lots of tears, but this time they were happy tears. It was good to see one another again.

She invited us to come back with them to her place on Schonwalderstrasse, across the street from the *Markthalle* (market hall) where we used to shop. She had just been given the apartment. Until then they had still been living in the *Erdbunker*. We walked back with them and found it hard to believe that there really could be a house left on that street to live in. It looked like the Laubes' house and it also felt very rickety. The apartment was on the third floor in the front of the building. They had brought the beds up from the shelter and set them up in the bedroom and living room. Frau Girndt and her girls were staying in the living room, while her sister Gertrud and her husband were sleeping in the bedroom. The other sister Frieda and her husband had moved out recently into a furnished room on Transvaal Strasse.

Again we sat together as friends and shared our experiences with one another. When Frau Girndt found out about our problem of not having any proof of legal residence, she asked us to come and stay with them. I cannot explain why we were drawn back to the old neighborhood. It resembled nothing more than a giant pile of rubble. It was dirty, dusty, smelly and very depressing. I am certain that we could have found a furnished room in Waidmannslust, but here we were accepting Frau Girndt's offer.

That very same afternoon she took us to the local police station and registered us as living at her residence. The police made out a temporary piece of paper listing our new address on (Liebenwalderstrasse) Schonwalderstrasse. It made us feel a whole lot better, not having to worry about not having any valid papers to show if we were stopped and checked. We were then invited to have a bowl of *Gemuse eintopf* (a meatless vegetable stew) with them. It tasted very good. Frau Girndt had come to our aid again. She was a kind and caring person, always ready to help someone.

Frau Girndt's brother-in-law, Heini, was a funny looking man. He was short and round, with a bald head, and was always muttering to himself. He spent his free time in the cellar fixing and rebuilding bicycles. Somehow he had managed to save a tandem bicycle, keeping it hidden from the Russians by taking it apart and storing the pieces in the bunker with Frau Girndt. When they moved into the apartment he put it back together. It had been put to good use ever since. He and his wife Gertrud used it to ride to work every day and also on other outings. They would ride out to the suburbs where small farms were located to buy vegetables and fruit. It was a blessing for them, especially the children, to have fresh fruit and vegetables to eat.

He tried several times to get me to ride with him around the block so that I could see how much fun it was. I finally agreed one afternoon. I was convinced that I would not like it and I did not, especially after we rode by a group of neighborhood boys and I heard their remarks. I felt embarrassed. Heini was not too happy with my performance either. He complained about my pedaling and he never asked me again.

The funny little man had done well by planning ahead. Frau Girndt had also done well by helping herself to a food supply in the bunker. The food was good for eating and valuable for trading for other needed items. She had always been curious about the room next to hers in the bunker. At different times she had seen people going in and coming back out carrying things, mostly bottles. When the Russians moved into the neighborhood and the guards had left the bunker, she rounded up some people from her floor and together they broke into that room. They found the room well stocked with all kinds of food. She carried away boxes full of canned meat and fish, condensed milk, cocoa, etc. The other people were more interested in the bottles of wine and champagne. She stored the boxes of food under the beds in her room in the bunker. It was not long before the Russians entered the bunker and emptied the room. For once the "loot" had fallen into deserving hands, and what a wonderful "find" the supply turned out to be.

Frau Girndt did well getting things that would truly be needed after the war before they were all gone. She helped herself to extra blankets and pillows from the linen room in the bunker. Right across the street from the bunker was the Woolworth store and a little farther down was the Kaufhaus Hertie (Hertie department store). They were good stores for finding things of practical value. Frau Girndt and her brother-in-law joined the rest of the looters and grabbed what they could from those stores—items that they needed like pots and pans, silverware, plates and cups. She also took some items that became valuable trading articles later on, like sewing needles and thread. When the war was over nobody wanted money in trade. Everyone, including the farmers in the suburbs where Heini and Gertrud bicycled to asked for something in trade. The sewing articles and other practical items came in handy.

Frau Girndt's sisters and their husbands had moved into a room in the bunker that had become vacant when the former residents left to stay at their homes. Those last days of the war were extremely unruly. People took great risks amidst the shelling from the *Stalinorgel* (Soviet multiple rocket launcher), running around on the streets in search of something of value. They all knew that for them the worst was yet to come.

When the Russians moved into the neighborhood only once did any soldiers come down onto Frau Girndt's floor. They looked into her room where she was sitting on the bed with her three girls. She thought that they must not have felt comfortable venturing several floors down below the surface. Strangely, they also would not use the elevator. She was thankful for this. The people on the top floors did not make out so well. They were bothered continuously day and night. Everyone told the same story—that the first group of soldiers, apparently the

Combat Units acted alright, almost civilized. But not the ones who followed. They were a group of barbarians.

That evening we returned to the Laubes' home and spent the night with them. The following morning we started on our walk back to Waidmannslust. We felt a lot better having the slip of paper stating that we were legal Berlin residents.[49]

When we arrived safely in Waidmannslust Oma and Opa were glad to see us back. They were also glad to hear that Tante Anna and Onkel Paul were alright. They were not too happy hearing our report about the neighborhood's condition and about our plans to move back there. They wanted us to stay near them. I was not so sure either about moving to live amidst the ruins and heaps of rubble. The air was also much easier to breathe around Oma and Opa's house. Oma was certain that her landlady would rent us a room that she was presently using for storage. She thought that it could be fixed up to live in. But my mother wanted to live near our old neighborhood and be with other people that were in the same situation as we were.[50]

---

49 In one way the situation really made no sense to us. We had always lived in Berlin. It was not our fault that we were made homeless. So why were we being treated like this?

50 As it was, events proved that maybe it was better this way after all. Not long after we left for our old neighborhood, Oma and Opa's landlady passed away and my grandparents had to find another place to live. Luckily, for them, Herr Gaebel, a *Gerichtsvollzieher* (bailiff) living one floor above them offered them a place live in exchange for Oma doing light housework for him. The location of the room was exactly the same as the one they had, just one floor higher. The difference in floors was not a problem, for Oma and Opa did not go anywhere anymore. Oma was able to buy the furniture they had in their room from the landlady's heirs at a very fair price. Oma and Opa then stayed with Herr Gaebel until they both passed away. They all got along well with one another. For Opa it would only be two years, but for Oma almost twelve years.

In time, another woman, Charlotte Resehausen, a widow, came to rent a room from Herr Gaebel too. She had been well off before the war, but had lost everything. She was a lovely lady. She had traveled extensively before the war, even to America. She had some interesting stories to tell. A few years later, Stan and I invited her to our wedding. She happily accepted our invitation but she felt bad that she could not afford to give us a present. We managed to convince her that we wanted her to come, and that her presence at our wedding was her gift to us. But she still insisted on giving us a few of the remaining pieces of silverware from the set she once owned. Stan had invited his work colleague Tom Reedy to our wedding and at the reception we had Charlotte sitting next to him. At first she did well conversing with him in English, but

Onkel Gerhard had been walking each day to the S-Bahn train station where he had worked before the war, trying to find out any news about when train traffic would again be resumed. He told us that the trains were at least running from Waidmannslust to Gesundbrumen, which was good news. It was not far from Gesundbrumen to Schonwalderstrasse. We would be walking right by the bunker at Humboldthain and then down Hochstrasse, past our destroyed house, across Gerichtstrasse to Schonwalderstrasse.

We did not encounter any problems on our journey. It took longer than under normal conditions but it still was a lot better than walking the whole way. The girls were glad to see me. They had the books and the games that they had brought along from the bunker play area all set up for me.[51]

Back in the Neighborhood

I was anxious to see my old friends, wanting to find out if and how they had survived the end of the war. I found them to be alright and with many interesting stories to tell me.

Guenter, my girl friend Ursula's brother, had just gone back to work with his father at a publishing company around Friedrichstrasse. Guenter was in his second year of apprenticeship, learning to become a *Drucker* (printer). At that moment they were all engaged in clean up jobs. The area had been heavily bombed and their building had been badly damaged.

Kurt J, another old friend, had not been called back to work at the AEG Company where he had been a *Lehrling* (apprentice), working to become an electrician. His older brother, Werner, had been called back to work for the

---

after toasting a few times with the delicious French champagne, she became slightly confused and her English language turned into French. Oh well!

51   The girls also loved playing school. The oldest of the girls had only attended school for about one year before they were closed because of the air raids. We tried to play school, but we did not have any paper or pencils. We could only do it verbally, and it was not quite the same. I do not remember how the school administration decided after the war how to place the students. Everyone who had remained in Berlin had lost two years of schooling. The *Volkschule* (public school) ended at the eighth grade when a student was normally fourteen years old. With the loss of two years the student would be sixteen years old. The war and the missed schooling certainly changed everything, including plans for entering a three-year apprenticeship or attending a school for higher education.

railroad. He was learning to become a locomotive engineer, but at that time he also was also doing clean up work. There was plenty of it everywhere.

My girl friend Ursula showed me her large selection of clothes. I could not believe my eyes. She had more dresses, skirts and blouses than she had ever had. They were all made from the same material, but in our circumstances who would care? At least she had something to wear. She told me how she and her brother Guenter had gone around and searched for things to eat and use. They brought home two bolts of material from the Kaufhaus Hertie. It was made into many nice garments, even shirts for Guenter and for their little brother, Manfred. I kept hoping that she would offer a small piece to me, just enough for a blouse, but she did not. I surely could have used it. My wardrobe selection was very limited. I became aware rather quickly how selfish people can become at a time like that. I had shared so many of my things with her in the past when she had never seemed to have anything, always complaining and crying that her father was stingy and a *Geizkragen* (miser). Just another disappointment.

The rest of the group was doing alright, just hanging around. They also told me about their adventure—a very dangerous mission, I thought. They were very lucky that they came back alive. They had heard about the food supplies that were stored in a huge storage building on an island at the Westhafen, which was surrounded by water. One could only get there by boat or by swimming, and a long swim it was.

They built a couple of floats and took turns swimming out to the island. The water must have been freezing. There they found that people with boats had already broken into the building. Nevertheless, the boys were able to bring a few bags of flour and sugar ashore. The less experienced swimmers stayed behind and guarded the loot. It went well for two days, but then the Russians moved into the area and took over the storage building. Plotzensee and the Westhafen were located at the end of Seestrasse. It really was a long way from the old neighborhood, and it certainly was quite a scary undertaking.[52]

---

52 I am reminded by this story of a Sunday during the summer of 1943 when our group came together outside after Sunday dinner. We were all dressed up in our Sunday best outfits, which meant that we were not to get dirty—a very boring situation. We were trying to find something to do. We had visited the museum at the palace so often that we thought the guards recognized us when we came. One of the boys came up with the idea to go to Plotzensee and rent a rowboat and ride around in Westhafen. It was quiet on Sundays, with no barge traffic coming to or leaving from the storage building. My girlfriend and I knew that we would never get permission for such an

My friends told me that they had heard the schools were going to reopen soon and that I needed to register. I knew that I could not afford the tuition at the *Mittelschule*, a private school, which made me sad because I liked going there very much. It had been spared from destruction. The *Volkschule* (public school) which I had attended for the first four years was still standing near the entrance to Humboldthain, but it had been declared unsafe. We had to go to another school. There were not enough children left in our old neighborhood or in the surrounding area to restart the old schools so they brought us all together to one centrally located school. It took me about forty to fifty minutes to walk there from Seestrasse. Riding the *Strassenbahn* (streetcar) was a little faster if the connections were alright.

When I went to my former school to let them know that I was not coming back and to get a release slip, which I had to take to the public school to register, I found out that half of my classmates from the other classrooms were still missing. All the girls, including my dear friend Elfriede Letter, had gone with the school to

---

outing, and neither would the boys. I was wearing a new outfit—a pleated skirt with a matching vest and white blouse—not at all something to wear on a boat ride. But they were very persuasive, telling us that we did not need to worry and that it would be alright. They talked us into it.

We had no problem renting two rowboats and at first it was fun riding around the lake. But then the boys rowed into the harbor area where the water looked quite dirty. When I saw a couple of rats swimming by, I was ready to go back to shore. Only then the boys were acting mischievous, trying to hit the rats with their paddles, getting us all wet, making the boats bounce up and down, and frightening us. Thank goodness we made it back safely before tipping the boat over. Falling into the dirty rat filled water would have finished me.

It was a very foolish thing to do. It haunts me to this day when I think of the consequences the boat ride could have led to. The boys were all good swimmers, but Ursula and I were not and I do not recall seeing life jackets in the boat.

When I stepped ashore I noticed that all the pleats had come out of my skirt. I did not know how to explain this to my mother. Luckily for me she had company and she did not want to show her disapproval of my appearance. By the time the company had left she had gotten over it. What a relief! I told her that we got caught in a heavy downpour. I never told her the truth and my conscience bothered me very much.

I was never a good fibber. As time went by I would forget what I had used for an excuse when I had done something wrong, but my mother never did. Her famous words were, "*Die Sonne bringt es doch an den Tag.*" ("The sun will turn it up some day!") It was better for me to tell the truth and accept my punishment. Though to this day I still do not know what the sun has to do with it.

Poland as part of a voluntary evacuation. I had wanted to go along too, especially the first time in 1942 when they traveled to Czechoslovakia. They were all so excited about going there and talking about the different things they would be able to do, like skiing, skating and hiking. It sounded like so much fun. When I asked my mother about it, she did not say yes or no, but instead asked me to write to my dad and find out his opinion on this matter. He wrote back saying that he did not think it was a good idea. He really did not like the idea of the three of us being separated in three different countries. He felt that it was best for me to stay with my mother. In all honesty, I must admit that I felt disappointed, but the feeling did not last long. Once the group was on their way I got over it. Later on I was thankful that I had stayed behind. It turned out to be a good decision.

The group returned from Czechoslovakia when the war began interfering with their safety. And then they went to Poland. Elfriede told me that they were well cared for and living within a school compound, protected by guards. They were only allowed to walk into town as a group. She also confided in me that she really wanted to stay home and not go to Poland. But her parents insisted that she and her older sister go along on the trip.[53]

Elfriede's family had been bombed out in 1943 and they went to live with her grandparents. I lost touch with them. I thought of Elfriede often, wondering if she had made it back home. Years later in 1948, I ran into Elfriede's sister at the city hall where I worked. I tried not to show how shocked I was at her appearance. The once pretty girl looked sickly and worn out. We all looked very thin and bony those days but her looks were different. She told me that she had recently been released and sent home from a labor camp in Russia because of ill health. The family had no knowledge of Elfriede's whereabouts, nothing whatsoever.

She told me that when the Russian Army came closer to where they were staying in Poland and they could hear the guns, everyone became frightened. Their leaders calmed them down and gave them reassurances that help was on the way. Trucks were expected to arrive the following day to take them all back to Berlin.

---

53 I met Elfriede in first grade. She was a sweet girl, always good-natured and very smart. She lived just a few houses away from me but she was never allowed to join my friends and me in any of our games. I used to see her looking out of her window, watching us. I felt sorry for her, although she never complained. We would walk together to and from school. Once in awhile, I would go to see her, mainly if I needed help with math homework, but I always felt very uncomfortable at their home. The parents were very old fashioned and strict. Her father was a teacher at a boy's school, poor guys!

They told them to go to bed, that they had nothing to be afraid of and nothing to worry about. When they got up in the morning, they found themselves all alone in the buildings. The safe in the office was open and empty. All the staff, teachers and leaders, including the guards, was gone, leaving the girls to themselves.

Panic broke out among them when they realized their situation—stranded in a hostile country with the Russian army not far away and no money and no identity cards. The school rules had been that the students' money and their ID cards were kept for them. If they needed money for something, they had to get it from the office. The girls were between ten and sixteen years old and they did not come just from my school. So there must have been many of them.

I was absolutely horrified, listening to her story and imagining their feelings at the time. She and Elfriede packed up a few things in a rucksack and left the school area along with some of the other girls, marching off into unfamiliar territory. They felt relieved when they came to a main road and found many German soldiers and refugees walking westward, all fleeing from the advancing Russian army. They joined them and for two or three days they were alright. But then the Russians caught up with them and what followed after that was disastrous. The Russians showed very little mercy. The two sisters became separated when the soldiers dragged the older one away, along with other girls her age. The Russian soldiers abused them before they were marched off to a railroad station and shipped to Siberia along with many other Germans, men and women. I could not hold back my tears as I heard this sad story. I felt so bad for Elfriede, her sister, and all the rest of the girls. They did not harm anyone. They did not deserve to be treated so horribly, so inhumanly. No one deserves such treatment.

I later met two more of my former classmates that had made it back to Berlin. It had taken them a long time. They had hidden out a lot and traveled at night. They felt at times as if they had been walking in circles and not getting anywhere. They too told me the same story as Elfriede's sister. How they found themselves alone and deserted and very frightened. A horrible experience for young girls. I was more than ever thankful that my dad had advised me not to go away. I missed two school years, seventh and eighth grade, but I would not have wanted to trade places with them.

When I registered at the public school I was told that I would be in eighth grade when the school reopened. What about seventh grade? Oh well, our attitudes had all changed. The things that we thought were important not so long ago, did not seem so any more.

Lehrter Bahnhof

I heard rumors that *Guterzuge* (freight trains) loaded full of German soldiers were arriving daily at Lehrter Bahhof, a railroad station that had been heavily damaged. The soldiers were sent being back to Germany because of ill health. They had been discharged from Russian labor camps. I went there several times in hopes that I might meet someone that may have known my dad, been with him or seen him in those camps or anywhere else. But I did not have any luck.

It was heartbreaking to see the condition those poor ragged soldiers were in, shuffling along shoeless, their feet wrapped in dirty rags. Many had open leg sores. I saw some awful looking feet, swollen and black, probably from frostbite. Others had amputated legs or arms and were hobbling along on makeshift crutches. Many of them were not even able to shuffle or hobble along by themselves anymore. They were carried out of the wagons and laid to the side on some straw. The Red Cross nurses tried to make them as comfortable as they could but they had very little to give. They carted the very sick ones away on small pull or push wagons to wherever they could find a vacant room in order to give them a little better shelter than the roofless railroad station. They even used the empty space in factories where the Russians had dismantled the machinery and shipped it off to Russia (before the other three Allied forces came to occupy the city).

I talked to some of the soldiers, but not everyone wanted to talk. Some just sat or lay on their sides with such forlorn expressions on their faces. They felt such despair and discouragement. They had been looking forward to returning to their homes, but now were told that they could not do so because the Russians, the Poles or the Czechs occupied their homeland. And they had no information about their families, their whereabouts, or whether they were still alive or not. It was a very sad situation. The cost of defeat!

I stopped going after awhile because it made me feel so sad and because I was not able to help. I never told my mother about these visits to the Lehrter Bahnhof. She just assumed that I was with my friends. If she had known about it, she would have wanted to come along and it would have been upsetting for her. She did not need any more of that sort of upset.

I read later on that 450,000 German soldiers, *Heimkehrer* (homecomers), arrived in Berlin between May and August of 1945. I do not know if this was a true statement or not. But there were many, many soldiers at the Lehrter Bahnhof.

Transvaalstrasse

Frau Girndt's sister Frieda stopped by one day and told us about an apartment that was unoccupied in her building. She wondered if we might be interested. My mother decided to go and have a look at it. She talked to the superintendent who told us that the tenant had served in the German Wehrmacht and that his family had been evacuated. We took a look at it and decided to give it a try. It was located on Transavaalstrasse, in the neighborhood named for the African colonies and one that had been spared from heavy destruction.

The superintendent gave us some paperwork to take along to our favorite place, the *Wohnungsamt*. The housing agency still was a busy place. We had to wait a long time before our number was called. When we walked through the open door my mother came to a sudden stop. She looked with disbelief in her eyes towards the center of the room.

When I followed her glance, I saw that terrible mean man sitting behind his desk just as if time had stood still. He must have recognized my mother, too, because he looked as if he wanted to quickly run away. But my mother did not give him that chance. She marched straight over to his desk, ignoring the clerk's call to come to her desk. She grabbed him by his tie, asking him, "Where is your uniform? Why are you not wearing it? And what are you doing here? After all the harm and pain that you inflicted on us and other people, you should be locked up!"

He made one attempt at telling her to calm down and not to cause such a scene. That was a mistake on his part because it really made my mother angry. The other employees came over and tried to pull my mother away. I told them to let her be, that she had all the reasons in the world to go after this obnoxious man, that he had made our life miserable, and that he had caused us lots of grief.

The commotion caused by my mother drew the attention of the other people in the waiting area. They started coming into the room, whereupon my mother proceeded to tell everyone about our encounter with this man. She told them how he had treated us when we refused the *Wohnungsamt* offer of a place to live in a *Ruine* and how he had thrown us out of the *Erdbunker* while he safely slept in his bunker apartment. When the people heard all the mean things this wicked man had done they were ready to throw him out. He picked up his *Aktenmappe* (portfolio) and was quickly escorted out of the office by two of the employees.

My poor mother was still very upset. I had never seen her so angry. All the stored anguish came to the surface when she saw this man sitting there after all the months we spent living in fear with nowhere to go. It had been too much for her to keep her anger in check. We never came across this man again. Perhaps they moved him to another district. I checked years later when I worked at city hall but he was gone from the *Wohnungsamt* in the Rathause am Wedding.[54]

Transavaalstrasse—Alt-Ruppin—Hamsterfahrten

After settling in on Transavaalstrasse, we decided to make a trip back to Alt-Ruppin to bring back some of our belongings we had stored there. During the spring and summer of 1943, my mother had started to take things to Alt-Ruppin for safe keeping, things like bed linens, towels, pillows, featherbeds and a few personal items like underwear and nightclothes. We were very thankful to have them now. My mother's foresight had been a good plan.

We inquired about train service and found that we could take a train from Stettiner Bahnhof to Neu-Ruppin, which we did. It left early in the morning and took us there without any problems along the route. We were warned beforehand that there was no guarantee of an uninterrupted trip. We were at the Russians' mercy. They might come along anytime during the trip and borrow the engine and return it whenever they wanted.[55]

We left the Neu-Ruppin station and walked to the police chief's house. He was the nephew of Frau Katerborn. She, along with his parents, had come to live with

---

54 **Entnazifizierung** People working in public positions had absolutely no choice but to join and belong to the Nazi party and most of them were not boastful about it. Right after the war ended people returned, if it was possible, to the jobs and positions that they had held before. But when everything became more organized the people holding any kind of government or city positions had to leave their jobs and take part in an *Entnazifizierung* (de-Nazification) program. If they were declared guiltless afterwards, they were reinstated in their jobs. I heard of some people leaving Berlin after the program—the ones who had been actively involved in the party—and settling in other parts of Germany. There they tried to start a new life where they were less well known. Maybe the ugly man from the *Wohnungsamt* was among them.

55 I do not know whether they really were in need of the engine at those times or if they were just being malicious. I did experience this game later on. It was very unpleasant being left sitting on a side track for hours, especially during the cold months of the year.

him when the Russians seized their house in Alt-Ruppin. She was so glad to see us and asked us all kinds of questions about Berlin. She did not seem to be the same anymore. She used to be so lively and quite imperious at times. It must have been a big disappointment for her, seeing all her hopes and predictions vanish with the arrival of the Russians instead of the Allied forces, and in particular the Americans.

Before we left her nephew the police chief came by and we talked to him. He wanted to know our reasons for coming back. After we told him, he asked us to stop by on our return and pick up a paper from him. He told us it would allow us free passage through the control gate at the railroad station.

We felt a little uneasy walking by ourselves through the woods but we did not have any trouble. The picture around the *Panzerkaserne* was unchanged. The Russians were still using the open-air toilet ditch. I never would have believed this display of unsanitary conditions had I not seen it with my own eyes. Everyone I knew appreciated modern systems, but not the Russians.[56]

Tante Grete greeted us warmly. They were all still living in the storage building. Nothing had changed in their life style. We spent the night with them and left the following morning loaded up with potatoes, vegetables, bread and some of our belongings. I do not recall the reason for not riding the train from and to Alt-Ruppin, but we never did. We always traveled the Neu-Ruppiner route.

We stopped at the police chief's house on our way back and picked up the piece of paper he had written out for us. We did not realize how much this piece of paper meant until we arrived at the Bahnhof. We asked when to expect a train and we were told that they were expecting one, hopefully soon. We purchased our tickets and approached the police checkpoint. The German police looked at our piece of paper and gave us an inquisitive look, but then proceeded to wave us through. That was when we realized that we were able to walk through without being checked, but everyone else was stopped.

It was a mean game they were playing, acting like bandits and stealing from their countrymen. They had instituted their own rules and procedures and there was absolutely nothing anyone could do about it. If the police needed or wanted

---

56 No wonder we had an outbreak of typhoid fever. I remember when we took turns being sick with a high fever and diarrhea and awful abdominal pains. The walk to the outhouse was sheer agony. Every step I took was painful. It was easier just sitting on a pail. It was exceptionally bad for an older person like Tante Grete's mother. It took her much longer to get over it.

any of the items that the people carried, they just confiscated the stuff. People from the cities who were coming back from the farming communities carrying bags full of potatoes had to worry that their potatoes would be taken away from them at the station. They were a cruel bunch. They showed no compassion, no matter how the people begged to leave them something to take home to their families. And to make matters worse, the people not only had to worry about this checkpoint but also the ones upon entering Berlin at Bahnhof Friedrichstrasse or Stettiner Bahnhof. It was a struggle in every way to survive all the hardships that the end of the war brought us.

We learned to take good care of that very valuable piece of paper. The police chief had done us a big favor and we were forever grateful. It spared us a lot of grief and trouble. It bothered us a little when we noticed the people standing nearby and looking at us curiously, but in time we learned to ignore them and became less concerned. Everyone, including us, had to look out for oneself in order to survive.

When the train arrived it was already full, but we managed to get on with a lot of pushing and shoving. We were standing so tightly together that we could not move or fall if we had tried. In times to come we took many train rides like that, never ever getting a seat to sit down upon. That time we were lucky to be inside of the car. Many times the only place left to ride was either on top or standing on a small running board alongside of the car.

I tried the ride on top of the car a couple of times. The roof was flat in the middle, which made it easier for sitting. Plus there was a place to tie the straps from my knapsack or bag to keep them from sliding off. The ride on the top of the car on a warm day was rather pleasant, much better than being cooped up with all the people on the dark and smelly inside of the boarded-up car. But it also had an unpleasant side when the wind blew the hot cinders from the locomotive back in our direction and into our faces and hair. It also became a little scary when we were approaching the suburbs of Berlin. There we had to lay flat to avoid all the wires criss-crossing over us, which was not a good feeling. I heard about quite a few accidents in which people were swept off and injured by the wires. They were very sad ghostly stories.

We also rode many times standing on the running board with one arm looped through a metal bar that was attached to the side of the car. When we did so we would have to continue to wear our *Rucksack* (knapsack). Then our biggest fear was falling asleep. We would watch one another very closely.

A trip to the country usually took three days, and sometimes as long as four days. If we were lucky, made all the right connections, and did not run into problems or troubles, we could make the tip in two days, but it did not happen very often. Riding the train was no longer a fun trip. People had become very ill mannered. Politeness, courtesy and friendliness had all vanished.

We would leave Berlin before daybreak, arrive in Neu-Ruppin, and then board the connecting train—a small train running back and forth between the little farming villages. We would get off at the third stop and walk as fast as we possibly could in order to get ahead of all the other people who got off the train. It was about two miles from the station to the village.

We had one place we liked going to first. The old Oma who greeted us at the door gave us potatoes almost every time. She never talked to us. She just listened to our sad story of having nothing to eat and then would nod to us to follow her into the barn where she would shovel the potatoes into our bags. She never took the money we offered, shaking her head "nein, nein". The money was not of any value to her, but we did not have anything else to offer in trade. She was a kind and caring old lady and I hope that she has found a nice resting-place in heaven. She deserved to be rewarded.

If our efforts worked out well for us then we would walk back to the station and hope for a train to come along and take us back to Neu-Ruppin. There we would spend the night in the waiting room until the next day or whenever a train arrived that would take us back to Berlin.

Hamsterfahrten (hamster journeys) became an important part of our life. *Hamstere*, we were called—the people traveling from the cities to the country in search for food. The poor overrun farmers would quickly lock up their houses when they saw us coming. Some would treat us down right mean, sending us on our way in tears and telling us to go back home and get busy planting potatoes in our roads. We understood their situation. It must have been frustrating for them dealing with *Hamstere* knocking on their doors every day asking for potatoes and other things. But we did not have any other solution to our food shortage problem. It was an awful feeling being hungry and having nothing to eat.

We had many *Hamsterfahrten* adventures. Some were good but most of them were not so good. Encountering a mean person happened to us different times, but I remember one particular day which bothered us a lot. We had been unlucky, walking from one *Bauernhof* to the next without getting any potatoes. When we came upon this farmer's house he was standing in the yard. He appeared friendly enough, so we approached him with our request for some potatoes. He listened to our story, acted almost compassionate, but then he gave us his advice for how to plant our own potatoes with an ugly smirk on his face. I have never forgotten that mean incident. It was better to knock on closed doors and get no response than to be treated like that.

Without the potato supplement to add to our daily allowance of 1100 calories, we would have starved to death. A lot of the older people did. We always shared some with Oma and Opa. It helped them survive on the meager rations. The potatoes we brought home would last us three to four weeks if we rationed them very carefully. If the potatoes were to be eaten peeled and cooked, they had to be washed and scrubbed clean first. The potato peelings were used for another meal. They were cooked until tender and then put through a meat grinder, formed into patties, and fried. The fried patties were not too bad. Eating reheated patties was not so good, but was at least filling.

On another one of our *Hamsterfahrten* my mother and I went with Hanna and Ursula. Hanna was an elderly widowed woman who lived in our building. Her son had been killed in Russia. She had lost her home during a bombing raid and came to live with her brother. Hanna was in poor physical shape. She walked with a limp because of one leg being shorter than the other, plus she only had one good eye. But despite these handicaps, she always insisted on coming along on the *Hamster* trips. She really was more of a hindrance to us, but we felt bad turning her down. We had to be very aggressive and bold when it came to getting on the trains that usually arrived already full of people. Having Hanna to look after was quite an additional burden.

On this particular trip we had been successful in obtaining some potatoes, but Hanna, as she often did, had taken on more than she could handle, refusing to listen to our advice. We were walking towards the *Bahnhof* when we met people coming back from the train station. They told us that the police were at the station and confiscating everything, all the *Hamster* goods, from everyone. These people were trying to walk to the next railroad station or perhaps all the way to Neu-Ruppin via the *Landweg* (path) that the farmers used to get to their fields. We decided to join them. We did not want to lose our potatoes to those bandits.

It had become dark by this time and we were worried that the police might come looking for us or for other *Hamstere*, riding their motorcycles with sidecars. After we started out on this path, we heard the sound of a motorcycle a couple of times and we saw the headlights shining in our direction. We all jumped into the ditch, trying to hide.

The whole situation made us very nervous. We were constantly turning around to check behind us. As we moved farther away from the village we felt much less worried and somewhat relieved. However, we were falling behind the group and soon found ourselves walking alone, just the four of us. The rest of the people disappeared into the night.

Hanna was holding us back. The path had big ruts in it and she kept stumbling from one side to the other, complaining loudly about everything, but especially her heavy load. We had no other choice but to help her carry it. There were lots of stars out that night which made it a little lighter. As we were walking along quietly, everyone lost in their own thoughts, we were startled when Hanna started lamenting loudly, calling to her deceased husband and son in heaven, accusing them of leaving her alone at a time like this. She carried on a regular conversation with her ghosts. "Do you see me from up there? Do you see how I am struggling? You promised to look after me when Father died." She kept this up until we reached the main road. We just let her be, poor soul.

We did not know what time it was. Nobody carried a watch anymore for fear that the Russians would take it away. We also had no idea where the train station was located.

All of a sudden we heard the sound of a car. We did not have time to find a hiding place. There we stood next to a tree by the side of the road praying that they would drive past without seeing us. We were certain that they were Russians. No one else drove vehicles on the roads.

Unfortunately they did see us—and they pulled to a stop. But when the driver rolled down the window we were pleasantly surprised to hear him speak German. He asked us where we were going and if we needed a ride. Inside the car were two young former German army soldiers, still dressed in the German uniform. They were the drivers for a Russian officer and were on their way to Neu-Ruppin to pick him up.

Their story seemed a bit odd to us, but they made such an earnest impression that we chose to believe them. We decided that Hanna and Ursula should ride along with them. They should also take our bags. That would be a big help to us while we walked on to Neu-Ruppin. Just before they drove away, the driver told us that they would come back for us if they had enough time left to meet their appointment.

With Hanna taken care of and our bags being carried by the car, we believed that we could quickly walk to Neu-Ruppin. To our surprise the two young drivers did soon come back for us. We were very glad after all that we would not have to walk to rest of the way. We were especially grateful when we realized that the road went right by the Russian occupied barracks. That was not a safe place to walk by after dark.

The young men told us that they both came from an area near Stettin, which was now occupied by the Poles. They were unable to return to their homes and they had no information about their families. They used to drive for German officers and now they were driving the Russian officers around. Very strange things happened in the days after the war.

They took us to the *Bahnhof* where we found Hanna, Ursula and the group of people we had been walking with earlier all gathered in the waiting room. They were clustered around the stove, roasting potatoes. Ursula already had some ready for us to eat. We were thankful, as we were very hungry. It had been a long day with only a couple slices of bread to eat. The potatoes tasted good. The coal fire had burned the skin black and made them crispy.

The larger group had taken up a potato donation for the poor people who had lost theirs to the bandits at the *Bahnhof*. By us doing so, they had at least something to take back home with them. The entire effort of traveling to the country and searching for food was very stressful. Too often we returned with just a few potatoes, hardly enough to last long enough to make it all worthwhile.

Of course we were not home yet. There still was the possibility of another control the following day, performed by the local *Polizei Banditen* (police bandits). Even if the local police bandits left us alone, we really were not out of danger of losing our potatoes and other goods until we arrived on our own doorstep. There were still other checkpoints to fear upon arrival at Stettiner Bahnhof or Bahnhof Fridrichstrasse. Sometimes, just to avoid these last few controls, we got off the *Eisenbahn* (train) at Oranienburg and rode the S-Bahn to Waidmannslust. There we stopped off at Oma and Opa's place. By doing it that way it was less worrisome. There were fewer checkpoints along the S-Bahn as compared to the train stations. Train passengers were more likely to come from the countryside, while S-Bahn passengers came more from the suburbs of Berlin.

Der Wartesaal—The Waiting Room

The waiting room was an empty room offering no comfort whatsoever, only a hard cold floor to sit or lay on. I do not know what happened to the benches, chairs and tables that used to be in the room. They were all gone. But the room did provide us with shelter, especially during the cold weather. It also protected us from the Russians who were always roaming around the station. The toilets, however, were in a separate building. It was not advisable to go there after dark and never alone. We heard some awful screams for help coming from there. They were very intimidating cries. Very few women were brave enough to step outside of the door, much less walk towards the dimly lit toilet building.

In the middle of the waiting room sat a small iron stove that gave out a lot of heat. It was fueled with *Eier oder stein kohle* (egg or rock coal, pit coal). Somebody always started the fire for us in the evening, leaving a pail full of coal sitting by the stove. It probably was the station master. He lived above the waiting room. It was very thoughtful of him and very much appreciated.

Right next to our waiting room was the *Bahnhof's* restaurant, reserved for Russian officers. The restaurant's big glass window was covered up with plywood except for a small opening in the center. I remember one particular day when Ursula and I had gone by ourselves on the *Hamsterfahrt*. The Russians had stopped our train and taken the engine away (probably for a joyride). When they finally returned it, we were late arriving in Neu-Ruppin and we missed our train to the country. That meant we had to spend the night in the *Wartesaal* until the following morning when we could again resume our journey. We considered ourselves lucky to have found a spot on the floor against the wall. It gave us a little support for our backs during the long, long night.[57]

We were both very hungry. We had brought along potato soup in a metal container, but we had saved it until we arrived at the *Bahnhof*, which was a big mistake. It had been made early in the morning by grating raw peeled potatoes into salted boiling water. While the soup was hot it was thick like pudding. Only by the time we reached the *Bahnhof* it had become a cold, runny and unappetizing soup. I had wanted to eat it hours ago, but Ursula kept telling me to wait, reminding me that it was all we had to eat. Now we were both sorry to have waited.

---

57   Many times we did not have the wall to support us and we would sit back to back on the floor, supporting each other. Like I said, it was a long night.

We walked outside, feeling pretty low. I cannot explain what happened next. Somehow I got the courage to walk up to the restaurant window and look inside. I saw the Russians sitting at small tables and eating. Whatever it was that they were eating, it looked good.

Ursula kept asking me, "What do you see?" Just after I told her, one officer who was sitting by himself and close to the window looked up and spotted me. I pointed to the loaf of bread on his table and mouthing the Russian word for bread—*Klebba*—and then pointed at myself. Ursula was ready to run away and so was I, especially when I saw him stand up. But we saw him take the loaf of bread from the table as he walked towards the door. I made her stand by me, threatening that I would not share with her if she ran away.

I was shaking badly with fright, but I managed to say "thank you" when he handed the bread to me. I did not understand what he said, but he smiled at us and then went back into the restaurant.

Once we regained our composure we were very grateful to have the round loaf of bread. We did not have a knife to cut it, but it did not matter. We simply broke off pieces to eat. We drew some curious looks from the people in the waiting room when we came in with the bread, but we ignored them and enjoyed our gift from a goodhearted Russian. The loaf of bread lasted us throughout our trip.

I do not remember ever again taking such a daring chance. Counting on a Russian soldier's good-natured conduct and understanding of our plight was a risk. I had learned to fear and mistrust the Russians ever since we had left our safe haven with the Americans. I tried to stay away from them as far as I possibly could. But it felt good knowing that there were some decent ones among them.

There was another day when something very unusual happened, especially considering the times in which we all lived. Ursula and I were walking from the village on our way to the *Bahnhof* when we decided to take a rest alongside the road. We were wishing that it was late summer and that the apple trees lining the roadside could give us some apples to eat. We heard the train whistle and not long after some people came walking past us. One woman, walking by herself, looked at us and nodded a greeting, which we returned. She then stopped a little ways past us and took something from her bag. She walked back to us and asked us if we would like to have her sandwiches. She had not eaten them and did not wish to take them back home with her. We were so surprised with her kind offer that it made us speechless for a moment, but we recovered and thanked her profusely for the sandwiches. We could not believe our good fortune. Just when we were wishing for something to eat this kind woman came along and gave us not just plain slices of bread, but real ham sandwiches. We enjoyed every bite of them.

I remember one other *Hamsterfahrt* quite clearly. It probably took place in late 1945 or perhaps early 1946. Again it was the four of us on this trip—my mother, Hanna, Ursula and I. Ursula was the one from her family who usually went on these. Her father and older brother worked and they could not take three to four days off from work to go on these trips. Jobs were hard to find and they had to do the best they could to hang on to their jobs. Her mother needed to stay home to look after her younger brother. She came along once in awhile, but only if she had someone to watch the boy.

When we arrived in Neu-Ruppin, my mother walked to Alt-Ruppin to get the rest of our things from Tante Grete. The remaining three of us boarded the train to the country. We had agreed to meet later in the evening in the *Wartesaal* at the station.

We had a hard time finding someone who would sell us some potatoes. They were all more interested in trading than money. Even at the old Oma's house no one came to the door. We had almost given up when we decided to go back to the Oma's house for one last attempt. This time she came to the door and nodded "yes" to our request for potatoes. She lit a lantern and motioned for us to follow her to the barn. We were so thankful that we would not have to return without any potatoes.

It had become dark and we knew we needed to get moving to make it back to the station. We had not gone very far, not more than half a mile, when Hanna started complaining about her heavy load. It was the same old story. She had taken on more than she could handle. Ursula and I took one bag and carried it between us, but we found it too much for us. We talked her into staying behind while we walked on to the station to drop off our bags. We promised that one of us would walk back and help carry her load. She agreed to our proposal and we left with the best of intentions to keep our promise. Only we ran into a problem when we arrived at the station. We confirmed after knocking on the stationmaster's door until he finally appeared that the last train had left and there would not be another one until Monday. What alarming news! It was Friday evening and we were stranded for a whole weekend. What were we to do?

I knew I could not possibly stay there. I had to at least get back to Neu-Ruppin. My mother would be worried sick. Ursula's family would also be worried about her. So we decided to walk to Neu-Ruppin, breaking the promise we had made to Hanna. We knew that she could not walk with us for that distance. We hoped that she would understand our situation.

We got onto the main road. It was the first time for us walking to Neu-Ruppin. We were moving right along at a steady pace when the sole loosened up on my right boot.[58] The loose sole changed my walking style. I had to pick my foot up with every step and then slap it onto the pavement. This was quite awkward and tiresome.

A couple of times we had to get off the road and hide in the trees when we heard vehicles coming. I am certain they were driven by Russians. We would move slowly around the trees to avoid being caught in the headlights of the vehicles. More anxious moments. I have not mentioned it often, but believe me I prayed often to God at moments like these, calling upon Him for help and guidance. I had been in some very frightening situations, but some help always came along. God did not forsake me or those I traveled with. He sent his angels to guide us and to protect us.

We walked through one small farming village, never seeing a living soul. It was not a very dark night. There was a little moonlight. Just a little way outside of the village we heard loud voices, Russian voices, coming towards us. We turned around and ran back to the village as fast as our load and my loose boot sole would allow us.

We stopped at the first farmhouse. We could see a little light on the inside, but as soon as we knocked on the window, the light went out. Everybody had become so fearful. We walked into the farmyard, trying to find a hiding place. We left our bags sitting on the ground and crawled up a small rickety ladder. It brought us right into a *Huhnerstall* (chicken coop). The chickens acted a little annoyed about our appearance, but they calmed down quickly.

We stayed up there a long while or at least it seemed so to us. We finally found enough courage to climb back down to have a look. We looked up and down the road and at first our imagination got the best of us. We saw movements behind every tree. We finally told ourselves that we were being silly, there was nobody waiting for us to come out of our hiding place.

---

58   They were the horrible Russian boots that the woman soldier threw back at me after stealing my pretty pair of pumps and walking off with them. I had been forced to wear them since my one and only pair of shoes had a big hole in their sole. My mother had been cutting new soles out of cardboard, but they only worked when the roads were dry.

When we came to the next village Ursula gave out on me. She could not go on anymore. We tried to see if we could rest for awhile, but as soon as we knocked on the door of the house, the lights we had seen went out again. We walked back out towards the road and Ursula sat down on a little bank by the entrance. The weight of her *Rucksack* pulled her backward into a ditch full of snow. It was not funny, but it did make me laugh. She then started to cry loudly.

I had a hard time pulling her out of the ditch. She looked like a snowman. Suddenly we heard someone behind us. When we turned around we found a young man standing there with a quizzical look on his face. We told him our story and that we were looking for someplace to rest for awhile. He offered to walk with us and help with our bags. He told us that it was too dangerous for us to walk by ourselves at this hour of the night past the Russian barracks. He went back to the house to get a coat and off we marched.

He told us that he was the son of the farmer and that he had lost an arm during the war. He had just recently returned from a POW camp in Russia. When we came closer to Neu-Ruppin, he told us to stay close to him and ignore whatever came along. We were to just keep our heads down and let him handle everything.

It must have been close to midnight but near the *Kaserne* we noticed here and there Russians popping out of the dark shadows. They would come right up to us and say things, but we did as we were told and kept our heads down. One of them even touched my arm. I ignored him and kept myself close to our new friend. He would say something to them in Russian, whereupon they would laugh and leave us. We never would have made it to the station without the help of that young man.

My mother was so relieved to see us walk into the waiting room. So was I. All I remember vaguely is thanking the young man for bringing us there safely. That is all I recall because I just collapsed in a heap on the floor. I was totally exhausted. My mother tried to wake me to get me to eat something but I did not respond. I did not wake up until towards morning when I heard a voice that sounded a lot like Hanna announcing loudly, "Here I am you good people! I made it!"

I opened my eyes and sure enough there she was. We were glad to see her! She seemed a little distant toward us at first, but after we explained to her our reasons for not coming back for her, she acted alright again. Then she told us her story about what happened after we left.

When she suspected that we were not returning, she left her bags by the roadside and walked back towards the village. I could not believe it when I heard her say that she went to the first house on the left, the one that sat alone, all by itself. We all walked a big circle around that house, doing our best to avoid it. We all knew that the police lived there. She said the house was all lit up and she could hear people talking and laughing as if a party was going on. The man who came to the door to answer her knock acted very friendly. He listened to her story and then he offered to walk back with her. They would get her bags and then decide what to do next. He called for another man to come along and off they went.

When they returned to the house he told Hanna that he was the police official for that village and therefore authorized to confiscate her goods. His advice to her was to start walking before he changed his mind and took stronger action against her. "*Hamstern* was considered unlawful," he declared. Poor Hanna, she had fallen into the hands of one of the police bandits, the cruelest of our own countrymen. What other description should I apply to these men, taking potatoes from an old woman and sending her off alone into the night?

We really felt sorry that she had this bad experience. But we knew we could not have made the trip with her, much less while carrying her bags. And knowing Hanna, she would not have left them behind willingly. Ursula and I agreed to share some of our potatoes with her so she did not go home totally empty-handed.

All told it was a very unpleasant experience.

School in the Winter of 1945–1946

I came to wish that I had registered at a *Schule* (school) located in my new neighborhood instead of the one I attended. It was very depressing to go back to the old neighborhood, always being reminded of the war and the devastation. It also was a long walk from Tranvaalstrasse to the end of Seestrasse, although the transportation network was slowly starting to work again. After a while I was able to ride the streetcar for part of the way.

I had hoped to find a few of the girls I knew from before the school had closed, but I did not know any of my classmates except for my friend Ursula. The eighth grade class was taught by the school's principal, a man who had spent time in a concentration camp for political reasons. He was a very bitter and discontented teacher. I do not remember seeing him ever smile.

Actually he fit right into the environment surrounding us at the school. The classroom looked quite dismal. The windows were covered with plywood except for a small piece of glass in the center that let in a little bit of daylight. On gray and overcast days it would be dark in the room, especially during the winter months. Only occasionally—thank to the Russian's generosity—would the electricity supply be restored so that we could turn on the lights. The electric power plant, the gas works and the coal mines were all located in the east sector and the east zone. They were all under Russian control. Such a great arrangement! They were totally in charge. They could do as they wished in supplying power and gas to the American, British and French sectors within Berlin. At that time, the people in the Russian sector were better cared for with food and heating material than we were in the other sectors.

We did have a blackboard. The principal had the one and only book for whatever class he taught. We did not have any paper or pencils to work with. Later on, we were given cut up German military maps (the backsides were blank) and pens to write with and we were taught to be very frugal with the material. Until then, our lessons were more or less done verbally, with our tests done out loud in question and answer sessions.

At first it was not so bad sitting in the unheated classroom, but then winter rolled in with a vengeance, intending to freeze us. That winter brought us such awful cold and freezing weather. There was lots of snow and an icy wind. It became almost unbearable. I would arrive at school half frozen. The wind would blow right through my clothing. I had several layers of newspapers stuffed into the Russian boots and my feet still felt cold. When it snowed on our way to school, it would become an ice crust on our coats and hats that never melted while we were there. We shivered and sat huddled close together. Trying to comprehend what the principal was saying was really difficult. Periodically we had to stand up and do a few warm-up exercises, moving our arms, jumping up and down, and walking around the room. I remember asking myself, "What am you doing here? What is the purpose in all of this? Why did you leave your warm bed for this?"

While we sat there so cold and hungry we had to sit and listen to our teacher's disturbing lectures. He would talk about all the evil and harm the Germans had done to other people and then tell us over and over again how ashamed we should feel for being German! I was very confused about it all. During my first years in school I had been told to feel proud to be a German. I had been told about all the good things the Germans had done and now I was being told the opposite. I did not know what to believe any more. Until the war ended I had never heard of the concentration camps, only about the labor camps. The principal was very bitter and full of hate. I felt sorry that he had been imprisoned because he disagreed with Hitler. But we believed that now he was wrongly blaming us. We were only children. It made all of us very uncomfortable.

The Red Cross had set up a kitchen in the school's entrance hall. Every day they would cook big pots full of different kinds of soup. It smelled delicious. The smell drifted throughout the school, making us realize more and more how hungry we were. But we were only treated to the smell. The soup was prepared for the younger children, up to about the age of ten years old. Only if they had some left over would it be distributed among the older children. I was never fortunate enough or lucky enough to get some of the soup. If this was not torture then I do not know what would be.

As much as I had always liked going to school and had missed it very much during the last two years of war, I really did not care anymore. I had lost all interest. I missed many days of school. I either was absent because I had gone on a *Hamsterfahrt* or the bad weather and the lack of shoes and clothing kept me from going.[59]

Care packets shipped from America were arriving in the city, but were mostly distributed in the American Sector to families with more than two or three children. I thought it was the same old story that we experienced during Hitler's rule. Families with one or two children needed the food and clothing just as much as families with four and five children. It was not fair. And then so many of the care packets ended up in the wrong hands, their contents being sold on the black market.

At some point our class was given three pairs of shoes. There were about thirty girls in the class. The shoes were beautiful high-heeled pumps. They were not at all what we needed but whoever was lucky enough to get a pair could use them in trade. The teacher made up some kind of raffle to at least give us all a chance. The lucky winners then took the shoes to the recently reopened shoe stores and offered them in trade for more practical shoes.[60]

---

59 I would like to mention that despite the cold weather and my inadequate clothing, I was never sick. I never even had a cold. It is difficult to figure out. Maybe the germs were also frozen and it kept them from infecting us. Or maybe they just took pity on us poor suffering creatures.

60 I remember that the stores charged a small fee for handling the trades. It was better to find a store in a lesser destroyed area in order to have a better selection.

The principal told me one day that because I had been absent from school so often that I did not need to come for my *Abgangs Zeugnis* (final report card) because he would not know what to write on it. I am sorry to admit that he was right, and so I did not stop to pick up a blank piece of paper. My *Abgangs Zeugnis* was not going to make our life easier or better, or keep us from starving and freezing. The tomorrows looked so bleak and hopeless, even more so now than during the war years. At least then we were able to hope for better days with the end of the war.

The French Occupation

Living in the French sector was very hard for the first two years after the war. We were reminded daily of who were the victors and who were the losers. We were issued ration cards, but that did not allow us to go to the stores and buy food items because the stores were only open when they had something to sell, especially the grocery stores. Just like when we lived in Alt-Ruppin we would have to watch for any activity which might mean something had been delivered. If we saw the shutters being pulled up we would quickly run and stand in line without even knowing what might be for sale.

It was the same at most of the other stores, too, except for the bakery. Bread was available there with coupons. The produce store had potatoes most of the times and cabbage leaves from *Weisskohl, Wirsingkohl* and *Rotkohl* (white, savoy and red cabbage). The French ate the good part of the cabbage and we got the outer leaves that were normally fed to the animals. During the winter months the potatoes were mostly frozen. They smelled rotten and tasted likewise. The rutabagas too would be frozen, but not as bad tasting as the potatoes. It would be years before we could buy quality dairy or meat products.

The butcher shop hardly ever had something to sell except for some soup bones now and then. The butcher always had a big barrel sitting outside of the store. The first time I lifted the lid off to see what it held I was really sickened. The barrel was full of herring fish heads floating in this horribly smelly brine. It was disgusting. Again, we were fed the waste while the French dined on the fish. My mother inquired about the fish heads, asking what we could use them for. She was told that they would add flavor to soups or gravy. We put our disgust of the smell aside and bought a couple of them to try changing our otherwise tasteless gravy. Even though we liked eating fish we did not care for the result.

The French considered this cruel behavior towards us as retaliation for all the bad things the German soldiers had done to them while they were stationed in France. Perhaps the soldiers who had been involved would have understood and been willing to accept the retaliation, but I had not done anything to the French for which I should be punished. As a result I felt angry and had a lot of resentment towards them.

They treated us very badly. On the corner of Transvaalstrasse and Mullerstrasse was a restaurant that the French had taken over. In front of the place stood several open garbage cans. Before the war it had never been allowed to have garbage cans at the front of a house or restaurant. The cook, a big greasy-looking guy, would lean out of an open window and light up a cigarette. He would take a couple of pulls and then throw it out into the street. As soon as some poor German man would bend down to pick it up, an armed *Gendarme* would come running out of the restaurant and challenge the German, shoving and pushing him around. The French in the restaurant would laugh and then repeat this act over and over. They got big kicks out of this. Standing in line at the grocery store, we were able to watch their game quite clearly. Sadly, they carried on much worse when they noticed people were watching them play their cruel game.

The same game was played at the garbage cans. The cook would come outside with a bowl full of something and dump it slowly into the can, all the while looking around to see if anyone was watching. Woe to anyone who tried to retrieve something from the garbage can after he went back inside. I once saw a man led away by the *Gendarmerie*, accused of stealing from the French. They were playing a mean game with people who were hungry.

Tegeler Wald 1945

As I mentioned earlier, winter arrived in 1945 with a vengeance, bringing us very cold weather. The Russians announced to the public that they would not be distributing coal to individual homes in our sector. Meanwhile they supplied the people in their sector with coal.

Berlin had many big parks like Humboldthain and big forests full of trees. The Americans and the British gave permission to the people to cut trees which they had marked in the parks and forests of their sectors. But the people in the French sector were treated with malicious cruelty. I am certain that a controlled felling of timber could have been done in our sector as well. Instead, the French announced that they would not allow any trees to be cut down in the parks or in the forest. In fact, we were not even allowed to go into the forest to gather wood off the ground. They patrolled the forest with guard dogs to enforce their decree.[61]

My mother and a couple of our neighbors decided to take a chance and go into the forest after dark and cut down a few trees. We did not know what else to do to keep from freezing and to allow us to cook something to eat on the stove. During the daytime hours we looked for suitable trees, focusing mostly on the smaller birch trees. An elderly neighbor lent us a small wagon to haul the wood back to the house and return we would share with him some of the wood we cut. It would take us all night. The wagon did not hold very much and we would have to make several trips to get all our wood back to the house.

The forest was within walking distance but it was also very close to the French barracks at the Quartier Napoleon. It was a dangerous undertaking. We would stumble around in the dark, trying to be as quiet as possible. A few times we heard dogs barking very close to where we were working. We were all afraid that they would find us. And on top of everything, we also had to worry about being seen and turned in by ordinary Germans. I could easily imagine myself locked up in a French jail.

The wagon finally gave out on us and we ended up pulling the logs back to the house. We would not cut the trunks into short pieces. We would tie a rope around the long trunks and then around our waists and pull them to our house. It was quite strenuous.

When we made a fire with the wood in the oven of our small room it often did not want to burn. It would just smolder and smoke because it was so fresh. But we would sit in front of the open oven door and watch it smolder despite our burning eyes. Those fires really did not give out much heat. It would have been better mixed with coal, but we had none.

Our apartment was on the fourth floor, with the attic immediately above us. There were double windows in our apartment and they still had glass in them, but they were all frosted over. It was very cold. We were so thankful that we had the nice thick featherbed which my mother had stored in Alt-Ruppin. I do not know what we would have done without it.

The Heinz Family Comes Home

We must have been living on Transvaalstrasse for about two months when one day someone knocked on the front door. Before us stood a very ragged and

---

61   Several years later they would build the new Tegel airport right in the middle of Tegeler Wald, cutting down hundreds of trees to make room for a runway.

haggard looking man. He looked just like the poor soldiers I had seen at Lehrter Bahnhof.

"Guten Tag. Ich bin Herr Heinz und ich wohne hier. Wo ist meine Familie?" ("Good day. I am Mr. Heinz and I live here. Where is my family?")

He was visibly shaken when we told him that his family was not there. Even though we had been expecting this at any time, we were hoping for our sakes that it would not happen so soon. Still, we were happy for him that he was able to return home after spending time in a POW camp in Russia.

He was a quiet man and kept to himself. I tried to talk to him a few times. I wanted to ask him questions about the POW camp and Russia, but he did not want to talk about those places. We left him alone.

It must have been two or three weeks later when his wife and their two children arrived home. They were a pitiful sight, dirty and exhausted. They had been on the road for weeks, making their way back home from Czechoslovakia, their place of evacuation. It was a very tearful reunion. Mr. Heinz met his fourteen or fifteen-month-old son for the first time and was reunited with his four-year-old daughter.

My mother returned to our favorite place—the *Wohnungsamt* (the housing agency). We had to find another place live. Our living arrangements became quite troublesome and very inconvenient once Mrs. Heinz and her children returned to the apartment. They still had some coal and wood stored in their cellar, enough to have a little fire going in the kitchen stove. The Heinz family decided to move their beds into the kitchen where it was a little warmer than their bedroom. It made the kitchen extremely crowded. My mother had just enough room to step into the kitchen and stand by the stove, which fortunately was located right by the door. It was then a challenge to get from the stove to the sink because of all their stuff. It was easier to go to the bathroom sink instead of trying to cross the kitchen. The living arrangements simply did not work any longer.

Not long after Mrs. Heinz and the children returned I was again scratching my head. My mother checked and found some head lice. Twice in one year, how lucky could I be? We were fortunate this time. It was not as bad as the first time. Perhaps the cold weather helped. The lice did not act as lively as in the summer. I knew that Mr. Heinz had been through a delousing station. All the returning POW's were required to do so. But Mrs. Heinz and her children had not and they were scratching their heads a lot. My mother mentioned our problem to Mrs. Heinz but she shrugged it off, denying any lice problems. Oh well, whatever!

The housing agency was having difficulty finding a place for us to live. We wanted to stay in the same area but that was looking hopeless. The French had taken several housing blocks for themselves and their families. What an unforeseen outcome for the people who had kept their homes throughout the years of war and bombing only to be forced by the French to leave their homes and all their belongings behind, several months after the war ended. It was another sign of the French cruelty and not much different from what had happened to us in Alt-Ruppin when the Russians needed lodging for their officers.[62]

I think that if I had been given a choice I would have preferred losing everything to the bombardment. It was difficult enough walking by a pile of rubble that once was our home, but I would have felt much worse walking by my home and seeing strangers living in it and using my things while I was homeless and on the street. In any event, many more people had joined the search for a place to live.

1945 Comes to an End

1945 was the year that brought us the long awaited peace and the end of the horrible and senseless war. The war was over and we were thankful to have survived it. We were grateful to be able to live a peaceful life again. It gave us new hope to look forward to be reunited with my dad and to again live as a family, together and not separated.

1945 was also a year full of sadness, misery, hardship, uncertainty, fear and danger. We had coped with the loss of our second home and then survived our incredible journey from Berlin to Alt-Ruppin to the American lines and then back again. Now we were hungry and cold, without proper clothing or shoes, and once again searching for a place to live.

If I had a birthday celebration in December of 1945, I do not remember anything about it. If there was a Christmas celebration that December of 1945, my mother and I could never recall it.

---

62   Too bad the Americans and the British did not leave more of the residential areas intact instead of destroying them all. Many years later the Americans built their own community in the Grunewald Forest. The Germans called it "Klein Amerika" ("Little America"). As far as I know, the French never built their own community. They continued living in the confiscated German homes until they returned home to France.

Willi Wittmutz camping in Tegeler Forest
sometime prior to marrying Frieda.

Frieda Wittmutz, Willi's mother and "Oma" to Charlotte.
This photo was taken on Mother's Day in 1936.

Willi Wittmutz's father's name was also Willi Wittmutz.
When Charlotte's father married Frieda Ida Luise she became Frieda Wittmutz.
Therefore, both Charlotte's parents and her grandparents
bore the names Willi and Frieda Wittmutz.

Willi Wittmutz in a more formal pose, taken perhaps in 1937.

Gerhard Wittmutz, Charlotte's favorite Uncle.

Frieda and Willi Wittmutz, Charlotte's "Oma" and "Opa"

Charlotte Lowe.
This second grade school picture was taken in 1940
at the Volksschule at Grenzstrasse am Humboldthain.

Willi Wittmutz (top center) and three comrades.
This photo was taken May 21, 1940 in Berlin at Potsdam.

This photo was taken at the hospital in Finland,
possibly at Jywaskyla, Christmas, 1941. Willi Wittmutz is
second from the right, third row up from the bottom.

Willi Wittmutz is second from the left, with rifle in his hand,
in this photo of him and a group of his comrades outside a bunker in Finland.

This photo of Charlotte, wearing a new outfit, was made
to mail as a gift to her father for his birthday.

Charlotte's Confirmation photo, March of 1946.

A photo of Charlotte's step-sister, Lieschen, taken in 1946.

Charlotte in October of 1947.

These two photographs of the Flakturm at Humboldthain were taken by Stanley Lowe in 1951. This Flakturm, located on the edge of Humboldthain Park, often served as Frieda and Charlotte's shelter during Allied bombing attacks. With concrete and steel reinforced walls more than one foot thick, it offered protection at any one time to as many as 18,000 civilians.

During the war the Flakturm stood six or seven stories high, towering over the park. After the war a portion was torn down and the remainder buried under tons of debris hauled from the surrounding neighborhoods. Today it is the focal point of the park. Its towers offer a view of the city, its walls a place for rockclimbers to practice, and its labrynth of inner corridors and partially collapsed spaces are a popular underground tourist attraction

Ewald Kendzierski, Tante Martha, Frieda Wittmutz and Onkel Hermann.
This photo was taken in 1953.

Frieda Ida Luise Wittmutz, Charlotte's mother, in 1958.

Stanley Lowe had one of the few American cars in Berlin in 1951.
Charlotte is in the driver's seat.

Charlotte and Stanley's wedding day, June 26, 1953.

PART TWO

1946—Moving to Swinemunder Strasse

The *Wohnungsamt* gave my mother an address for an apartment to look at. It was located on Swinemunder Strasse, back in our old neighborhood. The agency could not find a place for us near Transvaalstrasse, where most of the houses were intact, but they found a place in our old, badly destroyed neighborhood. Hard to figure out!

We had become used to the Transvaalstrasse neighborhood and would have liked staying in the area. It really felt better living in an area that was not as devastated as our old neighborhood. It was a lot less depressing.

My mother and I rode the streetcar from the corner of Mullerstrasse and Seestrasse to Badstrasse. Then we walked up Brunnenstrasse. This whole area was very familiar to us. We walked right past the school I was then attending. The private school I used to attend was only a couple of blocks away. We passed the upper end of Hochstrasse and the movie theater that we used to go to, now all burned-out, with nothing left of it any more.

We walked by Bahnhof Gesundbrunnen. While crossing the bridge over the railroad tracks we stopped to take a look at the bunker, our *Lebensretter* (lifesaver). It was still standing, looking as strong and indestructible as ever. It was also a survivor. The bombs had not been able to destroy it and neither had the *Stalinorgel's* constant rocket barrage.

We turned left on Ramlerstrasse and walked all the way down to the corner of Swinemunder Strasse. I saw that if we moved there I would not have far to go to attend confirmation classes at the parsonage.

My mother had been very quiet since we started on our walk. She had not been beyond Bahnhof Gesundbrummer since we were bombed out in March of 1945. She just looked around at everything. The area held a lot of memories for her.

We came to the house where my grandparents and my dad once lived. Too bad they moved away from there to Hochstrasse. We would all still have had a home and it would have spared us a lot of moving from one place to another. Although the houses on either side were gone, it had survived the bombings, the fires, and the fierce street fighting that took place around the Humboldthain area. The house looked intact with only the usual damage showing, like the glass gone in the windows, lots of bullet holes on the outside of the house, and so on.

This was the neighborhood where my dad grew up and where he lived there until he got married. Humboldthain, just across the street, had been his playground. It was where he went swimming and played soccer during the summer, and enjoyed sledding in the winter. That was why he knew so much about the *Rodelbahnen*. He had seen a few bad accidents happen there, mostly from carelessness, and knew how dangerous they were. That was why I was not supposed to go there until I was older.

My mother told me that Oma and Opa's apartment had been very nice, with a big garden in the backyard. My parents and I lived with Oma and Opa for a while after I was born. They had come home to their furnished room in Tempelhof to find themselves evicted, along with their landlady, who had failed to pay the rent to the owner of the house. My grandparents had felt for some time that my great-grandmother, Oma's mother, should not be living by herself anymore. It was decided that she should move in with them and that my parents should take her apartment on Ackerstrasse. And so it came to pass that we went to live there.

My mother told me that apartments that she and my dad could afford were hard to find. My dad had lost his steady employment with the Bergmann Company, where he had worked as a *Schlosser*, just before I was born. He was working odd jobs, whatever came along, on a daily basis. Oma and Opa helped them a lot during those bad times. Opa was employed by a tobacco company and had kept his job, which was a blessing.

We walked on down Swinemunder Strasse past many burned or bombed-out houses until we came to the one that had the vacant apartment. The superintendent showed us the place. It was located in the side wing on the first floor, not counting the ground floor. It was a small apartment, with one bedroom and a kitchen, but was big enough for the two of us. The only drawback was that it did not have a bathroom. The toilets were located in a separate building in the courtyard, one half for women and one half for men. The only other time I had seen this arrangement was at my first school on Grenzstrasse.[63]

We told the superintendent that we were taking the apartment and we would move in as soon as the legal work was done at the *Wohnungsamt*. I found it quite ironic to think that we would be living just a few houses away from where my dad, Oma and Opa once lived.

Swinemunder Strasse was a long street. It had been a very nice street before the war, with a promenade in the center of it that had lots of big shade trees and benches to sit on. It no longer resembled that description. We would be living only two houses away from the corner of Bernauer Strasse. That was where the French sector ended and the Russian sector started.[64]

Frau Katerborn's Bookstore and Lending Library used to be on Swinemunder Strasse. We walked up to where it had been and we could still make out a little bit of the sign above the shop entrance, "*Buch* ..." and "... *Leih*". It must have been a good-sized store. It took up a lot of space.

A little farther down the street, stood the *Ruine* (ruins) of the *Versohnungskirche*, the Church of Reconciliation, all burned out, including the parsonage. I had been baptized in that Church and later attended Sunday School there. I also took flute lessons from the pastor's wife, *Frau Pastorin*, as we were told to address her. My flute playing never amounted to more than *Tonleiter rauf und runter* (the up and down scale) and one tune—"*Hanschen klein, ging allein, in die weite Welt hinein.*" It was a tune about a bird that leaves home and wanders off into the far away world, all by himself. I used to feel so sorry for the poor bird. It would bring tears into my eyes when we were singing the song. Especially when we came to the part that told that he did not have a mother and father anymore!

The noise that I created while practicing with my flute did not sound very *musikalisch* (musical) to my mother's ears. After listening to my *gepiepse* for a

---

63   That was a very old school building, probably built before they had indoor plumbing. I remember not liking it then, especially during the winter months, when it was freezing cold inside the unheated building. But it still was better than an outhouse. After we moved into this new apartment we found out how inconvenient and troublesome it really was, especially after dark, trying to find the way in an unlighted building. I can assure you that I never went without my mother. I was not that brave.

64   That borderline did not matter much until 1961 when the East German government had a wall built to seal the East off from the West. Then Bernauer turned into a street of horror and sadness. Many people lost their lives trying to make it to the West to be free before they were totally walled in and cut off from the rest of the world.

couple of weeks she declared that I did not have any talent to become a flute player and that was the end. Shortly thereafter we lost our first home and with it my *Flote* (flute).

What I really wanted to play was an accordion. My school friend Waltraut had one and whenever I visited her she would let me play on it. I really liked it. I talked my mother into going with me to a music shop to see about one. They had quite a few for sale, but it was 1941 and we were told that we needed a special permit in order to buy one. To attain such a permit one had to be a member of a *Musikkapelle* (musical band) or a member of the military forces. As soon as I heard that explanation I knew who to ask for help—my dad! I wrote a letter to my dad, explained the situation and asked him to put in a request for a musical instrument, an accordion.

He wrote back saying that he was sorry about not being able to help me, as much as he wanted to, but he could not possibly request a musical instrument at that point and time. Knowing my dad's character and his good sense of humor, I am sure that he had himself a good laugh out of this. As a front line soldier a musical instrument was the last thing he needed in Russia.[65] Oh well, I tried.

As a young fellow, my dad used to belong to a *Musikverein* (musical society). He played a mandolin. When my dad came home on leave in 1942 he tried finding a used accordion for me, calling upon the help of his friends, but they did not find one either. Someone offered a Geige (violin), but I was not interested.

We walked to the corner of Bernauer Strasse and Brunnenstrasse. We stood there thinking about all the times that we had come there to shop. There used to be many small shops and big department stores along Brunnenstrasse all the way to Invalidenstrasse. In the past we would walk down Brunnenstrasse and then make a right turn on Invalidenstrasse. There we would sometimes shop at a big indoor *Markthalle* (market hall). Further along Invalidenstrasse we would pass the lower end of Ackerstrasse and a little further on the Stettiner Bahnhof. Then we came to Chausseestrasse. There we would make a right turn and walk back home. It was a long "walk around the block" with lots of interesting things to see. I loved going window shopping, looking at all the different displays in the store windows. If we got tired and did not feel like walking all the way, we could always take the *Strassenbahn No. 3* and ride back home, getting off *Am Gartenplatz*, one block from our house.

---

65 Perhaps it would have made a difference in his dealings with the enemy—the "culture-seeking" Russians.

Going straight ahead on Brunnenstrasse would eventually lead us to Alexanderplatz, taking us past several *Tageskinos* (all day movie theaters). They were known for not being so strict with the rules that allowed only certain age groups to see some movies. We would usually go there on Sundays after our noontime dinner and try hard to act older than we were. I do not believe that we fooled anybody. They probably laughed about us silly kids behind our backs. They were really stupid rules anyways. I never saw anything bad showing in the movies that we should not have seen or heard about. Although we made the effort to get in, I honestly did not enjoy going to those theaters because I felt very uncomfortable. Every time I heard the door open, I would turn around. If I saw something shiny, I just knew that it was the helmet of a policeman coming after me. But it never happened. We were always lucky, but it was hardly worth the trouble or the worry.

This time when we turned onto Brunnenstrasse I noticed immediately that the house on the other side of the street, the one with the small furniture shop where I had found our kitchen set and beds, was gone. So was the larger furniture store a little farther down the street, the place where my parents had bought their first new furniture, a kitchen set and a living room suite. I remember how excited and happy they had been about buying the new furniture to replace my great-grandmother's worn out things. I had been happy, too. During the fall months of 1941 my mother and I went back to the same store and together we picked out a beautiful bedroom suite. She had planned to surprise my dad with it. That was the time he was supposed to come home on leave for Christmas, but to our big disappointment he was not able to. When he finally came home in 1942 he was very pleased with the new bedroom suite we had selected.

We came to the building with the millinery shop. It looked intact, except for the shop, which was all boarded up. We were both reminded of the day when my dad was home on leave and he brought us to this store. He had decided that we both needed a new hat to wear to the theater, for which he had been given tickets. My mother was not a "hat-person". She must have tried on every hat in the shop. She looked quite funny at times and we all had a good laugh, except for the sales lady. They finally decided on one, a very pretty dark blue one with flowers on one side. My mother did not look comfortable wearing it, but she wanted to please my dad.[66]

---

66 I had found my hat right away, a plain, brown one that went nicely with my coat. My
    Oma was the one in our family who could put on any hat in a shop and walk away

We looked across the street at the huge AEG complex. It took up several blocks, yet it appeared unscathed and untouched amidst all the bombed and burned out houses. Again it was simply unbelievable and incredible. How could a big factory complex remain intact when every house around it was reduced to rubble?

On our way back to Transvaalstrasse we stopped at the indoor *Markthalle* on Mullerstrasse. There we checked out the bulletin board where people advertised things for sale. We saw that someone living close by had a bed for sale. It turned out to be a beautiful brass bed, in excellent condition, for only twenty-five marks. It was worth a lot more money, but the lady wanted to get rid of it and seemed glad that we wanted it. When she heard about our plight she gave us a small table and two chairs to also take along. She then helped us find a two-wheeled cart that we could borrow for our big move to Swinemunder Strasse. Every so often a kind and caring person came along to help us out of a destitute situation, as this lady did.

We were able to get all of our *Hab und Gut* (belongings) onto the cart. Off we pushed to Swinemunder Strasse. It was almost one year since we were pushing a cart like it with Opa lying on it. It was hard to believe that it had been only ten months prior. It seemed so much longer, considering everything that had happened in the meantime.

It took us a lot longer getting back to the apartment than we anticipated. We had to stay on the main streets. They had been cleaned up, the debris removed and the holes filled, making them more passable. It was also a very heavy load to push.

We were very glad when we reached the house, but unbeknownst to us, a very unpleasant surprise was waiting for us. My mother went to the superintendent's apartment to get the keys for the apartment. When she and the superintendent came back I could tell by my mother's expression that something had gone wrong. I found out that during the time it took us to get back, our apartment on the first floor had been exchanged for one in the basement—a *Kellerwohnung* (basement flat).

---

looking great. We used to tease her about it, telling her that she would look good wearing a *Nachttopf* (night pot) on her head, saving her a lot of money otherwise spent on buying expensive hats. When I was older and we were living under normal times again, I used to enjoy going shopping with her. We had a lot of fun together, especially in the hat department of the big stores. We liked browsing through the stores; something my mother never did enjoy. She would go to the store for whatever was needed, but not just for looking.

The superintendent acted like a guilty person, someone who had acted wrongly. He kept apologizing while trying at the same time to explain the reasons for the apartment exchange. Whatever they were, they did not make any sense. My mother could have complained about it to the *Wohnunsamt*, but I think that she had become very tired of the constant hassle and the trouble. And what could we have done at that point? It was January and cold, too cold to set up our brass bed in the park. She remained remarkable calm, accepting the superintendent's offer to help move our things downstairs.

The apartment was about the same size as the one upstairs and it was very clean, but it still was a *Kellerwohnung*. At least the two small windows still had glass in them. The apartment upstairs had only cardboard in the window frames. We were able to see legs walking past! It might even have been warmer living underground than above ground, but I was very unhappy about our new living place. I sensed that my mother was, too. She just did not talk about it.

1946—Moving to Seestrasse

We had been living in the *Kellerwohnung* for about five or six weeks when Hanna told my mother about a place on Seestrasse. It had been offered to her but she had declined because her brother did not want her to leave him. An elderly woman was living by herself in a Seestrasse apartment and she needed someone to look after her. She did not have any problems getting around, but her mind was not always good. She would be very confused at times and then again very clear. We understood that she had an accident during an air raid and had hit her head hard against the wall in the cellar. That caused her to have a concussion and it resulted in her condition. Hanna had worked with the woman at a tailoring business in Moabit. The woman who owned the business had been appointed by the court as a guardian, at the old lady's own request.

We decided to give it a try, check it out and have a talk with the lady. The apartment was located on the third floor in the *Hinterhaus*, the same location as the apartment we had lived in on Hochstrasse.

We must have caught the lady, Frau Michaelis, on one of her better days. She invited us into her home after my mother explained the reason for our visit. She showed us the apartment. Everything was very nice. She had some fine pieces of furniture. Her husband had been employed at a furniture making company, as a *Drechsler* (turner on a lathe), and he had made their furniture. She appeared to be glad and in favor of our offer to come to live with her and look after her. We agreed that we would move in as soon as we talked to her guardian, which we did. She, too, seemed glad that we would be moving in with the old lady. My mother agreed to pay the rent every month, including the gas bill, which did not amount to very much.

The apartment was the only one in the two houses that did not have electricity. Originally there were three houses and a church in this block. The houses belonged to a group of doctors and were built circa 1930, using gas lighting in all of them. Frau Michaelis and her husband were the first tenants to move into house No. 37. Later, when electricity was installed in the houses they chose to stay with the gas lighting. I was not looking forward to it. I remembered how it frightened me before, when we were staying outside of Kottbus.[67] But at least the apartment had a bathroom!

After we had made all the necessary arrangements, we were truly looking forward to this move and to again living in a less demolished area. The damage in our neighborhood had really affected our state of mind. It was very depressing, living amidst all the *Ruines*. It was also very weird living in a *Kellerwohnung*. We never met anyone else who was living in the house. We only saw their legs walking by our window.

There were several *Kellerwohnungen* on Ackerstrasse that were occupied by gypsies. We hardly ever saw them outside, but when we did I remember the colorful clothing they wore. Nobody else wore such bright colors as they did. We were warned to stay away from them because they had a reputation for stealing children. But curiosity would sometimes get the best of us, and we would sneak up to their windows and take a peek into their apartment. It always looked very nice and clean. The table would be covered with a tablecloth and on it often sat a vase with flowers, not at all matching what we heard being said about them. Perhaps my feelings about living in a *Kellerwohnung* relate to my seeing it as a place where gypsies lived. I was having a difficult time adjusting to our situation—being so

---

67   As it was, we lived with the gas lighting until about 1950 when we had it changed to electricity, at our own expense. We had received a reimbursement from the German government, a percentage of our estimated loss due to the bombing of our homes. It enabled us to do a little redecorating and to have electricity installed. It was great being able to switch on a light and not hear the hissing noise anymore from the gaslight.

poor and having nothing. I missed our nice home and all the things we used to have.

Back at our *Kellerwohnung* we packed a wicker laundry basket with all of our things. We had borrowed the basket from Frau Michaelis. As much as we would have liked keeping the nice brass bed, we had decided to leave it behind, along with the table and chairs. We just did not know how to move them. It was hard enough before when we had moved them from Mullerstrasse with a cart.

When we came back to the new apartment on Seestrasse we experienced the other side of Frau Michaelis. When we rang the bell she came to the door, but she would only open it as far as the safety chain allowed. She maintained that she did not know us nor anything about our plans to move in with her. We did our best to refresh her memories, but without having any luck. She stubbornly refused to acknowledge us and our agreement.

There we stood with our few belongings; once again feeling so rejected. My mother started to cry. At that moment the neighbor, Frau Galtke, opened her door and asked us what was the problem. After we told her, she went back into her place and got a slice of bread. She then used it as a bribe to convince Frau Michaelis to open the door.

This first encounter really created some doubts about our ability to handle her changing moods. It did turn out to be quite difficult at first, but eventually she became used to our presence and we learned to deal with her strange ways.

She was a small, thin woman, about seventy-five years old, but very agile on her feet. Each day she would go out into the neighborhood, bringing back all kinds of leaves and planting them in the flower boxes on the balcony. I followed her once to find out where she went. She almost got away from me, but I found her sitting on a bench at the entrance to the cemetery, about a block away from the house. She just sat there in her own small world. She did not even notice me. Poor soul!

The first thing we learned was not to leave any kind of food sitting around because it would be gone when we came back. Right after we moved in she ate up our week's ration of bread. When we confronted her about it she of course denied it, and maintained that she knew nothing about it. It was a long week for us without any bread to eat, but we learned not to leave food lying around. Instead, we locked our food in the pantry.

When Frau Michaelis had her accident, something must have happened that made her unable to tell if she had something in her stomach or not. We would often eat together. She would always be done before us, even though we were not slow eaters. She would get up, step away from the table and then stand there, rocking back and forth, looking at us with tears in her eyes, telling us that she had not eaten for days and that she was so hungry. She made us feel so bad that we were still sitting at the table with food left on our plates. We tried explaining to her that we all started out with the same amount on our plates, but this was a waste of time and effort. She just did not understand. Eventually we learned to ignore her behavior and send her away from the kitchen. At times like that we had to speak quite firmly to her.

In time we became used to one another and we got along alright. When she was normal, she would tell us some interesting stories and sing old songs to us. They were songs that I remembered from the records that we played on Oma and Opa's gramophone. But the other side of her was difficult to live with.

We wondered where everything in the apartment had disappeared to. It was very sparsely furnished for a home that had not been damaged during the war. Her wardrobe did not have much in it, and neither did the linen closet. Her kitchen cupboard contained very few dishes. Even the cellar was empty, not even a lump of coal or a piece of wood could be found.

Then we learned how people were always taking advantage of her condition, especially her cravings for food. She let them take all kinds of things for just a slice of bread. There were two wardrobes in the room when we moved in. We hung our few pieces of clothing in the empty one, only to find them gone when we returned, along with the wardrobe. It did not do any good asking her what had happened. She did not even remember that a wardrobe had been standing in the empty space. We asked our neighbor, Frau Gattke, for help in finding our clothes. She gave us a hint where to go to ask about the wardrobe. We found it there, only two floors below us. They told us that they had bought it from the old lady and had not noticed the clothes hanging inside until we told them. What a story!

Remembering By-gone Days on Seestrasse

My mother told me that she had often mentioned to my dad, while walking on Seestrasse, how much she liked the area and how she wished that they could live there one day. On Sunday afternoon outings we had often come to Seestrasse to walk along the promenade under big shade trees to Plotzensee or to the park, Rehberge. They had a big area fenced off in the park where they kept *Rehe* (deer). They also had an open-air theater, where they had concerts on Sunday afternoons.

I especially looked forward to stopping for *Kaffe und Kuchen* at one of the many outdoor restaurants along the way. Over the entrance to each *Gartenlokal* was a large sign welcoming guests to come in and bring their own coffee beans for the *Lokal* to prepare. *"Hier konnen Familien Kaffee kochen"* ("Here families can make coffee.") It was an old custom. People would bring their coffee beans and for a small fee the restaurant staff would prepare the coffee and return it to their table in a big pot. This was mostly done at the outdoor restaurants. Customers could also bring their own cake and sandwiches.

It may seem that the owners of the *Gartenlokale* would lose money on this very unique custom but I do not think that they did. Otherwise they would not have done it. Each *Gartenlokale* had a playground for children and musical entertainment for dancing. Families came to spend the afternoon and evening there and surely would buy other kinds of refreshments during that time.

I do not recall the reason that people would bring their own coffee beans. I can only guess that people wanted their own favorite brand of coffee. Coffee was very expensive and considered to be a treat. Therefore it was only offered at special times, like Sunday afternoons or when company stopped by and during special get-togethers with friends or family. The rest of the time everyone drank *Ersatz Kaffee*, usually made from roasted ground barley. Children were never served the "real coffee". I am certain that this is the source of the phrase, "Eine gute Tasse Kaffee" ("A good cup of coffee.")[68]

Although it was not the way she had wished for, we were finally living on Seestrasse.

---

68 My mother never fussed much over making coffee, but my grandmother did. I used to watch her grind the beans. Sometimes she would let me turn the handle of the *Kaffeemuhle* (coffee mill). Then it was measured accurately into the *Kaffeekanne* (coffeepot) and hot water was slowly added. It was a ritual, but everyone always complimented her on the good coffee she served.

Oma always set a nice table even during the meager times. When Stan and I started dating, I would take him for afternoon *Kaffee und Kuchen* on Sundays to my Oma's place. He never objected to going there, so he too must have liked her coffee. She would have a *Schweineohr* for him, a big crunchy pig's ear, which he liked. Nice memories. Much more enjoyable to write about than all the sad happenings!

1946—*Einsegnung* (Confirmation)

Several months earlier Ursula and I had been to see Pastor Werder at the Pharrhaus (parsonage) to find out about resuming the instructions that we needed for our forthcoming confirmation. It was really nice to visit with him. He was someone we were familiar with from better days in the past.[69]

Einsegnung was a very special event in the life of every Protestant 14-year-old girl and boy. It was when we confirmed our faith and received God's blessing. It was also the first time that *Abendmahl* (communion) was offered to us.

Until we were confirmed we had *Religion unterricht* (religious instruction) on every Monday morning from eight until nine o'clock. Meanwhile, the Catholic children would come to school on Mondays at nine o'clock, and I only remember girls from my class being of Catholic faith. They had an extra hour to sleep.

It was also the day when children became young adults. The familiar "*Du*" was dropped for the more formal "*Sie*", and "*Fraulein*" (Miss) and "*Herr*" (Mister) was added in front of one's first or last name. Girls no longer had to curtsy and boys did not have to bow when greeting grown-ups.[70]

Finally, it was graduation day from the eighth grade of the *Volksschule* (public school). But if I had stayed at the *Mittelschule*, I would not have graduated until I was 16 years old.

There were no undamaged churches left in our neighborhood. However, Pastor Werder informed our group that a church had been located in the Russian occupied sector where we could hold our *Einsegnung* on Sunday, the 24th of March. Normally, confirmation was held on Easter Sunday, but Easter was not until the 21st of April. For whatever the reason, it was held earlier that spring.

---

69 The parsonage was located right across from the bunker in Humboldthain Park. Walking back to Ursula's house we decided to take the road alongside of the park. It was a little shorter than the other way. The park was also not safe to walk around in yet. It had not been cleaned up and there were lots of fallen trees lying here and there along with other debris. But we soon wished that we had not chosen this way because it took us right by an area where large mass graves were being dug up. Seeing all the dead German soldiers made us feel sad and tearful. Hopefully, their families were finally notified so that they would know what happened to their loved ones and where they died. They must have been fighting around the bunker area during the last days of the war. I cannot help but wonder how many more were buried in the park and no one knows about them.

70 The rule we had been required to follow was stated as "*Madchen machten einen Knicks und Buben einen Diener*" ("Girls make a curtsy and boys a bow.")

My mother got busy trying to make this day as special as possible for me. We had all talked about it when my dad was home on leave. He had assured us that the war would be over by the time of my confirmation and that he would be home with us to help plan and celebrate my special day. The war was indeed over, but he was not to be there.

I had been looking everywhere for a dark blue or black dress to wear on my *Einsegnungstag* (confirmation day). I had almost given up hope of finding one when I walked by a small *Kurzwaren geschaft* (notions establishment) on Mullerstrasse. It was the last place I could think of to look for a dress but something made me go inside. And there it was, a pretty black dress, hanging on the wall all by itself, just waiting for me to come along to wear it. I begged the shopkeeper to hold it for me while I ran home to get the money and the *Bezugs schein* (ration coupon). I never even tried it on. The shopkeeper had told me that it was a size thirty-six, my size, and I was sure that it would fit me. I was so happy that I had at last found a black dress to wear.

My mother gave me the black pumps to wear on my special day. She had saved them and carried them with us for at least a couple of years. Regrettably, she had not anticipated that by then my feet would be bigger than hers. As I squeezed my big feet into the pumps I felt as bad as Cinderella's sisters must have, moaning and groaning with every step that I took. I also had to learn to walk with heels, but I was determined to wear them. I did not have any other shoes to wear except my pair of men's shoes from Tante Ilse's husband.[71]

It almost was impossible at that time to find fresh flowers, but I did not like fake ones. I would have rather gone without any. On the day before the *Einsegnung*, the lady from the flower shop in my former neighborhood took pity on me and came up with ten stems of *Maiglockchen* (lilies of the valley) for me. Just the kind of flowers I had wished for.

---

71 After my Confirmation Day, I took the pumps to a store in Tempelhof. I found an equally nice pair of pumps and traded for them. I know I should have chosen a pair of practical shoes, but by then I had been given a pair from Tante Ilse's husband, very sensible pair of tie-up men's shoes. I was very unfortunate to have big feet. I could not even borrow my mother's shoes. At this time in 1946 shoemakers were unable to repair shoes for lack of material. Later on, in 1947 or so, they started making sandals from wood. The shoes were very noisy but helped reduce the shoe shortage. Once I took a leather bag to a shoemaker and he made a nice pair of sandals for me. He covered the wooden wedge with leather, which made it look quite dressy.

The *Prüfung* (test) took place the Sunday before my confirmation. We all met at the parsonage, about twenty of us, and along with our family members we marched off together. Pastor Werder led his flock of sheep around the broken pieces of pavement, huge holes and other kinds of obstacles.[72]

It was a long and tiresome walk. I was also worried about failing the test and not being confirmed. I had studied the catechism from the first to the last page on Pastor Werder's advice, but I had missed some classes and had not fully kept up with my lessons.

When we finally arrived at the church, we met many other boys and girls there. We filled the three front pews on both sides of the *Kirche* (church). The rest of the *Kirche* was packed full with all the family members. Oma had come along with us. She had taken the S-Bahn to Bahnhof Gesundbrunnen where we had met her. I was wearing my pretty blue "Easter dress," which I had not worn since that tragic Sunday in March of 1945.

When it was time for our group's testing Pastor Werder climbed up the steps to the pulpit so that he could get a good view of us. He fired one question after another at us. I held my hand up for the answers at every one of them, but he ignored or bypassed me the entire time. I was so disappointed and I told him so afterwards. He just laughed and told me that after he warned me that I might fail the test he knew I had studied and that I had the answers for his questions.

For my confirmation my mother had been able to buy some extra items for us to eat from the black market dealers. She had paid a lot of money for some butter, eggs, and sugar, enough to bake a small cake. She had also obtained a rabbit for our dinner. She prepared the rabbit on Saturday along with red cabbage made from the outer leaves.

Oma came to our house very early on Sunday morning to cook the rest of the meal and have our dinner ready for us when we came back from church. The long walk the previous Sunday had been too strenuous for her and my mother had thought it would be better if she came directly to the apartment. We also needed someone to watch over our food and keep Frau Michaelis out of the kitchen or we would end up with nothing on our plates.

Saturday had been a nice, sunny day and we were hoping that Sunday would be likewise. But the weatherman decided to send us a chilly and windy day

---

72 The transportation system had not been restored around this area. In fact, in comparison to our area, the Russians had not done very much work cleaning up the roads in their sector.

instead. I could feel the cold through my gloves. My poor flowers nearly froze in my hands.

It was a very meaningful and festive service. I had been alright until I received my first *Abendmahl* (communion). Then I had trouble holding back my tears, wishing so much for my dad to be there with me. We came right home afterwards. There was no picture taking because nobody had a camera or any film.

Oma had our dinner all ready for us and it looked good. Although I was hungry I could not make myself eat a piece of the meat. It was cut up in pieces and all I could see, looking at it, were those cuddly, soft, furry rabbits that I used to take care of and play with. Tante Martha and Onkel Hermann had lots of them. They kept them in cages on their balcony. Tante Grete had a few and so did her landlord. I felt bad that I could not eat the meat after my mother went through so much trouble getting it, but I enjoyed the potatoes, gravy, and red cabbage.

After our dinner we fixed a plate with food for Opa and took it to him. I could tell when we came into his room that he had been waiting for us. He looked me over and he told me that I looked nice. He told me he had been wondering if he had to call me *Fraulein* from then on. For a man of few words, he surely talked a lot on that day. He also enjoyed the plate of food that Oma had heated up for him.

Oma then set the table for *Kaffen und Kuchen*. We had brought the cake with us so that we could share it together. It had been a long time since any of us had eaten cake and we thoroughly enjoyed it. Afterwards I went to see Onkel Gerhard and Tante Elisabeth to present myself. This was called *Vorstellung* in German. It was an old tradition where the newly confirmed and graduated young boys and girls would go to visit people and present themselves to them.

Under normal times most of the relatives and friends would have been invited to celebrate the *Einsegnung* with the *Konfirmand* (confirmee), but we were not living in normal times. *Ostermontag* (Easter Monday) was still a holiday but on Tuesday the *Konfirmanden* (confirmed) would go around to visit anyone who had not been at his or her party. Even the shopkeepers in the neighborhood expected a visit. They would have a gift waiting for each *Konfirmand*. I always thought that it would be terribly embarrassing and the last thing I would want to do. I was relieved that our present situation eliminated this old tradition of the *Vorstellung* and the "hand-out."

On Tuesday morning my mother and I went looking for a photographer to have a picture taken of me with which to remember my *Einsegnung* day. While hopeful, we were also very doubtful that we would find someone who had been lucky enough to have hidden a camera from the hands of our "liberators." We did know of a couple studios in our old neighborhood, but we found one of them bombed out and the other one without a camera. The second place did give us an address for someone living near Stettiner Bahnhof, which was located in the Russian sector.

We found the place, a partially bombed out house that really looked unsafe to enter. The photographer was at home and to our surprise, he still had a camera, film, and the rest of the equipment needed to take a picture and to develop it. We wondered if the unsafe appearance of the house discouraged the Russians from entering it. Perhaps they did not expect to find any treasures in such a bombed-out place and left it alone.[73]

It was a lot of trouble to go through just to have a picture of myself in memory of my *Einsegnungtag*. I wish I had not been so tired. By the time we found this photographer I was really worn out and it shows in the picture. The photographer had very little in the way of props. The background looks very plain and the chair by which I am standing is worn. But I got my photograph and I have it today.

On our way back home we stopped at the Girndt's place. The girls were glad to see me and asked lots of questions about *Einsegnung*. I told them that from then on they had to address me with "*Fraulein*" in front of my name and use the formal "*Sie*" instead of the familiar "*Du*." They looked rather intimidated until I told them that I was just teasing.

"*Fraulein Lotti*." It sounded strange.

After the *Einsegnung*

A new chapter had begun in our lives and the big, vital question was: "What do we do from now on?" Had we been living in normal times we would have been able to fulfill our wishes instead of doing nothing. I registered at the employment office for an apprentice job in an office or a shop, but I was told that my chances were not promising.

My mother had gone to work for the city of Berlin in a work program for the *Wiederaufbau* (reconstruction). Their first job was to clear away all the debris from the banks of the river and the harbor. It was considered *Schwerarbeit* (heavy

---

73 Normally when a house was severely damaged, a sign would be posted out front reading *Vorsicht Einsturzgefahr* (Caution-danger of collapse).

work) and she received a ration card accordingly, but the wages were very low. I believe that the equal pay for men and women had its start with this kind of work program. Until then, men were always paid more than women were and it was expected of them to do the heavier work. But with the equal pay arrangement, men refused to help the women with the heavy lifting, always pointing out to them that they were being paid equally. Therefore, the work assignments were also to be equal.

German men were changing drastically, becoming more and more impolite and disrespectful. It was noticeable everywhere, but especially when using the public transportation system. The men would push and shove to get onto the trains ahead of the women in order to get a seat. Then they would sit there and ignore the women, without ever offering them their seat. It never used to be like that, but it was the outcome of the equal rights and pay for women and men.

My mother experienced this difference at work. It was hard for the women to push the loaded lorries along the rail track and especially uphill, but the men would not help them. She had always worked with men and she had been able to count on their help, but not anymore. The times that we were living in were to blame. It was changing everything and everyone. She was convinced of the fact that all the good German men were gone, having become casualties of the war, and that we were left to deal with these rude and very self-centered characters.

The French Occupation Soldiers

Moving back to Seestrasse made us once again aware of the French occupation soldiers. On Swinemunder Strasse we never saw any of them. Now we were living one block away from the French Club which was located on the corner of Mullerstrasse and Seestrasse. It used to be a very nice German restaurant, with a large outside veranda in the front. The French redesigned the front and the inside of the place. They enclosed the veranda and decorated the interior in a very gaudy style using mirrors and chrome. It had a very cold appearance and totally destroyed the look of *Gemutlichkeit* (cozy atmosphere). The area had become a very busy place and we were not allowed to walk by the restaurant. They placed barricades all around the area and we either had to walk on the road or on the other side of the street. I believe that this was done for security reasons. The Americans had done the same around the Tempelhof Airbase.

The French soldiers always traveled in groups. They had also taken over the public transportation, which they did not have to pay to ride, and treated it as a form of entertainment. Most of them acted as if they had never ridden on a streetcar, subway or an inner city railroad. They would stand in the entrance doors on the U-Bahn and the S-Bahn and force the doors open after they had been closed automatically. They would hang out, acting very silly and irresponsible. On the streetcars they would stand on the steps and jump off and back on again. Surprisingly, I never saw anyone get hurt.

The worst part was their attitude towards the German people. If they did not feel like it, they would not let the people get off or on the trains at the stops. It was a mean game they would play, challenging people to a fight. Often it would be a very unfair fight, involving four or more French soldiers versus one lone German.

In the beginning of their occupation they carried automatic weapons. My mother and I witnessed a horrible incident one day as we were riding the streetcar to the Mullerstrasse and Seestrasse stop. The streetcar was very full and, as always, the platform had been taken over by French soldiers. As we approached our stop we were bounced around a little. This happened all the time on streetcars. It was never a smooth ride. All of a sudden, as we were leaving the car, a commotion started in front of us. Three French soldiers had pounced on a young fellow, not much older than me, accusing him of having stepped on their feet. The boy kept apologizing, saying that if he had stepped on their feet it was *Aus Versehen* (by accident) and not done intentionally. But the soldiers ignored his pleas and the other bystanders' comments. They were on a mission.

They dragged the boy out of the car and shoved him across the street. Quite a few people got off ahead of us and they followed the French soldiers and the young boy, forming a crowd in around them. When we got closer we could not see what was going on. We only heard loud shouting. My mother pushed herself through the crowd. When she saw what the soldiers were doing to the boy she became very angry. They had pushed the boy against the plywood-covered window of a small smoke shop, banging his head into the small glass piece in the center and shattering it. One soldier had his gun pointing at the boy's chest. They were all yelling at him. It was an awful scene.

When my mother saw this cruel treatment by the soldiers upon the defenseless boy, she marched right up to the one with the gun and pushed it away from the boy's chest. She told them what bullies and *Feiglinge* (cowards) they were and told them to leave him alone. I do not think that they understood German, but her gestures told them what she wanted them to do. They moved away laughing, mocking her and pointing their guns at all of us, making the sound of guns, "boom-boom."[74]

For once I was behind my mother's intervention. What they had done was a very cruel thing to do to the boy. The boy's actions had not been intentional. I cannot recall all the times when I had stepped on someone's feet or had been stepped on while standing on the platform in a streetcar. It happened a lot and was never treated by anyone as an aggressive act. The boy was visibly shaken and bleeding from where his head had been pushed through the glass. My mother and I walked with him to the hospital, which was only a couple of blocks away on Mullerstrasse.

This type of behavior by the French soldiers towards the German people happened quite often during the years after the end of the war. One group of French soldiers was called the *Rote Stiere* (red bulls) because of the bright red hats they wore and their mean and aggressive disposition, behaving just like bulls. They would walk six or seven abreast on the *Burgersteig* (sidewalk) and force the Germans to step aside into the road. If the Germans did not move fast enough, they would push them. German men were treated especially harshly. I saw them one Sunday afternoon going after an elderly couple. They had stepped aside, close to the curbstone, to let the bulls stride by, but they were not satisfied with the couple's polite move. They walked so close to them that the couple stumbled backwards into the street, falling down. The more I saw of the bulls and their cowardly ways, the more I came to dislike them.

Later on, when conflicts erupted between the Allies and the Russians, the French would go on alert. They would drive their army vehicles to Seestrasse and line them up under the trees, ready for whatever might happen. The Russian sector was only a few blocks away from Seestrasse. On one of those times I came out of my house just as they set off a tear gas bomb to chase the little children away who had been congregating around their vehicles. What a mean and nasty thing to do to the children. They were just little kids being *neugierig* (curious).

It was also was my first experience with tear gas. I had no idea what had happened when the children ran up to me crying that their eyes were burning. But then the gas vapor drifted towards me and affected my eyes too. I took the

---

74 I do not believe that they would have used the guns on us. They were just trying to intimidate us.

children along with me into the courtyard to the water faucet where we washed our eyes out, which helped a little bit. Before I walked the children into my house I could hear the soldiers laughing. They found it amusing watching us trying to find our way with our eyes closed. Later I had to go upstairs and change my clothes. They must have had absorbed the horrible stuff. My eyes looked very red, as if I had been crying, and they bothered me for awhile.

Later on, when I was working at the library, some of the older boys from the neighborhood would come by and hang around and talk, especially during the winter months. I overheard some of their conversations in which they expressed their hatred for the French soldiers and how they wished that they could get one of them alone, especially the *Rote Stiere*, to have some revenge for all their wrongful doings. But to my relief I never heard of any clashes between the German boys and the French soldiers, which was good. It would only have brought more problems onto the German people.

I do not know if problems like these existed between the soldiers and the German people in the American or British sectors. I have never heard of any. When we started going back to Tempelhof to visit Tante Martha, Onkel Hermann, Hilde and Lutz, my mother and I would often choose to walk the last three subway stops. We had done this many times before and we always enjoyed it, especially beyond the airport. It was such a pleasant walk along the promenade, with benches to rest on. On other times we would walk when leaving from their house, with them walking along halfway. We never saw or ran into any kind of problems, not even around the airport area, where there was always more activity around the entrance gates. The American soldiers always made a good impression on us. They looked sharp. Their uniforms were clean and neatly pressed, and their shoes or boots were polished. They gave a very impressive appearance, whereas the French soldiers gave the opposite impression. Their uniforms looked wrinkled, as if they had slept in them, and their shoes were dirty and unpolished. They also used lots of smelly gel on their hair, along with powerful cologne. Riding with them in a subway car was breathtaking.

Hamsterfahrten fur Fruit nach Werder (Hamstering to Werder for Fruit)

We were getting used to living on Seestrasse. My job was to keep the apartment clean and take care of the shopping for whatever the stores had to offer. I did alright except for starting a fire in the kitchen stove. I had the worst time with it.

When Frau Michaelis was at home, she would take care of the dusting. The same pieces of furniture got dusted off several times during the day. It did not bother us except when we had someone stop by for a visit. Then it became annoying having her dance around us with her feather duster.

My mother went to work every day at the *Baustelle* (building site) and came home looking very tired. It was a hard job without the help of some nourishing food. A couple slices of bread and a thermos bottle filled with *Ersatz Kaffee* was not enough to sustain someone doing such heavy work. It really was a big help and a wonderful treat to have some fruit to take along in her lunch bag. I do not recall that we were able to buy fruit at the markets in Berlin. So my friends and I decided to take the S-Bahn to Potsdam and then board a *Dampfer* (steamboat) to Werder to look for strawberries.

Werder was a suburb of Berlin, known for its fruit orchards, which used to supply Berlin with all kinds of fresh fruit. Before the war I would come with my parents for the *Baumbluten-fest* (tree blossom festival). After the war Werder was located in the Russian occupied zone, so consequently the fruit harvest went to the Russians. Nothing was ever distributed to the German stores to sell to us. We found a place that gave us jobs picking strawberries and at the end of the day they let us keep a market basket full of the fruit. And we could eat all we wanted to, which we did. We went back several times until the season was over. It was such a treat for us.

We did not do as well when the cherries ripened. We had tried a couple of times and came back home empty handed and very disappointed. We had walked for miles through the orchards and had seen the trees loaded full of cherries, but no one would sell us any, not even let us have a few to eat to quench our thirst. One time we had just been given another refusal, when we had to step aside to let a Russian truck by. It came to a stop at the entrance to the orchard. As we then stood watching, the same people who only moments before had sent us away empty-handed, loaded up the truck with crates full of cherries for the Russians. It really hurt our feelings. They saw us standing nearby and watching them but it did not seem to bother them. They were more interested in pleasing the Russians than in pleasing us.

The boys made plans to go on Sundays, when no one would be around and we could help ourselves. It worked out alright for a couple of Sundays, but then the orchard owners became wise and they hired men to keep watch over the orchards. We were not the only ones that were taking the fruit. There were lots of people on the steamboat with bags full of fruit. Then we almost got caught. It was quite a challenge to outrun a man on a bicycle. Luckily we were able to run into a small wooded area, where we found a hole to crawl into. We stayed hidden for quite a while before we found the courage to check if the guard was still in the area.

I was ready to give up on our Sunday trips. It was a lot of trouble and worry to go through, just for a bag full of fruit. However, the boys were not ready to give up just yet. They thought of another way to get some fruit. They planned for us to leave for Werder late in the afternoon, catching the last steamboat of the day. We would arrive at the orchards while there was enough daylight left to have a look around. Then we would wait for dark to pick the fruit and return the next morning to our homes.

It sounded quite dangerous and daring to me. I really did not like to take such chances. The thought of getting caught and ending up in jail in the Russian occupied zone was frightening. But I also did not want to be the only one admitting to having cold feet.

I do not remember what I told my mother, but I am certain that it was not the real plan or she would never have given her permission. When we arrived at the orchards we found ourselves a suitable hiding place in a small wooded area, right next to a footpath that led through the orchards. We noticed how full the trees were with different kinds of plums and pears. It must have been a good year for fruit. There seemed to be a lot of it.

Our group consisted of four boys and two girls. The oldest boy was seventeen years old and the youngest boy was twelve. We waited a long time before it got dark. When it finally did, we walked over to a spot in the fence where we had noticed some loose wires. They enabled us to crawl through. Werner, the youngest and the smallest boy, crawled through first and stumbled right into a big *Stachelbeeren Busch* (gooseberry bush) on the other side. He let out a loud squeal, which sounded extra loud in the stillness around us. We were worried that someone nearby had heard it and would come to check it out. We waited for a while, listening and watching, hearing our own hearts beating, before the next one crawled through the fence.

I remember feeling very apprehensive about the whole thing. I almost backed out of crawling through the fence. A second boy named Werner and I were the last ones. We were both hesitant. We finally crawled through. Thanks to the first boy named Werner, we at least knew where the thorns of the *Stachelbeeren Busch* were located.

We spread out a little and moved from tree to tree, feeling with our hands for the fruit. I found a tree with the kind of *Pflaumen* (plums) I liked and filled my rucksack full. They tasted so good that I ate just as many as I picked.

I remember noticing that it was not as dark as when we started. The moon and the stars had appeared in the sky. It made it a little easier to find our way back out of the orchard. Ursula came along with me, but when I asked her about the rest of the group she told me that the boys had found a patch of tobacco plants and had gone mad about it. I did not like hearing that. Getting caught with tobacco leaves could get us into more trouble than with just the fruit.[75]

The boys finally came to the fence. After they had crawled through the opening we fixed the fence as best as we could and then we walked to our hiding place. I remember coming upon quite a few huge, deep craters. I believe that they had been made by bombs.

It did not take the boys long to fall asleep, but Ursula and I were too nervous to sleep. We had too many things to think about, like how to get back home without getting caught. Eventually I dozed off too. Then a strange noise awakened me and I heard voices talking loudly.

I quickly woke everyone up and we moved closer together, hoping that whoever they were they would walk on past us. When they came closer to our hiding place we could see that there were two men. The strange noise that I had heard came from their walking sticks.

They were almost past us when one man decided to step to the side of the path and relieve himself. It splattered close to Kurt's head. We were all horrified and yet we were so thankful that we were not discovered. We were convinced that they were night watchmen hired by the orchard owners and out on patrol to find thieves like us.

None of us had a watch, so we could only guess at what time it was. We figured that it had to be well past midnight.[76] We waited for awhile after the *Nachtwachter*

---

75 The boys all smoked, except the youngest one. They had been trying all kinds of different leaves, drying them and then rolling them into cigarettes. The smell was awful and sickening. I had a hard time believing that something so bad smelling could taste good. Some of the adults would use pipes and fill them with dried, crumbled leaves and puff away like a smokestack. Maybe that is the reason why I never had any desire to smoke. Luckily for me—a *Nichtraucher* (non-smoker)—the trains had separate cars for smokers and non-smokers.

76 During the summer months it did not get dark until after 9:30 pm and it started getting light around 3:30 am.

(night watchman) disappeared into the night. Then we decided to move on and walk to Bahnhof Potsdam to take the train back home instead of taking the steamboat from Werder to Potsdam. We had lots of time and walking to the train station would take us away from the orchards. We felt uncomfortable and worried after those men came by.

When it started to get light, the orchard workers began to pass us on their way to work. They made loud, nasty remarks about us. We had agreed that if someone should question us we would say that we had missed the last steamboat in the evening and we had decided to walk to Potsdam.

About halfway to the train station a Russian military truck came along and stopped beside us, with only one Russian soldier as the driver. Guessing from his gestures, we gathered that he was offering us a ride. We were starting to feel very tired, so we decided to accept his offer. Normally we would not have, but with only the driver to cope with we felt that we were quite safe. He motioned for me to sit next to him in the cab and the rest of the group to sit in the back of the truck, but Kurt acted ignorant. He climbed up into the cab to seat himself next to the driver and then Ursula and I climbed in. The rest of the group sat in the back of the truck with our bags. The driver did not act too pleased at our seating arrangement. It almost looked as if he was going to order us off again, but then he started to move the truck.

The driver did not seem to be much older than we were. He became very talkative. Even though we did not understand a word, he kept on talking. He offered Kurt a cigarette, one of the very potent Russian cigarettes. I worried about Kurt because we had not eaten anything since we had left home except the fruit. I was afraid that his stomach could not handle the strong cigarettes. But he proved that he was tougher than Ursula and I. We both got sick from the smoke. We were coughing and hanging our heads out of the open window. We must have looked funny to our driver because he kept laughing out loud. Ursula and I did not think that it was funny.

The truck driver took us all the way to the Potsdam railroad station. We thanked him and gave him some fruit, which seemed to please him a lot. He was a pleasant kind of Russian soldier. Too bad they were not all like him. We waved *Auf Wiedersehen* and *Do svidanja* as he drove away.

We found a lot of people waiting for the train. It did not look very promising for us. We would need a lot of luck to get onto the train. We talked it over between us and agreed that each one of us would try to find his or her own place and not worry about the rest of the group.

When the train finally came puffing into the station, Kurt and I headed towards the front of the train, where the *Bremsenhauschen* (brakeman's cab) was located. Looking like a little house, it sat up high at the back of a car behind the engine. It had something to do with the brake system on the train. Climbing aboard, we thought that we had been lucky. We would have been right, if the windows had still been intact. The little cab was very small inside, in fact it was quite tight, but we were glad that we got onto the train. Lots of people were left standing behind on the platform.

Our spot had a great view. Whoever used the cab for his job had a good forward view of the back of the locomotive. After the train started moving, the vibration of the train caused the little door to the cab to open. We had to hold it shut. Before long Kurt gave out on me and fell asleep, standing up. Eventually he slid down onto the floor, which made it twice as crowded. Then I had to hold the door shut and also keep an eye on the small pieces of cinder that were blowing in from the engine in front of us. It kept me quite busy.

It was about one hour ride but it seemed a lot longer under the conditions. When we got off the train we saw that the rest of our group had made the trip too. We were all very glad and relieved to be safely back home.

My friends all lived within walking distance from the *Bahnhof,* but I had to take the subway to get from Stettiner Bahnhof to Seestrasse, about four stops. I remember that when I got onto the subway, I was suddenly overcome by fatigue. I was afraid to take a seat, though, for fear of falling asleep. When I got off at Seestrasse it took me twice as long to get up the stairs as it normally did. I was totally exhausted.

Was it all worth it for a knapsack full of fruit? If someone had asked me that question right then, I would have answered "no." But after I had slept for a few hours and eaten a slice of bread with the *Pflaumenmus* (plum spread) that my mother had cooked while I was sleeping, I felt differently about it. It was, however, our last trip to Werder.[77]

---

77 I would like to say that we never feel guilty about these trips. We did not feel like thieves. We felt that we were forced into doing it by the people working in the orchards. We would have preferred getting the fruit the proper way, paying for it or working for it. We kept telling ourselves that we were not taking the fruit from the German people but from the Russians, who were taking it from the Germans. Anyone

Being Hungry

Looking back, I remember the years after the war as being the worst for lack of food, clothing, and heating materials. I still continued going on *Hamsterfahrten* to the country to subsidize our small daily food allowance, even though I never went back to Werder. The trips helped a little bit. We had a few more potatoes and vegetables.

I was born with a sweet tooth. I liked candy and cake and everything else that was sweet. During the war years candy had become a very special treat. We had to use our sugar ration coupons to buy hard candy. My dad used to save up his candy rations and send them to me. They were always received with great joy. One time I received a box with one big lump of candy in it. It must have traveled through several changes in temperature, which turned it into a solid block of sweets. It had not spoiled the taste and I enjoyed it very much, even though I had to use a hammer to break off a piece. I also had to spit out the pieces from the wrappers. But it was still a treat.

At school we were given a vitamin tablet every morning. It tasted lemony sweet and I looked forward to it every morning. It must have been vitamin C, because citrus fruits were unattainable.

I would have preferred jam on my school sandwiches instead of luncheon meats, but my mother would not hear of it. So I used to trade with anyone who had a jam sandwich until the teacher found out about it and stopped me. Then I would take off the meat or cheese and only eat the buttered bread, leaving the rest in my desk drawer. I got away with it for a little while until it started to smell quite badly around my desk and my moldy, spoiled luncheon meat and cheese was discovered. A note from the teacher was sent home with me and I was in trouble! My dad was a very easygoing fellow except when it had something to do with food. He would become very strict. He would not let me leave the table until I had eaten all the food that was on my plate. He also would lecture me about food, telling me to be thankful and appreciate having food on our table. He told me to never take it for granted that it would always be there, as times could change

reading about these experiences might get the impression that we were looking for something exciting to do, some kind of adventure. But I can assure anyone reading this that I would have liked doing things that young people at my age were doing, instead of constantly searching for food to supplement our daily rations. I know that my friends felt the same way as I did.

quickly. A day might come, he would say, when I would wish and crave for just one bite of the food on my plate.

Of course I did not agree with him. I felt so sure that I would never crave for food. Well, perhaps the sweet things, but certainly not the meat products. He turned out to be right and I turned out to be very wrong. The day came when I remembered his words. How I wished and longed for the food that I had pushed aside. Many times I would wake up from a dream in which I was sitting at a table full of food, eating all the things I had pushed away, only to find out that it had been just that, a dream, and that I was still hungry and my stomach was still empty.

I remember distinctly one night during the awful cold winter months of 1946–1947. We were lying in bed, sleeping while wearing our coats and hats, trying to keep from freezing to death. I was dreaming that I was eating a *Wurst* (hot dog) at a *Wurst* stand. It tasted so good. My mother nudged me and told me to get back under the covers. I woke up and found myself sitting up and holding my hand as if I had a *Wurst* in it. *Wurste* were another meat product that I had never cared for and there they were appearing in my dreams to taunt me.[78]

During this time I also felt so sorry for my dad. I imagined him enduring a second time in his life without enough food to eat. The Russian prisoner of war camps had a reputation for starving the prisoners.

My dad was six years old when World War I broke out in Germany. It lasted four years and during those years living in Berlin was difficult. Everything became scarce, but food was the biggest shortage. Then it took a long time after the war ended before things became somewhat normal again. As soon as they did, along came the period of inflation when a suitcase full of money bought just one loaf of bread, with prices rising every day. After that period passed, my parents resumed living a somewhat normal life again, not counting the political side of Germany, which was an unsettled commotion. My dad was twenty-three years old when he married my mother and not long afterwards another catastrophe came over Germany—*die grosse Arbeitslosigkeit* (the great unemployment). My parents both lost their jobs and another struggle for survival began for them. I believe my dad had ample reasons for being so conscientious about us eating our food. His memories of those bad years did not fade away as time went by.

---

78 I have never forgotten that dream and I think of it whenever I eat a *Wurst*. How thankful I am that those awful times passed by. I hope and pray that they will never return again.

My mother's youngest brother, Otto, was serving in the German military in Flanders, France during World War I. He sent a picture of himself to his grandmother and on the back of it he wrote:

> *Dear Grandmother,*
> *Many hearty Greeting from your grandson, until we see each other*
> *again, God willing. Please send a little food!*

He too was hungry and forced to ask his family to mail something to eat to him.[79]

My mother had a different experience, growing up on the estate in *Schlesien* (Silesia). Although they had shortages of many things, they had enough to eat. That was the big advantage to living in the country. Footwear was a problem, especially during the winter months when lots of snow fell in *Schlesien*. Their gardener made wooden clogs for my mother to wear. They served her well in the summer months, but not during the cold and snowy season.[80]

Wars are cruel, bringing so much hunger, misery, pain, and suffering to everyone involved.

Wiedersehen mit die Bottgers (Reunion with the Bottgers)

We learned of our friend Frau Bottger's whereabouts and went to see her and the girls. We were all so glad to see each other again. Marlies was alright and she remembered her babysitter, "Rotti-Rotti," but Elfriede was doing poorly. She had always been frail but by then she had trouble walking for only a few steps without becoming breathless. They had been living with Frau Bottger's mother until it became too difficult for Elfriede to walk up two flights of stairs. The *Wohnungsamt* had found a small apartment on the ground floor for them. It was located in a partly bombed out house, quite dismal looking, but they could not be choosy.

Elfriede had come back to Berlin from the tuberculosis treatment center one week after we had been made homeless. Unaware of our loss, she had walked

---

79 My mother was very close to Otto. He had promised her that he would come back home from the war and take care of her, but it was not to be. He was killed on his eighteenth birthday by one of the last shots fired. The war was officially over, but word had not reached his unit.

80 She did tell me that the clogs worked real well for skating on the frozen pond.

from the train station to the still smoldering pile of rubble that used to be her home. She was utterly beside herself with worry about her mother and sister's whereabouts, especially after she was told by someone that everyone in the house had died. She was so relieved when she found that her mother and sister safe and sound at her grandmother's home. The bunker had saved their lives too.

The grandmother's house was located near the bunker, behind the S-Bahnhof Gesundbrunnen. It was not a good place to be at the end of the war, not only because of the bombing raids, but also because of the heavy street fighting that occurred once the Russians entered the city. The worst danger came from the *Stalinorgel's* constant rocketing of the bunker.

They had remained in the shelter throughout the last days of the war. Every so often a Russian soldier would come down into their shelter, supposedly looking around for German soldiers. The Russian soldiers kept reassuring the frightened people that they should not be afraid of them, saying that they would not harm them. They also said not to expect the same treatment from their *Kamerads* who were coming along behind them. They warned that their *Kamerads* were bad and merciless.

When the shooting stopped and it had become quiet, they came out of their shelter and found out, that the war was over, finally. Their house was quite badly damaged but they hung blankets over the open windows in the apartment. They took seriously the warnings about the Russian soldiers and their ruthless behavior. Frau Bottger's two younger sisters, along with their children, joined them at the apartment in the hope that they would be safer in a group than by themselves. They then made up a hiding place for Elfriede and her cousin. They pushed the bed against the wall in the bedroom and covered it with feather beds. One girl lay against the wall and the other one at the foot of the bed, under the featherbeds. The grandmother laid in the bed, with the small children at her side.

The adults would take turns watching and listening for intruders. As soon as they heard strange voices downstairs they would get into their hiding places. They experienced a few anxious moments when one of the soldiers came into the room and picked up one of the crying children from the bed. He almost sat down with it at the food of the bed. The Russian soldiers had a reputation for liking little children. They were probably the ones who had left children behind in Russia. German women took a chance on this assumption but it did not always work. Elfriede and her cousin were very lucky that they were not discovered in their hiding place and were spared the horrible experience of being raped.

Their mothers were not so fortunate. *"Frau Komm!"* ("Woman, come!)—those two words were feared by every woman and young girl, more than anything else that happened during or after the war. I heard so many heartbreaking stories from other young girls and women that that they created a permanent unforgettable place in my memories. Every time I see pictures of the Russian soldiers of World War II, I am reminded of the horrible time when they entered my country and brought such fear and misery to us.

On one of our visits to the country we had stopped to see Frau Katerborn. She told us that her young niece, the police chief's only daughter, had died, leaving behind a young child. When the Russian soldiers entered the outskirts of Neu-Ruppin, she and a group of women and children had fled into the woods to hide from them. They chose the worst place possible because that is where the Russians had set up camp. She was kept there for some time and when she returned home she was in bad shape. Eventually they found out that she was suffering from an incurable disease, syphilis.

In earlier years, based on the Russian soldiers I had met who were cleaning up around my old house, I had been very doubtful about the stories I heard about the Russian soldiers. I had found it hard to believe that people could be so inhuman and monstrous. I found out and learned otherwise, sometimes at first hand, not to trust but instead to fear them.[81]

Frau Bottger asked if she could come along with us on our *Hamsterfahrten* to the country. They needed a little more to eat. In time, she went more often than we did because she had another mouth to feed. Her husband returned from a Russian prisoner of war camp—ragged, malnourished and ill. But she and the girls were happy to have him back home with them. Marlies finally met her father for the first time. Sadly, he was no longer the friendly man I used to know, the man who always had something to say to me when I ran into him on my visits to Oma and Opa. His experiences at the prisoner of war camp had changed him into a different person. We went to see them a couple of times after his return, but we felt uncomfortable around him. He would not acknowledge us. He just sat and stared at us. It was so uncomfortable we stopped going.

---

81   I felt the same fear years later when the East German government took over the leadership of the former Russian sector and trained their police force, the *Volkspolizei*, or *"Vopos"*, into cold-blooded monsters. It was difficult to believe that they were Germans.

Frau Bottger worked hard to nurse him back onto his feet. She succeeded, only to be told by him that she was too worn out and that he needed someone younger and livelier. The poor woman was heartbroken. She did not deserve such treatment, especially after all the trouble and hardship that she had endured. It really bothered me when I heard about it. I wanted to tell him what I thought of him. They had always appeared to me as the perfect couple, happy and devoted to one another. I never expected this outcome. He moved in with a younger woman and divorced Frau Bottger. I wished him nothing but bad luck. He deserved nothing good. It was a very sad and disappointing end to a once seemingly very happy family.

Eventually something wonderful came their way. Elfriede's illness took a turn for the better. The tuberculosis went into remission and she enjoyed much better health. She got married and had a baby. It was so good to see her looking well and happy.

Frau Bottger and Marlies moved to another place in the Russian-sector, where she took the position of superintendent of the house they moved into. Her former husband later tried to come back, but she refused to take him. He had a lot of nerve asking her to take him back after being so cruel to her.

Herr Girndt also returned home from a Russian prisoner of war camp to be reunited with his family. I was very happy for them, but at the same time I also felt very sad. Where was my father? Why was he not returning home to us? What had happened to him? So many unanswered questions.

The Girndt family eventually moved away from Berlin to West Germany to a place near where his parents lived. We missed them, and then we lost touch with them. It was very regrettable.

1946—Visiting the Paulisch Family

My mother and I decided one Sunday afternoon to take the U-Bahn to Tempelhof to see Tante Martha, Onkel Hermann, Hilde and Lieschen. We had not been in touch with them for a couple of years, not since the daytime air raids became so frequent and everyone tried to stay closer to home. We got off at Ringbahnstrasse exit and found the neighborhood surprisingly intact, despite being so close to the airport. The Paulisch backyard practically bordered onto the back of the airport. Ringbahnstrasse was still there, showing some damage but nothing like the destruction of our street. Except for the house that I was born in, our street had been reduced to a pile of rubble.

In front of the Paulisch house was a big crater where a bomb had fallen. It had taken half of the sidewalk away and exposed all the pipes. The damaged pipes had been replaced with new ones but, for whatever the reason, they had not yet closed up the hole. They were very fortunate that the bomb had missed their house, just as the bomb had missed the Laubes' home.

We found them all at home and they were glad to see us. They had given up on us, having visited Hochstrasse and found everything gone. We met Lutz Kraus, Hilde's fiancé. He seemed like a nice fellow. They were planning to get married within the next two weeks. We had timed our visit just right to learn about and then take part in their wedding celebration.

Hilde's Story

Hilde and Lutz met in a very unusual fashion in the fall of 1945. At that time he was still an American prisoner of war and had been put to work repairing roof tops on factory buildings. The buildings were located conveniently close to Tempelhof Airbase. The Americans wanted to use the buildings for a motor pool facility and for supply storage. The factories were all empty. Before the Americans ever entered the city to take command of their sector, the Russians had busily dismantled the machinery and shipped it off to Russia. Lutz was working on one of the rooftops when Hilde, Tante Martha, and some friends walked past. They were on their way to the farmland outside the city limits to do some *stoppeln*, a word describing the act of searching harvested fields for something left behind, usually potatoes. On their way back that evening some of the fellows were playing *fussball* (soccer) in the yard, including Lutz. He came running quickly to the fence to talk to Hilde. And that is how their courtship began, very romantically, with a fence as a chaperone between them. The black American guards were quite understanding and looked the other way. Only once in a while would they order them to move away. Hilde was not the only one that came for a date with someone on the other side of the fence. "Liebe kennt keine Grenzen!" ("Love knows no fences!")

Just before Christmas of 1945 the prisoners of war were released and sent home. Lutz was offered a job working for the Americans as a truck driver. He agreed to take the job, but first he wanted to go home to see his family. Lutz (Ludwig) Kraus came from Odenwald near Heidelberg, where he was born on

May 14, 1923. His family owned a stone cutting business. He had been trained as a stonecutter before he was drafted into the military. His parents hoped that he would stay with them and work in the family business, but he returned to Berlin to work for the Americans, much to his parents' disappointment. I found out later that he had tried to get Hilde to go back with him, but she very sternly refused to leave Berlin.

Hildegard was born in Schlesien (Silesia) on November 25, 1923. She completed the eighth grade and graduated in Berlin from *Volksschule* (public school). Then she served her *Pflichtjahr* (a young girl's compulsory labor service for her country) at a local hospital. After serving her obligatory year, she was accepted as an apprentice office worker at the Lorenz-Gesellschaft. She completed her three-year training program and continued working there. She became engaged to a nice young man, a pilot who was a member of the German Luftwaffe. I remember meeting him once while he was home on leave and visiting with Hilde. I was quite enthralled with this handsome young officer in his sharp-looking uniform.[82] They invited me to come along with them to the *Eis-Cafe* (ice cream café) for a delicious treat. The cafes were still serving *Eis* during the summer months but we had to bring sugar ration coupons along for the *Eis*. Early in 1944 Hilde received the notice that her fiancé had given his life for the fatherland. She would never talk about it and I never asked about it. I felt sad that their short time together had ended so quickly and painfully.

For quite some time Hilde performed volunteer work for the Red Cross, located at Flughafen Tempelhof (Tempelhof airfield). The *Lazarett* (hospital) was moved underground when the daytime air raids began. Through all the bombing raids there never was a bomb dropped onto the airfield. It was a very safe place to be.

At first Hilde only volunteered for a couple of hours after work. But when the Russian army advanced closer to Berlin and her place of work was shut down, she stayed at the hospital without going home. They needed all the help available once the wounded soldiers and civilians began to arrive from the front. There were so many of them that every little space was taken.

When the first Russians were sighted in the neighborhood her superior sent her home, knowing that she lived close by. Hilde took off on her bicycle, pedaling across the airfield instead of the roadway, which was a good decision. She left the bicycle hidden in the elderberry bushes growing along the S-Bahn tracks and climbed over the fence into their backyard. She found Tante Martha in the air raid

---

82   One more example of my special interest for someone wearing a uniform!

shelter along with all the rest of the frightened women and children of their house. There she learned that Onkel Hermann had been drafted into the *Volkssturm*. A small group of *Schutzstaffel* (protective guard) or SS soldiers had come along and rounded up every man in the neighborhood. They were all handed a *Panzerfaust* (anti-tank rocket) and marched off to the front to fight the Russian army. Tante Martha recalled standing outside with all the women and watching the assembly of this most pitiful looking group. Made up of old and disabled men who could hardly move, it gave everyone watching feelings of the utmost despair and the end of hope.

It was not long after Hilde got home that the Russian soldiers were entering Ringbahnstrasse. Everyone hoped that the torn up sidewalk in front of their house would keep them away, but it did not. The soldiers that did not come through the front entrance came jumping over the backyard fences. It was impossible to keep them out.

Hilde had decided to use the *Hangeboden* for a hiding place. It was the small storage area above the front door entrance. She dressed herself in a black *Trainingsanzug* (sweatsuit) and crawled up into it and all the way to the back. Luckily for her, she was a petite girl who could easily fit into the small space. She told me how frightened she was when she heard the noisy Russian soldiers come stumbling up the stairs. Sometimes they made a lot of noise when they entered the apartment and on other times they were quiet, which was worse because she could not tell if they had left or not. She was so worried that one of them might want to check out the loft and come crawling into it to find her. Once they pulled a chair up close to have a look and pushed some of the stuff around that was stored in the little space. She buried her head into her pillow for fear that they might hear her breathing. It was a great help on those nights when the power was turned off. It was the one time when everyone except the Russians was glad that the lights could not be turned on.

Tante Martha found herself a hiding place behind an old cupboard on their big enclosed balcony. She often heard the Russian soldiers moving around the apartment, but only a couple of times did she hear them open the door to the balcony. Inside the apartment they rummaged through every closet and drawer. They had made a real mess of things, but that was insignificant. The main thing was that they had not found either Hilde or Tante Martha, for which both of them were forever grateful.

The Russian soldiers hung around near Tante Martha's house for awhile longer, celebrating their big victory with lots of drinking, singing, and dancing around their campfires. They had built fires in the middle of the street with tables and chairs hauled from the three pubs located on Ringbahnstrasse. The pubs also provided the *Schnaps* for their unquenchable thirst.

The SS Guards marched Onkel Hermann and the other old men out past Marienfelde, where the farmland began at the edge of Berlin. Before they reached the front, if one actually existed any more, Onkel Hermann and two other men were able to get away from the group. They hid out in barns or in wooded areas and slowly made their way back to the upper end of Ringbahnstrasse. There they took refuge in the small factory where Onkel Hermann had been employed for many years as a toolmaker. They hid there until they felt comfortable enough to take the chance of sneaking back to their homes under the cover of darkness. Once back home he kept himself out of sight for fear of being taken away again. Only the Russians would do it this time and the destination would be the dreaded work camps of Siberia. Fortunately it did not happen, and Onkel Hermann was safe after his brief service in the *Volkssturm*.

Lieschen's Story

Lieschen (Elisabeth) was born in Oderberg on September 16, 1925. She lived with her grandmother in Oderberg until she died, whereupon she came to Berlin to live with Tante Martha, Onkel Hermann and her sister Hilde. She was twelve years old when she made the big move from a small town to the big city. She had a difficult time trying to fit in at school while also trying to make up the big differences between a country and a city school. It was a known fact to everyone that the schools in the country were behind the standards of those in the city. But she worked hard and was able to graduate with the rest of her age group.

After graduating from eighth grade at the *Volksschule*, she served her *Pflichtjahr* as a domestic servant and a nanny for a doctor, his wife, and their three children. During her year of service she received a letter to report for work at Siemens just as soon as her service had ended. There she was assigned to assemble parts for *Rakete* (rockets). When the bombardment became so intense that it was causing too many interruptions in their production schedule, the Company officials decided to evacuate the department to Zwickau, not far from Dresden. The group consisted mostly of young girls and three older men, a foreman, a manager, and a handyman. There were also a couple of older women, acting as house mothers. They lived quite nicely in a former *Jugend-Erholungsheim* (youth hostel). Every morning they were escorted to work at a small factory and brought back to the youth hostel after work. It was very peaceful there compared to Berlin. There were no air raids to take shelter from, although they did see and hear big formations of airplanes flying over their town.

Onkel Hermann had relatives living in Bad Duben, not far from Zwickau. Lieschen would go there by train and spent Saturday night with them and return by Sunday evening. It was a nice change for her and she did not have any problems until about a week before the Americans entered their town. She could not get a train ride from Bad Duben to Zwickau on Sunday. The train had been canceled because they needed it for other purposes. She ended up walking and hitching rides with farmers and with German soldiers who were fleeing from the Russians. But mostly she walked back to Zwickau. She arrived there late Monday night and was glad that she had made it back

When she reported for work on Tuesday morning she wished that she had stayed in Bad Duben. Her foreman greeted her with nasty words and threw a fit. He accused her of negligence toward the German Reich. He was very angry with her, unreasonably so. He took her *Personal ausweis* (identity pass) away and locked her up in a room. She was to stay locked up there until he received further instructions from his superiors as to how to punish her. She told us that it was comical watching "*diesen aufgepusteten Truthahn*" ("this puffed-up turkey") jumping around and yelling. She could not be serious about it, so much so that she and her colleagues could not keep from laughing, which of course made it worse.[83]

About two or three days after this incident took place the Americans entered Zwickau. The housemother let Lieschen out of her locked room and advised every one of the girls to stay together. They moved their cots into the large residence hall.

The foreman had vanished. Lieschen was very concerned about being without an identity pass. The housemother and Lieschen searched throughout his office for her identity pass, but in vain. They did not find it anywhere. He also had

---

83   I remember that she told us that for quite some time before this incident they had not received any new supplies for their work. They had kept themselves busy by assembling the parts and then taking them apart again, then repeating the idiotic procedure again and again. It was very boring and made for long days.

taken their money with him. It had been kept in a safe. The girls received only a small weekly amount, similar to an allowance, while the rest of their wages were kept for them in the safe. Miserable cheat! Lieschen hoped that the Russians got hold of him and marched him off to Siberia.

American soldiers, black ones, came to their hostel and looked the place over. They proceeded to tell the housemother that they needed the hostel for their own lodging and that the Germans would have to move out. The girls moved into the factory, where they slept on the floor. They were allowed to take their blankets along, which was nice of the soldiers.

I do not recall how long the Americans stayed before they moved on and the Russians took over the territory around Zwickau. The war was definitely over by then. When the Russians moved into Zwickau it brought along the usual unpleasant changes. Life was quickly very different from when the Americans were there.

Lieschen and two other girls decided that it was time to leave and try to get back home to Berlin. They traveled only after dark because the countryside was crawling with Russian soldiers, making daylight travel very dangerous for them. They used the railroad tracks for guidance, as they did not have a map. They did not run into any problems until they came to a river and discovered that the bridge across it had been destroyed. While they were standing by the river's edge, trying to figure out what to do, a Russian soldier with a horse and *Panjewagen* came along. They tried to run away but when he shouted *Stoij* (stop) and pointed his gun at them they took no chances and stopped. Lieschen was worried that he would want to see their identity passes, something she did not have.

When he approached them they saw that he was an older Russian soldier. He did not ask for their *Ausweis* (credentials), but only demanded to know what they were doing at the river's bank. It took a while, but they explained to him that they wanted to go home. With the bridge across the river gone, they did not know how to continue.

The soldier motioned for them to follow him. They stumbled behind him through thick underbrush, wondering all the while where he was taking them. Finally they came upon a boat, hidden away. With a lot of gestures and words from him, they finally understood that he would come back and row them across the river. He wanted them to wait there for him. They did not know what else to do, so they decided to wait, hoping for the best.

Just before it became dark the Russian soldier returned, bringing with him the oars for the boat. He proceeded to push the boat towards the water's edge. The girls had trouble believing their good luck that a Russian soldier was actually helping them across the river to the *Amerikanski*, as he called the Americans. The old Russian soldier turned out to be true to his word and rowed them across the river.

The girls were so ecstatic for joy when they stepped out of the boat on the other side that they kept hugging the old soldier over and over again. One of the girls showed him a picture of her family, whereupon he took one from his pocket. It showed a woman and children. The picture looked quite weather-beaten. It must have been in his pocket for a long time. He had probably not been home for many years. It was a blessing for Lieschen and the other girls that this kind and caring Russian soldier had come along.

They continued their homeward journey without encountering any other problems. Eventually they came to a railroad station where they halted and waited for daylight. They then learned that a *Bummelzug* (slow train) heading towards Berlin would come along some time during the day. Eventually a train did arrive, although it was already filled to capacity. The only room available was on top of the train. The girls climbed on top of the *Zug* (train) and it moved on, ever so slowly. The train acted like it wanted to go faster but lacked the strength to do it. It really did not matter to the girls. They were thankful that the train was taking them closer to home.

Lieschen and the girls arrived in Berlin at Lankwitz, which was located in the American sector of Berlin. They must have come back sometime after July 4, 1945—the date that the Americans moved in to take over the occupation of their sector. They left the train station, feeling so excited to be back in Berlin.

It was after 7 o'clock in the evening and they wondered why the streets were so deserted. They were unaware that a curfew was in effect. They soon found out when an American military police jeep and a truck stopped beside them. They were asked to show their *Ausweise*. Lieschen had to tell them that she did not have one, nor did they have the special permit that allowed someone to be on the streets during the hours of curfew. So, they were loaded onto the truck and taken to the police station.

At the police station a German translator was located. They were then able to fully explain their situation and Lieschen's missing *Ausweise*. They were told that they had to stay at the station until morning when the curfew was over, but that they could continue on their way home. In the meantime they were treated to bowls of chili, sandwiches and bottles of Coca-Cola. Chili was a totally new food, and the sandwiches were made with soft snowy white bread. They had never had a Coca-Cola either, but thought it was delicious. Lieschen never forgot how good the chili tasted. Years later at the American *Volksfest* in Grunewald, she again had the opportunity to eat "chili" and she enjoyed it just like she had the first time. From then on she would look forward every year to having a bowl of chili when she visited the American *Volksfest*.

1946—Hilde and Lutz's Wedding

Hilde and Lutz's wedding took place on May 11, 1946. It was a double wedding. Lutz's friend Fips (I forget his real name) married Hilde's friend Liesbeth. They had met the same way as Hilde and Lutz did. Lutz and Fips had served together in the German Wehrmacht and were also taken prisoner at the same time. Liesbeth and Hilde lived across the street from one another.

I remember the evening before their wedding. The evening is called *Polterabend* (eve of the wedding). On *Polterabend* old pottery is smashed at the bride's front door to bring good luck. People would save their chipped pottery for just such an occasion. It was then the bridegroom's obligation to sweep up the broken pottery pieces. In normal times there would also have been good food and drinks to be served to every one that came by.

I thought Lutz and Hilde's *Polterabend* was hilarious. Lutz was kept busy all night sweeping the area in front of her door. He would have it all swept up and would go back inside just as a new barrage of pottery would be thrown at the door. It went on and on, all evening long. Poor Lutz did not get any rest while the rest of us were having fun.

On the following morning the two couples, along with their *Trauzeugen* (marriage witnesses), walked to the Rathaus Tempelhof (Tempelhof City Hall) where the marriage ceremony was performed by a justice of the peace.[84] My mother and Onkel Hermann walked with the wedding party to the Rathaus

---

84 My mother and father were also married at the Rathaus Tempelhof. When my mother died in 1988 and we reported it to the responsible official at the Rathaus, they located her file in the basement archives. The file contained her marriage license. They added the death certificate to it to complete the file. I believe this is referred to as "German efficiency."

Tempelhof, while I stayed with Tante Martha and Lieschen to help cook and then have the dinner ready when the newly wedded couple returned. Tante Martha was feeling very weepy. She had parted from two of her rabbits. We all knew that the purpose of raising rabbits was to have them for a meal, but it was never easy to part with them. Thank goodness that Herr Busch, the baker, was preparing them in his oven at the bakery located in the front of the apartment building. He also made two delicious looking cakes, which I anxiously waited to taste.

When the newlywed couple returned, looking very happy, we all sat down to a good meal. Considering the year and the times, we were thankful to have something on the table to eat. The adults had all done a lot of bartering and buying on the black market for this special occasion.

Later on in the afternoon the party became quite lively. Friends and neighbors stopped by to congratulate Hilde and Lutz and extend good wishes to them. There were very few presents or flowers. This was something missed, as it was customary to bring flowers to weddings as a gift. But flowers were very hard to find. The florist shops were still mostly closed.

Liesbeth and Fips later came over with their guests to join us. Tante Martha's place had more room for everyone. There were lots of toasts made with beer and *Schnaps*. The liquor must have been well hidden not to have been found by the Russians.

The last U-Bahn, our homeward transportation, left at 8:30 pm, while the party was still in full swing. It was decided that my mother and I would simply spend the night with them. I do not remember how long I lasted but I know I gave up before anybody else did. A bed was made up for me on the couch in my sister's bedroom—the bridal suite! There must have been some questioning about this arrangement. At the time I had no idea what the concern was, but of course I later figured it out. I remember my mother reassuring my aunt and my sister that they did not need to be concerned, as I was still quite the naïve, inexperienced, and unenlightened girl. I know that I went to sleep right away. I remember waking up once, hearing strange noises and realizing that I was not alone anymore in the bedroom. But I must have gone back to sleep because I do

---

In Germany, a civil marriage is obligatory and takes place at the local *Standesamt* (Registrar's office) in the presence of two witnesses. The church wedding, if any, then follows the civil ceremony. Therefore there may be not one but two records of marriage, one civil and one church.

not remember anything else. Kind of strange now to think that the little sister spent their wedding night with them in the same room!

Working at the Lending Library

I had been going to a neighborhood *Leihbucherei* (lending library) and getting books to read, when one day the owner asked me if I would be interested in working there. I was willing to try, as I was quite bored of sitting around at home. There was very little to do for me and it made the days seem twice as long. I liked to read and by working at the store I could take out books free of charge, which was great. And keeping books in order on the shelves was the perfect job for me. I had always liked things neat and orderly. The job did not pay very much, but every little bit helped. The owner and his wife lived behind the shop. That allowed him to drop in and out. If we became very busy, the owner's wife could also come and help out.

There was one other woman working in the shop who was about ten years older than I was. She came from Vienna, Austria, where she had married a German soldier from Berlin during the war. She came to Berlin to live with her husband's parents and was waiting for his return from wherever he might be. She had not heard from him for a long time. I liked working with her. She was very nice to me and helped me a lot with my first job. When we were not too busy she would tell me about Vienna and its palaces, parks, music festivals and so on. I heard so much about Vienna that after awhile I felt as if I had been there. I also had the feeling that she was very homesick. That was quite understandable, considering just the obvious difference between Berlin and Vienna. Berlin was a giant heap of rubble compared to Vienna. It was very depressing and despairing to look at every day.

We were kept quite busy most of the time at the shop. Many of the customers were elderly ladies who would take out two and three books at a time, mostly romance stories. The owner wanted us to offer the other, more classical, serious books to them, but they were not interested. The shop had not been damaged during the war, so it had a good selection, but a lot of books collected dust for lack of interest. I enjoyed working there and being around people even though a lot of patience was needed. Some of those old ladies were hard to please. It also became quite difficult to do the work as the days grew shorter and it became dark earlier in the day. We had to use candlelight because our electric power was still turned off.[85]

While the job at the library did not pay very much, I was hoping to add the money to the twenty-five *Reichsmarks* I was receiving monthly from the German government as my *Waisengeld* (orphan's pension), paid because of my dad's continued absence, and go to a private school. I had applied at the Harnack School of Languages and the *Haushalts Schule* (home economics school). I had been accepted for the fall semester. I preferred to go to the Harnack School to learn English and French, but the tuition was very expensive. It really was out of my reach without a miracle. If we had been able to withdraw from our savings account we would not have had any problems, but our accounts were frozen. Strangely, the same banks where our accounts were frozen had reopened their doors and were looking for customers to open new accounts. That did not make any sense to us whatsoever.

I met a nice girl, Marion Thiebert, at the school's office. She had been signing up for the fall semester. Even though I did not get to go to that school, we remained in touch and we became good friends. We were both at the same age. Her birthday was only two days after mine, and in later years we often celebrated our birthdays together. She managed to stay at the Harnack School for one semester but then her money ran out too. She had hoped that her uncle in America would send enough to keep her in school, but it did not work out. Her family had been receiving a care package every month from the uncle. At first Marion's mother was able to give her and her older sister Inge the nylon hosiery that came in the box. Marion would take hers to the black market and get a good price for them, which she saved up for tuition to the school. But later her mother had to use the hosiery money for other more necessary things to support the family, including the four younger children.

Marion and her sister Inge were born in Russia. Her family had been part of a group that emigrated from Germany to Russia when Catherine the Great was the ruler. They were called the Volga Germans. Marion's father died when she

---

85 The war had been over for more than a year and we were still living in the dark, thanks to the Russians and their control of the power plant. They were still only providing us with electricity and gas when they felt like it. They had also announced once again that private households were not getting any coal for the forthcoming winter. That made for a very bleak forecast to look forward to. The last winter had been bad enough.

was about two years old and her mother decided to return to Germany with the children. They lived for a while in *Ostpreussen* with relatives, until their mother remarried and they came to live in Berlin.

Marion never cared for her stepfather, especially as she grew older and realized what kind of person he really was. During Hitler's regime he held a high-ranking position in the party's office. They lived well in a nice house in the Grunewald area, with servants and a *Kindermadchen* (nanny).[86] Four more children were born of this marriage, two boys and two girls, and Adolf Hitler himself presented her mother the *Mutterkreuz* (mother's cross). It all came to a quick end when the Russians marched into Berlin. The stepfather traded his uniform in for civilian clothes and disappeared.

Marion's mother's knowledge of the Russian language proved to be very helpful when the Russian soldiers entered their neighborhood. The Russians confiscated their house and several officers moved in. They allowed the family to stay in an apartment above the garage. Frau Thiebert offered to do the cleaning and the laundry for them, which worked out alright for them until the Russians moved out and the Americans moved in. Then they were not permitted to stay at the apartment any longer. They were told to move out immediately. They walked around aimlessly until someone told them about a shelter for homeless people. They lived there for quite a while before a place was found for them. It was located Am Kreuzberg, about three houses from Flughafen Tempelhof. It was an empty apartment, but they were happy to move into it. They used the bunk beds from the air raid shelter, found a table and a couple of chairs, and settled into a very different way of life from what they had been accustomed to living.

1946—HW61 *Haushalts Schule*, Wedding

School started for me at the *Haushalts Schule*. I was a little disappointed that I could not go to the language school, but attending the one was better than attending none at all. The school was located in my old neighborhood, not far from the private and the public schools that I had earlier attended. The old neighborhood surely seemed to keep bringing me back.

---

86   Marion told me that she had often wondered who the real owners of their house were and what might have happened to them. The house had been fully furnished and they had provided only their personal items.

The *Haushalts Schule* was intended to provide guidance for young fourteen to sixteen-year-old girls in finding a profession. It offered a *Lehrplan* (curriculum) containing a little bit of everything, including German, English, social studies, history, cooking, sewing and gardening. I remember that some of my classmates were interested in dressmaking, dress pattern design, and becoming *Kindergarten* teachers.

It probably had been a very good basic learning institute in normal times when all the material needed for teaching the classes was available. Sadly, the times were to our disadvantage. We lacked everything. Almost everything we learned was done theoretically with the use of the blackboard and with only the teacher having a book. Mending and darning was taught using paper, which was extremely difficult to work with. It was hard to keep the paper from tearing. Despite the unusual method, I learned to be a good *Stopferin und Flickerin* (darner and patcher), almost as good as my mother.

The teacher, Frau Schuler, gave us the task of making an apron. It was to be a white one and we were to wear it at our planned *Weihnachtsfeier* (Christmas party). My mother gave me a pillowcase. I had to take the seams out and prepare it properly. It was a project meant to last for several sewing classes and I found it very boring. The biggest challenge was to put contrasting piping all around the apron, which we had to make from scrap material.

I worked diligently on it. I liked the teacher and I wanted to please her. I did not like her belief that if the seam was not perfectly straight—and I do mean straight—it had to be taken out and done again. She was a perfectionist. I had already done a few stitches and I decided to do it the easy way to achieve a straight seam. I noticed that the teacher was busy at the other end of the room so I felt safe to take the chance. I placed the fabric in the sewing machine and only turned the wheel with my hand. I guided it along slowly and it went well. I felt great looking at my straight and perfect seam until I hard Frau Schuler's voice behind me saying loudly, "Fraulein Charlotte, I am very disappointed to think that you tried to deceive me!" Whenever someone called me by my full name I knew that I was in trouble. At that moment I no longer felt very good about my straight seam. Instead I wished that I had never done it. I had made a big mistake. I had lost the teacher's trust and all interest in my apron project.

The classes on gardening were fun. We planted, weeded, and harvested potatoes and all kinds of other vegetables. The school owned a piece of property in a

Laubekolonie (garden colony) near the Bornholmer Strasse Bridge. The French sector ended there and the Russian sector began.[87]

Back at the school we learned how to make sauerkraut, how to pickle cucumbers and beets, and other such tasks. There were three or four kitchen units, very practically arranged with a table and benches, plus a stove, kitchen cupboard and sink. That is where we had our cooking lessons. We were divided into groups of six girls and we took turns being in charge of the preparing and cooking of a meal, along with the serving and the cleanup. We cooked mostly soups and stews using the vegetables from the school garden. We talked about baking but regretfully we did not have the ingredients needed for it. The teacher did show us how to decorate a make believe cake. We made mashed potatoes to use as icing.

I liked the English class, even though it was for beginners and I had studied it before. We had a male instructor and he made it a lot more interesting by teaching us words with which to have a conversation. He had spent some time in England as a prisoner of war and he had only recently returned to Germany. He taught us words describing food and other words commonly used in daily life. We begged him to teach us some popular English songs. He declined at first because he was concerned about *Herr Direktor's* (the headmaster's) opinion of our "sing along," but he eventually gave in. We learned quite a few songs like *Don't Fence Me In*, *Tipperary*, *You are my Sunshine*, and *Kiss Me Once*. It was a fun class.

I also learned how to dance the Waltz, thanks to my other classmates. I had asked my mother to teach me, but she gave up on me after two or three attempts, telling me that I was too stiff and clumsy. Her advice was for me to enroll at the dancing school on Mullerstrasse and take lessons.[88] I went twice to sign up but

---

87   Many years later, in 1984, I almost walked onto the bridge and into the Russian sector with my son, Tom. We had been riding on a bus, doing a little sightseeing around my old neighborhood, when the bus stopped at the end of the line. We got off and walked along with the rest of the bus passengers, but those people were living in the Russian sector and they were returning after visiting the Western sector on a special permit. By then the infamous and inhuman "Wall" that the East German police controlled had divided Berlin. Tom and I were talking and we were not paying any attention to where we were walking until just before entering the bridge. Thank goodness that we realized our mistake in time. We would have gotten ourselves in a lot of trouble with the *Vopos*.

88   My parents both were very good dancers. They looked nice together on the dance floor and I loved watching them. Many times they were asked by their friends to dance the "Charleston" because they could really do it good and fast. They worked

I gave up both times after watching what was happening in the dancehall. The whole procedure did not appeal to me. Plus there was not one tall boy in the group and I just knew that I would end up with the shortest boy in the group and look ridiculous on the dance floor.

No one looked as if they were having fun, either. It looked too formal. The girls sat on one side of the room and the boys on the opposite side. As soon as the music started the boys would jump up and move across to the other side as fast as etiquette allowed. They would make a proper bow in front of the chosen girl and ask them for a dance. The girls would stand up and accept with a proper curtsy. Then, under the direction of a very stern looking matron, they would try stepping "one and two and three and turn." I did wish that my mother could see them. They looked anything but agile.

I also noticed that there were more girls than boys in the group. Consequently some of the girls ended up dancing together. That also turned me off. I decided that the *Tanzschule* (dance school) was not for me. It looked too stressful for me.

I was therefore very happy that the older girls in my class at the *Haushalts Schule* agreed to show me a few steps. We started in the bathroom during our breaks, doing the one and two—humming the tune to ourselves, "*Die Donau so blau, so blau ...*" (The Danube so blue, so blue ...."). The school's regulations did not permit such frivolous actions during school time. And of course we were caught when we tried doing it in the auditorium where there was a piano. One of the girls could play the piano well enough for us to twirl around the floor. We were all enjoying ourselves, but we were interrupted by the *Herr Direktor* himself and given a stern warning not to do it again.

My school friends invited me to come along with them on Sunday afternoons to their favorite hangout. It was a dance hall located in the Russian sector, not far away from where my dad grew up. In fact, my mother remembered that my dad used to go there when he was a teenager. I was really not old enough to be allowed admission to a dance hall without parental escort. Neither were my friends, but they assured me that it would not be a problem. They had been going there regularly, buying their tickets with borrowed ID's from older sisters. My mother gave me permission to go along for the afternoon.

My friends purchased my ticket. I was told to look and act unconcerned and not show any of my apprehension about the whole deal. I tried but I felt

---

hard and long hours during the week, but come Saturday evening they would get together with friends at the neighborhood pub and have a good time.

uncomfortable. I never liked pretending to be something that I was not, and I was afraid of the consequences.

We entered a large hall. The dance floor was situated in the middle of the room, surrounded by tables. It reminded me of the *Tanzschule*, especially when the band started playing and I saw the boys coming across the dance floor to our side. I took off for the bathroom in a hurry. I did not believe that I was ready yet. I wanted a chance to watch a little before trying my "one and two." Besides, the band was not playing the kind of dance that I had practiced. It was a new dance—the swing—and I had not quite gotten "the swing" of it yet.

It did not appear that I would just be able to sit and watch. I also realized that I could not run off to the bathroom every time the band started to play. So I decided to tell whoever asked me to dance that I did not know how to dance.

The bands always played the music to three dances, followed by a short pause. The boy who came along during the next pause heard my story and then told me not to worry, that he would show me how to dance. And of course the band was playing the awful swing dance again. The boy was very patient and forgiving with me, no matter how often I stepped on his feet. He could have taken me back to my table after the first dance, but he endured the two following dances with me. I was exhausted after the three dances ended and ready to go home. My friends just laughed and told me to hang in there and not to give up, that it would become enjoyable. I was not so sure at that point, but eventually I became better and dancing became more tolerable.

I learned about another custom the hard way. If one refused to dance with someone, it was customary to sit through the following two dances. If the rule was not followed, then the girl would find a *Pfennig* (penny) at her place upon her return from the dance floor, left there by the boy with whom she had refused to dance. I found two *Pfennige* left at my place before the custom was explained to me. I did not think much of that silly custom and I collected quite a few *Pfennige*. I danced with whomever I wanted to and not out of duty.

I do not wish to give the impression that all I was interested in at this point in my life was to learn how to dance. Dancing was a big part of our social life. I honestly cannot remember anyone who did not know how to dance at least the most common steps for the waltz, the polka, the *Schieber* (slide) and the foxtrot. As a matter of fact, I decided that these early dance hall visits were too stressful. I was also so fearful that it would be discovered that I was underage and illegally in the dancehall. So I stopped going until many months later. But I did not give up dancing. I practiced whenever the opportunity came along. At our school's *Weihnachtsfeier* (Christmas party), I even felt bold enough to ask the *Herr Direktor* to dance a waltz with me. He accepted and I never once stepped on his feet. I struggled a little with the "left turns" but I hung in there.[89]

The *Haushalts Schule* offered a two-year program but I am sorry to say that I was only able to attend for one year. We just could not afford it any longer. When I started to go to the school I was hoping to be able to keep on working at the library, but because of my irregular schedule it was not possible. I do not know if I learned anything worthwhile to use later on in my life, but I liked going and I missed it and my school friends.

1946—September

After Hilde and Lutz got married, Lutz continued working for the Americans driving their trucks and delivering supplies to various bases in the American sector. He noticed from the time that he started his job that there was quite a black market business going on, mostly with coffee beans and sugar. Once or twice a week he was told to drop off certain bags at addresses he was given. He would later find some cigarettes or a small bag of coffee beans, never more than a half of a pound, left on his seat in the truck. The "pay off" to "keep silent" about the shady dealings meant a lot to him. The coffee beans were a good trading item for other much needed things. And the cigarettes were a treat to a smoker.

It went well for quite a while until one day the military police were waiting for him as he left one of the drop off addresses. He had one bag of coffee beans left on the truck. The situation quickly turned quite nasty because he would not tell them the address for the next drop off. They took him to the police station while other military policemen were sent to his home to search for stolen goods or property belonging to the American forces.

Hilde was at home in bed nursing Traudel, their three day old daughter, when the MP's walked into her bedroom and started to search through everything. It was very upsetting for Hilde, Tante Martha, and Onkel Hermann. Hilde tried talking to them, trying desperately to get some explanation about their rude behavior, but they ignored her and kept on looking. I am certain that the language difference caused most of the problem. I do not know why they did not send an interpreter

---

89   To dance the waltz *linksherum* (counter-clockwise) takes a lot more practice than *rechtsherum* (clockwise).

along. It would have helped the situation a lot. They left when they had searched everywhere and found nothing.

When Lutz did not come home that evening Hilde became more upset. The following morning she walked to Lutz's workplace, looking for information about his whereabouts. But she had trouble communicating with the American guard at the gate. She had taken a picture of Lutz along to show the guard and tried to tell him that he was missing, but it did not get her anywhere. He just shrugged his shoulders.

When my mother and I dropped in to see them that afternoon we found them all in turmoil, and justly so, considering all the things that had happened within the past two days. Not long after we got there, Lutz came walking in, followed closely by two MP's. They were unmistakably keeping an eye on him. When Hilde saw him and his escort she really became upset and started crying uncontrollably. I felt so sorry for her. Lutz looked very tired. He did not talk very much. He just told Hilde that he was alright and that he had come home for some clean clothes. He said that he would come home just as soon as some problems were resolved.

It was a very awkward situation with all of us in the small bedroom. We tried to leave the room but the guard at the door motioned to us to stay put. The MP's and Lutz left shortly thereafter and we were left behind with our unanswered questions, wondering what was going on.

It must have been difficult for Lutz to communicate with the Americans, as he only knew a few common words in English. Nevertheless, a couple of days later he returned home. He told everyone that the problems had been sorted out and that he had been cleared of any wrongdoings, calling them "black market dealings." Regrettably, however, he had lost his job. He felt quite badly about that, but the rest of the family was simply glad to have him back home. He did not talk about the affair, but neither did he seem to be bitter about it.[90]

---

90 It did not take Lutz very long to find a job as a stonecutter making *Grabsteine* (tombstones). He worked there for several years until his employer decided to move his business to West Germany. Again he was not unemployed for long before he was hired as a chauffeur for the Senate of Berlin. Many times he had to drive the car through the East Zone of Germany to Bonn, which was then the capital of West Germany. The "*Herr Direktor*" would fly to Bonn because he did not like the inconveniences that were involved in traveling by road through the East Zone. But he wanted his car there and at his disposal while he was attending government meetings.

The Fall of 1946—*Rieselfelder* (Irrigated Fields)

That fall my mother and I took the S-Bahn to the suburbs, where Berlin's *Rieselfelder* were located. All kinds of vegetables and some fruit trees were grown there. Before the war they had supplied Berlin's markets. By 1946 they made their deliveries to the Russian kitchens. Nevertheless, we hoped that we might still find something left behind after the harvest, although we had never been there and we did not know what to expect.

When we got off the S-Bahn at the end station in the Russian Zone, we noticed other people walking along with *Rucksacks* on their backs. We asked them about

---

It was a very scary experience driving through the East Zone from Berlin to West Germany and vice versa. Lutz did not have any special privileges just because he was driving a government car to West Germany. There were long waits at the checkpoints while every person and car was checked thoroughly. He had to wait in the long lines with everyone else. Western newspapers, magazines, and books were not allowed to be transported through the East Zone. If one was found during a search it brought severe punishment, and their jails had a horrible reputation.

The Autobahn through the East Zone was forever in need of repair. It made driving very dangerous. The East Germans were never in any hurry to repair it. They really did not care. They just waited until the West German government offered to pay for the repair work.

The East Germans knew how to frighten people and they practiced at it. The speed limit was strictly enforced and the changing of lanes was strictly prohibited. Stopping along the Autobahn was also prohibited. It was only allowed at controlled rest areas. The *Volkspolizei* (people's police) or "*Vopos*" watched everyone very closely and enjoyed catching motorists who were driving only one or two kilometers over the speed limit. They would impose big fines upon them and only collect payment in western currency. They also stopped people who drove safely and well under the speed limit. Any disagreement with the *Vopos* over why they were being stopped and the *Vopos* would only increase the fine. Some people were even escorted to the police station and kept there for however long the *Vopos* liked.

I traveled once in 1951 and again in 1953 on a *Reisebus* (tour bus) through the Russian Zone, as it was called then, before the East Germans took over control. I do not recall that the Russian controls were quite as bad as when the East Germans took over. The *Vopos* were well instructed in their harassment tactics towards people from the West. I almost feared the East German police, my own countrymen, more than the Russian soldiers, which was really very sad. It was indeed a nightmare driving through the East Zone of Germany, constantly being worried about being accused of something the *Vopos* concocted. It was a mean game the *Vopos* played with the people from Berlin and West Germany.

the whereabouts of the *Rieselfelder* and we were told to follow them. When we arrived at the fields I was amazed to see such a vast area under cultivation. As far as I could see were narrow ditches divided by two or three meter wide raised beds of dirt that were used for planting. There was water in the ditches, but it did not look dirty and it did not smell.

Sadly, everything had been harvested, except that in the cabbage rows the outer leaves had been left standing. We got busy cutting them off. We were glad to have them to take home with us. We had not been given a whole cabbage for a long time. We were used to getting only the outer leaves of a cabbage.

Our bags were almost full when we heard a yell from the only man in our group, who said loudly, "Here comes trouble!" Sure enough, we saw trouble coming too when we straightened up from our crouched position. A Russian soldier on a horse was galloping towards us, and there was no time and no chance to run away. He rode up on the main path and started shouting and gesturing to us to get out of the cabbage field. We gathered up our bags and walked out to the road, whereupon he ordered us to empty our bags and then get out of there—"*Daway-Daway!*"

We were very disappointed to have to give up our red and green cabbage leaves. The man from the group suggested that we walk on a little way and then sneak back to see if the Russian had left and maybe get our leaves back. We did not think that it was a good idea. He appeared to be a very angry soldier. He probably would not have hesitated to make use of his pistol.

We had walked on a little further when we came upon a bench with an old woman sitting on it sorting through a basket of greens. My mother recognized the greens as *Brennessel* (nettle) and she became curious, asking the old woman what she was doing with it. She told us that it made a good spinach if one used the young leaves. After rinsing the leaves well, they were placed into a pot full of cold water. The water was brought to a boil, then poured off. More cold water was added, with a little salt, and again brought to a boil. It was cooked until tender and then prepared just like spinach. Thanks to our chance encounter with this old woman, we learned to prepare a good tasting substitute for spinach.

While my mother sat and talked with the old woman, I got off the bench and walked over to an area where some fruit trees stood. They were all picked bare, of course. As I stood there looking into the ditch, I discovered two green apples lying hidden in the high grass, just waiting for me to find them. I picked them up and saved them for our ride back home, surprising my mother with my tasty find.

The people who had been with us in the *Rieselfelder* came to the train station with empty bags. They had gone back when they thought that the Russian soldier would no longer be there, but his horse had trampled the pile and made a mess of the cabbage leaves. We did at least share our newly learned recipe with them— "*Brennessel a la Spinach!*"

Back in our neighborhood we did not have any luck finding the nettles among our ruins. We had to look long and hard to find enough for a meal. Then one day I mentioned our search to Tante Martha. She suggested looking along the railroad tracks in back of her house. Sure enough, that was a good area for nettles. We found a lot there.

Tante Martha also told me about my grandmother and how she made a living after her husband died. She collected all kinds of *Krauter* (herbs), berries and mushrooms in the woods and in the fields. She would then dry them. Putting small bundles together she would then take them in baskets to the market to sell. Tante Martha and her older brother Fritz would go along and help their mother. The youngest boy, Otto, would stay at home to watch the little sister, my mother Frieda. Otto was only five years older than my mother was. It sounded like a very hard life and a backbreaking way to make a living. But of course there was no *Soziakhilfe* (welfare) available. Life was a lot different than it is today.

Meeting Inge, a School Friend

On one of my walks back from visiting Tante Anna's house I came upon a pleasant surprise—my friend Inge, a former classmate. She came walking out of a house that did not look habitable. Actually, all the houses on the street looked badly damaged.

The public school that Inge and I attended from the first grade to the fourth grade held very unpleasant memories for me, because of our teacher Frau Fritz. Early in the first grade she had selected Inge and Rosemarie as her pet students, always emphasizing to the rest of the class how much smarter they were than us. They never could do anything wrong, even when what they had done was obvious she would find a way to justify it. On several occasions during a test I would finish before Inge or Rosemarie, but I was afraid to raise my hand. I had raised my hand once before they did and I was treated so awful in front of everyone in the class that I did not want to repeat the experience. I was also doubtful about my answers. After all, how could I have the answer before the "Two Smart Ones"? What made the one occasion so hurtful was that my answer had been correct. Frau Fritz had insinuated that I had copied the answer from someone else. The accusation did not make any sense and she knew it, but she enjoyed putting me down.

I was friends with both girls. Inge had always been nice to me, but Rosemarie could be unfriendly at times. They both lived in the same apartment building, just a block away from the school, and they were both being raised by a single parent. I saw them often outside of their house on my visits to Oma and Opa's place and we would talk and laugh together. At school, however, they were very distant, especially Rosemarie.

Inge told me once that she could not understand Frau Fritz's behavior either and that she felt it was very unfair to the rest of the class. Maybe it showed that I was afraid of her, dreading every morning, wondering what the day might bring when she entered the classroom. I would hope and wish that an illness would keep her at home, but during the four years of having her for a teacher she never missed very many days.

It was like a holiday when she did not show up and, even though we had to squeeze in with another class, I enjoyed every minute of it. I envied the girls in the other classroom for their teacher. They acted so relaxed and content, and so different from our class. I never said anything to my mother about the problems I had with the teacher for I knew that it would only make it worse if my mother confronted her about it. I was not the only one who was treated badly, but I could sense pleasure and enjoyment in her cruel ways towards me.

In the early spring of 1942 I applied at a private *Mittleschule* (middle school), along with three of my classmates, my dear friend Elfriede Letter, Waltraut Haase, and Eva Marie. After we passed an entrance examination, which lasted all day, we were accepted for a six-week trial period, starting after the Easter vacation. I remember well the day when the reports were sent to our classroom. Frau Fritz had the task of telling us whether or not we had passed our entrance exam for acceptance at the *Mittelschule*. She knew that we had been anxiously awaiting the report, but she sat at her desk and took her time, deliberately keeping us in suspense. She finally called each one of my friends and told them the good news. She kept me waiting a longer while before she let me know that I had been accepted. She very sarcastically told the class and me that it would only be for a short time and that I would soon be back where I belonged. Then Frau Fritz sent a note home with me asking my mother to come and see her. She tried to convince my mother that I—"*die Charlotte*"—was not the studious type, that I would fail, and that it would be very disgraceful for us. My mother told her that we would deal with whatever happened and that she did not expect me to fail. What an awful woman to have for a teacher!

I remember the trial period as a very worrisome time. It was a long six weeks during which I lived in constant fear that I might fail. I wanted very much to stay at the *Mittelschule* and learn the English and the French languages, and I studied extra hard to avoid a return to Frau Fritz's classroom. We also had to work with Eva Marie a little and help her where she had problems. "*Gott sei Dank!*" ("Thank God!"), I did not fail the trial period and neither did my three friends. I felt so relieved and happy that I could stay at the Mittelschule.

Sometime after we left the public school, the *Schulamt* (school board) decided to change the regulations regarding transfers from and entrance to a *Mittelschule*. They gave the teachers the authority to select students for the *Mittelschule* accordingly to their academic performance. The tuition for a private school was also to be paid from then on by the *Schulamt*. They abolished the entrance examination, but not the six-week trial period. At the end of that period the principal had the option to decide whether the student could remain at the school or return to the public school. I never would have had a chance to go to the *Mittelschule* under the new rules. Frau Fritz would have had me in her classroom for two more years of her cruel treatment.

Naturally, under the new system Frau Fritz took advantage of the opportunity and sent her two favorite pupils to the *Mittelschule* I attended. But Inge and Rosemarie did not pass the trial period and had to return to Frau Fritz's classroom. I am certain that they received her fullest consolation, putting the blame for their failure on someone else. I do not mean to gloat about their unfortunate outcome, but it proved that they were not as smart as Frau Fritz kept telling us. Inge never mentioned to me the reason she was sent back to the public school and I did not ask her.

Inge and I had not seen one another for about three years. She and her mother had lost their home on the same night as we had in 1943. Inge had not seen Rosemarie since then. She invited me into her home to say hello to her mother. We were quite excited to see one another again and to know that we had both survived the war. We had lots to talk about.

When I left to go home, Inge came along with me for a ways. A couple of houses further along, a boy stood out front and Inge called a greeting to him. He came over to us and she introduced us to one another. His name was "Hotte," a nickname for "Horst." He appeared to be younger than us, a good-looking boy with dark curly hair. Dressed in ragged clothing, he looked as fashionable as we did. I saw him a few more times after that and he always waved. He was a very nice boy. Years later I read about a young movie actor by the name of "Horst Buchholz" who was in Hollywood making a movie with some big American movie stars—the Magnificent Seven. In his comments about his life story he told about growing up in Berlin, am Wedding, and that his nickname was "Hotte." The picture of him showed a young man with dark, curly hair dressed very smartly in a cowboy outfit. I am quite certain that he was the boy I met down the street from Inge's house. If so, his life was a fairy tale rags to riches story—a boy from Wedding, the working class district, becoming a well-known movie star. I was happy for him.

1946—My Mother Loses Her Job

My mother lost her job at the construction site. She had been expecting it, due to the arrival of cold weather and also because of the rumors that the City had run out of funds for such projects. It was nice to have my mother home, but it was not for very long. The unemployment office found her another job as a *Putzfrau* (cleaning woman) for a small business, a variety store, owned by a Jewish brother and sister. The store was located in a partially bombed-out building on Badstrasse, about two or three blocks from where I was going to school. The two owners appeared to be older than my mother. They sold different kinds of things. I remember pots, pans, silverware and other utensils. My mother purchased our small frying pan there. It had been made from a German soldier's helmet and it was the best frying pan we ever had.

She worked from early in the morning until after the store closed, very long hours for starvation wages. My mother was kept busy all day long with different kinds of jobs to do. Sometimes I would stop during my lunch break to see her. If I stopped in the evening I would wait for her and we would ride the *Strassenbahn* (trolley) home together. I did not like going to the store because the owners were very unfriendly and distrustful.

Early every morning my mother had to build a fire in a pot-bellied iron stove that stood in the middle of the back room at the store. The hot water had to be ready when the storeowners arrived for their coffee. She could always start a fire in our stove, but she struggled with this pot stove every morning. When they arrived they counted out the real coffee beans for each pot of coffee. They never offered a cup of coffee to her but they allowed her to take the used coffee grinds home with her. We were glad to have the grinds, and shared them with my Opa and Oma. We could brew coffee from the used grinds at least two more times and it would still taste better than our *Muckefuck*. A few times my mother was able to add a teaspoon full of sugar to the grinds and I would eat it with a spoon, pretending it was chocolate. Very hard to believe today.

1946—A Trip to Oranienburg

One day Tante Anna asked me to come along on a trip to visit Tante Ilse to check out some clothes that she had laid aside for me. With winter weather coming on, I desperately needed some warm clothing. I had outgrown the only two skirts that I owned, not to mention the rest of my clothes. There really was not much left to my wardrobe. It looked quite pitiful. But I was not alone in that situation. Many other poor souls shared the same predicament.

Tante Ilse seemed very pleased to see us. She looked as frail as ever to me. Their *Apotheke* (pharmacy) was still closed. They had nothing to sell. Her husband, the pharmacist, was working at the local hospital.

Tante Ilse made us lunch, potato pancakes with applesauce. It was delicious. I did not even mind the smell of the cod liver oil that she used to fry them. Their house was nice and warm. The Russians did supply their citizens with an allocation of coal, and they allowed the people to go into the forest to gather up firewood, which was priceless during these times.

Tante Ilse gave me several articles to wear—a winter coat, skirt, sweater, scarf, hat, and mittens. I was so grateful for the much-needed items. She also gave Tante Anna several worn sweaters for her to unravel. She could use the wool to knit new sweaters. Tante Anna was the "handicrafter" in the family. I was told that my great-grandmother also was a good one. I am certain that Tante Anna learned her skills from my great-grandmother but that they bypassed my Oma. She had never shown any interest in doing craftwork. Once before, in 1931, Tante Anna had come to my aid when I was in need of warm clothes to wear. She had knitted a sweater outfit for me and crocheted little dresses for me to wear later. It was during the time when my parents were out of work and very poor. Now here we were once again in a very similar situation.

I had never had very much contact with Tante Ilse and I was very surprised to find her so caring and sympathetic towards me. When we left her house we were really loaded up. Besides the clothing, she had also given us some coal and potatoes and a small bottle of cod liver oil, a gift from the old pharmacy.

Tante Anna later made for me a pair of pants from an old wool blanket. Very simple in style, they looked like a little like today's sweatpants. I was ever so thankful to have them, along with Tante Ilse's other donations, when the cold, cold winter of 1946–1947 moved in.

1946–1947 "Der Schreckens Winter" ("Winter of Horrors")

Winter came early that year. It was a horrible cold winter that brought us freezing temperatures from November until April, hunger and cold, and so much misery and suffering. Six decades have passed since that awful cold and merciless winter and I still shudder when I think about it, even after all the years.

Tegeler Forest

Inge and I went on a search for firewood into the Tegeler forest. We were getting desperate because we did not have any kind of heating material in the house. We could not even make some hot water for tea or coffee or to fix our meager meals. Whenever the Russians turned on the power people would know because their lights would come on, but we did not get the message with our gas lighting. If they turned the gas on during the night, while we were asleep, we had no way of knowing about it and we would miss our chance to make use of the gas.

We went to the forest and found some small birch trees about ten or twelve feet tall. With a very dull saw we fiddled until they fell. It took us quite awhile. Inge had not done any such strenuous work before this *Baum-fallen* (tree cutting) and it showed.

While we were sawing we were watching and listening for any kind of noise, vehicle, or people with dogs. Our biggest fear was getting caught by the French *gendarmerie*. A few times we heard vehicles driving close by and we hid in a nearby ditch until we felt it was safe to return to our woodcutting job.

We sawed the tree trunk into small pieces that we could carry in our knapsack and a couple large bags. We hid the rest of the sawed up pieces in the ditch, hoping they would still be there when we came back for them the following day. It was a very heavy load to carry. Nevertheless, we had decided to forego the trolley-car stop near the entrance to the woods. Instead we walked the back road to the next stop. That made our walk quite a bit farther, especially with the heavy loads we carried, but it made us feel a little more at ease. If we were stopped by the French *gendarmerie* and asked where we were coming from, we could try and make up a story. We had a small chance to convince them that we were coming from anywhere but the forest.

Inge had a difficult time carrying her load. We had to stop and rest quite a few times before we arrived at the Strassenbahn-Halte stele (Trolley car stop). She almost did not make it into the trolley car. On the last step her load pulled her backwards. Luckily for her, I was standing right behind her and was able to give her a good push, which sent her to the other side of the car. She slid down and sat on her bag. She looked exhausted and worn out. I could tell that I had a lot more stamina than she did and a lot more experience, all of which I had come by in the previous three or so years, out of necessity.

I was very surprised to see Inge show up the next day for another adventurous trip to the forest. We made several more trips and were lucky not to be caught by the French police. It could have resulted in serious consequences. The firewood was a big help even though the fire did not last long without any coal. At least it lasted long enough to heat up our water and cook what little we had.

Standing on the Corner

I met Inge a few times on the weekends at Brusseler Strasse Ecke Mullerstrasse, just around the block from where I lived. The corner attracted young people from around the area. I did not know anyone except for Inge, so I was like a new kid in the neighborhood. It was an odd meeting place. Because of the cold we would hop around from one leg to the other to keep warm while we talked. Sometimes a few of us would go across the street to a movie theater where at least we were sheltered a little from the wind. It was the smallest movie theater, long and narrow, that I had ever been in. They did not show anything but French movies, stupid detective stories or tales about the French Legion, all in their language with German subtitles underneath. It was very boring.

On one such "stand-around gathering", the discussion turned to music. One of the boys in the group mentioned that he had an old wind-up gramophone and a few records at his home. He invited us to come home with him and listen to the music. We took him up on his offer and marched about ten blocks up to the end of Mullerstrasse, past Quarter Napoleon. It was a long walk, but we were all used to walking by then and never questioned the distance. We walked everywhere.

His house was located in a devastated area. It reminded me of my old neighborhood. His parents were sitting in the kitchen and looked a bit surprised at all of us walking in. Their son explained to them the reason for our intrusion and they nodded their approval. We went to his room and sat around the floor listening to his records. This certainly was different. I had never done anything like that before. Everyone seemed to enjoy the musical evening. The lights were on, which made it extra nice. The boy's mother brought us cups of peppermint tea to drink, a wonderful warm-up treat.

Cold

As winter became much colder and brought ice and snow, our gatherings at the corner stopped. No one wanted to be outside more than they had to. My fifteenth birthday came and went, and so did Christmas and New Year's Day of 1947. They must all have been uneventful. I do not remember anything about them. All I remember is the awful, bitter cold and trying to keep warm, an almost impossible task.

Our apartment had not been damaged in the bombardment that took place in the neighborhood. Our double windows still had glass in them. They were solidly frozen over and remained so all through the winter months. The kitchen felt like a walk-in freezer. We had hung a heavy blanket in front of the balcony door. It was frozen stiff as a board. We spent as little time as possible in there, and this included the bathroom. Both the painted and the wallpaper covered walls sparkled and glistened from all the ice crystals that had formed all over the walls.

When the water pipes froze up, we had to carry pails full of water from a street pump around the corner, about two blocks away. There were always long lines at the *Pumpe*. Waiting for our turn could be extremely cold, especially with an icy cold wind blowing. By the time I would get home with my two pails of water, there would be a thin layer of ice on top. But it was a blessing to have the *Strassenpumpen*. I do not know what we would have done without them. They gave us precious water when other sources failed.

My mother and I slept together in a twin size bed to keep each other warm. We never undressed. We wrapped scarves around our heads and stayed under our covers. And we prayed that we would wake up the following morning. So many people did not, especially the elderly.

We kept our bread and a small bottle of oil in the dresser drawer in our bedroom, thinking that it might be better than the kitchen, but it too froze solid. We used every piece of furniture that we could spare for firewood, using it to heat water or to cook a meager meal. We were desperate.

Early one morning while on her way to work, my mother came upon a mob of people ransacking a truckload full of large pieces of *Presskohle* (pressed coal). My mother climbed onto the truck and was able to get about eight pieces of *Presskohle* into her bag. It was "precious black gold."

The circumstances under which we lived had made us into thieves. That was very sad, as was the fact that we felt no remorse for our action. We did wonder about the poor driver, hoping that he escaped punishment for losing the load of coal. It only took a few minutes to empty the truck. I wonder if he did not do this on purpose, leaving his truck unattended while he went inside a house. He surely knew how precious the load on the truck was and how desperate the people were for some heating material.

Our Neighbors—the Kirschke's

I liked our neighbors, the Kirschke's, despite all the stories that I heard about them. They had become members of the Nazi party and had taken advantage of the situation when Hitler took over the leadership in Germany. But I do not believe that they were fanatic believers or followers of the party. They never acted like it by crying over the end result or the defeat of the regime. They were simply a family, which, no matter how bad things were for others, always managed to somehow stay on top.

Herr Kirschke was a chauffer for a high-ranking SS officer and traveled between Paris, France and Berlin, Germany. They lived well throughout the time that the Nazi regime ruled and lasted. Frau Kirschke was a housewife. Their daughter Inge was married to an SS officer from Austria who was killed during the war. Their son Egon, who was about four years older than me, was terribly spoiled by his mother and sister. He was quite a charmer, but also a big nuisance at times.

Egon had been drafted him into the home guard at the close of the war. After his training he was stationed in the suburbs of Berlin, but he never took part in any kind of war activity. When the frontline advanced closer to Berlin, he managed to escape and to come home, whereupon his mother and sister hid him until the war was over. They were very lucky that he was not discovered. People told us how the SS soldiers searched the neighborhood cellars and ruins for German army deserters during the last days of the war. One soldier who used to live at No. 36 Seestrasse made it all the way back from Russia to Berlin and hid out in the ruins of house No. 38. He sent a note with a boy to his wife to let her know where he was and she brought him civilian clothes to wear. It went well for a couple of days until someone tipped off the SS search party and they came and hung him on the lamppost nearby. What an awful thing to do. That poor soldier did not deserve to die like that. There was no justification for such an evil act. Everyone knew that the war was over when the Russians entered Berlin and every German soldier that they got hold of would be marched off to their prison camps in Siberia. I am glad that I was not in Berlin during those last days of the war and was spared seeing such cruel lynching acts.

When the war was over Inge married a man of Jewish descent in order to escape retaliation for their affiliation with the Nazi party. He was a survivor of a concentration camp and also the only survivor of his family. The change of fortunes put him in a different position in society, whereupon he was able to help the Kirschke family. They were able to remain in their home and keep their belongings because he put a claim on them. I remember him as a quiet, pleasant man so different from the rest of the family, who were such a boisterous group.

After the de-Nazification period, Inge divorced the quiet man and married someone who blended perfectly into the family. He worked for a company that manufactured butter and cheese. He must have held a good position with a good income because he could afford to drive an American Oldsmobile at a time when most Germans were glad to have a bicycle to ride around on. Our family doctor drove an old Volkswagen. Even he could not afford anything better. They were also the only people at that time that I knew of who had a telephone. Very few private homes had one. It was very expensive to have it installed, plus there was the monthly fee. All of the neighbors in the house were well aware of the family's history and dealings but were willing to overlook them because they would never refuse someone asking for help.

During that awful freezing cold winter the Kirschke's invited my mother and me for a game of rummy. Neither one of us knew how to play the game, but they promised to teach us. I played while my mother chose to watch. It was a lot of fun. Inge was my partner while I was learning. We played for *Groschen* (ten penny coins). I remember how excited I would get when I won. Looking back, remembering their smiles and facial expressions, I am quite convinced that they let me win. Still, it was wonderful to put our own misery aside for a couple of hours and enjoy a warm room and nice company, despite the cigarette smoke, which made my eyes burn. It was very nice of them to invite us into their home. My mother and I needed a little change from our otherwise very depressing lifestyle.

The Mercedes Palast Movie Theater

Now and then my mother and I would go to the movies, to the Mercedes Palast, which was located around the corner from us. We always had to wait in long lines until fifteen minutes before the starting time in order to buy our tickets. Many times they were sold out when we finally reached the box office, causing disappointment after the long wait.[91] The theatre were still only showing French movies with German subtitles and they were still stupid, but it felt warm inside the theater with so many people crowded close together. Almost everyone would bring a blanket to wrap around themselves. Before the movie started there would be a little variety show, which was the best part of all. Someone would sing or tap dance, juggle or do magic. Whatever it was, it was always nice to watch.

The Mercedes Palast was a beautiful movie theater still intact after the bombing raids. It had comfortable, plush seats. A piano rose up from below the front of the stage and someone would play it before starting time. During the last weeks of the war the theater had been used as a shelter for the homeless people in the area. We too had been told that we could use it because many of the designated shelters had been destroyed. The Red Cross had set up a food distribution center and a first aid station in the lounge. My mother and I had checked it out, but it was very crowded. We had instead decided to stay with the Laubes in the air raid shelter.

In the American sector the theatres were showing American movies with German subtitles underneath. Hilde and Lutz invited me to go with them on several Sunday afternoons. The first American movie I saw was "Thirty Seconds Over Tokyo." A war movie!! But I liked it much better than the French movies. There, too, Lutz had to wait in long lines for tickets. Lots of people were looking for a change in their otherwise drab and cheerless everyday life. Of course the

---

91   Another sign of the French superiority over us was that they received their tickets free of charge. American soldiers did not patronize the German *Kinos* (theaters), at least not in Berlin. They had their own.

other reason for the long lines was that many theaters had been destroyed during the war.

Parting From My Beautiful Watch

Many times that freezing cold winter I would go to bed cold and hungry. I would dream about tables laden full of all kinds of good things to eat; and then I would wake us and realize that it had only been a dream. Our food rations were very skimpy. The French kept our rations at a subsistence level, just a tiny bit above starvation.

To add to our misery, we discovered that our ration cards had been stolen. My mother had kindly allowed two people to stay with us overnight and that was their thanks. There were still three weeks ahead of us before we could obtain new cards and we faced them without even the meager food allowance that the cards allowed. We did not know what to do for three weeks without food. We turned in a report at the police station but getting the cards back looked quite hopeless. Our fears proved to be correct, for when the police found one of the culprits the ration cards were gone. My mother's kindness had turned into a very unpleasant situation for us all.

In utter despair for something to eat for the next three weeks, my mother decided to look up an old friend for help. They had only recently met after many years of not seeing one another. Her name was Wally and she seemed to be a very likeable woman. When my mother encountered her she had told us her reason for being in our neighborhood, but we had a difficult time at first believing her story. The proof of her story was in the bag that she carried—two 1500 gram loaves of bread (two to three pounds of bread). She had worked out a scheme whereby she would seek out bakeries where young apprentice girls were working behind the counter. Somehow she would confuse them so badly with the coupons that she would end up walking out with one or two loaves of bread and without giving them a coupon. An incredible story. She traveled all over the city, two or three times a week, and most of the time she was successful. I tried it once in our bakery, where I knew the girl working there. I engaged her into a conversation after I told her what kind of bread I wanted, but she never went to get it until I gave her the coupon for the bread. I would have liked being present when Wally pulled off her scheme.

I remember going along with my mother to Wally's home on Mehringdamm, not far away from where my friend Marion lived. Wally had just come home from one of her bakery trips and there were three loaves of bread lying on the table. She was in a good mood, along with her husband, who we met for the first time. I could tell that she was doing this *brot-hamstern* for this man. The bread that she brought home was used for all kinds of needed things. It gave him a nice warm place to sit and amuse himself playing cards with a friend, puffing away on cigarettes and drinking real coffee. All the while, she was walking around and searching out bakeries where she could try her scheme.

I did not like that man, especially the horrible cough he had. I stayed far away from him, because I was convinced that he had tuberculosis, a disease I did not want to get. He looked like he had it. He was very thin and his color was sickly. But he was definitely in charge of their household.

When my mother told Wally of our problem and she asked her if she would sell us a loaf of bread, she looked to him for an answer and he shook his head "no" to a cash deal. He became more interested when we mentioned trading my watch for the bread. He looked the watch over and offered us three loaves of bread, each one weighing three pounds. We would receive one loaf then, another loaf the following week, and the final loaf the week thereafter.

I did not like parting from the watch that my dad had chosen for me and I hated to give my watch to that man. When we were being searched on our return trip to Alt-Ruppin I had been so lucky hiding the watch from the Russian soldiers. I was convinced that he got the better deal of it, but we had no other choice but to accept his offer. It helped a little thinking about my dad's words to us that we were to use the jewelry for whatever we needed. We were certainly in great need. We had to have something to eat for the next three weeks.

Our treasure was, however, getting smaller. My ring had floated away in the river and now someone else would wear my watch. I still had my necklace and my earrings, but I did not know for how much longer. My mother only had her watch left. Everything else had been traded for something.

My mother told me that Wally never would have made such a deal on her own. She had always been very kind and helpful when my mother had met her years ago. But she had fallen under her husband's influence and it made things different.

My mother told me that Wally and her parents had been very nice and helpful to her when she came to live in the big city. She had come to Berlin in hopes of making more money than she could in Oderberg. She needed to support her two children. She had made a big mistake at her divorce trial, listening to her mother and older sister Martha and following their advice not to ask for child support and just rid herself of the "no good bum". It certainly was an easy way out of his responsibilities as a father and a difficult one for my mother to fulfill. They never had any contact with him again. Hilde never saw or heard from her father or her grandparents after they left Silesia and Elisabeth never met them.[92]

Wally and my mother worked together and became good friends. Wally was always inviting my mother to come along to some kind of amusement taking place on Saturday nights. As much as my mother would have liked to, she could not afford it. She did not have the money or the time to spare. She was living with her sister and brother in law, Tante Martha and Onkel Hermann, in Tempelhof. She either worked on weekends at a second job or she took the train to Oderberg to see her daughters. Her mother was taking care of them.

Finally, she agreed to go along with Wally and her parents to a costume ball in Schoneberg. It turned out to be a very special and fateful moment in her life. My mother had very dark hair and it was decided that she should go as a *Zigeunerin* (gypsy woman). Wally's mother made her costume.

My dad attended the ball with his parents and with his fiancée and her parents. It was quite a sensitive situation. He was dressed as an *Ulanen-officer* (King's guardsman). My mother remembered how awkward it was to dance with him because of the long saber he carried. It kept getting in their way. He kept asking her to take off her mask and let him see her eyes, but she refused to do it. She left the ball before the magical hour when everybody took off his or her mask. After searching for her unsuccessfully, my dad was able to talk Wally into giving him her name and address. It sounded a lot like Cinderella's story. My dad told me, whenever I asked to hear the story of how they met, that my mother was the prettiest "gypsy" he had ever seen, and that he knew at the time she was the girl for him. Wow!! I loved hearing that story!

My parents were very happy together despite all the problems they encountered along the way. As I wrote earlier, my grandparents did not agree to their marriage.

---

92 I thought it was all very sad. I asked Hilde once how she felt about this history and she just shrugged it off. She told me that as far as she was concerned he never existed. I am glad that she felt this way, but it still was sad. He must have been a very heartless person. Many years later my mother found out that he had also remarried and had children and was living in Berlin.

They wanted their only son to get married to his fiancé Else and not marry a divorced woman with two small children. But my dad had made up his mind and they got married without his parents' blessing. Thanks to Wally, the *Ulanen-officer* found his *Zigeuner Madel* and we became a happy family.[93]

I never accompanied my mother when she went to pick up the bread. She did not go back again after picking up the last loaf of bread. As much as she would have liked visiting with Wally, she would not do so because of the husband being around.

I would not have mentioned the ugly incident about our ration cards but I wanted to explain the reason for trading in my watch for three loaves of bread. Eventually my mother gave her watch to me. I wore it until we had another crisis. It was a never-ending struggle for us as we tried to survive.

1947—My Opa Passes Away

Whenever I went to visit Oma and Opa that cold winter, I found Opa all covered up in bed. He had become very apathetic and listless. He hardly acknowledged my greeting. Oma told me that he only got out of bed when he had to use the bathroom.

Towards the end he became more and more withdrawn and lost all of his will to live. Opa died that spring of 1947. He was 67 years old. My grandparents' landlord had a telephone because of his job at the courthouse. When my Opa passed away, the landlord called the police station in our district, which happened to be across the street from our house. They notified us about Opa.

1947—Spring Arrives in Berlin

We waited a long time before spring arrived. Then it took a long time before we thawed out, along with our homes. It would have helped a lot if we could have opened our windows and balcony door to let the warm outside air come into our cold home. But they had been so completely frozen shut that we were afraid to

---

93 As I related earlier, my arrival brought the family back together. My grandfather was very pleased to have a granddaughter. I have always complained about not having any talents. Not long ago a friend told me that I do have a talent. My talent is bringing people together. I never thought of it that way, but as I was writing this part of my memoirs it made me wonder if maybe there is something to his observation.

break the already fragile windows by pulling on them. We kept busy mopping water off the floors. It was dripping off the walls, taking off some of the paint and the wallpaper too. It was a real blessing when the water pipes thawed out and we did not have to carry water from the street pump anymore for our daily use, especially for the toilet.

After Opa passed away, Oma came more often to visit with us. I remember one Sunday afternoon very well. Sunday afternoons were enjoyed by drinking a cup of good coffee and eating a piece of delicious pastry. Because of this tradition the bakeries would open on Sunday afternoons between two and four o'clock. They were only allowed to sell pastries. At our first home we were quite spoiled because we had a bakery in the house. My mother very seldom baked. It was so much easier and convenient to get whatever everyone wanted at the bakery.

On this Sunday we were sitting together and reminiscing about the good old days, which seemed so long ago. We could only reminisce and wonder if we would ever see such times again. During my childhood years, ice cream was only available during the summer months and it tasted more like Italian ice. We would start watching in late spring for the *Eis* (ice cream) flag to be hanging above the entrance to the *Eisdiele* (ice cream parlor). That would be the sign that the ice parlor was open for business. It was always something to look forward to in the springtime. They would stay open until late summer when they would close. When the cold temperatures came along, they would reopen the store and sell wild game and poultry (rabbits, ducks, geese, chicken, venison, etc.)—a seasonable alternative due to the lack of refrigeration.

I remembered having seen an *Eisdiele* around the corner from us, on Mullerstrasse. I offered to go and check it out. I had heard that they were selling some kind of fluffy cream for which everyone had to bring their own bowl, and that no coupons were required. I took off for the corner to have a look if the *Eis* flag was hanging in front of the store. I saw that it was, so I ran there quickly and joined the long line. I overheard the people talking about this mysterious white, fluffy stuff and how good it tasted and how filling it was.

When I got my bowl filled, I was told not to take too long getting home with it because it melted quickly into liquid. I hurried home as fast as I could. We did not even bother dishing it out into separate bowls. We each just grabbed a spoon and started eating it. It was like foam and very sweet. It did not taste bad and it was very filling. But not long after we finished eating it, we noticed this awful aftertaste. It was very bothersome and it was followed by visits to the bathroom.

None of us felt very good for the rest of the day. Oma even spent the night with us. We never had that stuff again. Just mentioning it made our stomachs cringe. Even after all these years, I still wonder about that white foam and what it had been made from.

A New Dress

Something joyful came along when my sister Hilde gave me a piece of white crepe material to have a blouse made. My sister had saved the material for her wedding gown but had then decided that wearing one was inappropriate. She gave me some, had a blouse made for herself and the rest was used to trade for other much-needed things. We instead decided to use my black confirmation dress with the white material and have another dress made from it. Tante Martha's neighbor was a dressmaker and she made a beautiful dress for me. She took the black part of the top of the dress off and replaced it with the white material. It turned out very nice.

It really felt good to have a nice, new dress to wear along with the shoes for which I had traded my confirmation shoes. However, it turned out that my shoe trade had not been a good one. They were pretty, but the thin soles were soon worn through on the bottom. My mother the cobbler kept cutting soles out of cardboard to fit inside the shoes. That worked fine until they became wet and soggy, and then the inserts dissolved.

Whenever I had time I went to Tempelhof. I liked being around my sister Hilde. She was fun to be with. She never made me feel that I was in her way or that I bothered her. I took my niece Traudel for long walks in the baby carriage that we had bought for her when she was born. It was a used one, but it was in very good condition. It held up for two more children after Traudel.

I do not recall seeing or visiting with Lieschen very much. Even at times when she was around, she never had much to say to me, other than a greeting. Perhaps she still held a grudge towards me from an earlier time when I had not been nice to her.

1947—Fred and Helga Get Married

An exciting event took place in Tempelhof on Ringbahnstrasse sometime that spring of 1947—the first marriage between a German girl and an American GI.

The newspapers all reported in on the front page. The Mayor's office even sent flowers, along with the Mayor's good wishes. It was treated as the beginning of a hopeful relationship between our two countries.

Helga, the bride, was a friend of my sister's. She lived in the adjacent house with her mother and grandmother. Helga had been employed at Tempelhof Airbase, where she worked in an office and where she had met Fred. He had been stationed at Tempelhof with the military police and he came from Alabama. Everyone in the neighborhood was well aware of the fact that Fred's home was in Alabama. He must have given Helga the record with the song "I come from Alabama with a banjo on my knee ..." because she played it a lot, over and over again.

After the wedding Helga and Fred left for Alabama. When the first letter from Helga arrived, it was not a happy one. Her grandmother read it to Tante Martha and they both ended up crying. She wrote about how homesick she was living way down south in Alabama, with fields of cotton all around and very few white people. Fred's family operated a gas station and a repair shop for cars. They lived together in a big house with all his brothers and their wives and children. Before long, babies started arriving and she complained about having a difficult time making ends meet. After 1949, when things began looking better in Germany, the grandmother started mailing packages to Alabama to help them out. The last report from Helga was that she finally convinced her husband to move to a bigger city where they both could find employment and make a better living for themselves and their children.[94]

Bad Duben

That spring of 1947 Tante Martha had asked my mother and me to come along with her to the country on a visit to Onkel Hermann's relatives. I do not remember anything about the place, only the *Bauernhof* (farm). These relatives

---

94 I wish that I had paid better attention to where she was going in Alabama, but I had no idea at that time that I would ever travel through Alabama. When I did, I thought of her and wondered if one of the small villages we were driving through might have been the one where she had come to live. It must have been a drastic change for her coming from a big city to a small southern town in Alabama in 1947. Hopefully their life improved when they moved to a bigger city. Before she left Berlin, she gave me her English lesson books and a dictionary, the latter of which I still have. For something to do I used to practice translation from German into English. I liked doing it, and the books were a big help to me.

were the same people that Lieschen visited on weekends when she was evacuated to Zwickau. They were nice people, working hard to make the farm productive, an almost impossible task. First, they had to fulfill a quota that had been set by the Russians. Only after that could they keep whatever was left for themselves, which was usually very little. If the quota demanded twelve eggs and their chickens only laid ten eggs they were forced to buy or trade the two missing eggs from another farmer. It was an ongoing, frustrating occurrence. I felt very sorry for them. They looked so tired and exhausted when they came home in the evening.

I only went along this one time, but Tante Martha went quite often and my mother joined her whenever she could, especially at harvesting times. On this visit the three of us helped with jobs around the house and yard and had supper ready for them. It was not the kind of food that hard working people needed to keep going, but it was better than nothing at all

I have never forgotten this one and only visit because I became very ill after eating too much *Ruben Sirup* (sugar-beet syrup). They had cooked up a big barrel of syrup, something I had always liked spreading on my bread for breakfast. The barrel was stored in the room where we slept and I had trouble resisting the smell. It was too tempting; so I would take a ladle full and lick away. It tasted good, but my poor stomach did not like it in such a quantity. It became very upset. I spent a lot of time in my favorite place, the outhouse. Many years went by before I tried it again as a spread on bread.[95]

---

95 In the years to come their lifestyle never changed. They continued to struggle, trying hard to hold onto their farm. Tante Martha tried helping by taking things to them, especially after the Berlin Blockade had been lifted and we were able to again buy things in stores. Eventually, however, the controls at the railroad stations became so strict that it was difficult to travel to Bad Duben or anyplace else in the eastern part of Germany. They struggled on for a while longer but life became intolerable under the harsh and unreasonable Russian rules. I believe they left their homestead in 1951 and came to Berlin. In order to escape punishment for disobeying their rules, they fled their home after dark and left everything behind. They walked all night on country roads, avoiding the main roads for fear of getting caught. They stayed with Tante Martha and Onkel Hermann until they were granted a residence permit to stay in Berlin. Onkel Hermann found them a superintendent job that came with an apartment in a house just a couple of houses away from theirs. It worked out well for them, thanks to Onkel Hermann's help. Jobs were hard to find, especially for an unskilled laborer, as were apartments.

It was a very caring deed that Onkel Hermann and Tante Martha performed for these people in their time of need. Eventually a few more of their relatives arrived on

My Mother Changes Jobs

My mother quit her job at the Kaufhaus Gutfeld and took a job with a French family. She was a little hesitant about it, but the meals that went with it were very appealing to her. It meant that we had her daily ration for a little more to eat. Our neighbor, Frau Gertrud Hampel, had been employed as a *Putzfrau* (cleaning lady) with French families for quite a while. She kept telling my mother to do the same, mainly for the benefit of the meals.[96]

My mother's French family consisted of Monsieur and Madame Ducy, their young daughter and a puppy dog (a male boxer). Monsieur Ducy was a young good looking man who was an officer in the French gendarmerie. He was quite pleasant. Madame Ducy, I am sorry to say, looked completely the opposite and not at all like the stereotype about French women. Her overall appearance was very disappointing. Their little girl was about three or four years old, an adorable, pretty child. She also had a pleasant disposition and my mother enjoyed taking care of her. She was the reason that my mother kept going back every day. Madame Ducy was difficult to deal with because of her moodiness. My mother dreaded going there every morning, wondering all the way from Seestrasse to Sansibarstrasse what kind of mood Madame would be in. But the little girl was always so happy to see my mother that it made up for Madame's unpredictable and rude behavior.

---

their doorsteps, asking for a place to stay. They came from the Spreewald area, where Onkel Hermann originated from, and from Oderberg, where Tante Martha and my mother were born. It was mostly the younger generation that was fleeing from the harsh lifestyle that the communist rulers had imposed upon them. It was very sad for them to leave their families, homes and belongings behind, not knowing if or when they could return. I was told that the men gave avoidance of being drafted into the People's Army as their main reason for leaving their homes in East Germany. As for Tante Martha's relatives, I have wondered at times if the family returned to Bad Duben to again take possession of their homestead after the unification of Germany.

96 The German government paid the wages for the people who were employed by the dependents of the occupying forces. It was quite a nice arrangement for the French, British, and American families. Sometime in 1951 or 1952 this arrangement was discontinued and they had to pay their help out of their own pockets. Needless to say it ended up that many German people found themselves unemployed because their employers could not afford paying their wages. I offered to take a job with the French as well. Gitta Hampel, our neighbor's daughter, had gone to work for them. She was a couple years older than I was, but my mother would not hear of it.

Apparently her husband had the same problem with Madame Ducy. My mother witnessed almost daily arguments with loud shouting, things flying through the air and doors slamming. It usually happened while they were having supper. It was very disturbing and it was very upsetting for the little girl. She and the little girl would hide in the kitchen. My mother never found out the cause for these tantrums. She did not understand their language.

Some mornings, when my mother arrived at the apartment, Madame would tell her what needed to be done and then disappear into her bedroom. My mother liked those days. She would quickly do her assigned duties and then get the little girl ready for an outing to the park, along with the dog. Otherwise the little girl and the dog would spend the day indoors as they usually did. Madame never took her anywhere. She was not a good mother. She cared more about the dog than she did for her own daughter. The dog had the habit of nipping at the little girl's legs. She wore dresses all the time and her legs were exposed. He was just a puppy dog being playful. But it hurt her and she would cry out. Madame would ignore her cries and never try to discipline the dog. It bothered my mother a lot and she tried to teach the dog not to do it. He did behave as long as Madame was not around.

Warmer Weather

As the weather grew warmer and people shed their winter clothes it became obvious that many people were afflicted with horrible carbuncles on their legs, arms and necks. They were ghastly looking, like an open boil that had been broken. I had first noticed them on people the year before. Apparently it was an illness that did not go away. I was every so thankful that neither my mother nor I contracted this awful disease. People were standing in line all the way to our house from the doctor's office, which was a block away.

Tegeler-See, Freibad Tegelsee

My friends from the old neighborhood asked me to go swimming with them in Tegel, a place I used to go with my dad before the war came along and interrupted our good times. We all met there and we enjoyed ourselves. The boys were such good swimmers and I envied them for it. I wished that I had learned to swim better. I was not afraid and I surely tried, but somehow I had problems with the breathing technique, something I never was able to learn.

We all looked very stylish in our self-made bathing suits. The boys had taken printed blue neckerchiefs, which were worn as a trademark by carpenters and masons, to make their slip-on bathing suits. They looked like today's brief style underwear. They seemed to work well enough. At least they did not lose them while jumping around in the water.

Someone had given me a dark blue skirt made of wool fabric. I made myself a two-piece bathing suit out of it. Luckily, the lining held it together; otherwise it could have expanded to twice its size after getting wet!

Tegel held many wonderful memories for me. I loved going there with my dad. We would leave very early in the morning with a basket full of food that my mother had prepared for us the evening before. There would be potato salad, fried breaded pork chops, *Bouletten*, and many other delicious things to eat, but there never seemed to be enough. I had to be reminded at home to eat. I never seemed to be hungry. But it was a different story when I visited a beach. I craved food all the while we were there and I have never changed. I am still that way today, more than sixty years later.

It was a long ride on a streetcar to Tegel, but we made it there much faster by bicycle.[97] I sat on a seat behind my dad on his bicycle. I believe that the age limit was five years for that kind of transportation and I know that eventually I was considerably too old. It did not help that I also was quite tall for my age. So my dad kept watch for policemen, who usually were seen standing on corners. When he spotted one he would tell me to make myself as small as I could and we would hope to be lucky. We were never stopped. It was not because we had fooled the policeman. It was more likely a kind act of overlooking our unlawful outing.

My dad knew all the little shortcuts and once we got to Tegel, leaving the city behind, we rode the rest of the way on a road through the woods. Before my dad got married he used to go camping in the Tegeler forest. He had a small tent and a collapsible boat that he paddled around with on Tegeler-See. He had lots of fun with it. Freibad Tegelsee had also facilities for *Nackedeis* (nudist naturists). They hid behind a huge wooden fence! We tried finding a peephole without being successful. We never saw anything.

---

97 My mother never came along because she dreaded spending her only day off from work on a crowded streetcar for the long ride to Tegeler See. She rode the S-Bahn every day to Tegel and Eichborndamm, where she worked for DWM, Deutsche Waffen Munition. She preferred staying home and having a quiet and relaxing Sunday.

I had lots of good memories. We always had a good time except for once, when I accidentally stepped on a sharp piece of glass. My dad had given me money to buy myself an *Eiswaffel* (ice cream cone) at the kiosk. It happened on my way back. My dad had been watching for me. When he saw me sit down so suddenly he guessed that something happened. He came running to me. When I showed him my foot he picked me up and rushed me to the first aid station. The nurses laid me down on a table and tried to take my melted *Eiswaffel* away from me but I would not part from it until my dad promised me a fresh one. The following I remember best of all. The nurse asked me to be a very brave little girl while they were getting the glass out of the bottom of my foot. To help ease my pain I was supposed to look at our beloved Fuhrer Adolf Hitler's picture that was hanging above me on the wall. I remember looking up at the Fuhrer's stern look and deciding that I would rather hold my dad's hand. It was a painful experience but I do not remember having any problems with my foot afterwards. Once they pulled the piece of glass out and bandaged it up, it must have healed alright. And I did get a fresh *Eiswaffel*, which made everything better right away.

On a Constant Search

I had noticed that a *Damenmode* (ladies fashion) shop had opened its doors. I took a closer look and found a woman inside, unpacking and hanging up a few dresses. I felt as if I was dreaming. It was something I had not seen for years. It was quite dark inside the shop. The big window was still boarded up with only the small *Guckloch* (peephole) in the center and the electricity was probably off. But what I could see looked very good to me.

I asked the woman what was needed to purchase one of the dresses. She told me that I only needed a coupon, a specific amount of rags to be used as a trade-in and, of course, money, which was the easiest thing to get. I went to city hall and was able to talk the nice *Beamter* (official) out of two coupons, one for my mother and one for me. I managed to get the needed rags, too, with the help of Tante Martha.[98] I took the rags to be weighed. They gave me a piece of paper stating the

---

98   I would really like to meet the person who made up such a ridiculous requirement. In our case, where were we supposed to get rags from, other than the clothes we were wearing. It was a really dumb rule.

I would also like to mention that the ridiculous requirements for purchasing clothing continued until 1949. I often wondered if they had a similar system in West

amount I had brought in. With those papers in our hands, my mother and I went shopping for new dresses.

We were so happy to get new dresses to wear. My mother's wardrobe was very sparse, especially her winter coat. It was threadbare. Having worn it for at least four years, plus having used it for a blanket, the coat was showing its wear.

I am wearing my new dress in a photograph we had taken in 1947. I had been visiting my friend Marion when she came up with the idea to have our picture taken. She had noticed that a photography shop had reopened in her neighborhood. So we got ourselves all spruced up. Mainly we fussed with our hair. Then we went to check out the shop. The photographer seemed glad to see us. I had the impression that we were his first customers. It was a silly idea, but we had fun doing it.

Doctor Krause

I finally went to see a dentist to have my teeth checked. I had been very concerned about them. My back teeth were becoming loose, especially one that wiggled back and forth. The dentist who I visited told me that my teeth were detaching from my gums due to poor nutrition. I had some form of nutritional deficiency in my diet. He pulled the very loose one and he was ready to pull the rest of them, but I stopped him in time. I told him that I would rather wait and let them fall out, than to have them all pulled out ahead of time.

I was very upset about this prognosis. I had always taken care of my teeth. It was a promise I had made to my dad. To lose them in this way seemed so unfair. The thought of false teeth in my mouth had the same effect on me as a horrible nightmare.

After a while, I could tell that my teeth were again tightening up to my gums. I went to see Doctor Krause, who had been highly recommended to me as a very good dentist. He checked my teeth thoroughly and he told me that they were alright and that he did not see any problems, which was a big relief to me. During the examination he asked me a few questions about myself and I mentioned to him that I was looking for an apprentice job in some kind of office. When he was done with me, he asked me if I would like to come and work for him as his receptionist.

Germany. I cannot help believing that we were treated like poor orphans in Berlin while the people in West Germany were able to buy things a lot easier than we were.

I was quite surprised at his unexpected offer. Before I accepted, I made certain that his office had a modern setup. I had tried once before to work in a dentist's office, but there I had to empty and clean out a holding tank underneath the chair and into which the saliva drained. That was a very unpleasant and nauseating task. I had tried hard to overcome that feeling, but I could not handle it. I had to give up the job after one week. But Doctor Krause had a very modern office and so I accepted.

I learned that Doctor Krause was leasing his office while the original dentist was waiting to be "de-Nazified" before he could return and resume his work. He was well liked and respected around the neighborhood. He had served in the German military as a dentist and had been stationed in Paris, France during the war. He was married and the father of a little boy. Doctor Krause was a truly nice man, just like everyone said, but he also had a dark side which surfaced eventually. He fit perfectly the description of a member of Hitler's elite group, a true Aryan. He looked especially so when he wore parts of his former uniform—the black boots, gray pants, white shirt, gray cardigan, and army coat.

Thinking now about his appearance and how much he looked like a former German officer, it seems strange that he had so many French military members and their families for patients. There must have been a dentist of their own kind available to them, yet they chose Doctor Kraus. I do believe that he spoke French fluently. I never heard him hesitate or search for words during a conversation with French people.

The French people were treated like private patients and given an appointment, whereas other people came and waited in the waiting room for their turn. The French patients would sign a form after the treatment and about once a month, depending on how many he had treated, Doctor Krause would travel to Frohnau, where the French headquarter was located, and turn in the forms to collect his fees. He would also present them with an order form for his needed medical supplies. The form had to be signed by the French authorities. Then he could go to the warehouse to get them. Doctor Krause took me along once, on a Wednesday, when the office closed at noontime. I was surprised to learn how much time was involved just waiting for them to see him and take care of his requests. It really was quite a roundabout way to deal with the fact that he treated French people.

I liked working for him and we were kept quite busy, which suited me fine. I hated sitting around with nothing to do. It was too boring.

Because of my age I did not earn very much money for my work. The employment agency made up the pay scale for juvenile apprentice employees. It was considered to be an allowance while in training. It paid thirty marks per month for the first year, then forty marks per month for the second year, and fifty marks per month for the third and final year of the apprenticeship. The juveniles were only supposed to work 35 hours a week and they had to attend a *Berufsschule* (vocational-technical school) one or two times a week, depending on the nature of their training. It was somewhat like a work-study program, but it started after eighth grade graduation from public school, a much younger age than work-study.

Frau Michaelis

The last two years had not been easy for us, living with Frau Michaelis and her ever-changing moods. Whenever Frau Michaelis had some good, clear moments, she would ask my mother to go with her to see a lawyer to make out a will. She wanted to make sure that all of her furnishings in the apartment would go to my mother. Well, those rare moments never lasted very long, not long enough to visit a lawyer. And we never thought that a court would acknowledge a will from someone in her mental condition.

I remember coming home to a locked-up house door and having Frau Michaelis come to let me in. That would only happen when she was in a clear state of mind. Many years before, my father had told my mother that he did not get a house key until he was eighteen years old. That supported her decision to do the same with me. It did not make any sense to me, but whatever her reasons were, she stuck to them. Locking a house door up at nine o'clock during the summer months was really too early. It would still be daylight, with lots of people out for a nice, cool stroll in the evening. It did not matter very much during the winter months. Then the house door was locked up at eight o'clock. But these had been the rules forever and ever. I did not like the rules, but I grudgingly tried to obey them.

Sometime during this time in 1947, Frau Michaelis suffered a slight stroke during the night, after which she could no longer move her legs. We called a doctor for help and he promised to find a place for her in a nursing home, but we had not heard from him and it was becoming harder for my mother to deal with her needs. Our neighbor Frau Kirschke had also called the guardian to let her know of our situation, but we had not heard from her either. It was entirely left up to my mother to take care of everything.

Frau Michaelis was a small woman and she did not weigh very much, but she still was a heavy load to carry to and from the bathroom. It was extremely tiring during the night, when the old lady would constantly call for us. If we ignored her, she would get louder and louder, disturbing not only us, but all the neighbors around us as well. We made ourselves a bed on the floor in the small spare room but it did not help much. We could still hear her crying for us to come and help her. It really was a sad situation and we felt so helpless. It also really was not like her to be so demanding and inconsiderate. She had been forgetful and confused and she had been known for making up stories, but we had become used to one another and we did not like seeing her this way.

When I arrived for work one morning, Doctor Krause looked at me and asked in a teasing tone if I had been out late the night before because I looked very tired. When I heard him say this, I lost my composure. I started to cry and I told him about our problem at home. He offered to call his friend, who was a doctor, and ask him to stop by our place to see what needed to be done.

Doctor Krause's friend was able to find a nursing home where Frau Michaelis could get the needed care. He took care of all the arrangements. I was told that only a few nursing homes had survived the war and very few ambulance vehicles. It was therefore difficult to obtain a place in a nursing home as well as an ambulance to transport a patient to it.

We were very grateful to Doctor Krause and his doctor friend for their help. We felt bad for Frau Michaelis, but we were unable to give her the care that she needed. But before she departed, we had to deal with another one of her outbursts of difficult behavior.

My mother had told Frau Michaelis about the arrangements that had been made for her and she had agreed that it would be better for her to go to a nursing home. But when the ambulance attendants came to take her away, she refused to go. No matter what my mother or the neighbors said to her or how they tried to make her realize how much better care she would receive, she refused to go along with them. Of course the attendants refused to take her against her will, not even after her mental condition was explained to them. They were ready to leave when my mother tried one more time to change her mind. She got a slice of bread and told her that she could have it if she agreed to go along with the attendants. She left smiling, holding on to the slice of bread as if someone had given her a present. We felt relieved, but also very sad. It was not the kind of outcome we had anticipated. We had become used to one another and missed having her around.

My mother visited Frau Michaelis at the nursing home and found her asleep every time, with her food untouched on the bedside table. She would wake her up and ask her why she had not eaten her bread and drank her tea and she would reply that she was not hungry or thirsty. That was a big change for her, she who had been hungry all the time.

I do not remember anymore how long she was in the nursing home before we were notified that she had passed away. We notified her guardian and were told that all the arrangements for her funeral had been taken care of previously. She did let us know when the funeral would take place. My mother, Frau Gattke and Frau Kirschke went to the funeral service where Frau Michaelis was buried next to her husband. It was the same cemetery where I had found her sitting on a bench near the entrance. We had not known the connection until the funeral. The only other person attending the service was her guardian. She took my mother aside afterwards and told her that she need not to worry about the apartment, the furnishings, or anything. She said that she would take care of everything as she had promised my mother when we first agreed to move in with Frau Michaelis. Before long we found out how well she had taken care of everything.

Doctor Krause's Dark Side

I felt a debt of gratitude towards Doctor Krause for coming to our aid in our time of need. I considered him a truly nice man, always acting correct and professional. Therefore I was totally unprepared for his other side.

One evening I walked the last patient to the front door. When I turned to go back to the office to finish up my book entries, it happened. He came towards me and he took hold of my arm, trying to pull me up close to him, saying words to me that were not nice at all, and very improper. I had never seen him like that and it really frightened me. Somehow I was able to get away from him and I ran out of the office, hearing him laughing behind me, calling me a silly girl. I ran home crying, feeling very betrayed in my trust and respect for him. I could not understand what had just happened to me. I was only fifteen years old and he was close to my father's age. Why would he treat me that way? And as I had done many times before, I was wishing that I had my dad to run to. I needed him so much. I believed that these things would not have happened if my father were around.

I ran right into my mother who was standing in the hallway with Frau Peters, a neighbor. She had been the one who recommended the doctor to me. Both of them looked at me quite questioningly, asking why I was running and crying and not wearing my coat. When I blurted out what had happened to me, they both looked bewildered. They kept asking if I was absolutely certain about what had happened. Frau Peters was very adamant with her questions. She had trouble believing my story, for which I did not blame her. I had the same problem. It was very hard to believe. My mother did believe me. She knew that I would never even think of making up such a story. I told her that I was not going back. She agreed with me and said that she would go and pick up the coat that I had left behind in my hurry to get away.

The following evening Doctor Krause appeared at our door, bringing my coat and asking why I had not shown up for work. It was unbelievable seeing him standing there and behaving as if the past evening had never happened. He did all the talking, while we just stood and listened. We really did not know what to say. It was very confusing. When he started to leave he turned to me and said that he expected to see me back at work the next morning, since he saw that I was not sick. He also wanted to let me know that he had hired another girl to help me with my work.

The whole situation was incredible. I liked my job and I knew how difficult it would be to find another one, but I feared that the ugly incident might happen again. It was a difficult decision and I gave it a lot of thought, but knowing that another girl would be present gave me the courage to give it another chance.

When I returned to work the next morning, the doctor's personality in the office was as it had been before the awful evening. It was as if nothing had happened. The new girl was about my age and we got along alright. Her presence did make it a little easier for me. It allowed me more time to assist the doctor when he was working on a patient, especially when he was extracting teeth and had the patient anesthetized.[99]

---

99 Anesthesia called for fast work. A couple of times I witnessed how strong a person could become under an anesthetic and how silly they would behave. I remember two people, a man and a woman, who were both small of build. They were each given an ether-anesthetic to have many of their teeth pulled during one session. We usually strapped them down with a belt around their chest, arms, waist and legs, but at this

1947—Another year comes to an end!

One day in late 1947 Madame Ducy told my mother that she was expecting a baby and that it had better be a boy because she did not like girls. What a sinful thing to say! My mother hoped that it would be a boy, for the well-being of the child. Perhaps Madame's continued moodiness was caused by her pregnancy. I certainly hope it was not caused by any dislike of girls, much less her own sweet little girl.

The year 1947 had not brought us any changes for the better and I do not remember doing anything special on my sixteenth birthday. We were still living with shortages everywhere. But we were hoping and praying that the new year would bring us what was needed to make our lives a little easier and better.

Madame Ducy invited me for Christmas dinner, which was very thoughtful of her. I was looking forward to it because she was a very good cook. I do not remember what she served, only that everyone had a bottle of wine at his or her place, including the little girl, who sat next to me. I could not believe my eyes. Until then I had never even had a glass of wine. Watching the little girl drinking it like water I knew that I had a lot of catching up to do. I felt lightheaded after one glass of wine and despite all the good food that was being served, I asked to be excused. I had to get home. My head was spinning and my stomach was not doing so well either from all the rich food. Sadly, I missed the desserts, my favorite part of a meal. I made the three blocks back to our home and collapsed on the sofa, where I found myself the next morning. My mother had tried to wake me up when she came home, but I was out. This happened after only one glass of wine, proving that I was definitely my father's daughter. Based on the stories that my mother told me I believe that my father and I were very much alike. At parties he never lasted to the end either. He always managed to disappear before it was over.

---

time, judging by their size, we kept the one around the legs a little bit too loose. It turned out to be a mistake. They both developed great strength and kicked up their legs. I tried to tighten up the belt around their legs, but they would not hold still. It took both of us girls to hold them down by lying across their legs. The little man had become very powerful. The woman did not become quite as strong, but she behaved very silly towards the doctor. It was quite amusing, especially since I knew her as a very proper businesswoman. I never forgot about that experience and I always wondered about myself and what my reactions would be under an anesthetic. Years later, when I was given gas to have a tooth pulled, I remember seeing the amused expression on the faces of the doctor and his assistant. I must have been silly too.

1948

My mother helped Madame Ducy get ready for a big New Year's Eve party that she and her husband were hosting. When my mother came home we both went to bed. We did not have anything to celebrate. It was good that we were not able to look ahead. We would have been very discouraged. 1948 brought us more privation, unpleasantness and inconveniences.

On New Year's Day my mother went very early in the morning to the Ducy's house where she found lots of cleaning up to do. The little girl was very happy to see her. My mother and the little girl did not see Monsieur and Madame Ducy until late in the afternoon.

In early 1948 Monsieur Ducy was transferred to West Germany. Madame told my mother that she was going home to France to have the baby. Her parents lived outside of Paris, where they owned a small hotel. Hopefully the little girl's grandparents were nicer to her than her mother ever was.

A surprise visit!

One day in either late January or early February I decided to go home during my lunch hour, something I did not do every day. I knew that my mother was at home because she was between jobs. When I came around the corner on Seestrasse, I saw a truck parked in front of our house and I wondered who was moving.

As I came closer I recognized a couple pieces of the furniture and I started running. Our front door was wide open and through it I heard my mother's voice, arguing with someone. She was holding onto a tablecloth, which a woman was trying to take from her.

When my mother saw me she started to cry, telling me that these awful people were Frau Michaelis' relatives, her brother, his wife, and their son. They lived in the Russian zone and they had come to claim the furnishings in the apartment as their inheritance. My mother had been caught by surprise when she opened the door and found them standing in front of her, showing her a paper that supported their claim. Their appearance was so unexpected because we had been told repeatedly by Frau Michaelis and her guardian that all her relatives had died and that she was the only one living. Looking at these people, they appeared to be anything but dead. I wondered where they had been keeping themselves the past two years while we had cared for Frau Michaelis.

My mother had tried to talk to them, explaining our situation, but they were unapproachable and would not discuss letting us buy the furniture from them. They would not even consider leaving us at least a bed to sleep in, or a table and a couple of chairs. The old woman was especially greedy. She had started to pack up everything, including our bedding, when my mother had stopped her. She was going by what my mother had told her earlier, that we had lost everything during the war.

The small white tablecloth had been lying on a round table by the window. Her argument was that we could not own anything anymore, especially not the tablecloth, and so this old woman was trying to gather it up. My great-grandmother had handcrafted the small white tablecloth. It was the only one that we had left to us after the destruction of our home because it had been stored in Alt-Ruppin for safekeeping.

It was a terrible situation. Our neighbors tried to talk to them, but it was useless. The Michaelis relatives did not even want the furniture for their own use. Instead, they had promised it to some other people.

I ran back to the office and told Doctor Krause about our ordeal. I reasoned that he had many connections and I hoped that he would be able to help us. After listening to me, he made a phone call to City Hall, which was located about two blocks away, on Mullerstrasse. He spoke to someone who told him that he was in luck, because the official in charge of such affairs just happened to be present and would gladly come check out the situation.

We hurried back to my house, arriving at the same time as the official pulled up in his car, stopping right behind the truck just as the Michaelis relatives were closing it up and preparing to leave. My mother and a few of our neighbors were gathered outside our house. They had been watching the greedy relatives load up their truck.

The man Doctor Krause had summoned was the official in charge of preventing any kind of goods from being taken out of the French occupied sector of Berlin into the Russian occupied zone of Germany. He must have held an important job because he was driving an official car, something very few people were doing at that time. He asked to see their papers. He looked at them and found them unacceptable. He told them that he had the authority to stop this move because it was illegal to take the furniture out of the French sector into the Russian Zone, and he ordered them to unload the truck.

They were furious and they tried to argue with him, which only made matters worse. When they started to unload their anger onto my mother, accusing her of being an *Ero schleicher* (inheritance sneak) among other things, the old woman was the worst. The official told them to stop their insulting ranting or else he would confiscate their truck too.

This unpleasant affair had drawn quite a lot of people from our house and the next one. They all stood with us, giving us support, and helping us to carry the furniture back upstairs. The official stayed until the Michaelis relatives left with their truck. He told my mother that he would take care of the necessary filings with the court and that we would hear from them.

Doctor Krause went back to his office, but he gave me the afternoon off. Thanks to Doctor Krause and his connections our apartment was again filled with furniture and we were sleeping in a bed instead of on the floor. It had been such a disheartening thought that we might again have to live in an empty apartment.

We had been living with Frau Michaelis for two years and had never heard or seen anything about any relatives. The guardian had never mentioned them to us. She had always emphasized to us that Frau Michaelis was all alone in this world and how glad she was that we were looking after her. The guardian certainly turned out to be a conniving and very dishonest woman. We never heard from her again.

Major and Madame Hollebeke

When Monsieur and Madame Ducy left Berlin, the employment agency quickly found another family for whom my mother could work—Major and Madame Hollebeke and their two young boys. They were residing in an apartment on Liverpoolstrasse, surrounded by German people. They were the only French residents. This was quite different from the other French families, who mostly all lived together in one area.

My poor mother was not as lucky as Frau Hampel, who always seemed to get good placements with nice families. My mother liked the Major. He always treated her respectfully and was nice to her. The boys were not any trouble either, but Madame was hard to please. She told my mother that she knew all about the tricks used to fool someone about one's work-habits. She said that she had worked as a maid in a hotel and that my mother should not try any of them. My mother told her that she was new to this type of work, never having done it for other people, and that she had no idea what Madame was talking about. Madame did not act too pleased with my mother's answer and looked for other ways to be hurtful. Before long, Madame had found one, a real nasty one—she accused my mother of stealing. She had told my mother not to bother peeling the tiny potatoes, just to throw them away with the peelings. She had also given permission to my mother to take the peelings home with her. One day she went through my mother's bag, dumping it all out on the floor and calling her a thief. My mother reminded her of what she had said, but she denied it. It was quite an ugly scene. When Major Hollebeke walked in something was said between the Major and Madame. She ran off, slamming doors. The Major was very apologetic and he pleaded with my mother to forget about the incident. It did become a little more tolerable afterwards, at least for a while.

The Major must have had a position at the Quartier Napoleon where he was able to do some black market dealing in coal. Many evenings after dark, when my mother was leaving the house, she saw a truck parked outside and men carrying full sacks into the basement. On other occasions she saw men bringing sacks out and loading them onto a truck. Whatever was going on was of no concern to her; nevertheless, if the Major was present he would call her aside and fill her bag up with four or five *Presskohle* (coal). Her bag would not hold more than that. Then one day he told her that he would come by our place and bring us a sack full of coal. He was well aware of our situation and what this meant to us. We could not thank him enough for this precious coal. Later on we met a few of his neighbors at a dinner party which he hosted, and they were full of praises of him. They told us how much he had helped them with coal and other things, especially during the cold winter months.

Madame showed her mean streak one other time on Easter Sunday of 1948. Normally my mother had Sunday off, but this time Madame wanted her to come on Sunday. When she arrived early that morning, only Madame was at home. She told my mother that she wanted the sheets on the beds changed, with clean sheets put back on and the dirty ones washed. My mother could not believe what she was hearing. This was normally done on Mondays, never on Sundays or holidays. My mother told me how she fought back the tears, she felt so humiliated. Madame disappeared into the kitchen and my mother started doing what she had been told to do. She was in the bathroom, washing the sheets in the bathtub, when the Major walked in. He just stood there for a minute without saying a word, before he walked away. Even though he had closed the door behind him, she could hear them. My mother finished her work. She never saw Madame again, but she found the Major waiting at the door for her. He again apologizing for Madame's behavior and he put a twenty mark bill into her hand, wishing her a happy Easter. He also told her not to come on Monday to make up for coming on that Sunday.

Purchasing the Furniture

It took quite awhile before we heard from the court. A *Gerichtsvollzieher* (bailiff) came and took inventory of the furniture. He put an *Anstecker* (sticker) on the back of every piece. The sticker read that it was unlawful for an unauthorized person to remove it. Some time later we received a letter from the court that itemized each piece and its price and gave us the chance to buy them. The money from the purchase would go into an inheritance fund. We did not care whatsoever about that. We were just glad to put the worry behind us.

The settlement offer came at a bad time. There had been a currency change and our funds were extremely low. But the court agreed to let us buy the furniture with monthly installment payments. When we had it paid off, the bailiff came and removed the stickers. It was a really good feeling to know that we owned the furniture.

Wahrungs (Currency) Reform

The currency reform and exchange was announced without advance notice and it came as quite a surprise to everyone. I remember hearing about it and learning that it would take place, for our district, at a school around the corner from our house. Long lines formed on the evening before the exchange took place. By the time that we joined the lines, they were already in front of our house. My mother and I took turns standing in line, all night long, along with everyone else. I do not remember the reason for doing so. I cannot believe that they did not have enough money to make the exchange. It never made any sense to me.

The exchange was limited to fifty marks and was made on a one for one basis. After this exchange, we all had the same amount of cash money and we were all very poor. Whatever old money anybody had left became worthless. Fortunately, we did not have very much money left to lose, but some people did.

Giving Up My Job with Doctor Krause

Sadly, my job at the dentist office ended. Doctor Krause had another weird moment in which he chased me around the office. Luckily for me, he tripped over the cable of the x-ray machine and they both crashed onto the floor. It gave me a chance to run out of the door, almost knocking a lady down who was coming up the stairs. I can still hear her crying out loudly, "*Aber, Aber mein Fraulein, was is denn nur passiert?*" ("But, but miss, what has happened?")

I had become a little alarmed when the last patient left at noontime and I was told to put the sign on the door, "*Heute keine Nachmittags-sprechstunde.*" ("Today, no afternoon office hours.") He had done this before, but then he had given us the afternoon off. But not on that day. He gave the other girl a list of supplies to go and get from the warehouse, a task that would take her most of the afternoon.

It was the first time that I was alone with the doctor since the first incident. I felt very uneasy. To be honest, I was afraid. He went into the lab to work on the molds for dentures. I was doing the paperwork, sitting in an armchair that was pushed up closely to the desk.

All of a sudden he was leaning over me and breathing down on me. I felt captured, but then relieved when the telephone rang. But when he stopped me from answering it by putting his hand over mine, I knew that I was in trouble. Somehow I found the strength to push the chair backwards as hard as I could to allow me to get up and out of the chair. That is when the chase around the room started, and I got my lucky break when he stumbled over the cable.

Quite an ordeal for a sixteen-year-old girl to go through. And it has bothered me throughout my life, wondering what I did to bring on that kind of attention. I certainly never wanted it.

This time I was convinced that I would not go back to his office. My mother agreed with me. Enough was enough. He had been very helpful to my mother and me and it mostly had been a pleasant relationship at work, but then he would change into this other person who was anything but pleasant.

My mother went to the office to have Doctor Krause sign my employment booklet to show that my employment with him had ended. But he had refused to see her. He told the other girl to tell my mother that I had to come personally to get it signed. I had no other choice but to go back to the office, as I needed the booklet for the employment office.

When I got to the office he asked me to come in, but he told the girl to stay outside in the hallway. He was busy with a patient. He acted very calm, and agreed to everything that I said, which really surprised me. But when I moved a little closer into the room I could see the reason. The patient was a French woman who did not understand German. He had been mocking me the whole time.

He signed my *Arbeitsbuch* (employment booklet), but he wrote in it that I had ended the employment on my own accord. I had hoped that he would write that it had been his decision. It would have been better for me, but he would not do it. It was left up to me to explain my reason for leaving his employment to the agency.

Shortly after I left the job at the dental office, I heard from Frau Peters that the former dentist had finished the de-nazification program and had reclaimed his office. Dr. Krause had to find himself another place. Frau Peters also told me that the young woman, whose job as receptionist I had taken, had been involved in a relationship with the doctor and that he was the father of her baby. That certainly explained her monthly visits to the office.[100]

I dreaded going to the employment agency. The people working there were very unfriendly. It turned out to be another unpleasant episode for me. The woman who waited on me would not accept my reason for leaving the doctor's employment. She kept after me until I finally told her the real reason for leaving. And that was a big mistake, because she did not believe my story. She became very angry with me, raising her voice so that everyone in the room could hear her, accusing me of trying to damage the good doctor's name and his reputation. It was awful. I wanted to run away. These people honestly believed that I made up the story to draw attention to myself. Their judgment was very poor. I learned one thing from that awful experience—that I should never mention it again. The outcome was too humiliating.

---

100 About three years later, when I was working at Osram, a light bulb factory, a colleague mentioned having an appointment with this great dentist. She could not say enough about this good doctor. When I asked her who her dentist was, I was very surprised to hear that it was Dr. Krause. He had not moved far away. He had opened a dental office very close to our neighborhood. She must have noticed the surprised look on my face, because she asked me if I knew him. I told her that I had worked for him a long time ago. The following morning she wasted no time to look me up to tell me that the doctor had told her to say hallo to me, and that he had asked her if I was still so naïve. She wondered what he had meant with that remark. I just shrugged it off. What a character that good doctor was!

The clerk gave me an appointment for a job interview in the juvenile department at City Hall, *Bezirksamt* (district office) Wedding. I wondered why she chose that place. Perhaps she felt that working for a social worker would help me with the problem that they had created. It was not my fault that she did not believe my story. I had told them the truth.

I was hired as an office helper by the head of the department, a very nice man, around fifty or so years of age and a bachelor. We were situated in a large office with three other social workers, who were about twenty years younger than my boss, and two girls like myself. I did not care for the social worker who was sitting at the desk next to mine. He had a very arrogant attitude, always making smart remarks about people or cases that he was working on. Being seated so close to one another, I could not help overhearing the way he handled their cases. He acted very insensitively and unfairly. My boss had to caution him many times that it was very unprofessional and that he needed to better control himself. I felt sorry for the young people and their families.

I attended a *Berufsschule* (vocational school) twice a week in the afternoon. I found it to be quite boring. I did not like shorthand and they did not have enough typewriters for everyone, so we had to take turns. The *Schreibmaschinen* (typewriters) were well used. They constantly broke down. With repair parts hard to get, we were without typewriters a lot. The other classes were a little better.

My boss' district was in an area where blue collar workers from working-class families lived. It also was an area that had been heavily devastated during the war. Therefore, the living conditions were very poor for most of the families.

I did not like making house calls or serving a summons to someone who had missed an appointment with the social worker. I never had a problem, but I felt very uncomfortable with this task. Most of these young teenagers had gotten themselves into some kind of trouble with the law in 1945 and 1946, right after the war ended. The charges included burglary, stealing food, coal and other needed things, or being involved in the black market. It is easy to risk the possible punishment for stealing when you are hungry or freezing. We had all been involved in some of those things, only we had been lucky not to have gotten caught.

After being caught a couple of times and then having ignored the warnings, they would be turned over to the juvenile department. They would become a ward of the department until they turned twenty-one years of age. The court would appoint a social worker as their guardian and the ward was asked to check in periodically with the office.

I remember one case. In my opinion it was handled very unjustly by the social worker I did not care for. It concerned a young couple who had come in to see the social worker, who was the young man's guardian, to ask for his consent to get married. The young man was about twenty years old, had finished an apprenticeship and was employed with a steady job. He had not been in any kind of trouble with the law since he had become a ward of the juvenile department. His girlfriend was expecting their baby and they wanted to get married. They had their parents' approval, but they needed the guardian's too. The guardian told them his decision, which was final, that the young man was not mature enough to get married. He would not change his mind, despite their pleading. It was a very upsetting and tearful scene. At the same time it was very enlightening for me because I had not known that a social worker had such power over another person. I did not agree with the decision, especially coming from a man like him. It was very wrong.

Our daily work was not entirely without a little fun. The City Hall building had a great elevator system, called a *Padernoster*. It was a constantly moving elevator with small, individual cars without doors. As the cars, at a slow pace, went up or down past your floor, you just stepped in or out, at floor level, to enter or leave the car. The cars were big enough for two people. We liked being sent on errands so we could make use of the elevator. We played different daring challenges and took some chances, but it was fun riding on those silly *Padernosters*. I never had the courage to stay on the car into the attic or into the basement and ride it as it switched to the other side. I would always jump off at the last minute.[101]

1948—*Hochzeit* (Wedding)

We celebrated another *Hochzeit* (wedding) in our family in the spring of 1948. This time it was Lieschen's turn. She married Ewald Kendzierski in a civil ceremony at

---

101 My husband Stan later told me that they had the same system at Tempelhof Air Base, where he was stationed. Needless to say, it did not take him long before he investigated the stories that he had been told about what happened to the cars when they reached the attic. Of course he solved the mystery. It was very simple. The cars just rolled over the top in an upright position to the other side. Not at all as mysterious as I had been told. No matter what, a ride on a *Padernoster* was quite a challenge.

the Rathaus in Berlin-Tempelhof on April 10, 1948. Lutz Kraus and their friend Liesbeth stood in as *Trauzeugen* (witnesses) to their wedding.

It turned out to be quite a chilly morning and the bride was shivering in her light summer dress. She had made the dress herself, from an old bed sheet, sewn together by hand. She had finished it with embroidered borders around the neck, sleeves, and the hemline. It looked very nice. She was very talented with such things. Sadly, she never received the proper training to make a career of it. She did not have a decent looking coat to wear, so she borrowed my mother's coat, which was still in better shape than hers was. That good old coat, along with mine, had certainly served us well in good and bad times. If only they had been able to talk. They would have told some interesting stories.

Ewald Kendzierski was born June 22, 1926, in Pommern (an area of Germany given to Poland after the war in 1945). His father had been employed as an estate manager. The estate had been owned by Hermann Goering, whose home "Karinhall" was nearby. It was located about 60km from Berlin, the capital of Germany.

Ewald had four brothers and three sisters. When he was 17 years old, in 1943, he joined the *Kriegsmarine* (German Navy). A fortuneteller had told him that the Navy would be the safest place for him to survive the war. He trained on land and he never went aboard a ship. They assigned him to a job where he was guarding a poison gas depot until the end of the war. When the news reached his base that the war was over, he changed into civilian clothes and headed for home. He managed to avoid being caught and ending up in a prisoner of war camp. He was very lucky. The fortuneteller had given him good advice and it was fortunate that he had followed through with it. For this he was spared a lot of hardship, perhaps even saving his life.

With the help of the Red Cross' *Suchdienst* (search service), he was reunited with his family at their new location in Gollin-Schorfheide. They had become *Heimatvertriebene* (displaced persons). The family had fled their home in Pommern to escape the advancing Russian army, hoping to be able to return when the war was over. But that hope was shattered with the Allies' decision to give that part of Germany to Poland.

Ewald and Lieschen had met about one year prior to their wedding. She and her friend Liesbeth had gone to a movie theater. Ewald and his younger brother Ottie came in and sat in front of them. Back then the few movie theaters that had survived the bombardment of the city were always filled up to the last seat. It did not matter whether it was a good movie or not. People were starving not just for food, but also for some kind of change in their otherwise very drab lives. Movies were a place where they could forget for a couple of hours. At the movie theater the two girls, especially Lieschen, were confronted with a problem. Ewald was wearing a wide brimmed hat that blocked her view of the screen. She told me that she tapped him gently on the shoulder and asked him nicely to remove his hat so that she could see.[102]

The chance encounter in the theatre was the beginning of their courtship. According to Lieschen, it was quite one-sided at first. Lieschen was not interested in dating him, but he was very persistent and kept coming by her apartment to look for her and crying on Tante Martha's shoulder, trying to gain her help.

His persistence worked. Normally, Tante Martha was very nice and easy to get along with. I never had any trouble with her and neither did Hilde. But she could be very resolute, especially with Lieschen, who she saw as a troublemaker. As a result, she would periodically get after Lieschen. One day Tante Martha went to the movie theater and waited outside until Lieschen and her date came out. She confronted her, boxed her ears (*ohrfeigen*) and said a few harsh words to her. She then marched her home, much to Lieschen's embarrassment. After that, Tante Martha saw to it that Lieschen stayed home and waited for Ewald's visit. Knowing her character, when Lieschen told me about this episode I was surprised that she went along with it.[103]

It was a small wedding with only the family present. Ewald's family, except for his brother Ottie, was unable to attend. Before the wedding Ewald had made a trip to Gollin and he had brought back a few things to be used for the meal on their wedding day. His family did not have much to spare except for some potatoes and vegetables. Tante Martha provided the meat. I believe it was the last of her two rabbits. We did not have a cake for them or a bottle of wine to toast the newlywed couple. It was kind of sad. Three years had gone by since the end of the war and we were worse off than ever.

The following day, on Sunday morning, they departed on their *Flitterwochen* (honeymoon). Not exactly! They boarded a train to Gollin, which was located

---

102 Knowing Lieschen and her direct approach to handling problems, I doubt strongly that it was a gentle tap.

103 It does not sound like a very romantic beginning to their courtship, more like an arranged marriage, but in time she learned to love him. They had been married for forty years when he passed away in 1988.

in the Russian occupied zone of Germany. There they planned to start their new life together as *Neu Bauern* (new farmers), as they were called under the new East German leadership.

Ewald's family met them at the railroad station in Gollin and took them home. There his mother greeted them with a cake she had baked for them. That was a very special treat. One that they shared with everyone. Later, they were taken to their new home, a small cottage with a large kitchen and living room area, a bedroom and a storage room.[104] A barn and an outhouse were located in the backyard, and included for their own use was a small garden. The cottage was sparingly furnished, but it had a bed to sleep in and a table with two chairs to sit on. They were also given one cow, one piglet, and a few chicks. With this generous donation, they had become *Neu Bauern*. What more was needed for a start?

They did not expect it to be an easy task, but they found out in a very short time how hard it was to work in the fields from sun-up to sundown. The leadership had set quotas to be filled, no matter what. Excuses for failing to meet the quotas were not accepted. It was a harsh system to work for.

They had named their cow "Bella". It was also expected to work a full day in the fields and then give plentiful milk at night. The milk was collected every morning. The can was then returned in the evening. It would contain a little bit of *Magermilch* or *Blaues Wasser* (skim milk).

The skim milk was mixed in with the piglet's food. It needed a little more nourishment to grow quickly into a pig. When the piglet reached a desirable size, it was picked up and they were given another piglet with which to start the whole process all over again.

When the chicks grew into egg laying hens, Lieschen and Ewald were expected to turn in a certain number of eggs, whether the hens laid them or not. Many times they were forced to buy or trade with another farmer to fulfill their quota.

Lieschen and Ewald had noticed that every time they delivered their harvested goods to the collecting place, it was loaded onto Russian trucks parked behind the building. I always knew that the Russian army that was stationed in Germany was being fed with German food. I remember laughing at a statement that I read about the Russians shipping food to the starving German people. It was just propaganda to make themselves look good.

---

104 There were several of these cottages. They had been built for the farm workers who were employed on the estate and their families; and of course they were built by the previous estate owners and not by the East German leadership.

Seeds for planting were also very hard to come by. Lieschen and Ewald had planted some *Zuckerruben* (sugarbeets) in their garden. My mother and Tante Martha happened to be visiting them when the beets were ready to be cooked into syrup. To keep the syrup from being noticed by the people who were always watching for unusual happenings, they had to do the cooking after midnight and by candlelight. My mother and Tante Martha took turns standing watch outside over the syrup. What a life!

1948—Trouble Brews

As I mentioned earlier, my mother had bad luck with her Madames. The first one had been very moody, but at least not mean like Madame Hollebeke. Madame Ducy always made sure that my mother had enough to eat and sent leftovers home with her for me, something that Madame Hollbeke never did. She would rather dispose of it instead.

1948 was turning out to be a troublesome year. There were lots of problems with the Russians, which made everybody edgy and nervous. The French military decided to relocate its dependants to West Germany to secure their safety. Madame Hollebeke and her boys left Berlin and relocated in the French zone of Germany. They only took their personal belongings.

The Major asked my mother to continue to come by the apartment once or twice a week, but he wrote into her *Arbeitsbuch* (workbook) that she worked for him every day for four hours. He knew that she needed the extra hours to receive the working class ration card. He really was a very caring man.

Two or three times we were invited, along with his neighbors, for a spaghetti supper at his place. He was a good cook and a great host. Everybody would have a good time, including the Major, despite the differences in our language. The differences made it more fun and gave us something to laugh about. My mother believed that he was enjoying himself without Madame's presence.

The agency asked my mother to help out at another French family's residence because their regular helper was ill. The family lived in a house, one of several three or four story high houses adjacent to Quartier Napoleon, formerly the Hermann Goering Kaserne, in a well-hidden and wooded area. They used to be the residences of the German officers and their families who had been assigned to the Hermann Goering Kaserne.

One morning when my mother arrived for work, she found the lady of the house supervising a couple of men who were rolling up a large Oriental rug from the living room floor. She must have noticed the questioning look on my mother's face, because she told her laughingly, "We are retaliating. When the Germans came to France, they did lots of *comme ci, comme ca*, and now it is our turn." My mother thought, "Whatever makes you happy." Nothing really surprised her any more.

After that incident, she paid more attention to what was going on around the area. She noticed that the French families were not just leaving with their personal stuff. They had moving vans parked outside of their buildings.

When the family left, my mother had to go back to clean the place and she asked me to come along. I was quite impressed with the apartment. It must have been beautiful when it was fully furnished. There was not very much left. All the movable items were gone, including the draperies.

That was the last job my mother had with a French family except for Major Hollebeke. She continued to work from him until August of 1948, the latter part only on weekends.

1948—The Blockade of Berlin!

On June 24, 1948 the lights were turned off in the western part of Berlin. The Russians, who were in control of the power plant located in the Russian occupied zone of Germany, had turned the power off. They also closed all the roads leading into Berlin, as well as the railroads and the waterways. And so the Russian Blockade of Berlin began. They were in control of all the main entrances to the city. Only the air routes were outside their control. With their actions they turned Berlin into an island completely cut off from the outside world.

We had always believed that the Russians wanted control over the entire city, not just their sections, even though their sector was much larger than what the other three Allies controlled. They were a greedy bunch. We also knew that our very own people in West Germany would have liked nothing better than to be separated from us. We were a burden to them. They had already decided to make the city of Bonn the capital of West Germany. At the time I thought it was quite unfair to be treated like that. After all, it was the people of West Germany who had cheered for Hitler and his nationalism. The Berliners had openly opposed much of his leadership. They had also suffered greatly throughout the war years and still there was no end in sight for them. It did not seem fair.

A couple of days prior to June 24 we wondered what was going on when the French military moved into our street with all their armored vehicles. They had done this many times before, but this time the soldiers acted differently. They were more disciplined and serious. It had been just the opposite on the other occasions. Then the alerts had turned into loud and boisterous all night parties.

Well, we found out the reason for their movement on June 24. We were stunned and very frightened about the situation. We feared that this could mark the end for us and for our city. We also feared that we would become slaves to the Russians. Everywhere one went on that day there were groups of people standing together and talking about our frightful doom.

What little hope we had left rested with the Americans. The American military governor, Lucius D. Clay, described our situation as one of the cruelest attempts in modern Russian history to use mass starvation as a means of exerting political pressure. But thanks to the Americans and their allies, who did not desert us Berliners, we were saved from starvation and from freezing to death. They took care of us for eleven months, flying supplies into Berlin under unbelievable conditions. They showed the Russians what they were capable of doing.

Flughafen Tegel

In late June or July of 1948, my mother was notified to report for work in Tegel. She joined a workforce building a runway in Tegel to help with the airlift. The Tempelhof and the Gatow airports were not enough to support the massive air traffic. More runways were needed to allow more airplanes to bring the much needed supplies to Berlin.

I wish that I had listened better and asked more questions about the job at the Tegel airport. I remember her leaving very early in the morning and coming home late, looking very tired. The job was mostly done with shovels and picks. She mentioned that they had two pieces of heavy machinery to help them and that was all. Yet the job was completed in three months.

The area where the runway was built had been an exercise ground amidst the Tegeler Forest. In 1909, Count Zeppelin's airship had landed there. In 1931, Werner von Braun and Hermann Oberth fired the first liquid fuel rockets from there. To make room for the new long runways, they had to clear out many trees.

The French overseer in charge of the job gave his permission for the workers to take away the small pieces of wood, which was very much appreciated by everyone. My mother brought home a bag full every evening until they were done with the clearing.

I came home earlier than my mother did. Anyone under the age of eighteen only worked a thirty-five hour week. The small pieces of wood were a big help in getting a fire going in the kitchen stove, which was my job. I had the worst time with building a fire. No matter how often I was shown how to do it, I never found it to be easy.

I also had to take care of the shopping and the preparing of our meal for supper. Neither one of these two chores was difficult to do. Our meals were simple. We had almost the same thing every evening. It was easy to prepare the meals, except for building the fire in the kitchen stove. That sometimes brought me to tears.

Our evening meal usually consisted of boiled potatoes, peeled or with the skin left on, gravy made from flour, and sometimes some boiled cabbage leaves. However, during the blockade we regularly received food items that we had previously only received when it had been the Americans' turn to supply us with food rations. Perhaps they had abolished the old rules and were supplying us every month, instead of every third month. Whatever the reason, it surely seemed a little better. We were receiving dried egg powder, grits, dried potatoes, carrots, and peas. At first, some of the foods were strange to us, but we learned quickly to use these new items. We were very thankful for every little bit that was given to us.

Good-Bye to Major Hollebeke

My mother's job with Major Hollebeke had only been part time since his family had been relocated to West Germany. In late summer her job came to an end. The major had been told to move into Quartier Napoleon and give the apartment back to the German people. He gave one last party, to which he invited his neighbors, my mother and I. He served us spaghetti, which was very good. My mother and I were unaccustomed to drinking wine with our meal—or at any time—and we both felt quite wobbly within a short while. As soon as we politely could, we excused ourselves and went home.

The major was a very attentive host and well liked by his neighbors and they felt sad about his leaving. The following morning, my mother went back to clean up the place before it was turned over to the Germans. The major told my mother that the rest of the partiers stayed quite late. She could tell by the many empty wine bottles that the party had lasted a long time.

The major gave my mother a bag full of *Presskohle* to take home, a priceless gift to receive in anticipation of the upcoming cold winter months. Of course the Russians announced later on that private households were not to receive any coal rations from them. We were not too surprised by their announcement. We used the major's coal in the kitchen stove to cook our simple meals or to heat up some water.

Tempelhof Airport

The area around Tempelhof Airport had become a very busy place. Visiting with my girlfriend Marion on weekends became quite exciting. There was so much activity going on, in the air and on the ground. Airplanes were landing or taking off, while a steady flow of trucks rolled out of the gates and headed off in all directions. We were not used to seeing this kind of traffic. It really was quite an operation, and fun to watch.

We also saw a strange looking game being played on the square in front of the main entrance to the airport. A small group of fellows were hitting a small ball with a stick, then running in a circle and sliding in the dirt and so on, all to the watching fellows' loud cheering. Whatever kind of ballgame it was, it surely looked strange to us. We found out eventually that the game was called "baseball."[105]

"Party"

I attended my first "party"—as the gathering was called in America—in 1948. It was a different kind of party than we were accustomed to because it was very informal.

---

105 The square where the game was played used to be a small roadside park with benches and a rose garden, but it had been destroyed during the last days of the war. Then it had been used for a temporary burial ground for some of the dead German soldiers. After the war ended, the soldiers' bodies were all dug up and properly buried in a cemetery. In 1951, the Airlift Memorial was erected on the square. It was dedicated to the men who had given their lives during the blockade. And it is again a nice roadside park.

Marion's sister Inge was celebrating her nineteenth birthday. Inge and her girlfriend were dating a couple of airmen from the airbase and they brought along a few more fellows. One of them brought his guitar and it turned out to be a very delightful afternoon. Everyone had a good time singing along. Most of the songs were new to us, but Marion and I enjoyed listening to them.

One of the fellows was a cook at the base and he had made a cake for Inge, which tasted delicious. They had also brought Ritz Crackers and jars of Velveeta Cheese Spread and Coca-Cola in bottles. What a treat! Marion and I feasted on those crackers and the cheese spread. It tasted so good to us, along with the coke.

Inge and her friend's living room had one small, worn-out sofa. They had moved their rickety kitchen table into the living room to hold the refreshments, but otherwise the large room was empty. We all sat on the floor, except for the guitar-player, who sat on the sofa. We sat in a circle and the only part missing was a campfire. It was quite a picture.

It was fun being with Americans. They acted so carefree and jolly, as if they did not have a worry to be concerned about. It was different when we were together with our German friends. Sadly, everyone had forgotten how to laugh and be jolly.

A baby boy!

During these unsettled times, my sister Hilde had her second child. The baby was born September 3, 1948 and he was named Wolfgang. The baby was born at home with the help of a midwife. My brother-in-law Lutz, who always acted very "macho," was asked to stand by Hilde and hold the candle during the birth of the baby. Well, Lutz tried, but he did not last very long. He almost fainted. Good old Onkel Hermann had to take his place.[106] Fortunately for baby Wolfgang, his father's family sent a big box of used baby clothes and other much-needed articles from West Germany. It was very much appreciated because they had practically nothing for him to wear, and no one around them had anything left to help them with.

---

106 After this episode, whenever Lutz acted too boastful about his strong manhood, he was quickly reminded of that night. But he always took it in good humor. He was a very easygoing fellow. The only time I ever saw him get excited was at a soccer game, which was his passion.

1948—Memories of Hunger

Whenever I write about these mostly gloomy years, one time in late 1948 keeps flashing especially well through my mind. I see my mother and me sitting in our cold kitchen with a warm 500 gram loaf of rye bread on the table, which I had just brought home from the bakery. I had been able to talk the salesgirl into giving me the loaf and accepting my coupon, even though it was not valid until the following week.

We were very hungry. We knew better than to eat the loaf up all at once, but we did not have any willpower. We did not stop eating when we should have, and we ate up the whole loaf of bread.

During the months of the blockade we tried our best to carry on. If I remember correctly, our ration card allowed us 100 grams of bread per day. It was not enough when it was the only food one had to eat all day.

December 14, 1948

That winter the Russians allowed us two hours of electricity per day. It was turned on whenever they felt like it. It could be at any time during the day or night. They were masters at chicanery. The gas was handled the same way, but it was more difficult to know if it was on or not. Neighbors would alert one another by yelling from their windows when they found out that the gas was on. Nevertheless, we missed out on the gas ration a lot, especially during the night.

I turned seventeen on December 14, but it must have been like any other ordinary day because I do not remember anything about it. The same goes for Christmas and the New Year. My mother and I probably went to bed, pulled the covers over our heads and dreamed of better times to come. What else was there to do on these dark and cold winter nights, without heat or lights, but with a rumbling stomach?

It is so hard to believe that I experienced in my young life all of what I have written down, but it really happened.

1949

My mother and I had been struggling with our small income ever since the currency reform took place, especially when she was not working. The job at the

Tegel airport had been completed and she had not found another job since then. She had received unemployment benefits for six weeks and then had been switched to "Alu," which was another type of benefit for unemployed people. It amounted to only *zwolf Deutsche Mark* (12.00 DM) per week, a very small amount to live on. She had to go weekly to the unemployment office to check in, which was called *Stempeln*, and to see if another job was available for her. If she failed to show up on her *Stempeln* day she would lose her twelve deutsche marks.

I received a monthly wage of 40.00 DM for my apprentice job, which was not bad for an allowance, but hardly enough to live on. I was also still receiving *Waisengeld* (orphan's pension), a monthly 25.00 DM pension, from the German Government. That would end when I turned eighteen. My mother would have been eligible for a war widow pension, but the government refused to pay her because she would not sign the paper that declared him as deceased. My mother was unable to make this decision. It was too painful for her. We were still hoping for his return from Russia.[107]

My grandmother, too, was just getting by with a small monthly widow's pension. Her landlord, Mister Gaebel, had been very kind to my grandparents. He had never charged them rent for all the years they had been living with him. In return for that kindness, my grandmother did a little housework for him and she took calls for him when he was out.[108]

Because of our financial problems, my mother and I decided to part from our last piece of jewelry—my mother's gold watch. It was not an easy decision, but we did not know what else to do. She had given the watch to me to wear after we had traded mine in early 1947 for the three loaves of bread. All of our other pieces of jewelry had already been traded in, mostly for food.

I took the watch to Wenig's Jewelry Store on Mullerstrasse and a couple other stores in the neighborhood, but Wenig made the best offer. Since the end of the war, jewelry stores had started doing this kind of business. They would buy jewelry from people and then sell it for more than they had paid. They gave me 150.00 DM for the watch and later displayed it in their window for 195.00 DM. Quite a

---

107 Ten years after a soldier was reported as missing in action or presumed to be a prisoner of war, the government automatically declare the soldier deceased. It never made any sense to me why the government was paying a monthly pension to me and denying one to my mother. It was a really stupid rule.

108 Eventually she received her own pension for the years that she had worked and she was able to do much better.

profit. I walked by the store every day on my way home from work and checked on it, but after one week it was gone.[109]

May of 1949—the Blockade Ends

No words can ever express the gratitude of the Berliners to the Americans for their efforts and their caring support in our time of need. My generation will never forget it. I do not know how much longer they could have kept up the airlift, but after eleven months the Russians gave up. On May 12, 1949, the Russians lifted the blockade of the city. Many trucks loaded full of supplies were lined up at the border. As soon as the barricades were lifted, they started rolling down the Autobahn towards Berlin.

When the trucks reached Berlin and entered the western parts of the city, they were greeted by Berliners lining the streets. The people waved to the truck drivers and shouted out loud. The drivers in turn answered by honking their horns. Everyone was jubilant and happy to witness an end to the horrible blockade.

Overnight, the stores were filled up with goods that we had not seen for many years, and they could be bought without ration cards or coupons. All that was required was money. Yes, only money. As my mother had predicted a long time before, if we were fortunate enough to see the stores filled up with goods again, we might not have the money to buy any of it. So true! We felt the lack of money especially hard. We did not have the money to buy much needed things. We both needed shoes and clothing. Everything was worn out. But it felt good to know that the goods were available again, and that we would not be hungry anymore. It had been a long, long time since we had been able to buy milk, butter, eggs, meat, vegetables, and fruit in the stores. We had forgotten what it was like to have these food items available. The years since 1945 had been very lean and meager.

Applying for a Job at Osram

A friend of mine, Erika Bruning, who was looking for a better paying job than her apprentice job at a beauty shop, told me that the Osram factory might be hiring. Her father was employed there and he had heard it through the grapevine. He

---

109 It was over two years before I got another one. My grandmother gave me a new watch on my twentieth birthday. It looked a lot like the one we parted from.

had told her that if she was interested she should be at the factory on a Monday morning at 6 am. The office would be open at 7 am. She asked me if I wanted to go along and give it a try. She was aware that I had been considering a job change for financial reasons and also for another reason. I wanted to give it a try. My mother and I really needed some help with our financial situation.

When I told my mother about our plans, she was very much against it. She gave in a little after I told her that I was not happy anymore with my present job. But she kept telling me that I should stay there and work out whatever I did not like. I could not tell her my real reason for wanting to change jobs.

I met Erika Monday morning in Moabit and together we walked to the factory, where we found long lines of people already waiting. We felt quite discouraged. We did not believe that we had a chance. When we reached the office, they handed us several forms to be filled out, a lot of questions for a factory job. Then we were called for an interview by an official, who kept asking more questions. I noticed that he kept looking at Erika's hands. I had told her to hide them and not to let them see her red fingernails. I did not think it was a good idea to apply for a job at a factory with red fingernails. But Erika could not talk without the use of her hands.

We left the place not feeling very hopeful. The official told us that we would hear from them, but we really did not expect it. Surprisingly, I did receive a notice to report back to their office for further instructions and to get a physical examination, performed by their own doctor. I was then scheduled to start work within a few days. It was getting serious and I had not mentioned anything to my boss about my plans. My mother was still trying to talk me out of this factory job, but I had made up my mind to go ahead with it. Little did I know what changes lay ahead of me.

When I went to see Erika, I was shocked to hear that she had not received a notice from the factory office. I felt so bad. If it had not been for her, I would not have known about the hiring. She assured me that it did not bother her and that if she really wanted to work at Osram she could ask her father to put in a word for her. Instead, she had been thinking about it and she had decided to stay at the beauty salon. I think she made a good decision. As I was about to find out, she would not have lasted for very long.[110]

---

110 Erika and I remained friends until she got married and moved to America, the land that she had always fantasized about. My mother and I had some good laughs over

Leaving City Hall

I did not look forward to telling my boss about leaving my job at City Hall. I waited for him in the morning in the lobby at City Hall because I wanted to tell him in private. He was surprised and he appeared to be genuinely sorry about my leaving, but after I explained to him my reasons, he understood my situation. He offered to take care of the required notification to the employment office, which I gladly accepted. He was such a nice, old gentleman. I liked working for him, and I was going to miss him. All the while that I worked for him, he had presented himself as a caring and kind social worker who was trying to help the young people.

I was glad and relieved that I did not have to go upstairs to the department and face the rest of them. I was a little worried about my big job change, but I was also relieved at not having to be near the awful older male social worker at the office. I would not have lasted one day working for him. He had acted so obnoxiously and so totally out of character for a social worker towards me. Whenever he had a chance, he would make mocking remarks, even whispering them across the desk to me. It was very unpleasant for me.

The situation at work had become much worse after an unpleasant incident. He must have overheard a conversation I had with my boss in which I mentioned that I was going to be home alone on the weekend. My mother and Tante Martha were going to visit with Lieschen and Ewald in the country. When I left the office on Friday, he followed me out and caught up to me in the hallway. Then he very casually told me that he might stop in to visit with me the following morning. He said he had to make a house call to a young man living at the same address as I did, only in the side building.

I remember standing there utterly speechless and watching him walk on with a nasty grin on his face. It was not unusual for a social worker to make a house call after office hours, because it was a good time to find someone at home. But in this case I did not believe that it was necessary to make a house call. Everything seemed to be quite orderly. The young man was about nineteen years old. He lived with his mother, a war widow. He appeared to be a nice fellow who went to work everyday and led a perfectly normal life. This obnoxious man was just using

---

some of her wild ideas. Hopefully, she made out alright. I am sorry to say that I never heard from her again.

the visit as an excuse. It was very improper behavior, especially for a social worker who was also married.

I was so nervous for the rest of the day. I kept thinking about his comment and hoping that he did not mean it and that he was just trying to upset me. But I really knew better.

I slept very little that night. I was up and sitting by the window, behind the curtain, long before it was necessary, watching the entrance to the courtyard. About 10 am I saw him walking through the door. He stopped and looked up towards our windows before he walked to the side building.

I had the window open a little. In my nervous state of mind I closed it after I saw him walk to the side building. Maybe I wanted to make sure that I was locked in and he could not get to me. I should have gone to stay with my grandmother for the weekend to spare me from this unpleasant annoyance. It might appear that I was overreacting a little, but I was afraid and I did not know what to do about the situation.

It was not too long before I saw him walking towards my building. Our doorbell started ringing, again and again. After a while I watched him leave. He turned around by the door and looked up to our windows. He was so obnoxious.

I dreaded going to work on Monday morning and facing him. I knew already that he would have something to say about his visit. Sure enough, he confronted me as soon as he was able to, telling me that he had stopped and asking me why I did not open the door. He said that I must have been afraid to let him in. I answered that I was not at home, to which he just grinned and commented that I must have an automatic window operator.

I could have tried arguing or debating further, but I just let it be at that. I did not know how to deal with someone like him. I had learned to keep quiet after the problem with Doctor Krause and the employment agency. No one would believe me in this case either, if I told about it. Who was I to accuse a social worker of improper behavior?

After I left the department, I ran into him one last time on a subway train. He approached me in his usual manner and said to me that he had not given up being appointed as my guardian. He said that he knew that I would sooner or later stumble and become a ward of the juvenile department. What a nasty thought! It bothered me to think about it, and he had again managed to make me feel uncomfortable. I wondered if I should write about this unpleasant incident, since he was a social worker. But I decided to tell about it, to show that characters like him can be found anywhere in our society.

My New Job at Osram

I started my new job with Osram. It started at 6 am and lasted until 5 pm Monday through Friday, plus Saturdays from 6 am until 2 pm. It was a long day. I caught the streetcar at 5:10 am and I came home a little before 6 pm. We had a twenty-five minute lunch break and a fifteen minute midmorning break. I was paid eighty-one *pfennig* per hour and I brought home about 40.00 DM per week after the deductions. If I worked weekends, I made 50.00 DM. The pay for my first week at work was held back and it was very hard for us to get by until I got paid at the end of the second week.

I noticed on my first day at work that only a few other young girls were present to start for work. It did not look like many new people had been hired. We were also told that the job might only be for three months, and perhaps at most for six months. It depended on the kind of contracts that might be sent from their main plant in West Germany. A rather dim outlook with which to begin my new job.

I was taken to the department where light bulbs were being made. The *Vorarbeiterin* (forewoman) seated me at the end of a conveyor belt between two women as old as the place itself. They were so engrossed in their work that they hardly looked up to acknowledge me. The forewoman showed me what I had to do—solder two places on the top and on the side of the light bulb. After soldering the two spots, I had to blow on the bulb to cool it off and then put it on a rack.

The task seemed to be quite easy, but the two old women were speed demons. Sitting between them and seeing all the bulbs piling up in front of me made me extremely nervous. I tried to keep up, but in my hurry I came too close with my nose to the hot solder. It burned the tip of my nose and hurt! I let out a shriek, loud enough to get the two old women's attention. Surprisingly, they took pity on me and helped me with my pile of bulbs.

It took a couple of days before I was able to keep up. What a job. The only change was the different sizes of the bulbs. Otherwise it was the same work for ten hours. After two weeks, the woman whose place I had taken came back and I was relieved of that monotonous job. I was instead given the job of supplying three machines that made the glass bulbs. It kept me quite busy, but I liked it better than the soldering.

For the first days after I started to work there, I do not know how I found the strength to go home. I was totally exhausted, especially when I attended the machines. I was always glad when one of them broke down or when a change over was necessary. It allowed a little rest for me.

My mother was always waiting for me at the trolley stop. I tried very hard not to show how tired I was, but I do not think that I fooled her. She knew from her own experience what it was like working in a factory. My mother also always got up with me in the morning. She made my lunch and tried to make me eat some breakfast. I never seemed to have time. I would just drink some coffee and grab a slice of bread, eating it on the run to catch my trolley.

Working at the factory was very hard for me, a big adjustment. At the end of the day I just wanted to lie down for a half hour before eating supper, but then I would never get up again for the rest of the evening. When I was a little girl I remember my mother coming home from work and being tired. She would say that she just wanted to sit down and lay her head down by the kitchen stove for a little rest before starting to fix supper. I would beg her to let me do her hair. While she fell asleep I would put lots of waves into her hair, using lots of water. My poor mother would wake up from all the cold water dripping off her head—but she had nice waves.

In time I became used to working in the factory, although I never felt comfortable. It was a different atmosphere from what I was used to. Many times I wished that I had a better job in a nicer place. I worked very hard for the money, but I had to be content to have a job at all.

The money that I brought home was a big help to us. We were able to buy a few much-needed things. My mother finally got a new coat to replace her worn out winter coat. Actually, it was a second-hand fur coat which looked like new. I paid 50.00 DM for it. The coat looked very nice on her and it kept her warm.

I also got a new coat. A tailor that my friend Marion knew made them from wool blankets. My coat was dark brown and Marion's was a burgundy red color. They turned out nice, and they kept us warm. They were also quite durable. Mine lasted for several seasons.

As soon as we were able to, we purchased four new chairs to replace the ones we had. They had caned seats that had worn out, making it dangerous to sit on them. We picked out the chairs at a small furniture store across the street from us. The owner put them aside for me and I made weekly payments on them. When I had paid for one, she would let me take it home. It took about four months. I was so happy to have good chairs to sit on again. It was also a good feeling to be able to buy things. We needed to refurbish everything and in time we did.

It was difficult for my mother to stay at home and to have me be the breadwinner instead of her. She never openly talked to me about it, but many years later when she had a small savings account she told me that she was saving it for me as a "thank you" for the years when I took care of her.

1949—Celebrating My 18th Birthday

It was a government policy not to have young people under eighteen years of age working the night shift. So for a while I was spared that shift, but no time was wasted to arrange for me to work the night shift the week that I turned eighteen. And that was how I celebrated my 18th birthday—working the night shift. For the first two nights I spent every free moment holding my face under cold water, trying to stay awake. It was especially hard after midnight. During our break, my colleagues had a small cake for me, which was very thoughtful of them.

Lieschen and Ewald Return to Berlin

Lieschen and Ewald's stay in Gollin lasted about one and a half years. It eventually became intolerable. The demands were unreasonable and being constantly under the watchful eyes of the government was unnerving.

For some time they had been seriously talking about leaving Gollin and their hopeless situation. Then a friend had warned them and told them that their name was on the black list. The final decision for a getaway was made after an ugly incident with the village official, who had been appointed by the Russian Kommandant and who took his job very seriously. This arrogant character happened to be Ewald's oldest brother. He was someone who was more concerned about pleasing the Russians than his own people. He had come by their place just as Lieschen and Ewald were coming home, tired and hungry after a long day working in the fields. He complained to them about their unfilled quota and threatened them with punishment.

By then Lieschen had enough of his arrogance. She lost her temper and went after him with her *Holzpantoffel* (wooden clog), hitting him with it and chasing him out of the barn and their yard, all the while telling him what she thought of him and his job and his employer. Of course, that was the wrong thing to do and they knew they had to leave.

The following day, they went about their chores just like any other day, in case they were being watched. They brought the hay into the barn, milked the cow, and fed the animals. Then they sat in the dark cottage until after midnight and all the lights were out in the houses around them. They loaded up their bicycles with their few belongings and started out on their walk back to Berlin, praying not to be seen or heard by someone, especially the dogs. They avoided the main roads and only traveled over fields and country roads. It took them all night.

They arrived safely at Tante Martha and Onkel Hermann's home, where they stayed until they found a place of their own to live. Apartments were, however, still very hard to find. They rented a furnished room near the S-Bahn Tempelhof, right across from the airfield. On one of my visits, I remember their landlady telling us about the airlift and all the airplanes flying over her house. Ewald and Lieschen did not mind the constant noise and the vibration. They found it to be a reassuring feeling to hear the planes, knowing that they were taking care of the people in Berlin. They lived there until they finally got an apartment in a newly built settlement in 1954 on Mariendorfer Damm.

Ewald found employment in a factory that manufactured different kinds of ironworks. He was trained as an *Eisenbieger* (ironbender). He bent and formed reinforcing rods for some of Berlin's most well known structures—the Kongresshalle in Tiergarten, the Airlift Memorial at Tempelhof Airport, the Europa Center am Ku-Damm, and the American Library am Kreuzberg. Lieschen found employment in a factory that manufactured *Wassermesser* (water meters).

Osram Moves from Moabit to Seestrasse

Osram decided in 1950 to move our department to a newer factory on Seestrasse. I was very much in favor of this move as it was within a twenty-five minute walk from our house and it would allow me to save on trolley car fare. I was told to report to the Osram plant on Seestrasse for a temporary placement in the *Kolbenwascherei* (laundry room) while the machines were being set up at their new location. As soon as they were in operation, I was to be called to return to my former job.

I found out that the *Kolbenwascherei* was the worst place to work in the whole factory. It was where the glass globes were washed with chemicals, then dried and prepared to be made into light bulbs. It was a damp and smelly place to work.

About twenty women and three men worked in the *Kolbenwascherei*. One man was in charge of this department, *der Meister* (the master). The other two men attended the drying ovens and they did the heavier lifting of boxes and so on. It was difficult to get people to work in this place and once they got someone, they held onto them. I was a good example of their hold. I kept asking to be sent upstairs to my old job, but I was told that I could not leave until a replacement was found. Of course no one wanted to trade places with me. I lasted in that awful place for over a year until I finally found myself another workplace in a different department.

Many employees at Osram lived in the East Sector of Berlin. They had been working for Osram and other companies in the western sectors for years. It had never been a problem, but then the currency reform took place. Thereafter they were paid in East German currency, which made a big difference in their income. They started to bring all kinds of goods to work and sell it to their western sector colleagues for West German currency. Both parties involved in this trade were getting a deal. It was a big help to the *Ostlers* (easterners). They were paid in western currency for their goods, which allowed them to shop for things that were not available in the East Sector. I bought a few things from them, mainly houseware items, like dishes and silverware. They would bring some samples to work. We would choose from them and they would take our order. It would cost about one-third less than in our western sector shops. The exchange rate of one western deutsche mark for six eastern marks made a huge difference.

Eventually this trading came to a halt. The East German police checked the *Ostlers* too thoroughly at the border crossings and threatened them with severe punishment if they were caught taking goods out of the East Sector.[111]

---

111 Two or three years later, I went to a shop called the "Glashutte," located on Friedrichstrasse in the East Sector of Berlin, with my husband, Stan. It was well known for its glassware from Bohemia. We were looking for something special to send to his mother for Christmas. The shop had beautiful *Kristallglas* (cut glass) at affordable prices. However, we were not able to buy anything. Only people living in the East Sector could make purchases. A friend of Tante Anna lived in the suburb of Berlin that was located in the East Sector and she met us at the shop. We had to let her know discreetly what she should buy for us. The salespeople in that shop were so unfriendly. They made us feel very uncomfortable. But Tante Anna's friend purchased

1950—My 19th Birthday"

For my nineteenth birthday, my colleagues from the *Kolbenwascherei* gave me a beautiful *Fruhstucks-Kaffeeservice* (breakfast-coffee service) for two. I was told to find myself a suitable "mate" to share it with. They treated me as an old maid. Unbeknownst to me, at that time my mate was still very far away, living in another country across the ocean.

1950–1951—*Weihnachten und Neujahr* (Christmas and New Year's)

As 1950 came to a close we were actually looking forward celebrating the holidays. It had been a very long while since we had felt like doing so.

Hilde and Lutz had finally moved into an apartment of their own. It had taken a long time and countless visits to the *Wohnungsamt* (housing agency) before they found one for them. One more child had joined the Kraus family, a little girl, and her name was Brigitte, born November 9, 1950. As a result, it had become quite crowded living in Tante Martha and Onkel Hermann's home, although they never complained.

Tante Martha and Onkel Hermann invited my grandmother, my mother and myself to spend the holiday with them and the rest of the family. It was the first Christmas that we could afford buying a few small gifts for the children. It had bothered me that I had not been able to give Traudel something in the past as I was her *Patentante* (Godmother).

The adults had agreed to exchange a *Bunten Teller*, a plate filled with sweets, cookies, nuts, and fruit, which was always found under the Christmas tree. It was an old holiday custom.

This was also the first Christmas in years that Onkel Hermann decorated a tree. It looked very nice and brought back a feeling of festivity. Many years before, when I was a little girl, Onkel Hermann was the first one I knew of who decorated his tree with electric candlelites. It was so different and a lot less dangerous than lighting trees with real candles. He would also trim his tree with lots of sugary

---

a cake plate, a bowl, and six wineglasses for us. We later went back a couple of times and purchased a few more pieces. After we left Berlin and came to America, my mother continued going there, at least a few more times. But again the East German Police started checking too thoroughly at the subway and S-Bahn stations. It became too risky. All of the *Kristallglas* pieces I own today came from the "Glashutte."

candies. Then he would invite the children to help him untrim his tree. Did we ever enjoy helping him! He always left the tree standing until sometime in February. I believe it was his birthday then.

The children's presence also made our Christmas more enjoyable. The holidays in the past had been so disheartening. At midnight, we went to a nearby Catholic church. Tante Martha liked their candle lit service.

We also celebrated New Year's Eve together. At midnight, we revived another an old custom—*Bleigiessen*—to see what lay ahead of us in the coming new year. We melted a special kind of lead, held on a spoon over a candle, and then dropped it into a pan of cold water. This special lead could only be bought at this time of the year, like all the other New Year's Eve amusement games. My melted lead very clearly resembled a ship, whereupon Tante Martha and everyone else foretold my destiny, that I was to sail across the ocean. Oh my, I laughed a lot, never expecting it to actually come true in only a few short years.

We enjoyed ourselves and we spent a wonderful holiday together. Perhaps we were at last resuming a normal life and leaving behind us the awful and dismal years that had followed the end of the war. It gave us a good feeling of hope for better years ahead.

Changing Jobs at Osram

In 1951 I left the *Kolbenwascherei* very abruptly. My leaving had to do with our new forewoman, who was sent to us from another department. I remain convinced that our small group did not need a forewoman and that the company just wanted to get rid of her. They did so by dumping this meddlesome woman on us. Our *Meister* was well liked and respected by everyone. I liked the *Meister* and the rest of the people I worked with, but I did not like the forewoman and neither did anyone else. The *Meister* did not have any problems that he could not solve with his people. But it all changed when this woman joined us.

One Monday morning when I arrived for work, the *Meister* took me aside and he told me to be more discreet during working hours on the night shift. I was to find myself a place away from the window to read my book. I was speechless. It had to have been around two or three in the morning when we had a break because something happened upstairs with the machinery. I had grabbed my book and sat by the window to read while others went to the restrooms to have a smoke and some found a dark corner to take a little nap. I ended up being the only one who was spotted doing something wrong on company time, shame on me. It did not take me long to figure out who the informer was. She only lived one block away and only someone like her would spook around in the middle of the night to spy on others. The *Kolbenwascherei* was located at street level, but in order to look into the place one had to stand across the street on a step stool because the lower half of the glass in the window was milky. After work, out of my own curiosity, I had to check it out. I was not able to look into the place without a step stool and I was taller than the forewoman. There was no need whatsoever to act like she had because the *Meister* could figure out by our worksheet how busy we were during the night. She just was a troublemaker.

Each year when doing our annual inventory we had very little work to do. It was hard trying to look busy when you were not. I had been dusting shelves for the second time around and it was still morning. I was wondering how to fill the rest of the day when the forewoman walked by and accused me of not putting a little more effort into looking busy. She said that I could get fired for that. She was right of course, but I was trying my best to look busy and I did not like her telling me that. I had never missed a day of work, never been late, and I had never refused doing any kind of work. I resented her remark and the way she had talked to me. I was upset enough to disregard the rules and regulation and walked off to find myself another place to work.

When I asked the *Meister* from the lab about a job for me in his place, he looked a little puzzled, but he told me that he could use me. When he heard where I was working, he laughed and wished me good luck in getting out of there. I needed lots of it, because trouble was waiting for me when I returned to the *Kolbenwascherei*. The forewoman was threatening to take me to the administration office to report my unruly behavior, but my *Meister* stepped in and settled our dispute. He also gave me permission to leave the department for another one.

1951—The *Wendel* (Filament) Lab

As I mentioned earlier, I had already found myself another job in the filament lab. It was a glass-enclosed room. To keep it dust free as best as it was possible, we had to wear satin-like lab coats. I had passed the lab many times on my way to deliver bulbs and I thought that it looked like a neat place to work. At this lab the filaments for the different size bulbs were spread out onto a small table. Then, using tweezers over a lighted glass plate, faulty filaments were sorted out. The rest were then counted and boxed, one hundred to a box.

Sometimes a microscope had to be used to spot flaws, especially when working on fifteen watt filaments. They were like fine hairs. And it all had to be done quickly because we worked *Akkordarbeit* (piecework). I became quite good at it and I never had my inspected work returned to me, but it did put quite a strain on the eyes. I also made more money, which helped a lot. Our situation had not changed. I was still the breadwinner.

1951—*Pfingsten*, a Two Day Holiday

Pfingsten (Pentecost) was celebrated as a spiritual and a joyous holiday. By that time of the year, spring had arrived. The trees were sprouting new leaves and flowers were popping up everywhere. It gave everyone, both young and old, a happy feeling. *Pfingsten* was the opening date for all the garden cafes, and besides being a very important day in the life of the church, it was celebrated also as a day when families went on outings together to again enjoy the outdoors after a long, cold winter season. New clothes were also worn on *Pfingsten*, and they were seen everywhere.

My girlfriend Marion and I had planned to spend *Pfingst-Montag* together. We traveled via the S-Bahn to Lake Schlachtensee, along with many other people, which was to be expected, as it was a sunny, warm day. We were wearing our new outfits and we were feeling great. Schlachtensee was a lovely lake. A path led all the way around it, with many outdoor cafes inviting a thirsty *Spazierganger* (walker) to stop and rest for awhile.

Marion and I walked a little bit until we found an empty bench where we could sit and watch the people sailing by on their boats. On the way back, we found a table in a garden café. We ordered a *Kannchen Kaffee* (small pot of coffee) and selected a piece of cake from a large menu. A small band was playing familiar tunes and several elderly couples were dancing.

Next we decided to go and visit the Funkturm, a radio tower with an observation tower and a restaurant halfway up. It offered a spectacular view, day or night. We rode the elevator up to the top for a great view of the city and then on our way down we could not resist the temptation to stop at the restaurant for a delicious *Eiscremebecher*, a fancy sundae.

We did not talk much about the bad years. They were finally behind us. But we did not try to forget them either nor how quickly everything could change, for better or for worse.

We were enjoying ourselves. It had not been so long before when we had sat in front of her house and only dreamed about such times.

Michael's Epilogue

My mother did not know that I would take her notes and, with the assistance of my friend, Mary Jo Gibson, and my daughter, Elizabeth, turn her notes into a published book. Mary Jo and Elizabeth did the hard job of converting my mother's hand written notes into electronic form, and then I worked to edit and smooth the text, doing my best not to lose Mom's voice or style. My father, Stanley, helped find and scan the photos that appear in this book—and he did it without giving too much away to my mother!

Of course, there is much more to tell of my mother's life, but because I wished to keep the publishing of this book as a surprise, I was unable to find a way to convince her to write more. For the readers of this memoir—and especially those of you who are related to Charlotte or who are her children or grandchildren or great-grandchildren—I will tell you a little bit of what was to come.

All four of the young women—Inge, Eva, Marion and my mother—ended up marrying Americans and moving to the United States. Inge was the first one of the four to get married. Marion was the next one. They both married professional soldiers in the U.S. Army. Marion's younger sister, Eva, married an airman in the U.S. Air Force. My mother stayed in touch with them for quite some time.

Not too long after the point where this book halts, Charlotte met Stanley Lowe, a young U.S. Air Force radar technician from Middletown, New York. They met at the German-French Club in Berlin and they fell in love. They were married in a civil ceremony on March 4, 1953, and again in a church ceremony on June 26, 1953. My mother says that in May of 1953 she returned to Lake Schlachtensee with her "mate". She and my father sat outside in the "Alten Fischer Hutte" on a nice Saturday evening and enjoyed a bottle of "Crover Nacktarsch." She remembers that it was very romantic, despite the presence of some hungry mosquitoes.

I came along in April of 1954 and not too long thereafter my father's time in the Air Force came to an end and they moved to America, as my mother's *Bleigiessen* (fortune) had foretold. Onkel Hermann did not like the idea of my mother going across the ocean to America. He still considered it to be a wild country and he was worried about her.

My sister Diane was born in 1957 and my brother Thomas came along in 1964. In June of 2003 my parents celebrated their 50th wedding anniversary. Now living in Florida, they are proud of their five grandchildren—Elizabeth, Andrew, Brian, Steven and James.

Not very long after Ewald and Lieschen left Gollin in 1949, his parents, two brothers and two sisters also left there and resettled in Berlin. The oldest brother, the one that gave them so much grief in Gollin, resettled in West Germany. One sister also went to live in West Germany. Ewald's parents managed a kiosk, where they sold newspapers, magazines, cigarettes and candy.

In 1968, Lieschen and Ewald both came to visit my parents at our home in Dansville, New York. It was their first and only visit to America, and they also are the only relatives of my mother, other than my Oma, to ever visit her in America. Sadly, Ewald started to show signs of multiple sclerosis in 1968. He fought it bravely for nine or ten years, until walking became impossible for him. Lieschen took care of him to the very end, which came in 1988. Lieschen continued to live in the same apartment complex until her own death in 2005.

At my mother's wedding, Lutz took the place of my mother's father and walked her down the aisle. Her sister Hilde was my mother's Maid of Honor. Hilde died in 1991 from leukemia. She was then 68 years old. Lutz died of heart failure in 1998, on my mother's birthday, December 14th. He was 75 years old. Waltraut and Brigitte are still alive and living in Germany. Wolfgang passed on in 2006.

My mother's grandmother—"Oma" in these memoirs—had a horrible experience in 1955 or 1956 when she was kept in the East Zone of Germany for three days and nights on suspicion of spying activities. She had been hurrying up the steps at the S-Bahn station in Waidmannslust to catch her train into Berlin. There she was to meet Frieda (my mother's mother) and Tante Anna for lunch and some shopping. When she reached the top of the stairs, she saw two trains sitting there and she mistakenly chose the wrong one. By the time she noticed the mistake she had made, she had entered the East Zone of Germany without the proper permit.

The East German police entered the train at the first stop in the East Zone to check the passengers' identification papers. They would not accept Oma's explanation that she had in her hurry chosen the train going the wrong direction. She begged them to let her go back, but needless to say they would not hear of it. They escorted her from the train to a guardhouse at the station. There they searched her bag and found a letter written by my mother, who by then was living in America and married to a former U.S. Airman.

They took her from the guardhouse to a police station in town and for three days and three nights they asked her the same questions over and over again. They made a big fuss over something that my mother had written in the letter that they said meant that Oma and our family were all involved in spying. My mother does not remember what she had written in that letter. The only thing she can think of is that she might have written about Stan's summer job—installing electronic equipment for a new government radar facility.

When my grandmother failed to show up for the luncheon date, Frieda and Aunt Anna were not too concerned. They just thought that Oma had changed her mind. The next morning the police came to Frieda's door to let her know that Oma's landlord had reported Oma as missing. The news was quite a shock. Frieda and the family had absolutely no idea where to look for her. They spent some very anxious days worrying about her and searching for her.

Finally the East German police released Oma and put her on a train back to Waidmannslust. They warned her sternly not to make the same mistake again. The warned that the next time they would not be lenient with her. They kept my mother's letter and all of Oma's money. She had quite a lot of money with her because she had planned to do some shopping. My mother comments dryly that they were never too proud to take someone's western currency.

It took quite awhile for Oma to get over this horrible experience. She completely avoided traveling on the S-Bahn. She was too afraid of repeating her mistake.

Oma passed away on March 14, 1958. Uncle Hermann passed on in 1961 or so. Tante Martha died in 1969.

In the midst of editing these memoirs I asked my mother if she knew what army group my grandfather, Willi, had served with. She responded that she did not. I asked her to look over her meager records and even to examine his photos with a magnifying glass to look for an insignia on his uniforms. But there was nothing. All she knew was his *Feldpostnummer* (field post number). This coded number was placed on mail addressed to her father and it always got to him.

My mother's response got me to thinking. Using various search engines I spent several long nights on the internet. To my delight, I found three websites that had sections devoted to *Feldpostnummers*. It turned out that a *Feldpostnummer* identifies a very specific German military unit. With the help of a man in Norway who had a copy of an out of print book which deciphered all the *Feldpostnummers*, I learned that my grandfather was a member of the 6th Company, Infantry Regiment 310, 163rd Infantry Division, Army of Norway (later the 36th Mountain Corps).

This unit participated in the invasion of Norway and the subsequent occupation of Norway. In the summer of 1941 it moved across Sweden to Finland by train (setting off an international diplomatic uproar since Sweden was neutral). In Finland it was placed under the control of Finnish officers and participated in the June 1941 attack against the Russian forces northwest of Leningrad as part of Operation Barbarossa. When the attack bogged down the unit settled into three years of static trench warfare. All of this matches my mother's recollections, my grandfather's stories, and even the captions on the few photos we have of his time in the service.

My grandmother, Frieda Wittmutz, whom I always called "Oma", traveled back and forth across the Atlantic many times in the 1950's and 1960's, staying in touch with her widespread family. I traveled with her, my mother, sister and brother in 1965 to Berlin to visit Lieschen and Ewald. That was my first opportunity to meet many of my German relatives and to see, with my mother as tour guide, many of the neighborhoods and places she writes about in these memoirs. I traveled again to Berlin with Oma in 1969, the summer that Tante Martha passed. Oma and I attended her funeral.

Oma chose to live with my parents and spent most of her time with them through the 1970's and 1980's, living in Dansville, New York. She got to see her three grandchildren grow up and she got to hold her great-granddaughter, Elizabeth Lowe, and her great-grandson, Andrew Kiefer. Oma passed away peacefully in her sleep in 1988.

And so this memoir of my mother comes to an end. However, I heard recently from my father that my mother may have picked up her pen and started quietly writing some more of her recollections and memories. Let us hope that is true!

Michael Lowe
February, 2007

978-0-595-43793-1
0-595-43793-1